Jill Johnston, art and cultural critic and autobiographer, is the author of *Jasper Johns: Privileged Information*, *Secret Lives in Art*, *Paper Daughter*, *Mother Bound*, *Gullibles Travels*, *Marmalde Me*, and her revolutionary manifesto, *Lesbian Nation*. She lives in New York City.

Admission
Accomplished:

The *Lesbian Nation* Years (1970-75)

by **Jill Johnston**

Library of Congress Catalog Card Number: 97-062053

A catalogue record for this book is available from the British Library on request

The right of Jill Johnston to be identified as the author of this work has been asserted by her in accordance with the Copyright, Designs and Patents Act 1988

Many of these essays first appeared in *Lesbian Nation*, *Gullibles Travels*, and *The Village Voice*.

First published in 1998 by
Serpent's Tail, 4 Blackstock Mews, London N4

Cover design by Rex Ray
Book design by Amy Scholder
Set by Avon Dataset, Bidford-on-Avon
Printed by Mackays of Chatham

CONTENTS

I dedicate this book to my children Winnie and Richard, and my grandchildren Amanda and Benjamin, Lori and Marissa.

Introduction

Aroused is Aroused is Aroused

The essays in this collection appeared originally in the *Village Voice* between 1970 and 1975. In 1973, several of them were republished in *Lesbian Nation*, and a year later a much larger number — 39 in all — were brought together and printed under the title *Gullibles Travels*. In this current much expanded collection, some of the clamorous political writing I tended to eliminate from *Gullibles Travels* in favor of my loftier literary ventures has been reintroduced. Tones of unvarnished rage, of didactic hyperbole, and of unapologetic disregard for every conventional nicety in the political pieces were never pretty, I'm sure, and may be less attractive than ever at this remove in time. But no picture of that moment, when women like myself had done the hitherto socially unthinkable and suicidal — come out publicly as lesbians — can really be complete without these rantings.

By 1970, a year during which my writing shows I was warming up for an existence dancing on a political and literary precipice, I had already had two rather distinct writing lives with the *Voice*. Beginning 1959, I wrote serious dance and art criticism for the paper. Gradually from the mid-1960s on, after cracking up and then somehow losing or misplacing my former life, I subverted my arts coverage, turning the space allotted me into a personal chronicle, adventure story, travelogue, confessional romance, anecdotal assemblage, bully pulpit or soapbox, and experimental writing outlet. This last was more important to me than anything, until the advent of politics between 1969 and 1971 when I found out I was a woman and a lesbian.[1]

Then the dada-like style I had been cultivating and which was rooted in the vanguard art I had championed as a critic — an art of high amusement and contempt for authority — often seemed

---

[1] I mean that I had not known I belonged to a *class*, a political class called women, differentiated from the privileged class called men. As for finding out I was a lesbian, likewise and prior to Stonewall, with no consensus, no 'identity' had been possible. In an important sense, we didn't exist.

unserviceable for serious political rhetoric. Entertainment and political passion have never been thought to blend well. As my rage escalated, attaining full bloom by 1971; and my ardor for scribbling absurdly or outrageously continued unabated, I entered a strange period — torn between writing for fun and writing to save the world.

Depending on my circumstances and my whereabouts, my moods and the literature I was reading, I plied one modality or the other, sometimes having a windfall: the unexpected interface. By and large I was alternately silly and furious, writerly and inflated, diverting and dogmatic, devil-may-care and paranoid, whimsical and pontifical, cool and megalo — often at lightning-speed shifts within a single column.

I wrote generally as if there were no tomorrow. The *Voice* never tried to stop me; on the contrary, the paper must have thought, judging from the quantity of letters-to-the-editors they printed about my column, and the hundreds of fan letters I received, that I made good copy. It was a different paper then. Its current incarnation is the *Voice* only in name. Founded in 1955 by Norman Mailer, Ed Fancher and Dan Wolf, the first "underground" weekly in the US, the paper reflected the radical political and cultural events of the heraldic '50s, the culminating '60s, and the tailend whiplash early to mid-'70s. The founders were dedicated to representing many diverse points of view and writing styles. Once on board, writers were considered family — in the sense at least that they were never found to be expendable. In my case, as an example, the paper even printed pieces I wrote during my incarceration in the mid-1960s, as well as during later phases of mental instability.

Although I probably knew that the paper had been sold in 1969, with the founders/editors retaining control for five years — sure sign of an uncertain future — I never thought for a moment that my new-found fame (infamy to many) and wide berth for both political and literary outrage would ever end. A fan on the street at a gay parade once asked me, clearly with more foresight than myself, what I would do when I was no longer so visible. I answered blithely oh I would continue reading and writing just as before. Not until the editors lost their controlling interest in June 1974, and my column was slowly shut down commencing around that time, did I begin to suspect that another life somehow awaited me — a beclouded speck on an imperceptible horizon. At the same time I had to be dimly aware that I had become a media junkie (as addicted to my column and the attention it wrought as the many readers who wrote me claimed to be); and would begin to feel the trauma of withdrawal.[2]

Yet even by June 1973, right after *Lesbian Nation* was published, I showed signs of beating a retreat myself. I was not well-disposed to the fabulous hostility I experienced on the road on a book tour, or wildly happy over the loss of close lesbian accomplices and friends, who perhaps found it difficult to tolerate my new giantess misshapen profile rigged up in the glare of national publicity. And while I might have savored the inevitable adventures of my increased visibility, especially as grist for new columns, I was also thrown by the attentions of strangers, whose personal demands I was badly equipped to meet ("I have a feeling a lot of people love me and nobody loves me." — "Anybody Dying of Love"). Heightened exposure threw a searchlight on the "false self" of stardumb, placing a strain on my already fragile sense of authenticity, but even flimsier — so recently constructed — identity as a lesbian feminist. Attacks by non-literary often working-class lesbians for my writing style and perceived privilege were disconcerting as well. The class conflicts and race issues within lesbian and feminist communities, never mind normal jealousies and competitiveness, often seemed to be tearing all of us apart.

Disgruntlement in the ranks over my manner of writing was

---

[2] Our revolution, in the meantime, was being funded and promoted by the male-owned and -run media. The guys were eager to make a buck off us, and curious to know what we had to say. The lock we had on their attention was provisional at best. For a while, money was more important to them than the threat of our existence. I do not mean to underestimate the influence and reach of the many underground feminist and lesbian feminist publications that had upsprouted then. These came into existence, however, only in the wake of coverage by established media, and they tended to disappear like dying stars when planet media had had enough of us.

perhaps the least of my problems or worries. In fact, judging from my work throughout 1973 when *Lesbian Nation* was published, I gloried more and more in writing for the hell of it — my feints and retreats and rude movement awakenings paying off for me literarily. My true colors as a writer at heart and a politico in drag must have been showing through.[3] A line in "Great Expectorations" — a magnum opus of 7000 plus words making fun of an appearance junket in the midwest — indicates a motivation I had for skewing the cause I went on the road to represent:"i had the usual quota of horrible revolutionary experiences on this particular trip . . ." With its immense length,"Great Expectorations" showcased the two most obvious features of the signature style I was able to consolidate during 1972: consistent lower case, the whole text in a single paragraph.

A less obvious stock-in-trade well developed by then was my use of appropriated sentences and phrases — a form of plagiarism, of quotes without attribution, rooted in that venerable dada tradition of the "found object." As I say in "Do it Yourself","... i did it in the beginning making up . . . sentences as though a sentence was an old bed or bottle in the gutter." The non-sequitur arose simultaneously, the inevitable way of linking up these lines. Frequently I began a piece with a series of such lines, creating a kind of collage of unattributed quotes; but I used them also in the middles of pieces as transitional devices between anecdotal or narrative passages. Either they came across as nonsense or as "collage" parts with interpretable connections. Beginning "Mary Kissmass & a Hippy Nude Year," I wrote: "there is no god and mary was his mother. the steam was coming off the roofs and i thought we were on fire. she couldn't undertaker anything. too much light darkens the mind. there's some tactical insignificance about doing anything but living. what somebody found was incontrovertible evidence that it all means zero.

---

[3] I mean by politico an activist in the sense of someone who goes to meetings, organizes rallies or marches, pamphleteers, belongs to parties, etc.; or who becomes a political writer professionally. I made forays into the former, and while showing signs perhaps of becoming the latter, always undermined the tendency by striking out in literary or memoirist directions.

that phrase predicts the pattern of our ruin . . ." More follows, forming a preludial sort of fanfare or flourish announcing, as it were, the text proper. My lines were drawn from everywhere: spoken or written, by the people or the pope; and were chosen, it appears, for their aphoristic resonance. We lived, then, not only in a civil revolutionary period but in a neo-religious or zen and rumdum[4] sort of time, and the epigrammatic quality of the quotes as well as the mysterious links between them satisfied aspirations I had to transcend everything, to say or establish one thing in one breath, then contradict or cancel it out in the next.

Sometimes I grouped bunched of lines into riffs, or litanies, like this aggregate taking off from a woman called Judith I happened to know: "judith calls her store the perfect union. these ecstatic unions imply a joyful liberation from sanity. she always went without herself. she fell into some ark on the way in and there was light thru the portholes. she thought her thin arms and sturdy legs were peaceful and exciting. she saw mansions in the sky of lavender doors and gold knockers and thought it was a very corny dream. she pretends if she's not looking at anybody they can't see her either. she lives in a purely symbolic world and magically solves her problems. she knows there's certain conventions they'd all greed upon and she becomes inexpensively happy attending to nothing more interesting than her own thoughts . . ." ("Resurrection for 40 Cents").

". . . all greed upon" in this sequence barely suggests the intense plays on words that were also a hallmark of my style. The neologism or compound word formation — unlikely ever to have been used or seen before — was central to my sense of literary brinkmanship. My whole mission it seems was to mongrelize the language, deform and debase every convention, create a freak of culture, engender a misbegotten blot on the authorial landscape. In addition to lower casing and deparagraphing, thieving quotes, standardizing the non-sequitur, decontextualizing narrative and glorifying the neologism, I enjoyed writing unpunctuated run-on sentences, and habitually

---

[4] My nickname for Baba Ram Dass, alias Richard Alpert, the American Harvard professor, one-time associate of Timothy Leary, turned Eastern guru.

twisting grammatical norms and common usage.

As a picture or projection of self, such a miscegenated language suggests some extreme condition. Art is a biographical imprint, as well as an outgrowth of its own traditions. Some stamps may be hard to trace to a biographical source. In this case it seems easy. An art form of pure novelty and invention might naturally be expected to issue from someone undergoing the birth of an historically unprecedented (lesbian/feminist) identity. A serious defection from society was involved. Enclaves (of renegade women) were precariously established. A consensus now existed for asserting that we were something we had never been before. No integration at that moment was possible. We were called, and called ourselves, lesbian separatists. We were at war with a society that, if it had opposed us before (when our feelings for our own gender were *secret*), was now scandalized, assaulted, by the unbelievable appearance of *identity* — that clear marker of coming out. The literary transposition I see that I made was quite direct: a "defection" from language customs; the molding of an "enclave" locution, like ebonics, representing a group apart.

I had been schooled already in art outsiderness. I lugged dada forward with me into the lesbian feminist arena. Two alien entities merged in my style of the early 1970s — resulting in an excessive compound. One perceptive reader, a man, wrote in a letter-to-the-editor, 1971: "My initial reaction was that Jill Johnston's flowing sentences were an adroit deviance — a concomitant realization that to exist as a radical lesbian in America is not to exist within a social majority. Hence, I believed that Johnston's sense of writing was simply a needed demarcation from that social majority and served as a disparate characteristic for her within the movement." He concluded that in getting used to my writing, it became "natural" to him.

It never became natural to me exactly. No guides or precedents existed for organizing my particular assemblage of narrative fragments, found phrases, twisted grammars, colloquialisms, political discourse and matriarchist myth-making into an aesthetic whole. Writing fast, every week, could stretch my need for form and order. Repetition of phrases or sentences, usually by variation, was my one reliable device for establishing a through-line. Rarely did I try to fix a narrative through-line. If I had one story to tell (and normally I had many), I would break it up into anecdotal fragments littering the piece. Aesthetically, I counted on the surface "all-over" unparagraphed and lower-cased look to convey unity; and for internal cohesion, on some instinct for balance, for equal emphasis in progress on each part or element. Compositionally, the pieces are a form of weaving, of webworking or interlacing.

Nothing, at this remove, relieves a certain embarrassment I can have over a lack of detachment in my political diatribes. I was unable, it seems, to rail literarily. Yet I can also be surprised at how much I still agree with myself ideologically. The centrality of the lesbian position to feminist revolution — wildly unrealistic, or downright mad, as it still seems to most women everywhere — continues to ring true and right. The struggle of lesbians with feminists is a major theme throughout this work. In the next "phase," lesbians should be a much stronger force. Many hetero-feminists came out during the '70s and later. Many who could not come out understood the intelligence of the "woman-identified-woman" premise for undermining patriarchy. Many stood fast to resist the obvious: that they undercut themselves (and us) trying to get a better public deal from men while continuing to service them in private.

The alliance of lesbians with gay men disturbs me now as it did then. Not even the strong gay male feminist faction that existed then convinced me that we had a sound basis for coalition beyond our mutual civil rights interests. Women were our natural partners in revolution, and I saw lesbians as much more woman than straight women, the women who, after all, spend much more time with men, and for whom of course the marginalized lesbians were vermin. Oh it was a very divided time, with lesbians essentially stranded between straight feminists and gay men, and with powerful disadvantages in relation to each constituency. No doubt I felt I had to scream in order to be heard. This howl seems to reverberate through much of the political writing here.

The anti-family, anti-monogamy leitmotif that runs through the work, centric to feminism then, and a self-evident position for lesbians — the traditional family outsiders — ceased to interest me by at least 1980. A family movement by lesbians and gay men had commenced by then. With the nuclear model breaking down, and a postmodern pluralism growing up alongside it, many of us saw an opportunity to create or recreate family. With my life-partner, whom I met in 1980, I became a belated parent to my two children, who dot the printscape of these early '70s essays like fugitive presences. "The Yearly Mellowdrama" is an exception: a study of myself as an anxious stressed-out young mother — one of my looks back at some earlier personal history. "naturally," said I, "whenever the children are involved there is always a little trauma." A clue to my motivation for writing the piece can be found embedded in it — "I had a call yesterday from richard [my son] from caspar california. I'm organizing his trip by remote control." He was fourteen then, and no longer sheltered by his father. My apprehension over his sudden precocious independence evidently made me dwell on the past, when I was often overtaken by the same fear and foreboding.

Before Stonewall, before 1980 really, motherhood and a lesbian existence were a contradiction in terms. My pitch in "Lesbian Mothers Ltd." and "The Myth of Motherhood" was for lesbian motherhood through reclamation of historic or historically-imagined Amazon communities — woman supported, maintained, and legally sanctioned. Under patriarchy, I had lost my children. Under a weakened patriarchy — during the 1980s (and notwithstanding the backlash) — I was able to reclaim them to some extent. The fate of our children remains a major issue for lesbians, as it should for society.

It seems impossible to imagine leading the life I did during the decade 1965–75, had I not been a disenfranchised mother. I was not only "free," but free and on the loose with the rage of my failure as a woman. Then with the corrective rage of knowing I had been cast in a role for which I was unsuited. Not as a mother necessarily — but as a mother for whom a career and motherhood had proved mutually exclusive. And just as importantly as a mother for whom motherhood was rigidly predicated upon living with a man (for me a violent one at that) — indeed in a legally binding arrangement called marriage.

The pen which is said to be mightier than a sword was in my case a guided missile. A man who wrote to the paper in 1972 seemed to know something: "With muddy tear-stained cheek and swollen-throated warcry, Ismene gathers up her troops. The attack is on and Jill may retake Thebes after all these centuries with her many Amazons." A woman, clearly among the troops, wrote that it was "only too sad that I will never get the chance to sleep with [Jill] and be her friend." Her letter was titled: "Ma Nuit Sans Jill." Two other letter writers, one a woman, the other a man, struggled over which was more important — my writing or my sexuality.

"All that crap you print about Jill Johnston," said the woman, "Why doesn't someone say she's the first American literary genius since Gertrude Stein? Who would be interested in her wild life and her controversial sexuality if she weren't a great writer?" The paper titled this one, "What is the Question" — the last reported words of GS before she died.

"I would like to answer that presumably rhetorical question," went the letter by the man a week later, "with this rhetorical question: who would be interested in [Jill's] wild life or writing if it weren't for her controversial sexuality?"

The *Voice*'s title: "Aroused is Aroused is Aroused."

— *February 1997*

In Her Altogether Also

She stood up from a hot tub and passed out under the sink and broke a rib or two. I like to fall asleep myself in the middle of a story. Come again when you can't stay so long. And bring camera. My blood is thin, my heart is made of tin tonight. I didn't remember signaling with my foot my intention of dying with her and my foot isn't even stuck in the door. I'm stuck on the hi-way. Clapping my hands I am not singing joyfully in the moonlight. Frigid cold out as witches' tits. I stopped because of an interesting noise. Flapflapflapflap . . . Slowing down it does flap-flap-flap. Get out inspect the rear parts. It isn't the dislodged metal thing or any other hanging thing, it's a hunk of rubber on the wheel detaching itself from the parent body, so I stand some special helpless looking slouch leaning longingly in the direction of oncoming vehicles my Havid scarf arranged at some attractive chest spread. Wish the photographer was here. Whiz, whiz. Nada nobody. Whiz whiz. Bastids. If I were dead praps all the problems that bothered her would be settled. What was the great catastrophe before the drying up of the oceans? The coming of the snows. I should be pacing back and forth looking like I have no appointment at the end of the world. Last year this time according to a *Voice* office index card I was "envolved in many strange and wondrous adventures . . ." I should be leaning on my sword describing my defeat. I'm leaning on my car watching a bright red sports number slow down a few yards in front of my hood. Two smiling muscle boys are walking toward me. I hunch into my scarf and meet them halfway and stare at the snow and mumble about a disintegrating tire. Ye-s-s. And as they're into the jack and spare boy scout act I'm noting their Massachusetts license plate. It reads SOS. Terrific. I've been saved. I love being saved. Maybe while she was standing up from the hot tub and passing out under the sink I was backing into a snow bank stuck solid and gaily hacking away at the white stuff with a dust pan in order to find my way back to "grandmother's house" under the nothing night no stars even and falling into the embankments leaving the vehicle to be hauled out by the various rescue operation teams. I need photos of this business.

No, I'm telling her, I'm not hiding my forehead, I'm showing my bangs. So she's clicking some pix of my bangs and other parts inside and outside but the ". . . strange and wondrous adventures" are not being recorded. Like looking out this window and seeing some abominable bird tracks and this leaning tower of silo and this deadduck apple orchard and many obscure but timeless traces of the great catastrophes before and after the drying up of the oceans. At that time according to certain prominent bioanalysts I became a female because another much stronger animal *also* anxious to return to the aquatic existence of which we had been deprived managed to bore a tube into me in order to create a passage to get into the puddle which became my uterus. Amazing. And I don't even have any callosities on my forward extremities to facilitate the clasping of any other weakling who got bored into. But I'm sitting in my vest and shirt and pants and pipe at a table looking at a chess set opposite my opponent in her altogether also staring at the chess pieces about level with a pair of great knockers before the separation of creation from nothing there was probably something. Flap. I'm leaning on my elbow describing a checkmate. The photographer is 5 yards away. This was my brilliant dephallible idea to get a shot like the original Duchamp at chess with the chick in the buff a blubbler possibly detaching itself from the parent bodily situation to which the organization of the female accommodated itself in alternate projections apropobly. I make a move. Assault with intent to ravish. The set belonged to the master and his widow themselves. She loaned me the set. She didn't want me to make the picture. You don't play chess, she said. It doesn't matter, I play lots of games. My opponent's hair is black like the original but five inches longer and it's covering the profile. I don't care for my own. No, I'm showing my bangs. My blood is thick, my heart is made of doodlebugs tonight. If she were dead praps all the problems that didn't bother me would be unsettled. Let's shoot this one out in the snow she said. Yeah let's do it on the way to the road. Now sit in the chair. Now stand on the table. Now the hands. The bangs. The tie. The dingle dangle. Now take off your clothes. No I don't do that. "He looked at my naked body and found that it was perfect and therefore destroyed his sketches." There's no padding interposed any more between life and the word. This is not a strange and wondrous adventure. I'm not terrible enough to be beautiful and I'm not a streaming pillar of orange wax as a girl in a tangerine dress rising up out of a hot tub and melting away under the sink and I don't have an appointment at the end of the world. Either. Where's the SOS car? She said she was available, she'd never leave me, she has a beautiful soul too and she's very good with crazy people and how could I resist her. Come again when you can't stay forever. I find myself suddenly within the Unthinkable Itself. The lens is two yards away. Jesus she's foreshortening some part of my bare extremities and possibly even boring another tube into me somewhere and I don't need another puddle or any other substitution for somebody else's aquatic existence. But it's dramatically decadent. Capote on the couch. Just one frame, for her she said. Sure, one frame. Then let's do it on the way to the road. Then let's go up in that leaning tower of silo and make some abominable bird tracks and find our way back to grandmother's house under the nothing night no stars even and break a rib or two and wait for the SOS boys and the cameras to record each small catastrophe each infinitely small thing is as large as large things can be isn't it grand?

—January 29, 1970

Springjoyce

The moon outside is a Ryder; the rainbow in here is the chalk on a
Dutch blackboard. All the nickelly nacks are pieces of Egypt. And a
barkboat carrying a clod of moss and dade yellow flower and another
pitch of bark. Anyways a verytableland o junkle jeaps for a miniataur
tiger to roam and roar around in. The woods outside is a shambles.
Medusa madmess. Spring on the pathways is just a warm day and a
blue periwinkle butterfly and spring in the timberstalks along like
skinny miles of gray arms, snakevines, veering vetching varicose velly
awful looking interfuckulating strangulation by encroakment. What
is growling up here? The age of shrivelry is all over me. I shall eat
grass and die in a ditch in the browny bracken water where the
rotted leaves have deaded. I shall set on a rockofaggots foliaceous and
fuming flesh a new feenix up a flamin mamie a surefire baby; her
birth is uncontrollable, her funferall is a celebarktion by kindlelight.
By Zen and by Zoos the begin the beguine of the unifirst is rite
now if all tinks are at this momentus being cremated, and the end of
the unihearse is allso now if all thinks are at this momentum passing
away we went, to see The Inedible String Bean. We went to see the
Dairy of a Skinzopretty Girl. We went to see the saw strafe the
spring-dried denseyland disbarking benches of millentury old trees.
And by wishingwell and waterfall willie winkle watched pretty peter
pumpkineater wairing his feet in a pink sock on one and on the
other an orange sock and little annie ruiny she heard go spashing
and pooling and laffing down to the bottom go davy locker herself
down da bottom foriver and iver. Omen. So wail us. And up near the
approach toward the summit of its climax where the waterocktrees
all meet to crushendo din your drums appeared a parition of Christ
Christself in a visionee epigonee gonny glummy gloriation in
exseltzer madst the follyages. Ge bone! Gralloch! Graptotite! By grog
I'm disembered. I set down on the pathway and wrap me arms about
me knees and crosseye the welter woods into a worldwide web woven
by my eye in the loom of the branch. Misticalling me. Jungly time. I
akst wee willie winkle wheather she was going away for summari-
time? She doesn't no, she hasn't famished with her winter yet. Mr

4

Anklemine wood 'end her however to Ecuador to see some head-hunters and excheat X numbers of beads for eggs or voice reversa. But it don't adder at all becaws all her spriggity spring lovers are asparagas and strawberries and so sexing she went away leaving me to swallow in the skunkabbage in here the forest is a Rousseau; the rainbow note the above is the chalk on a Dutch blackboard. Outside I stole a log and dropped it in the mud and looged it up a high hell and lay its muddy soggy side sunny up and BLT and go ananny Gretel reddied up fine and ruddy for the conflammation. Too out and walking and walking, walking looking walking and looking as a woodsfan waking pyromaniacts I go ashenutely aghost and aggalled at the sites befort me. This ere tree 'as gone stark razor naked. This one ere is a merrible tress o flakes, its hole skin scalloping up as a mummy wrapping come loose all over itself. And this ere one is a mobster leviathan than which no less ten trunks in one or one trunk holding up ten and every trunk a them a mori memento. Macrophagocriticalciumbrage of some sort. So solly. Solong.

—May 7, 1970

Bash in the Sculls

East Hampton — One acre of love sun and sound at the Sculls. Drive along a Georgica road where the rich inherited the earth of East Hampton. An open sesame table at the head of the gravel driveway. Smiling women for equality. They say well look at list five other people called in to come for The Voice. Barbara Guest parries all checkshuns and leads me dancing and singing by the hand down the yellow brick road to the Crossbones. No she didn't but she was just charming and also flatterfull of good will too. This party I think Tom Wolfe would identifry it as Radical Chick for Women Striking for Equality, later on this month after reseiving the necessary funds from such parties as these that Bob and Ethel Scull sponsered at 25 grubs a poison to see their premises. That's not true but it's the way Bob himself now striding tord me cross his greeny lawn in his ducky white pants and candy striped shirt open at a mossy chest and his new Commander Whitehead beard under a rich smile did put it that people would be paying to see the place. He's happy to see me and so am I. Nice little bungalow you've got here Bob. Mmmm. I can't give you the style number and we're not allowed in, it's a lawn party, but it's a right angulated one story black and white and windowy modern minimal everybody's building/Some are building monuments/Others are jotting down notes. All my colleagues in the crime of reporting I never meant. Charlotte Curtis. *Time. Newsday.* Swiss Television. United Press International Syndicated News Service. Once I mingled in a group of five of which four of us were taking notes. My editor (there too perchance) said it's the ultimate sort of party where nobody shows up except the people who write about it. I tried interviewing Charlotte Curtis who was interviewing two men who might've been interviewing her while a lady was interrupting to interview me about whatever went wrong between Betty Friedan and me. What went wrong between Betty Friedan and me was a lapse of sexual interest. I liked her below the chin and was ready to talk at that level but she got super huffy when I arsked if there shouldn't be a pub(l)ic conjuction between Women's Liberation and the Gay Liberation Front. Her eyes went big 'n bulgy and her lipstick leered crimson and she said crisply enunciating each word that "it" is not an issue. What? She repeated. *And*, there's no relationship between the movements. Well, and she softened a moment. I *am* against all oppression. Good, but don't you think . . . — and she waved me off, excuse me I have other important things to do as she spun on her maxi and I called out after her you mean "it" is embarrassing. And Scull standing there looking at his feet his hands folded at the duck white pants behind over the coccyx. He wanders me a tour of the lawn garden fountain sculpture layout. Here's a tomato red tube fabricated Alexander Lieberman. It matches your napkin Bob. Mmmm. A stainless steel Walter de Maria cage. A neon number. A gray minimal Morris he called a do-nut, it has a square hole. A wood beam di Suvero faded weathering beautifully into driftwood. A fountain of three di Suvero cast bronze hands, and the story to go with it about how the one hand where the water sprouts out of its palm was supposed to cost 400 and Mark demanded 4 thou and got it and Scull says to me you know that Mark insults me, calls me a robber baron and the worst names — and I love him. He's beaming. Unhhuh, . . . you've changed Bob. *Yeah* I feel *great*, just great. He looks yachtsman cocktails. Tanned and supersuccessful. His wife Ethel is standing near the mikes by the pool in a quilted maxi looking slim and Betsy Ross-ish. He turns and smiles and says fondly you know we've been married 26 years. By the pool. The pool! Don't Go Near the Water! The pool is the centerpiece here the perfect aqua rectangle undisturbed by its peripheral human slow motion of cameras cocktails interviews. Back in the bushes by a road bordering the lawn sits a barefoot guerrilla. Why donchu come in I called out. Because I don't have $25. I was near him and I turned and scanned my sister and fellow guests and when I saw the host of the Philistines I was afraid and my heart greatly trembled. No it didn't. But *lo* a voice from heaven, saying, This is my beloved Daughter in whom I am (not) so well pleased. It was time. Something had to happen here. A new historical folks pass. In a flash I turned into a One Eyed One Horned Flying Purple People Eater. No I didn't. I continued interviewing and being interviewed. I talk to Edith de Rham who wrote *her* book one year after (in '64) Betty Friedan did and who saw that women didn't have the freedom she had in being able to pay for a maid. I say then you must've had an experience that wasn't so pleasant to make you that sympathetic. Yes, she was married before her present marriage and with*out* the money for a maid and she wanted to jump off a bridge from it. Right. It had eluded me that the movement had so much to do with maids. We need a better distribution of maids. Maids for everybody. Maids for the MAIDS. I decide to test her on the gay issue which Betty Friedan said is not an issue. She isn't hysterical like Betty but torrentially defensive. You see we don't hate men and so forth. And a story about a "queer" designer who was always describing his fabulous mother. I register that she's had gay men figured out for some time. Mother will never be duplicated. I change the subject and suggest that the women who hate men the most (and vice versa) are those who go to bed with them. She doesn't like any of it anyway and gives the old one-two about being normal or natural in preferring her opposite. "I'm not narcissistic you see." St John of the Cross where are you: / There is in every perfect love/ A law to be accomplished too: / That the lover should resemble/ The belov'd: and be the same/ And the greater is the likeness/ Brighter will the rapture flame — Narcissime: qui consiste a se choisir soi-meme comme objet erotique. — Our interview was being interrupted by another. Edith's book by the way was *The Love Fraud* and I'm sorry I don't know what it's about a fraud I guess. She said she's happily married now. Who can I seduce here. Betty wears lipstick. Ethel is busy being hostess. Barbara disappeared. Charlotte is taking notes. My editor is here with her boyfriend. So I'm talking to Scull again over a manicured hedge. Admiring his Commander Whitehead beard, just the right dash of distinguished gray-white in a black brush as clipped as the hedge. Schwebbers Electronics has that kind of beard now too. Scull is expansive suddenly: I can't *wait* to see my depressions in Nevada. Your *What*?- My depressions. — Oh. My sculpture in the desert in Nevada, by Mike Heizer. Oh. Say Bob who's that? I've spied my quarry across the pool. Pale blue cycle shades. That's Gloria Steinem. Gloria! Terrific. I made haste round the pool through the cameras cocktails interviews. She's in a bare-back and just as pretty at eyeball distance. Our past and future is settled immediately. Midwest-Smith-India-*New York Magazine*. And I disclose my unscheduled pool event. Return in peace to the ocean, my love; I too am part of that ocean, . . . we are not so much separated . . . — We are instantly by an introduction from Betty Friedan who's been giving a pep talk at the mikes about Women for Equality. She introduces Gloria. I wander back the other side of the pool, the hedge side. I was coming into that abnormal condition known as elation. I would cast my swine before pearls and give that which is unholy to the daubs. I would return my body to the water (Gene before he died said he was returning the earth to the land as he threw his flower pots from fifth story to sidewalk). And I lectured my brethren: the proper posture is to listen and to learn from lunatics as in former times. No I didn't. I sat down to organize the explosion. Removal of pants shoes socks hardware. I had to leave my notes behind. Too bad. I walk quickly to the center of the shallow end. Almost fall skidding on the slippery edge. Last Chance Balloon. Tarzana from the trees at cocktails. I didn't cross myself. I didn't yell geronimo. I dove in and did my lengths. I hoped my colleague reporters would be noting my 10 point Australian crawl. I did a little exhibition breast stroke as well. The second time round I got rid of the faded blue railroad shirt with a hole in the sleeve (Yes it was a calculated costume). She's terrible, she's beautiful. She isn't beautiful, she isn't terrible enough. Anyway I was alone in the aquarium. Water lovely. No rubber ducky (in the tubby). I emerge. Slippery edge. Jill tombe pour la seconde fois. Scull is waiting eagerly with big yellow towel and so happily I think he's my trainer and I just won the race. I go beyond the hedge into the trees. A maxi lady is lurking in the buses WHY DID YOU DO THAT? I mean but extremely furious. I'm wiping the chlorine out of my eyes. It isn't self-evident. Well . . . I was . . . uh . . . hot—and drunk. HOT. And DRUNK. —God, where's my notebook. The other notebooks are coming tord me fast now. They're saying you were hot and drunk. *Were* you hot and drunk? Yes. Were you protesting? Yes. Are you a woman . . . ? Yes. Were you part of a Red Stocking Plot to Sabotage this Party? Yes. Were you showing off? Yes. Are you a radical lesbian? Yes. Do you like the Sculls? Sure. Did Mr Scull put you up to it? No. He neither endorsed nor discouraged the exhibition but I did get permission from my editor. *WHY* did you do it? Well . . . I think one should be serious in one's purposes but not necessarily solemn. Well . . . Have gun, will travel. See pool, will swim. Well . . . It was a Conceptual Swim. Well you see I have this reportsibility to make my life interesting to my readers each week. And then I stormed the mikes and lectured my brethren again: Except ye become as little children ye can in no vice exit the killdom of haven. No I didn't. I went behind a tree to write up my swim. Scull appeared. They're saying I put you up to it. Well just say I was hot and drunk. And offer me a dry shirt please. He gets another blue workshirt. Where's Gloria? They're not even thanking me for the awful time I gave them. No, it's getting all changed around. You were great. Terrific. Sensational. Verweile doch, du bist so schon. But Gloria won't dance. Betty is still put out. Ethel and Edith and Charlotte disappeared along with Barbara. A voice on the mikes is saying Ladies and gentlemen the party is over. Radical Chick is over. One acre of love sun and sound. Was there any perfecting of spirits here this afternoon? I'd like to leave my clothes impaled on a souvenir spear. Tell it all, brother and sisters. Dinner at the Silver Sea Horse. The Wheel of Wandering On.

—*August 13, 1970*

The Kingdom of Holy Insecurity

Dear Charlie, I'm sick today. I'm writing in G. Segal's studio of white plaster pieces of bodies in Jersey. I can't breathe. I began sneezing on 59th Street at *Five Easy Pieces*. I received yr letter that morning and had been in New York just two days. I woke up wrecked from a hangover. The morning before I woke up in bed with a girl who didn't understand why I said I should've slept in my car. This trip I found sex in the provinces. The last trip I had it good coming back to New York. I don't know if I need it or not. After coming I wonder what I'm doing there if I'm not in love. My night dreams are satisfying and my masturbation fantasies are virtuosic and interchangeable. Used to be I couldn't get it off if it wasn't a single plot with a beginning a middle an end. Then if you got stuck halfway you had to begin at the beginning again. Peter and I discussed a lot of these matters over supper the night I arrived. Girls don't talk much. Peter turned 36 two weeks ago. He said I could say so. I sent him a Libra book with two fall leaves turning red and orange. Departing a remote place in Vermont I went searching on the road after the perfect dead leaf. I wonder if he minds if I say he's a virgin to women. I wonder if I should tell my James Taylor story. Or the dream I had making love with the girl I was in bed with . . . Some female heavies were poking fun at me and reminding us of my history which made me say that most aspects of my life are common knowledge. The trouble with this girl was that she didn't have a cat. Every girl I shack in with has a cat. The two who married me gave their cats away. It doesn't work just to lock the cats out. Unless they're not psychotic and they usually are. If you define success sufficiently vaguely I'm doing all right. I don't manage in New York at all and I'm writing to you because your letter arrived in all its mythological splendor just as I was despairing of spending as much even as my recent limit of a few nights at a time on these battlegrounds of sex and business. Now I'm sick out at Segal's. Helen is away on an errant. George is talking into a tape recorder with Jan. Helen isn't sympathetic. George gives me aspirin and vitamin C. My glands are swollen. I'll never feel segzy again. I'll just talk about it with Peter. I tried explaining the sensation of anal orgasm and thought he should know more about it than me but he doesn't. I told him 36 is a significant age. Shakespeare changed dramatically at 36. Dante awoke to find himself alone in a dark wood (or at 35). So did Leary (at 35). The universe ultimately is a dream, isn't it, a product of the mind. It's raining today too. I had a rain dream in Sandgate. I was swimming in a lake of painted wooden statues like Egyptian effigies floating face up. Being afraid I woke, and saw myself as all the statues which I was, lying stiff asleep on my back in the van under the rain we were awash. I've not yet been given like Coleridge a page of undisputed splendor in a dream. I prefer what I'm doing to Kubla Khan however. And I relate to the difficult quotes you sent from Buber's *Daniel*. I'm too sad in my common cold to say more except I appreciate your message and the knowledge that you too feel the necessity of the myth and symbol. I was dissolving over the last quote when a neighbor walked in and asked me what I was upset about. I said I only appeared to be upset. I mean I don't think I cry for myself personally these days. What do you think of events. Janis dead. Jimi dead. Angela captured. Bernadette released. Trudeau in trouble. Timothy in Algiers. In New York people look right through you as though nothing had ever happened between all of us. And you do the same so's not to be misunderstood. We behave like the scattered fragments of the god that we are. (What greater glory for a god than to be absolved of the world.) I'm not however overly sentimental like some extravagant people who are overwhelmed by our own actions without knowing how to enjoy themselves. Far north this last trip I enjoyed what Time described as the exuberant breasts of a Lachaise statue. On Sophia? — The inventions of sex are no less fantastic than those of art. One a.m. after orgasm I went to sleep again and dreamt I was walking with a friend down a childhood street in a black gauzy shirt nothing else, an old recurring dream of embarrassment, and I asked my friend to pull the shirt down in back while I tried buttoning it in front and turning to her at the same time said you know I used to have dreams like this. — The day before I'd been reading some authority on the occurrence of a dream within a dream (when one dreams that one is dreaming), which they analyze as referring to a theme a person wishes were "only a dream," i.e., not true. — I don't know. I don't think I'd be writing like this if my letter was private. I'd be saying only the public things we understand. At Goddard a couple of weeks ago a student flattered me by saying my writing was schizophrenic. The students are quite advanced. That's where I found the exuberant breasts. In New York Yvonne asked me if I liked that and I said I think I prefer boobs like myself. She snorted. I'm hopelessly narcissistic. I stopped at Goddard to drop Scheindi and son Miles whose older sister Laurie is a new student there. The girls and boys shared living quarters. I had the impression that contraceptives are supplied by coin and button next to the coke machines. The youthful president is living in a dorm to see what it's like. They have courses like Revolutionary Anarchism and Police Repression and the Justice Department and Women's Action Projects and Draft Counseling and Beyond and Politics and the Family and Radical Studies and Cain the Irreconcilable and Arthur and the Need for a Hero and Existentialism and Zen Buddism and Studies of Style and Temperatment in Pottery. I visited a course in Homosexuality and hope to've stirred a homophile movement on campus, a possibility suggested in the catalog anyway. In the cafeteria a student asked me if I was a girl or a lady. I said I didn't know. I mean are you over 20 she pursued. I'll have to ask my son whom I introduce as my father sometimes. We children went to see the Fortune Quackser movie where we were embarrassed at the gooey parts. During a preview advertisement for a movie of incestuous rape and murder and naked perversions of every sort Winnie turned to me and said coolly this one will be rated X. You'd like them I think. To Richard I said pleasant dreams the rest of the week old man when I left them at home. He had told me about a dream of gran'ma asking him go to someplace, but she appeared in my image. He's dealing with a small problem of gran'ma taking his sister to the West Indies tomorrow. His dream occurred *before* I told him I'd fly him down to Mexico when I'm there if I have the bread, which I told him *before* he related the dream to me. I want to remember to tell Peter that Apollinaire was honored in Paris by a banquet when he was 36 and that last week I slept in a room containing exactly 36 horse show ribbons. I don't think I'll tell the James Taylor story. I don't think there's such a thing as fact on the one hand and fiction on the other. Nor that we "condense" in our dream formations while we "decompose" in our myth formations as some psychology people say. I think we condense (fuse, merge, superimpose) images and ideas and also decompose (disunite, multiply, dissolve) in both dreams *and* myths, *and* art and fantasies we the undivided divinity that operates within us in all these forms of it are dreaming the world. Some nights I dream a procession of all my old lovers. They fuse and disunite endlessly. And I rejuvinate them and let them die and rejuvenate them again and they are me and I am them and we are together celebrating our collective miseries and splendors in our dissolving and merging images and identities. I feel better today. Even in New York. As you quoted: This is the kingdom of God: the kingdom of danger and of risk, of eternal beginning and of eternal becoming, of opened spirit and of deep realization, the kingdom of holy insecurity. Love, Jill.

—*October 29, 1970*

The Roles of the Passion

Go get a jacket and do it up and don't waste yr time worrying how you can't save the world. What was I doing in Rochester. Making but wild and whirling words again. I was doing in Rochester in order to drive back east and south towards Syracuse and Albany and break a piston rod near Syracuse to wait in a cold drizzle for a rescue squad while recalling a breakdown of 1955 or so in an old Nash near the very spot I steamed to a stop over the piston rods and abandoned the wreck and transfered boxes of somebody's dancing costumes to a greyhound which I took to New York where I am going right now in another greyhound convinced I went to Rochester not to save the world but to experience the remembrance of an incident from another life. Moreover I stayed overnight in Syracuse with the sister of a friend of mine who are interesting people. Tess and Marianne. I went to Rochester because of another interesting person I met in New York at di Suvero's place one day a sculptor Linda Benglis who's up on a teaching gig at the University in Rochester. I haven't talked publicly in a while. When I was an authority on painting happenings dancing & whatnot I was invited to sound critical and knowledgeable. Since I've become an authority on myself the category is not on file yet so I have to concoct a subject like Women's Liberation and Homosexuality in order to advertise when I get there a topic of special concern to anybody — the self as the center of the universe. If we are intelligible spheres whose centers are everywhere and whose circumference is nowhere we are not limited by any one of ourselves so long as we know this to be true we can experience our divinity together. An ego of expanding awareness radiating from a contained center is an ego in fluid contact and understanding with all members of itself. To celebrate our unique names forms habits interests is to exercise maximum pleasure in exchange. A deprived ego strives for power and control in the literal and negative sense of bondage and stricture. Politicians are deprived people. We don't live in a society in which politics is defined chiefly by service. The concept of service is rhetorical and not an ideal informing political action. The extraordinary contrast between power as inner and expanding awareness and power as political murder and repression is beautifully and terrifyingly exemplified in *Performance* — a movie damned by conventional critics who can't relate their own activities as critics to the awful truth of the movie; or who read the relation unconsciously and attack the truth which would undermine their own position if consciously understood. This is not a trip movie. I mean a pyschedelic box office spectacle. It's a morality play for our time. It's the first flick I've seen which represents a common fantasy of every head here and abroad. A fantasy boldly and perhaps immorally realized by Ken Kesey in his electric kool-aid acid test. Still, I think everybody out there *knew* that the punch was laced with acid. The great fantasy is the unannounced pollution of a water supply for a whole city or the secret infiltration of a White House congressional cocktail party to trick our leaders into the treat of true power. Yet every head knows the danger of exploding the consciousness of deprived oppressed and repressive people a number of times removed from their own independent power sources. In 1966 I imagined a political coup involving the deposition of LBJ through acid intoxification which made him so ridiculous to the people that they humored him awhile and then put him away. I was assuming an enlightened public. If a politician can't handle being God at the worldly level how could he comprehend himself as the God that he really is. He could go bezerk and push all the buttons. Every enlightened head is prepared to offer himself as a guide when he offers the drug itself. The criminal of *Performance* is accompanied by the magicians of his undoing. He becomes a possible creature of love and pleasure in the bizarre setting of three people who feel forced apparently to "turn on" one of the civilized monsters they've been living in creative exile from, a privacy bound to be invaded, and destroyed if they were unable to convert the menace into a member of their paradise. The criminal is converted by the explosion of his consciousness in a place of guidance and comfort. But the conclusion is that the rest of the gang come to get him and by so doing destroy the basement paradise anyway. Jagger and Fox in the movie represent the real polarities of our society as they continue in our post-war confusion — the criminal (i.e., politician) exercising real, external power; the crasher enjoying the power of love and fantasy. It's so clear. It's so sad. In the movie the polarized people meet, and ruin each other. The two types of performances are games that can't thrive apart from one another. The party (the part of the mind, body) which has to succumb to integrate ourselves is the part(y) we have been developing all these centuries to survive materially and growing monstrously outsized unbalanced to our neglected and shriveled up insides of magic and spirit and fantasy which a functional society permits and even unconsciously projects in the form of certain types of tolerated freaks like artists. In any revolutionary showdown the freaks will go with the rest. The part which *must* succumb for any survival purged of materialistic cruelty is the part which looks so strong and healthy which made so many of us materially comfortable. The part which has already succumbed, which does so in every generation, is the enslaved portion of the general criminal — a sacrifice to the system of comfort which he (the enslaved) is granted in some form to keep him mollified and in place. (Marcuse is great on this subject.) The revolution of the enslaved as they rise against their oppressors is a civil war of the head and results in a new oppressor, the tables being merely turned. There has *never been* a revolution. A true revolution would be the catastrophic (re)integration of mind spirit and body. Our political isolation from each other is a mere reflection of the isolation of ourselves from ourselves. *Performance* is about a crash program for change in a society now literally equipped for genocide. Drugs have been scandalized by the media. Drugs are as dangerous or as beneficial as they are intended to be. Drugs in all their hallucinogenic forms are the agents of instant and radical change in a society that can't afford to wait even for a new Messiah. People are doing their best with Yoga, Buddha, Zen, psychoanalysis etc. The drugs are quick and certain and lead people also to Yoga Buddha Zen and other disciplines of enlightenment. I'm saying all this and I just had a terrifying drug experience. I went through Woodstock on my way to Rochester. For All Hallows Eve I went to a *Performance*-like dream womb where my friend Lee is living now at the home of Zubin the tie-dye king. It's a commune of 14 people or so. They were cooking rice and making barrels of salad and inserting coins into the centers of apples and hanging up a total interior of billowing cloud droopy tie-dyed satin or silk of mandalic magnificance in preparation for a halloween bash. Lee produced a bag of mescaline pills donated by the landlord. I thought it over. I trust Lee. I trusted the place. I've never taken the chemical. I mean mescal or acid or the mushroom. I manufactured my own mind bender three times for three extended (weeks, and the third time months) joy rides of death and resurrection which I never tire of describing and explaining. I've been wanting to correlate the effects of the ingested chemical with the effects of the chemical I produced spontaneously. I've made the correlation. They're the same. The tremendous variety of known and recorded effects are manifestations of the same experience of surrender to the great forces of our own centers which are everywhere. But when you go out of your mind naturally the graph curve is a gentle diagonal sloping upward into a long horizontal crest where I believe it's possible to stay if conditions are supportive it's a beautiful nothing everyplace of cancellations to be but I came down each time on the gradual slope to complete the graph. On the drug the graph is a dizzy vertical. The highest hill of a roller coaster trip. I'm not experienced in the fast trip. I went up and out and called for bread and milk. I left my body and wanted to come back right away. I couldn't so I wrestled with it. Fear. Pain. Nausea. Incredible energy. Unable to go with it. Got locked in a stuggle of holding it inside. Couldn't look at faces, all glowing iridescent colors. Couldn't accept the enormous sound of a guest merely swallowing a swig of cider. The energy of the place itself too much. Good vibes. Drums. Dancing. Beautiful people. Witches. Goblins. Fairies. Ghosts. All Hallows Eve. 1970. Exorcism. I made myself a victim. I suffered in the kitchen. I suffered in the living room. I suffered in a bedroom. I couldn't walk because I had no body. I creaked into an ancient age of myself. I was all bent over and my hands went crooked. I told Lee in this crusty weak old faltering voice I was a hundred and twenty nine. He said at least. And he said I should try to let go and sleep. I said I couldn't because I'd die like Jimi (I'd had four tranquilizers). But I was dying anyway and I knew it. I remember talking about the universal trip, how we have some silence called death in between fucking ourselves to bring each other back. I said it was too painful to know so much and I was in a physical agony from it. Unnameable agony. I mentioned *Performance* a lot. I kept saying help me and there was no help until the chemical left my body or I went to sleep which I did at last they drove me a half mile away to a tiny cabin of friends in a quiet grove I passed out under care of Lee and two other gentle people Sharon and Brock. A fantastic trip. I learned once more how ancient I am. I learned how pathetic we are. And how beautiful if we believe it. And I tried driving on to Allen Ginsberg's place between Woodstock and Albany day after I said I'd be there. Allen has a mushroom growing on his land he told me he'd like to ask Cage about. I said Cage is only interested in the cooking mushroom. Certainly I wasn't interested in his mushroom myself at that moment. Nor am I interested in winding this up just now as though I knew what I was doing I was just on a greyhound for six hours and I'm going to say to be continued since the columns have a habit of doing that anyway I post a thought in continuance of a favorite fantasy for a movie script based on a Christ on acid idea modernizing *He Who Must Die* set in Westchester with Yale and Harvard alumnae just freshly on Wall Street commuting in from their debutante wives newly graduated from Smith and Vassar. The roles of the Passion.

—November 12, 1970

The Wedding

LEUCADIA: 20 miles north of San Diego . . . because we're sitting
here splitting fields and relaxing together and Pauline Oliveros is
playing me a tape of a performance of her Composition to Valerie
Solanis and Marilyn Monroe in Recognition of Their Desperation.
The friends of our friends are our friends. Dear Everyhead at home,
this is happy gay land. Can you believe the place is a Leucadia where
a Pauline who is another American and musical Gertrude Stein lives
with her recently wedded wife on the Pacific near the cliff of a
sunrise ceremony this July 4th performed by a minister of the
Universal Life Church which makes the difference between the
generations between say ours and Gertrude's merely one of great
pride in announcement. I told Pauline that the name of the World
War I model-T-Ford owned by Gertrude Stein and Alice Toklas was
Aunt Pauline. And that Pauline is the name whose bearers I collect
on my grandmother journey toward some place far below the
Northern Sea or like Persephone arriving from Hades to join her
mother Demeter when the spring is timing to go through the world
together but unlike Persephone not having to hear anyone say Ah
my dearest you ate those pomegranate seeds and therefore must
return some part of the year to sit in the dark places on the throne
of yr lord and master. Nah, this is 1971 in Leucadia which is the
ancient name of one of the Ionian Islands and the place Sappho is
said to have ended her life by a heroic leap off the summit of a
magnificent cliff. (At Lesbos she was the head of a great poetic school,
for poetry in that age and place was cultivated as assiduously and
apparently as successfully by women as by men.) You can't go
anywhere you can't get back from. Before and after follow each
other. Picture a lesbian estate on the cliffs of California where doors
open green and bodies open blue . . . Pauline married Lin Barron
who she is also a music person a cellist and composer and student at
the University of California at San Diego where Pauline is a professor
of electronic music and composition. For the two days preceding
the wedding she stayed at the minister's house in quite seclusion. Till
death do them unite or in life they can part as in all things only

perchange when we cease to have any motives at all can we comprehend the magnitude of the event. I fell in love in Los Angeles the night of the brinking day I was planning to leave and didn't stay because of it. That's the way isn't it? You're takin a very big gamble on gettin some sorrow. So last night happy new year I made the gay rounds in San Diego by invitation a pretty opera singer who later did me in good so I felt as well treated in a strange city I'd never seen by day as I imagined one would as the recipient of an Eskimo wife offered by her old man who makes a stranger feel at home in this manner and custom I've heard it sounds fine any old way you get done . . . You wiped me out I mumuranted. Happy New Year she said. So today January 1 in Leucadia I arrange drive L.A. tomorrow to meet the one I glimpsed many hours over body and loving and not even concerned to be getting it off by the light of a bottled blue candle of a Duccio Madonna captioned Our Mother of Perpetual Help. Is this the beginning of a new civilization or the symptom of a dying one. Demeter saw the chariot approaching and like a wild bird she flew to clasp her child. Sappho's painting of passion . . . has never since been surpassed (in antiquity her fame rivaled that of Homer). The only boy Daphne ever loved was a boy disguised as a girl. The day of the wedding Pauline went out below the cliff about 4 a.m. to hide out there with her conch shell trumpet and wearing her muslin gown toga Greek style made by the minister's wife. Pauline is impressively round and solid and good humored like Gertrude for whom she dedicated a piece in 1966 called Participle Dangling. The one I just heard, for Valerie Solanis and Marilyn Monroe, in Recognition of Their Desperation, is scored for string quartet, bass, three flutes, organ, and Buchla Electronic Music System. Many male composers think of her as the only female in their field. She wrote an article in the *New York Times* this summer on the subject which should be an encouragement to the other active women. In L.A. Alison Knowles was deploring the artistry of Charlotte Moorman whom I said we must cherish in all her vulgarity. Charlotte has no respect for cock in the desperation of her sex to sit on the stage of history. A magnificent woman Charlotte. Tits and teeth and all. And better latent than never. Even if she becomes more and more absorbed in some difficulty we can't fathom. Her hair was unbound as she ran down the slopes of the Mountain Ossa. Daphne saw him (Apollo) standing upon a peak with the light striking his quiver and she knew him for the most beautiful of the Olympians but when he called to her she fled from him for she had vowed that no God nor no man should possess her. Madam, your breakfast plate waits for you. The decision reached itself really. Mascula Virgo. Going against the grain of her sex. Do you think the time has come to share with a waiting world the names of the prominent people whose lives have been changed by taking LSD asked Leary who answered yes which I answer to the same question I would terminate by saying who would have taken homosexuality for the news is urgent to the health of the state in which the girl on the run and her pursuer become alternate versions of the same plight. In San Franscisco in a gay bar they told me it was a place that Janis Joplin frequented. Dear Kate Millett, thanks for your letter, I'm sorry too about the unpleasantness of our encounter, I meant to withdraw my challenge since everybody is working on different phases of a personal comeout program. We'll try to materialize the tellie show for March, I'll let you know. Gregory you met will be on it. We'd like Paul Goodman and Gore Vidal and Allen Ginsberg and Susan Sontag and I asked John Cage who doesn't think it's important. Pauline and Lin here will come if possible. Sappho is rising. As the sun was coming up Pauline emerged from underneath the cliff at the sound of the conch shell trumpet of her mate arriving above also garbed in the muslin gown toga they were married by the minister who rang a bell and symbolized their union by wrapping them round together in a long cloth and releasing two doves to inform the animal world. The newlyweds and company of friends descended the cliff to the beach to celebrate. Apollo wears Daphne as a laurel around his brow. For as she felt his breath upon her neck and his hands upon her shoulders she swayed; she knew herself changed, and rooted in earth, and safe from pursuit as the blood in her body flowed down to become sap and her limbs and the flesh and the flowing hair become branches and leaves and Apollo mourned for her where he stood and loved her now as a tree even as he had loved her as a maiden. The country of Lesbos is very fertile.

The country of Leucadia is luscious too. You can hear as I did after driving back up to L.A. as I sd to join the one I loved by the light of Our Mother of Perpetual Help the sound of one ocean clapping. Pauline played me her record of the Songs of the Humpback Whale. I wish we could arrange transportation for all far below the Northern Sea or anyway a fantasy I'm developing of triumphal re-entries such as Pauline Oliveros in full concert returning to Houston where she came from. Gertrude arriving New York 1930 or so or when by steamship a celebrity was said to have baffled reporters by making herself clear. (Alice cackled and giggled perhaps a little maliciously.) Isadora scandalized herself by flaunting the red flag of her Russian boy poet husband. Janis Joplin told Cavett and America on the tubes she'd been laughed out of her class, out of the town, out of the state, "so I'm goin' home man". I've got my eyes on a royal barge setting out from Calais to Dover. My fabled father is waiting. Ah Persephone (sd Hades), strive to feel kindliness in yr heart toward me who carried you off by violence and against your will. It's okay dad we're feasting on the guacamole and the oysters on the half shell and passing up the pomegranate seeds this trip around. *The Female Freeway*, a book of poems just out here by Lynn Lonidier who engineered the rituals of the wedding. Dear Lee, Pauline did a tarot reading for me. The first or basic or significator card was the four of wands — two laurel wreathed females under a laurel arch. The outcome card the knight of swords. In a dream I called a reconciliation-with-women dream I appeared as identical twins in the denim jacket laughing bent over slightly on the road under weight of a backpack. I tell Pauline not only is the coincidence of her first name a cropper but the first two syllables of her last name belong as well to my last livid maternal relative. And do what you will you will with the eros in it, and the olive, as in branch, this part of the Pacific coast between L.A. and San Diego is very Greek somehow.

—*January 14, 1971*

Lois Lane is a Lesbian

I plotted this augmented "confession" driving out of New Orleans at 5 a.m. with a broken left shoulder feeling cosmically sorry for myself and the world. I could've been some river boat rake shot up in a gambling game and crawling off to die in a swamp, that's how bad it was. At midnight I fell down a flight of stairs in the unlit landing of a warehouse where some kids had been showing me how they manufacture water beds. At 12.10 out on the street there, after broadcasting my agony sprawled over a car hood, I heard this nice clean American male heterosexual hippie who had been my escort explain that we should sleep in my vehicle together. At 12.15 I figured I couldn't have been in worse shape if the concussion I had just sustained had been administered by the billy club of a cop who was now offering to rape me as a reward for being so attractively destroyed. At 12.20 I climbed over the frying pan into the fire where I signaled through the flames the message that we both liked the same sex. At 12.25 my ex-companion of the water bed company was in greater shock than me and I left him gaping and fuming there to go on and win a medal for driving or careening through enemy territory in critical condition to a hospital where for four hours I waited in vain for somebody to determine the extent of the damage. At 5 a.m., as I said, I was on the road. I didn't look back. New Orleans was a disaster area called Mardi Gras. At 2 p.m. when I arrived there the French Quarter I thought was the most exotic area every side of St. Mark's Place and Carnaby Street and Telegraph Avenue and Commercial Street in Provincetown. By 7 p.m. I had lost and/or been ripped off of eight bills, I hoped I would never see another peace emblem or insignia ever; I had paid $2.55 for a ginger ale in a low class strip joint, and 25 cents to pee in a normal restaurant; I had been inadvertently charged by a troupe of longhairs pouring out of a lavender bus demonstrating for more pay for their local police force; I had declined the advances of a New Yorker who recognized me in a coffee shop, and passed up the subtler advances of a girl called Jill cruising me in a head-shop; the American eagle on my van had come loose and askew; and I had read in my own newspaper that I was part of a phony new industry of interpersonal technology of which my confessional gush is consecrated to the proposition that we must all abandon the privileged privacy of our most precious relationships or perish from emotional constipation and that these confessions are becoming increasingly profitable, both culturally and financially, and that I have been publicly exhorting every pretty girl in America to come out of the closet and into my bed (yeah) and that I want to look good so badly that I wind up making every else around me look bad.

If I hadn't been so upset over the new evidence that some of us are still finding it so difficult to celebrate all the things we are I would have been more astonished and flattered that a successful white American male heterosexual film critic had invested that much time and energy and rhetorical diligence to pay so much hostile attention to the meagre outpourings of the most oppressed and confused and unrecognized minority in every country of the world. It is as much your privilege to think I'm exaggerating as it is mine to believe I'm stating the case to fit the facts. Each of us is a barometer of social conditions which we observe through the perceptual screen of our needs. Reviewing and re-reviewing my experience of growing up and sort of surviving in a male dominated heterosexual world I am now prepared to say that a female who is a lesbian in this society is about as well off as a Sabine woman trapped in a camp of black corporals. I am, by the way, more in sympathy with the black cause than ever before, and in fact with all causes, for it has recently occurred to me that all causes are the same cause (as my critic said, we are all in the same boat) and that what we're doing here then is educating all the members of ourselves to certain needs which have gone unheeded or unrecognized or worse damned and vilified and thrust underground so that we can all coexist more happily together. My initial reaction to the women's movement was a classic. The line was "What's the matter with *them, I've* been doing it all these years." You can hear this same line from accomplished females all over the place. It's an elitist capitalistic attitude which blesses the fortunate and condemns the ignorant. My initial reaction to the black movement was hey wait a minute I didn't *choose* to be born white, and let me tell *you* about the problems of a white homosexual female in a . . . et cetera. Now I suggest you go up to a black person and say White People Have Problems Too and see what kind of response you get. I'm going on record here to notify every heterosexual male and female that every lesbian and every homosexual is all too aware of the problems of heterosexuals since they permeate every aspect of our social political economic and cultural lives. That we were in fact educated on these problems. That we were brought up and spoon fed or pitch forked on the crucible of the problems of thousands of Romeos and Juliets radiating outward from all our sublimely miserable and broken families into the movies and the funnies and the histories and the psychologies and the novels and our great Western classics. It is, in fact, the heterosexual problems which create a gay liberation movement or any movement to end the artificial social construction of sexual specialization which makes some of our members ill and confused. It is the heterosexual problem which creates this tremendous body of clinical literature to brand some aspect of sexuality perverse and abnormal. It is the heterosexual problem which creates the monstrosity of transsexualism, surely the most pitiful operation going, to "help" some gullible people *not* to be homosexual in a society far from convinced that all the equipment we are born with is perfectly beautiful. It is the hetersexual problem which creates therapies designed to "cure" people of their natural sexual interests. These therapies and those clinical studies belong to the same market of a disease called normalcy. A healthy society would enjoy and encourage all of its perversions by which in fact the society would be defined. Poly-morphous perversity is the norm. There is no norm. Unless it's Mailer, who perfectly embodies the heterosexual problem. I think all of us are authorities on the heterosexual problem. Knowledge on the subject is instantly available, in case you've missed out, in every daily newspaper with their front page accounts of the Wars. We are bored with the news from the heterosexual fronts. We want to hear from the lesbians and the homosexuals now. I want homosexual movies and novels and funnies and histories and songs and classics. Even problem stories. Certainly the songs. Let all those gay rock artists come out from behind their phony lyrics. But the movies! The big medium. I don't expect the next batch of gay ones to show us nothing but the doomed clandestine affair of Therese and Isabelle in boarding school, and the wrecked life of Sister George whose girlfriend leaves her for a great white witch of the west whose cold clawing sexual advances constitute the only sexual revelation in the film, and the huge tree of D.H. Lawrence's well equipped *Fox* falling on one of his two heroines to effectively wipe out the contender to his hero's object, or the girls in *Persona* never getting to the point, or the sisters in *Silence*, and the boys in anybody's band parading their sterotyped images to a public greedy for their distress and martyrdom. — Andy Warhol could give us a few straight stories. Eight hours of Nancy and Little Lulu in bed. Or Blondie and Lois Lane. I don't care much about endings one way or another but the homosexual movies could begin by making up for all the years we grew up watching Gary Cooper and Richard Greene ride gloriously into the purple sunset with Myrna Loy and Mrs Miniver etc. to live happily ever after. This film critic a few months ago wrote in the context of some review that "although I don't belong to the happy-endings-for-homosexuals club . . ." which made me ask him when I saw him "why *don't* you belong to the happy-endings-for-homo-sexuals club?" Exactly. The question is why we don't all belong to the happy endings (and beginnings and middles) for everybody club. Can you imagine me saying, in any context, "although I don't belong to the happy-endings-for-heterosexuals club"? Can you imagine anybody saying "although I don't belong to the happy-ending-for-black-people club"? Can you imagine any intelligent observer at this moment in history writing an article damning the blacks and their social agonies? Or suggesting that James Baldwin or Eldridge Cleaver or LeRoi Jones were something *more* or something *other* than their blackness — that they were not so much black people who happened to be fine writers as fine writers who happen to be black? We are not *any* of us something more (or less) or *other* than *anything* that we are. We are the sum total of all we are and we are all of what we are in every thought and in every action we manifest.

The Western habit of separating everything and of constantly defining our own spaces by the creation of an enemy is the habit that projected a profession called criticism by which people glibly judge and assess the complications of the lives of others. I never woke up one morning to say Ah now I am going to write something culturally and financially profitable called a confession. I don't share our film critic's obsession with careerism in the forms he describes it as Looking For An Edge. Confession isn't a luxury, it's a necessity. By any American standards none of us is rich. When any artist in this crazy pragmatic country begins to survive by doing just what he wants to do, his art, it seems to me an occasion for rejoicing. That the artists themselves should be attacking each other for arriving at this precarious position of a tenuous security seems to me the height of insanity. In New Orleans that apocalyptic afternoon I picked up the James Taylor cover pix issue of *Rolling Stone* along with *The Voice*. Taylor is quoted: "It is very strange making a living out of being yourself." — and the writer goes on: "which neatly defines the personal confessional school of songwriting which promises to supplant much of the hard rock of the '60s." — Confessional literature in any form hardly needs an apology for its current expressions. One shouldn't have to refer to our honorable ancestors St Augustine or Rousseau or de Quincey. The form is a misleading one in any case, for one might always ask what is *not* a confession? Still, there is a kind of religious consciousness, awakening, by fire and shock, which powers the necessity, an inner compulsion, to forge a confessional style. Nerval and Rimbaud and Artaud are such artists in the French tradition. The French historically have seemed especially susceptible. In any country the tradition can be related by a short mental jump to the religious ecstasies and confessions of a Theresa of Avila. At the present moment in America there's an activity we might call confessional journalism which is practiced along the whole gamut of profit at one end and revelation at the other. It's interesting to me that our film critic should express his distaste and displeasure over the medium while practising it in the same breath. If I had anything to do with stimulating his interest in himself to the point of public display I'd be pleased since I believe the entire practice of criticism is a pathetic projection of personal terrors and inadequacies and suppressed ambition. The rhetorical expertise of some of its practitioners is the best educated refusal to deal with the central problem of the world — the Self. My "confessional gush" is consecrated to no other proposition than that of collecting all of my selves that I can raise to consciousness in the shape of current experiences into some form of literary energy at the moment I sit down most every week to write that damn column. Sometimes I get a masterpiece seizure and work very hard for a structural coup. Sometimes I'm unsuccessfully trying to merge my literary ambition with my cause concerns. It's *always* a dilemma. What to say and how to say it. And you have to perpetuate the illusion that it means something to somebody besides yourself. Otherwise why the hell would you be publishing it? Why the hell am I bothering *here* to regress to an old academic style to answer a person who feels that his own myths and feelings are being ridiculed when he sees an exhibition of another way of life? Because that's the way I feel *right now*. I have straight friends whose lives I honor and respect and *they* don't feel ridiculed by the difference they discern in *me*. If it's anybody's turn to feel ridiculed, and by the massive heterosexual culture, you know who it is, and that's what the gay liberation is all about — to end this ridiculous posturing about anybody else's sexuality. My first and final line if I had only one on the subject would be that if you can't walk out your door and down the street and into the park in any familiar embrace with the one you love the whole society is in trouble. Men will have to give up the idea that every female is their potential mate. And women will have to abandon their designs on every male. Gay people are now expecting and demanding the same sanctified regard for *their* sexual interests and unions as they have rendered for as long as they can remember to the weird forces that endowed them with life in the first place. Now there is only one way for this social change to take place. And that is for all gay people, those who know it and accept it, to stand up and speak for themselves. There is no other way. The laws and discriminatory practises will alter according as the attitude does, and the attitude continues absurd as long as the society tolerates its aberrations by successfully pretending that it doesn't know what it already suspects. Ask any gay person about their traumatic confrontations with their families. Everybody *knows* everything. That is, we are in constant telepathic communication. But society is an iceberg. Most of it is under water. Knowledge which would reveal our most ancient archetypal terrors and taboos, our collective sins and guilts, is rigorously repressed. When this unconscious material erupts and surfaces we become the animal I can only imagine we once were — an animal all of whose parts were in mutual and open-ended communication. The human animal is, perhaps, in the tragic position of having to surface all the way up in order to go all the way back down, or vice versa. Total conscious knowledge means clear traffic from the depths of the unconscious to the rational parts of the functional forebrain. If the iceberg of society surfaced completely we'd be living in a painful but compassionate utopia. I believe with Freud and Brown and Reich etc. that sexual polymorphous perversity (you *can*, by the way, reconcile Reich with the others) and all its social consequences is the paradise we most profoundly wish to recover. Specialization (sexual, technological, etc.) is the monster that civilization visited on itself to sustain its material needs. We're working now for an aerial view. We need to know what we already know. Not enough can be said to inform people of what they already know. A secret is an archaic hoarded treasure. Secrets mean borders and barriers and codes and passports and thick walls and frontiers between people. Just a year ago I permitted Rosalyn Drexler at a small dinner party to convince me I'd been a dope for revealing myself at an artists' colony where I'd been I was not being self protective as Rosalyn pointed out "Oh Jill, can't you keep a secret" and I was not yet able to reply immediately "Do you keep your marraige to Sherman a secret?" — But if you think I'm having fun being a blabber mouth lesbian you're mistaken. The field is thick with clashing swords. The ground is already drenched in blood. If you think I'm feeling sorry for myself you're right. But I'm greatly in favor of people feeling that particular emotion. It's against the grain of the fearless Protestant ethic. Yet you don't know you're a human being until you feel sorry for yourself in a very grand way. Then you look around you and see possibly for the first time how we're all in it together and then you'll feel that big cosmic emotion and that's how you discover with a certain shock that you're religious even though you've read the French existentialists on the death of God.

I know the media thrives on our petty intramural battles but we really want something bigger for ourselves don't we? Why, in any event, would a quarterback want to tackle his own center? I've got enough trouble. I'm persona non grata with every "group" in the country, just for openers. The women's lib people don't like the way I swim. The Gay Liberation Front says I wouldn't get any support from *them*. Both organizations think I'm a male chauvinist pig, probably because I take more girls to bed (or want to or pretend to) than I have a right to — as though nobody was ever luring *me* to bed. — A black man once told me that LeRoi Jones and the like wanted my head on a platter. The artists were never pleased that I began to find their lives more interesting than their work. The religious groups accuse me of grubbing around on a fame and art trip. The artists coalition types begrudge my sudden minimal independence in my old age. All radicals dismiss me as an idle dreamer. Gay newspaper says I'm an exhibitionist. And I suppose the Aubudon society has it in for me too. Anyway I'm on everybody's list as number one menace to the universe. I have a case of the most exquisite paranoia. It's a wonderful feeling. For a female lesbian bastard writer mental case I'm doing awfully well. The only movement I'm dedicated to myself is finding out what anybody is calling me so I can say yeah that's me. For example: Co-opting the names in the name-calling dictionaries called psychoanalytical textbooks would finish a profession which defines its existence by an occult terminology of names branding whatever it isn't — that is, the enemy. Schizophrenics, Unite!

—March 4, 1971

On a Clear Day You Can See Your Mother

Some old lines and some new ones thrown on to each other for the Town Hall affair

The title of this episode is new approach: All women are lesbians except those who don't know it naturally they are but don't know it yet I am a woman who is a lesbian because I am a woman and a woman who loves herself naturally who is other women is a lesbian a woman who loves women loves herself naturally this is the case that a woman is herself is all woman is a natural born lesbian so we don't mind using the name like any name it is quite meaningless it means naturely I am a woman and whatever I am we are we affirm being what we are the way of course all men are homosexuals being having a more sense of their homo their homo-ness their ecce homo-ness their ecce prince & lord & masterness the 350 years of Abraham intersample Abraham lived for 350 years because the bible ages are only a succession of sons and fathers and grandfathers intensely identifying with their ancestors their son so identified naturely with the father that he believed he was the father and of course he was as was Abraham and Isaac and Jacob and Esau and Reuben and Simeon and Levi and Judah and Joseph each one lived for 350 years, but who are the daughters of Rachel and Ruth and Sarah and Rebekah the rest we do not know the daughters never had any daughters they had only sons who begat more sons and sons so we have very little sense, from that particular book, of the lineage and ligaments and legacies and identities of mothers and daughters and their daughters and their mothers and mothers and daughters and sisters who were naturally not lesbians if they had nothing of each other save sons so now we must say Verily Verily, I say unto thee, except a woman be born again she cannot see the Kingdom of Goddess a woman must be born again to be herself her own eminence and grace the queen queen-self whose mother has pressed upon her mouth innumerable passionate kisses so sigh us . . . There is in every perfect love/ A law to be accomplished too: that the lover should resemble/The belov'd: And be the same. And the greater is the likeness/Brighter will the rapture flame — even as John there St John of the Cross raptured on his pal Jesus whose son he was his father his son as when Jesus in another time said to his lovers and haven't you heard it a deluge of times And he saith unto them, Follow me, and I will make you fishers of men. And straightway they left their nets, and followed him. Ah lover and perfect equal! I meant that you should discover me so, by my faint indirection; And I, when I meet you, mean to discover you by the like in you . . . I want she who is the tomboy in me . . . I want she who is very female in me . . . I want she who is British about me . . . I want she who is ugly American about me . . . I want she who is mayonnaise about me . . . I want she who is the cunt and the balls and the breasts of me and the long straight browny hair and the gangly boarding school adolescent in a navy blue blazer and gold buttons of me . . . narcissme, qui consiste a se choisir soi-meme comme objet erotique . . . and I want the men to carry my boxes of books for me and carry me upsy daily pigback and pay for me everywhere and adore me as a lesberated woman . . . Over the inevitable we shall not grieve . . . This is the body that Jill built . . . Ecce Leda the Lesbian . . . Ecce Greta the Gay the gay Gertrude the gay gay gayness of being gay, of being, to be equal we have to become who we really are and women we will never be equal women until we love one another women and say Woe, and behold, a voice from Hera saying This is my beloved daughter in whom I am well pleased O Women of America the World you are your own best friend, your own closest friend, you are the best company for yourself . . . you should go through and study even right back to your childhood, and of course if you have the great ability to go back to your previous lives you should do so Women of America the World you are your own best friend . . . These are the series of sayings we are saving the world with: the lamentations of Mary and Marilyn Monroe. Lord help you, Maria, full of grease, the load is with me! Her smile is between her legs and her moustache is in her armpit and she ordered that history should begin with her with her this is a muster of elephantal cuntsequence the lost and foundamental situation of the feminine is the primordial relation of identity between mother and daughter the mysteries of Eleusis of the reunion of Demeter and her daughter Persephone to be born again and again and Arethusa and Artemis and Hebe and Hera and Diana and Daphne and Doris and Dora and Dolly and the Danaides all but one murdered their husbands on their wedding nights our case revives their stories for more than a hundred years I wander about in it without coming to the end of her body the most we can do is to dream the myth onwards, and rewrite the stories we will reunite Electra and her mother Clytemnestra and Jocasta will be well pleased in her daughter Antigone who will be more involved in her mothers and her daughters than in the proper burial for her brother and we will remember the histories of say how Eleanor of Aquitaine made a crusade to the holy land and dressed all her ladies in waiting as Amazons in leopard skins and dressed herself as Pan Athenea and that's how they rode through Greece for the queendom of heaven *is* as a woman travelling into a far country who called her own servants and delivered unto them *her* goods for Whole the World to see a woman finds pleasure in caressing a body whose secrets she knows, her own body giving her the clue to its preferences giving each the other their sense of self tracing the body of the woman whose fingers in turn trace her body that the miracle of the mirror be accomplished between women love is contemplative caresses are intended less to gain possession of the other than gradually to recreate the self thru her own self among the women and the women the multitude on the way to the way the world was before it began it is now the world is heading definitely towards a matriarchy more often to return to the source of things we must travel in the opposite direction, Wring out the clothes! Wring in the dew! Before all the King's Hoarsers with all the Queens Mum Her birth is uncontrollable and her organ is working perfectly and there's a part that's not screwed on and her education is now for by and about women and presided over by woman All women are lesbians except those who don't know it of course since whereas both sexes (even as Sigmund sd) are originally more attached to the mother and it is the *task* of the girl to transfer this attachment to the father naturally they we are but don't know it yet that woman is now approaching her ancient destiny as woman I am and therefore lesbian which means nothing we could say it over

and over again over lesbianlesbianlesbianlesbianlesbianlesbianlesbian-
lesbian — Special from the White House, the President of the United
States announced last night the appointment of a lesbian to his
cabinet . . . it's nice if you can invite them in, they usually come in
without knocking . . . Womens lib and let lib new official position
on lesbians: Hey ladies it's okay, like Red China is there so we might
as well recognize it . . . yupyop . . . Liberal Schmiberal . . . Maybe . . .
uh . . . we should invite . . . uh . . . her . . . uh . . . one of them to
dinner . . . One of what, dear? Uh, well, uh, she is a bit odd isn't she?
I mean, you know how we'd feel if a black man was interested in our
daughter — Aaaaaaaaaaaaa . . . Oh god, and she might make a pass at
my wife . . . Agh . . . But if she just doesn't *talk* about what she is . . .
We could pretend . . . Whaddyou say to the naked lady please please
sorry thank you we are getting to the bottom of women's lib we are
going down on women's lib I am beside myself with love for you
when you are beside me my love the beginning of the unifirst is rite
now if all tinks are at this momentum being cremated and the end of
the unihearse is right now for all thinks are at this momentus passing
away we went to see the Dairy of a Skinzopretty girl O why dint
her mother straighten out her teeth when she was young O she is
envolved in many strange and wondrous adventures O in short she
had come into that abnormal condition known as elation O she did
not yet love and she loved to love; she sought what she might love,
in love with loving . . . O what can she say now that is not the story
of so many others O do not fail me she says you are my last chance,
indeed our last chance, to save the West . . . and who vants the Moon
ven ve can land on Venus . . . and O how would you like to be the
heroine of yr own life story (she's looking forward to it extremely)
and O don't be nervous be mermaid be she whom I love who travels
with me and sits along while holding me by the hand she ahold of
my hand has completely satisfied me o natural woman woman
vinmim virmin woreman woeman of America the World until until
women all the women see in each other the possibility of a primal
commitment which includes sexual love they will be denying
themselves the love and value they have readily accorded to men,
thus affirming their second class status for within the heterosexual

institution no woman can be the equal it is a contrafiction in terms the heterosexual institution is a male institution a homo ecce homo institution and you can't ever change the absoluteness the institution is political is built out of the institutionalized slavery of women so it *is* a contradiction in terms — such an institution must only collapse of its own accord from within the heterosexual institution is over spiritually over and the new thing now that is happening is the withdrawal of women to give each other their own sense of self a new sense of self until women see in each other the possibility of a primal commitment which includes sexual love they will be denying themselves the love and value they readily accord to men thus affirming their second class status. *Until all women are lesbians there will be no true political revolution* until in other same words we are woman I am a woman who loves herself naturally who is other women is a lesbian a woman who loves women loves herself naturally this is the case that a woman is herself is all woman is a natural born lesbian so we don't mind using the name it means naturely I am a woman and whatever I am we are we affirm being what we are saying therefore *Until all women are lesbians there will be no true political revolution* meaning the terminus of the heterosexual institution through the recollection by woman of her womanhood her own grace and eminence by the intense identities of our ancestors our descendants of the mothers and the daughters and the grandmothers we become who we are which is to say we become our own identities and autonomies even as now we are so but except those who don't know it yet will be quite upset about it for some time to come as I would more properly be as majorities would have it leaning on my sword describing my defeat some women want to have their cock and eat it too and lesbian is a label invented by anybody to throw at any woman who dares to be a man's equal and lesbian is a good name it means nothig of course or everythig so we don't mind using the name in face we like it for we can be proud to claim allusion to the island made famous by Sappho the birds are talking to us in Greek again and continue on making a big thing out of it over all these centuries time we can do that we don't mind it's nice in fact for we all all of us women are lesbians why not and isn't it wonderful what a lot of devotion there is to us lying around the universe especially to those all envolved in some penis they're wrapping their cunts around . . . Oh well . . . Lillian over and out . . . he sd I want your body and she sd you can have it when I'm through with it . . . Keep yer hands off me you worldwide weirdo, I just want to be noticed, not attacked — we had a big argonaut about it . . . The age of shrivelry is abonus again . . . A Lord was not considered defeated in a local war until his flag had fallen from the main tower of his castle . . . svastickles falling outen da sky . . . the current dispute would be settled if the central figure was no longer present (*at this moment our leader Norman Mailer askt me to read my last line and I said I'd like to forego the question and my friends appeared on stage and I made love before notables and my circuitry got overloaded and the men in the audience voted they dint want to hear me no more and I don't remember too much except leaving and wishing later I'd kissed Germaine before we walked off*) . . . Flash from the White House: last night the President of the United States, clad only in a scanty tribal costume, announced the resignation of the American Government . . . His life was an empty record of gambling cockfighting titting balls and masques vimmin and vine clothes . . . Better latent than never . . . aliquem alium interum . . . there's no such thing as sexual differentiation in the spiritual nature of wo(man) . . . This is the problem passion play of the millentury . . . O this Restoration Comedy — it's going to be a beautiful reunion . . . plunderpussy and all spoiled goods going into her nabsack and some heroine women in wings of Samothrace . . . Is it to drown her passengers that you have bored a hole in her? Rubbish, what bunkum these people talk . . . Events are preshipitaking themselves in the harpiest confusion . . . cunnilinguist . . . Listen. If you recognized an aspect of yourself that you love in these ancient new womens heads I too have recognized an admirable aspect of myself in your willingness to be as beautiful as you are who you are My mother was a vestal, my father I knew not no prince nor lord nor master-ness but the nipples and navels of a whirld a wonderwoman the mothers and the daughters and the great grandmothers and daughters of Rachel and Ruth and Sarah and Rebekah the rest we will know now the daughter the mothers and sisters will have daughters who beget daughters so we will more sense, from this time, of the lineage and ligaments and legacies and identities of our mothers and daughters and their mothers and mothers and daughters and sisters who are naturally of course lesbians if they have of each other and saying Verily Verily except a woman must be born again she cannot see the Queendom of goddess a woman must be born again to be herself her own eminence and grace the queen queenself whose mother has pressed upon her mouth innumerable passionate kisses . . . Sail away where the wind blows sweet . . . and take a sister by her hand . . . Lead her far from this barren land . . . ON A CLEAR DAY YOU CAN SEE YOUR MOTHER.

—May 6, 1971

Hic et Ubique

It was the sort of trip you spend much more time coming and going than you do there. Then too all living leading inevitably to the supreme adventure of transition we crossed by ferry more times than you might ordinarily if you were just making a single trip to an island for the weekend, which we were. Things just really happen to me. I don't think my life was any the less interesting before I took on this terrible responsibility of leaving myself behind for a fiction. Actually more like Apollinaire I appear to be carrying everything along with me jilly nilly fact legend gossip glory and gore. Words are very very heavy magic. So everything you say is true. The necessities of style distort both fact and fiction. For sample I lied about Illinois. Besides flying my maiden voyage as a co-pilot I spent a part of one of those days way off when everybody is quiet and smiling and walking thru doors and walls because it's a sunny afternoon in the woods and the house is outrageously beautiful. I mean I made it all up that I had had an awful time prior to my flight in order to convince myself that I experienced a great drama. It's a renaissance trick of creating backgrounds to project a central figure. This is an ongoing essay with its own revision. You know that Apollinaire wrote a column called "La Vie Anecdotique" for *Mercure de France* in 1911 & thenabouts. Constantly he was trying to lug into the future with him the curious exotic treasures he found in the past. His manner became increasingly eccentric and he often filled his conversation with erudite and vulgar allusions, forgetting nothing he saw or heard. Like a photographer with her camera we interpose our notebooks between ourselves and the world. I suppose I was almost killed at an intersection a truck was bearing down on me passenger in a chevie coup C. who was driving asked me what was i doing just after we didn't collide I was writing a line about a man I saw seconds before the intersection this man who is the sort of man you see year after year a recurring image this time his appearance evoked a line about himself so I could immortalize his only aspect to me is a tall gentle einstein walking a city street and he always has a bunch of flowers in hand or a beautiful daughter or some sad thing, that's the way I framed him up or shot him dead the moment after I suppose I was almost killed at an intersection a truck was bearing down on me passenger in a chevie coup C. who was driving asked me what I was doing just after we didn't collide I was writing a line about a man I saw seconds before the intersection this man who is the sort of man you see year after year a recurring image it is possible to believe that none of these details come into being at the moment they appear. The line out my window leads to the Sun, the ox, the child, and to all of us becoming worms. Angels and ministers of grace defend us. I've met somebody more outrageous than me. The initial is P. stands for Polly. She said I could say so. It's about time somebody did. I wasn't dreaming she was driving my van in a blue latex bra. She did everything there was to do in my van since it was the sort of trip you spend much more time coming and going than you do there. Then too all living leading inevitably to the supreme adventure of transition we crossed by ferry more times than you might ordinarily if you were just making a single passage to an island for the weekend, which we were. The plot the ferryboat people devised for us was the separation of our bodies from our vehicle which they promised to reunite on the island the morning after the bodies part of the bargain had arrived to shift for themselves because the ferry is too small to carry both bodies and their vehicles on a Memorial day schedule we were waiting therefore in the early a.m., having crashed in a house of strangers and walked the morning misty sunny unreal roads of the aboriginal birds and bushes and looked at some red starfish and barbuncles leeching on the pier trunks and made love in the ants and grass weeds by two infant Xmas trees sharing a silent harbor excepting a gull streaking out close to the surface squawking like a baby crying for milk I never knew a gull made that sort of sound having waited in all these interesting ways including asking Polly to bring a scrap of paper on the way to the ants and grass weeds and Xmas trees to note none of these details since I was too busy doing them and moving my body to the pier to reunite with my vehicle as the ferry arrived there was every damned thing on it except the promised wheels so we rode back in a heat with the four boat bastards who were just altering the plot on their own initiative by claiming that the keys we left the day before in the ticket house didn't fit the van. We were besieged with diseases. Cramps and headaches and other symptoms of a desire to kill. The bull and the eagle unite to defeat the dragon. She has an eagle eye and my official sign image embarrasses me so I thank whoever anonymously from Brooklyn sending such a delicate miniature version of it all white already in the china shop. Stopping in Hartford to see important people who invited us to their museum for a function Polly asked me if they were ready for us. I guess we both have the inexhaustible strength of unbalanced people. Ca n'empeche pas d'exister. I don't know what a historian meant by saying Apollinaire ran the constant risk of turning his private life into a public performance. Risk? Whither we rides, and why, we do not know, only that the business is important and pressing. In the unstable compound of fable and fact that passes for our lives. I could tell you I saw oval colors coming off the sun walking down the clouds into the sea while I held her breasts under the blue latex she was hovering to obscure my vision of all save her head by the harbor. I could tell you she began kissing me dangerously while I was driving because I mentioned the Ti-Grace jail story as a sudden inspired line of Ti-Grace spread-eagled and shackled naked to the cell bars by the men after she constitutionally refused to strip and squat to be searched by the women but she said she didn't, begin kissing me because of my sudden sexual eloquence. Nor can I distinguish my early memories from the photos of them. We went to Bertha's house on the island. This is the house and I am a photo. A child with a stick and a sheep in the rugged backyard. A child in sneakers and a striped shirt and solid pants climbing the rocks that constitute the cliff separating the house from the ocean. A child in a small boat on the way to the house this time I cried somewhat under my shades clouding the glass or the plastic so she couldn't see I was once furious to receive as a present a box worth of kleenex held together by an iron bolt thru the center a sculpture I suppose I knew the significance of receiving kleenex when my lover got a drawing of a bird on the same occasion it is now more sensible to me there is nothing to hold on to like birds for sample but we might as well cry when the vision of an old house and maternal memories by photo or whichway and the current disjunction on a car ferry between you and a friend and lover who doesn't immediately look with wonder and admiration when you childishly point and yell "the house, the house" reminds us of the moral shock of the sudden ghastly disclosure of our mothers true nature. That was Hamlet's problem, actually, and not ours. I meant to lie so I could present the confusing nonsequitur of two such unhappy products in shock over ghastly disclosures blundering beautifully on to destruction by filling themselves inside as well as in an infinite number of positions in a rectangular space like sentences not too abruptly rotating their angular facets as cut stones or the multicoloured ball we lost to the tide in the harbor waiting for the ferry playing volley catch and fist serve and tap and such on some slabs sloping down to the water we watch ourselves in metamorphosis in sunglint floating out to sea I can't find the really classy line I thought I wrote to describe the pleasure of losing your game to an interesting disappearance anyway this is an ongoing essay with its own revision. On the ferry returning to the mainland to bring the wheels to the island ourselves I opened at random the boat bible stashed in with the life preservers to point and get the passage "forgive them their iniquities" so although I was still besieged with diseases or symptoms of murderous impulses I sat steaming silently on the other side even when we still couldn't abridge their extended plot by making the same ferry back by loading both our bodies *and* the vehicle because the lady with the keys to the ticket house within which my van keys were locked up was at church and Polly was running back and forth from captain to phone to old red-hat the macho-est one of all very angry at us for all the trouble he was causing us I realized too late that if I had bothered to avail myself of his name other than "red-hat" the revision of all emotions would have facilitated our earlier arrival or departure, but then we might not have had the opportunity to make more love while waiting in the rectangular womb on the mainland, and we might not have exchanged minor revelations on the trip back to Boone's fish place in Portland Polly noted the connection of my name obsession, as I described its origin learning hundreds of names in the funny farm six years ago, and my thinking to ask what was the name of old red-hat because he was so tall looming fearsome in his fury; and I noted for Polly to add to her Sylvia Plath fact and lore how Sylvia as Esther in her novel *Bell Jar* began obsessing suicide immediately after the psychiatrist she was visiting, by her mother's wish, in Boston, committed her to shock treatment. Like Sylvia, through a prolonged suicide Alfred Jarry clung to the moment of total freedom that precedes death. According to some historian Apollinaire's death in 1918 brought a timely end to his career since his creative powers were declining and he began to entertain vain hopes of official honors. He didn't actually die. The necessities of style distort both fact and fiction. He was creative even in his simulated death and forged disappearance and equally fictitious resurrection. The head wound he sustained in the war occurred in a trench while he was reading the latest *Mercure* from Paris. The blood encrusted *Mercure* and the ripped helmet became his most precious souvenirs. The central figure is always either a dead knight on a bier or a wounded king on a litter. Apollinaire arranged his own incredible revision of himself. I imagine arriving Hartford that although of course they're never ready for us we too might excel in balancing natural charm against intentional outrage. I don't know. The week before in some other hinterland all I had to do was pass out while she took the wife of a business associate of mine into the shower and committed other inconceivable transgressions against propriety and decency. In Hartford I guess we were more of a team. She told the museum director that his daughter was a brat and later I snatched the museum director's wife in her black maxi at the quasi-formal dinner sheik style pulled her over my lap horizontal to do something to her god knows what while she tittered and sort of screamed and kicked her legs pitty patty and feigned squealing for her husband or she meant it or whatever. Polly reminds me someday I'm going to be an elderly nude. I'm lying again because I didn't want to say I thought that myself. What she really said was that she never violated a certain park in the winter because she didn't want to see her foot break the snow. I can't think of a better way of saying I really like to be fucked by a woman and walk like an ostrich that's lost its eggs from expiring over a number of cosmic or cataclysmic orgasms. Hic et ubique. And exploit like Apollinaire our expansive personalities by celebrating them in our works and saying that around this composite creation unites a conflagration of dream and reality. C. observes that this horses jaw is two angels of God. She says also her mother would now consider finding a female lover. B. says yesterday Mercury and Venus were in conjuction. Angels and ministers of grace defend us. She made a gibson with nine onions. She showed me her Lacrosse stick. She spilled my coffee in the van over and over. She embarrassed me by being apparent to truck drivers in her blue latex bra. She excavated my seat belts from the ruins of my crevices. She burdens herself with these saddle bags that only Hermes would carry. She says we need a helicopter to cut short all the time you spend coming and going more than you spend there. She says I didn't look good posing on the island for a memory a photo next to the James Joyce died 1898 tombstone. She drinks peptobismol like milk or gingerale. She buys expensive champagne and shares the first rounds with your garage attendants. She's outrageous. Tears hearts and crosses raining down out of the eye holding up a totem of web and woman. Virginia Vita too tuo. In somno Eve ecclesia nascitur.

—*June 10, 1971*

The Making of a Lesbian Chauvinist

Lesbians who are not chauvinists are monogamous. The new liberation front is the lesbian chauvinist movement. A lesbian chauvinist is a woman who enjoys a variety of affectionate and sexual experiences with different members of her own sex. If she marries another woman she no longer qualifies as a chauvinist. Gregory Battcock is the only pure male homosexual chauvinist I know. He says he doesn't try to mess up his boyfriend's minds with love, security, false promises, fidelity, and the like. I asked him what does he do if a lover develops more interest in his person than his attitudes can tolerate. He says then he makes himself as obnoxious as possible, even developing bad breath if necessary. Revolutions are all about language, inventing and distorting your terms to suit the new strategies of survival. Male chauvinism is now a dead phrase. The new lesbian is co-opting it to define her positive attitudes of polygamous independence united with an exclusive interest in her own sex. Such an absurd but real position might more accurately be described by the term chauvinism than the attitudes of the heterosexual male who won the term in its pejorative sense in our time through its revival by the feminists in their proper instinct for a word just obscure enough to express an educated disdain for the cause of their social and private distress. I stopped using the word when I heard the musical "machismo" on the Coast. Now I'm bored with machismo too. I'm bored, in fact, with the problem or the concept. I'm very interested in this new idea of lesbian chauvinism. Derived from Nicolas Chauvin, a soldier of the First Republic and Empire, whose demonstrative patriotism and attachment to Napoleon came to be ridiculed by his comrades, the word has as much relevance to the polygamous lesbian as it did to the American male of choice in the ongoing battleground of language. I wish I had thought it up myself. I'll be satisfied if I demonstrate its usefulness to define a situation already long in existence but not socially comprehensible until truly invented by the whimsical dislocation of language to express reversal of value attending the same phrase. It isn't easy to be a lesbian chauvinist. Lots of people still think you're as wicked as the male of that description who owns and runs the world through the elaboration of his sexual preference into the various patterns of subjugation and captivity much noted by the polemical feminists who have realized at last the intimate connection between power, economy, property, and sex. I don't own or run anything except a deteriorating '66 VW van. The most difficult aspect, however, of being a lesbian chauvinist is the problem of maintaining the life style appropriate to our new definition by warding off the temptations of monogamy in a society in which the prime unit of its functioning as a warring nation is its embattled family. Next week I'll redefine my position as a lesbian monogamist. This week the revolution is the liberation of the lesbian chauvinist. The grand edifices of theory and speculation are elegant smokescreens for personal tactics of destruction survival and renewal. I've been a happy chauvinist in spirit since the summer of '68. A lapse or two since then into the exquisite agonies of feudalism or monogamy is not an aspect of my journey I go around boasting about: Not that it matters to anybody. People are learning to ignore the exaggerated claims and denials of their friends and various exhibitionists. People are learning to despise all problems and solutions that aren't their own. People are learning to be severely disappointed by the slightest deviation from any problem or solution that sounded good the week before. As people myself I feel the same way naturally. All we want to do is to dictate our own thrilling letters. All I'd like to do actually is write the feminist version of *My Secret Life*. I've been postponing an account of my amorous adventures in London '68 because they seem, at this date, embarrassingly harmless and meagre, and/or because I needed the revolutionary context of the new lesbian chauvinism to make the experiences pertinent to current or ancient issues. In connection with Lois Lane I mentioned that my momentous visit prompted my return to America as "a roaring lesbian". I meant that I discovered I could sleep with a woman and not feel like it was the beginning or the end of the world. Meaning that it was possible to just go to bed and have a good time and get up and share a cup of coffee or not even do that and say goodbye and thank you quite amicably like any self respecting male chauvinist for whom the pleasures of the body are not necessarily complicated and constrained by the emotions of greed envy fear guilt anger jealousy etcetera all the defensive-aggressive equipment attending the onset of romantic love. The British taught me this lesson. They were very hard on me. I arrived a gaping tourist and left a hardened sexist. Not really, I cried all the way home. I don't remember why. But I remained as mushy as I ever was which was pretty mushy. Possibly I hadn't grasped yet that it wasn't a crime to fall in love with every British princess who seemed as interested as I was in the mere pleasures of the body. Actually, there were only three. I think. That was enough. For a three week visit the average was outstanding. For a pure innocent virginal American it was lurid and licentious. For a victim of lesbian monogamy it was a revelation. Having dutifully tramped through Westminster and St Paul's and Charing Cross and the National Museum and Trafalgar Square and Picadilly Circus and the subway system and Soho and the Tower and around the Palace & so forth one day I decided impulsively I had to visit a gay bar. I had never done this in my life before. Except once as a very young lesbian naturally not connecting my thinking with my activities, therefore imagining I was a nice normal person, I went slumming with a friend to a Village place, meaning a low down dive, to watch the freaks and get excitedly aghast at *members of the same sex dancing together!* By the summer of '68 if you can believe it I guess you can I was still disconnected in this way my thinking or my attitudes or prejudices and my true nature were distinctly and neurotically separate from each other. I was a walking contradiction in turns. I just couldn't see myself as a freak. It was bad enough I was too tall for my age and wore my freckles when the sun came out. I was even strolling around in those fashionable gabardine culottes or leather mini skir's, I must have looked ridiculous. A lesbian still pretending she was available for invasion. Anyway, I went all out for some inexplicable reason and learned about a place called the Gates or Gateways Club. George Brecht located it for me. Very reluctantly. He said he was disappointed in me. I guess he thought he had an exclusive patent on chauvinism, not that I knew at the time that's what he was. I assumed all men had the right to drink a lot and insult womankind and drag as many as possible off by the hair into their caves. So naturally he was not enthusiastic about being an accomplice to my initiation as a rival chauvinist of the lesbian variety. Not that either of us knew the ultimate significance of his innocent investigation. The Gates, by the way, is the bar that figured as the freak joint in *The Killing of Sister George*, which I saw a few months later in New York. The entrance had a speakeasy feeling about it. You'd never see it if you didn't know where it was exactly. The door opened directly on a flight of stairs leading down to I imagined a dark den of sin. It was just a smallish well lit rather cheery basement room with comfortable round booths, a bar, a jukebox. The woman at the bottom of the stairs was a hardened something or other. Dressed high femme lipstick earrings stocking heels etc. with an incongruously low dark voice and garish features. The bartenders were handsome heavy set butch a type that has always repelled bewildered and frightened me. I sat down and waited. Eventually the only other customer addressed me sort of luke over her shoulder from her position turned three quarters away from me. I could appreciate her brown blond straight short hair and middling cockney accent. Hearing my own American she warmed up and even not too much later turned round to face me. She introduced herself as Maureen. She got so warm in fact she was inviting me to her place to meet her roommate who "likes American girls" and her own lover who was an ex-patriot American. I said I'd like to do that but later on if possible after I found out what this bar was all about. Soon I found out. It seemed the entire gay woman population of London must have decided this was the place to be that night. I had no idea there were so many gay people. I was very embarrassed. I didn't know what to do. I suppose I just sat there transfixed with horrified curiosity. I had a very snobbish attitude. I'm sure I didn't think I was a lesbian too. Yet I was rigged out to conform to one of the two stereotyped roles obtaining in conventional gay society until recently. Excepting my long hair. But they overlooked the hair because of my tie. The tie seemed to guarantee my role as a female who would play the part of a male. In my three lesbian marriages I had never played any part whatsoever unless it was all parts, so I regarded the attitude with amused toleration, thankful to be attractive to one half of the jam-packed room for inadvertently wearing the right thing. A year later I returned sans tie and was so confusing apparently to everybody that I became a model wallflower. Or else I had aged considerably. Or they had caught on to me. Or some damned thing. I didn't seriously figure any of this out until recently. Some experienced friends have by now explained the customs. I don't like any of them. No self respecting lesbian likes them. Aside from the exorbitant mafia prices of drinks or minimum the bars are corroded with long centuries psychologies of self hatred addressed to everybody. And the frantic behaviour of excessive monogamous thinking, quite naturally, since self hatred breeds extremely precarious relationships and the lesbian is not yet liberated into her chauvinism. I learned fast at the Gates. I asked someone the time and was threatened with murder by her girlfriend. I supposed she was desperate. It was a good thing I just asked the time. I realized right then I'd better not make a move to talk or dance or anything or they'd be flying me home as a corpse. So I waited. I didn't wait too long. I was pretty popular as I said. Thus there were a succession of sidewise or bizarre approaches. All femmes. I was a butch! The most exciting proposition was a note pressed into my hand by the femme I thought to be the most beautiful in the place; she was so expert in her treachery, passing the message on the run as it were and no doubt while her "steady" was collecting their coats and momentarily out of sight. It was really dramatic. A sequence in a spy movie. I repaired to the ladies right away to read it and find her name and a telephone no. scrawled in pencil. I took the names and numbers of two others who weren't as spectacular in their looks or approach and left to go to Maureen's flat to see about her roommate who "likes American girls". I felt saturated by London lesbiana. I felt I had learned something. I didn't know what exactly. Probably my unconscious was fast at work transforming me overnight into a raging chauvinist. One thing was certain. It no longer seemed bizarre for two members of the same sex to be dancing together. One other thing was certain. There were lots of lesbians in the world. Maybe half the world were lesbians. And I suppose I left with the faint suspicion that I too might be one of them.

—*June 17, 1971*

Who is the Father of Her Child?

After a ridiculous weak I waked up to write the making of a lesbian monogamist and decided instead on the celebration of a lesbian celibate. Certainly I no longer qualify as a chauvinist. I declined a weekend country invitation because it sounded too complicated sexually. Just chickened out. And it was me all along who was saying we should share the same lovers. As for monogamy, Frederick Engels may still have the last word on this archaic form of bondage: "And if strict monogamy is the height of all virtue, then the palm must go to the tapeworm, which has a complete set of male and female sexual organs in each of its 50–200 proglottides, or sections, and spends its whole life copulating in all its sections with itself." — This is ideal, but it isn't monogamy, it's a super auto erotic inter-fuckulating parthenogenesis. Anyway, Engels goes on: "Confining ourselves to mammals, however, we find all forms of sexual life — promiscuity, indications of group marriage, polygyny, monogamy, and polyandry." Please read the Engels (*The Origin of the Family, Private Property, and the State*). All women must read this outdated masterpiece of fanciful anthropology. The reason I never read it before is that I'm an uneducated female. I was encouraged to read *Black Beauty* and Nancy Drew and *The Snow Queen* when I could have been finding out about the Decline and Fall of the Roving Empire of My Own Sex. And other tidbits. Recently someone reminded me it's weird to spend four years reading plato, sappho, sophocles and like that and never mention homosexuality. I studied philosophy with an old man who mistook me for Alcibiades. A boy disguised as a girl, or vice reversa. As a 20th century Platonist out of Manchester, Heidelberg, and Harvard the old man has long forgotten the true sexual origins of his own discipline. By now the histories of the glorious ages of Greece are a disgrace to the proper understanding of our extravagantly beautiful perversities and the nowhere nothing of women. As for Sappho the only woman who was something more or less than all the raving Delphic priestesses, how could I really get to her when all that survives are the fragments altered over the centuries to conform to such as some early victorian scholars who went around changing the case endings of her lovers from feminine to masculine. I didn't know Sappho and Socrates and all the rest were gay until it was much too late to destroy the educational systems perpetrating all that trash and omission. What do you think Socrates was *really* on trial for? Who do you think Plato was really in love with? Why did I have to spend so much time studying the love affairs of boys and men? Imagine what Norman O. Brown is doing right now to the heads of his women students by not even so subtly invoking the exclusive male tradition, saying "It is all one book (he means the literature of the world), which includes the gospel according to Ovid, Saint Ovid the martyr; and Petrarch, and Marvell, and Keats, and Andre Gide, and Pound. Also the ravings of every poor Crazy Jane. Every poor schizophrenic girl is a Delphic priestess; or a Daphne, saying 'I am that tree.' 'That's the rain — I could be the rain. That chair — that wall.' It's a terrible thing for a girl to be a Delphic priestess. In the cave the priestess raves: she still resists the brutal god, to shake from her hapless breast his breast: all the more his pressure subjugates her wild heart, wears down her rabid mouth, shapes her mouth into his mouthpiece." He's right of course. But he's wrong too. We do have a real live tradition of women with names and great works and everything, but at women's colleges like Bennington the President is a man and the faculty is 80 per cent male and they now have 110 male students and the catalog of courses reads like an inventory of male histories and almost all the women become the wives or mistresses of the faculty before or after a short interim of freedom and adventure working as a secretary or messenger girl to a male corporation in the big city. Engels has satisfactorily explained this odd situation to me. I suppose anyone reading it now understands that he was talking down to the "savages" and "barbarians" by analyzing the origins of the modern family as a civilized advance over the more primitive forms. Yet occasionally he glimmers the contradictory insight that every step forward was relatively a step backward, "in which prosperity and development for some is won through the misery and frustration of others." Every clear thinker now realizes that a return to the savage conditions of the various types of "group marriage" is the sine qua non of a bewildered new world. The two contemporary expressions of our childhood awaiting us out of the debris of civilization's autodestruct are the longhair communes and the unsettling withdrawal of both men and women from the institutions of male-female patterns of domination-submission that thrive even in the communes, for the true equality of the sexes can only reoccur through a massive social upheaval involving customs and consciousness brought about by the revolt of women combining tactics of withdrawal and that re-assertion of mother-right by which the woman maintained an honorable position in relation to her own sex and to her brothers and fathers in the certainties of maternal parentage. The withdrawal of both men and women mentioned above is of course what the gay revolution is all about. The promiscuity in the gay world is the natural expression of all peoples pre and post-dating the legal binds of property rights that resulted in our abnormal closed monogamous family structures. The far greater activity and promiscuity of gay men is merely the outstanding expression of the advanced sexual mobility of all men, who have retained their rights of promiscuousness within the same institution of monogamy by which their sisters are deprived. The married man is polygamous. The married woman is monogamous. Engels clarified for me the single absurdly simple historical reason for this repression of women. I never saw it myself because I'm too much a product of the very situation that made me too outrageous to believe that my strange birth was actually a condition for something much better than the social psychosis they had laid out for me in the textbooks. I was supposed to be a deprived child. As it turns out I was that marvelous anomaly of a female relieved of the tyranny of paternal preeminence. As such I grew up in an unreal world of self revolving maternal identities and never properly understood the submission that was expected of me when I met the male corporation. Thus I had a precocious sense of my divinity. Given five years or so in the shadow of the greatest phallic masterpieces of urban civilized accomplishment I became the pathetic female of the textbooks. Five more years and I confirmed all their expectations. An official mental case! It was perfect history. But in 1964 or is it '65 we were moving into the Aquarian Age. We were dying and being reborn in droves. New tapeworms all over the place. The fugitive invisible second city of the psychic outlaws arising from the ashes of the atomic bomb destruction of shattered minds. I saw the beards and flowers and lollipops and the resurrected heros of *Howl* and I didn't foresee the revolution of the women and the explosion of the homosexuals. History is now the Everlasting Present. The repressive social structures belong to the real histories of recorded time and monuments and these are the paternal histories. The revelation I just lugged out of Engles is the simplistic explanation of the origin of history to be found in the transition from the "group marriage" in which whole groups of men and whole groups of women mutually possessed each other, living together indiscriminately in many large families, to the emergence of the patriarchal family and the establishment of the exclusive supremacy of the man in order to secure the fidelity of the wife to insure the clear and legal paternal identity of the children. It's so silly, but you've heard it a lot in the past few years. How many a woman in a longhair commune is uncertain who is the father of her child. It was this situation in savage and barbarian communities that naturally made mother-right (matrilineal descent) the order of inherited identity and substantiated the honor of the woman in an otherwise historically always difficult position of relative physiological immobility in her child bearing capacity. As the daughter of a Virgin I am now happy to assert my normal birthright as a barbarian. "Among all savages and all barbarians of the lower and middle stages, and to a certain extent of the upper stage also, the position of women is not only free, but honorable." The overthrow of mother-right was *the world historical defeat of the female sex*. It was apparently the elaboration of the means and tools of production that created this momentous shift in the relation of the sexes for since the man was in charge of obtaining the food and the instruments of labor necessary for survival and he *owned* these instruments and eventually also the new sources of subsistence in the form of cattle and slaves, it followed that the man would at least insist on the undisputed claim of paternal identity to stabilize the inheritance of wealth and property in his own image. The confined woman is merely the woman to whom access is limited or guaranteed to the expectant father. All the Danaes in the Towers. We're moving backward now. We can't go back fast enough. I'm going to England to buy my maternal birth certificate again. I have my father's name in my mother's country and my mother's name in my father's. I am now a citizen of my mother's country in my father's equally phony name. My mother was precociously independent. From the present vantage circle even the incestuous barbarian group marriage would be a form of bondage for the women. The woman bought her way out of the fearful chaos of belonging to every man by sacrificing her sexuality her mobility in the *apparent* securities of monogamy — the situation that made her *either* the Virgin Goddess *or* the Bitch Whore, both of them impoverished in mind and spirit and deprived of material autonomy. Woman now has the supreme task of withdrawing her services to wrap them unto herself. To reclaim her identify, her sexuality. The lesbian woman and the homosexual man are the frightening vanguard of the disruption and ultimate collapse of all modern archaic forms of bondage and warfare through the purchase and captivity of the woman who no longer remembers, unless she goes on a huge acid bender, how she got into this state which she has been conditioned to believe is desirable, especially in its current hypes of token liberties and promises. Please read the Engels and then read Virginia Woolf's *A Room of One's Own* and *Three Guineas*. I suppose you have already. It's another measure of my ignorance as a woman that I read all of Woolf as a young tapeworm who just enjoyed reading right through her novels and stopped short at her two feminist masterpieces. Nor did I ever hear of Harriet Taylor Mill. Or Mary Wolstonecraft. The women in the country will soon be pressing for their own education, for by and about themselves in order to learn a new history of the world. All over the country the women are still being educated for by and about men in preparation for being more intelligent helpmates and companions. For the reason that I assume the absurd position of righteous confusion over my polygamy and my monogamy and my polyandry and my celibacy all prefaced by my essential natural and political lesbianism I refer anybody to another masterwork of sexual politics and revelation: Sandor Ferenczi's *Thalassa* subtitled *A Theory of Genitality*. From this book I acquired a healthy sense of depression and tragedy in regard to the weird evolutionary adjustments our fore-species made to certain global calamities like the drying up of the oceans. Ferenczi's fabulous bio-analytical speculations leave no doubt that the ongoing warfare between the sexes is a perennial reenactment of the primeval warfare in which the animal divided itself by attacking itself and by constant obtrusion and recession creating an instrument of aggression whereby one half was forced to submit and be worn away into a cloaca for the eventual deposit of the other half in its frantic and successful efforts to evolve an aquatic substitute in the form of a womb. Where we are headed from there is perfectly clear to me. N.O. Brown's "Silence" in *Love's Body* brings us full circle. I'm disillusioned with Brown because I located his inherited misogyny and actually saw it in person in his house in California over his dining table his wife was the silent obedient mistress occupying one fourth of the space in remote and isolated control while her brilliant husband held forth and Robert Duncan and me were polite contributors and admirers. But N.O.B. can't help it. Nobody can. We're evolving back to our tapeworm selves and then over and out into our primeval slime and eventual silence so we might as well relax and enjoy, enjoy, in our beautiful journey to extinction. Anyway this is the week of the new worldwide celebration of being Gay!

—*June 24, 1971*

Could I Kiss His Wife?

LONDON DUBLIN NEW YORK: Enroute the Dublin stop. The reason being that my ticket now says I can. Instead of making a perfect circle back to Paris for New York. Once you're some ways across the globe it seems the air people can manipulate your fares and flights quite irresponsibly like the pins on a strategy map. It's a sensible derangement when you don't care where you're going. Once there, some of us think our presence or absence is important enough to announce. London had a dependable distraction called Yoko and John in the suburbs at Ascot. Any impressionable artist from America might want to see how a working class hero from Liverpool and the daughter of a banker from Tokyo had decided to live it but near the premises of the Queen at Windsor Castle. I think John knows the Queen or the Queen's son or somebody. Nobody knows anybody whom they do not know. I knew I had one more encounter on the timetable of toleration for mutual suspicion and sexual incompatibility. I knew it must have occurred to Yoko by now that I don't service people any more doing what I once did that got me in as much trouble as what I do now. I knew they knew we have nothing to offer each other except ourselves. I knew they knew I knew they don't have much time or aptitude for ourselves. So if *they* had no motives left, mine were hopelessly suspect. How could I not know or even not know that I would want to write about the hour I spent alone in the back cushion cavern of their white pullman mercedes benz limousine from Dorset Square picked up by the chauffeur to ride out thru London and Windsor to Ascot behind darkened glass like shades you can see out they can't see in and listening to Help acoustically stereopulent on some mysterious aspect of the console equipped an eight-track cassette radio record player stereo cassette taperecorder & watching people pointing at the car and schoolboys making thumbs up for peace or penury or puck you Violet Paget alias Vernon Lee reigned for 41 years over lesbians dressed as Botticelli pages I thought how could I fail to be impressed by my own imaginings and by a lavish solitude I translate instantly into a letter back home is indistinguishable from the experience or in some voids the letter home is the experience itself if you see you do you do you see how my this letter and the experience is the letter the experience the same all etcetera and I do want to see Yoko and John as just people I know and we know they have no more use for me unless I could do what I once did that got me in as much trouble as what I do now is of much more interest to me than to them. So we are thrown back on ourselves. Our mutual suspicion and sexual incompatibility. I like John a lot through the haze of his fame I can see him a regular charming fun loving chauvinist. I like Yoko but I want to like her better so I put her on sexually, and the banter from that is the best of our exchange. I wait in the huge sterile ultra new kitchen of their remodeled very white house. John comes down a spiral metal staircase, and kisses me in some weird patchcolor shorts and says he's got my number, when I go anyplace if nothing happens I make something up. Yoko comes down wearing metal studded shorts she doesn't kiss me and asks me if I want to go swimming. She changes her shirt several times and later even the whole outfit. She says she likes to wear what John likes a see-thru thing looks okay to me too. Yoko suggests a tour of the grounds. We climb onto a golfcart and John drives us bumping down a lawn to an artificially made lake we're followed by a team of cameramen and Julian John's son and four chauffeur's kids and possibly the workmen erecting a pre-fab miniature house on the island in the lake. It was a lot of commotion. Everybody seemed much more like an audience than a company of people. I felt a hush of obeisance or fear you might experience in the presence of a Sultan or a Judge arriving in a mighty place to dispense the law. I was giggling and ready to do something awful. Later on I was wondering about the money and the morality of it all. Sitting against the wall on thick woolly white rugs in their sumptuous bathroom I asked John who sat the edge of an enormous white circle crater bathtub if he thought this made people happier or feel better. He thinks so. "Your environment, y'know." Yoko was excited and mobile explaining the voyeurism of the plumbing how she and John can see each other on the toilet from the bed in the adjoining equally deluxe bedroom. Bumping down to the lake John explains that the movie is to accompany his new record to be released in

September. One of the songs is "Imagine No Possessions" and they're going to display all their possessions in the movie. It's awfully hard for a body like me to think money is money when there is more of it than anybody can count. Anyway I don't think of people owning these things that are apparently bought by the money nobody can count. Especially when John himself can't remember a car that was bought for short excursions into town. He was scratching his head trying to remember while Dan was saying don't you remember and describing it to him. What I see is the whole business is the decor for a play with intermissions of trips abroad by the protagonists. I'm a visiting actress improvising a part. The director says to leave the golfcart and board a rowboat and doesn't hand me a script. Whatever I do I won't be invited back. That's the essence of my social life. Gregory said so in New York. Gregory said at a dinner party oh Jill you'll never be invited back. By saying so he clarified the nature of my social life for that I was thankful. At a meeting of women uptown, I had never been invited before to a meeting of women up or down town, they spent an hour or so deliberating whether they should send me away, this was an interesting modification of the pattern, to be sent away before I got a chance not to be invited back. They were quite right of course. Until everybody writes their own column we'll be oppressed by our present limited available distortions. But I was impressed by the women there and wanted to stay. Gloria Steinem was helpful. She said she didn't think they should worry because I write fiction anyway. Gloria! — I invited Yoko to that meeting thinking that if I can no longer assist in vindicating her career as artist I could expose her to some advanced women of America who might throw her paranoia into a new dimension — the shared world of women in the same bateau. Yoko is a woman now in an extra-ordinary predicament. Although it's reasonable to assume that if she were not with John she would be as (un)-recognized as other artists who have worked in the same genre as herself, all of whom have remained relatively obscure, not only in respect to the world at large but to the art world itself, excepting a Walter de Maria, who had his day with what might be called the minimal immaculate conceptual stuff of which Yoko's examples are as tough and as good as Walter's or anybody's, and that Yoko would be in the greater traditional twilight of obscurity accorded a woman, it is another terrible fact of the present that no amount of recognition now granted her could convince anyone much less herself and she's a very smart person that the attention she receives is not because of John but for the work itself. The power base is John's. That's the ultimate steel-trap issue of women's liberation. She brought John to the women's meeting. I told her she couldn't. She said she had to. It's like they're Siamese or something. That must be because they are their selves only with them selves since everybody else has the ulterior motives that could obviously be ascribed to them in their relation to everybody who can and does assist in making them even more inaccessible to ordinary everday human people contact. Like me, now would I be writing like this about the big expedition in their rowboat 10 yards or so from shore to island of the lake if it was Henry Geldzahler and Christopher Robin and their son? Do they have a son? Well, the vehicle thing of pop affluence is like taking a cab to cross the street and a helicopter from curb to doorway. They'll get out of shape and the tennis courts are dilapidated. They like to play pool. I said it's *the* lesbian game, but I don't play it. I play tennis. If I were rich I suppose I'd play pool. So I plunged gingerly into the rowboat still giggling nervously. I had to pee and I could see the island we were just embarking for 10 yards away had only one tree on it and all the cameramen were coming along in a rubber raft and the children were gawking along the shore and the workmen were unloading the pre-fab house from a truck. Yoko and me weighted down our end so the boat tilted at an absurb angle and John said he couldn't row. Yoko got very personal. "Aren't you embarrassed to have such large breasts . . . I mean as a lesbian . . ." I guess she thinks lesbians aren't supposed to have breasts at all. Since I think of myself as just pleasantly medium. "Really Yoko, lesbians like breasts you know." John began talking about food. Yoko said he talks about food whenever breasts are mentioned. So do I I said. And Yoko asks me later to be one pair of 360 in her new tits movie. I don't want to. They've appeared already in *Time*. I know Yoko thinks something is wrong with me. She wants to know why I got married and had kids and everything.

The only explanation for the modern world is a seduction. It's the game of the afternoon. I reassured John by telling him that my first male lover was from Liverpool (that's true). I admired all his toys. I admired their 85 acres of magnificent arboretum of trees from all over the world planted by the former tenants. I admired their new secretary (John said he never even saw a *man* look at a woman that way). I played his incredible white grand piano Steinway. "This Morning A White Piano For Yoko From John With love 18.2.1971." I removed my shoes and socks to enter the white white sanctuary a large room Yoko's permanent exhibition of white and clear plastic conceptual objects. In that condition I climbed as commanded the ladder leading to a dangling magnifying glass thru which I had to peer at the word "yes" on the ceiling or on a canvas up against the ceiling which is what John did at the fated exhibition in London the day they met. I gave his son and the chauffeur's the stickers I had bought for my own. I wore the patriotic shoes I permitted him to purchase in America where I had said it felt like I was shopping with my mother again. I listened to his new record in the studio in which he made it I was absolutely stoned saturated penetrated envelopiated in the super frequency clarity opulence of its sound. I said I wanted to see Yoko's Rape movie. I permitted myself to be filmed pulling my pants up after peeing behind that tree on the island the cameramen were waiting naturally. I didn't tell them I had had some bad moments wishing they wouldn't be so upset at one of those dudes riding the golfcart shooting the geese and us and wotnot who might or might now have been responsible for not shooting the magnolias while they were still in bloom and John and Yoko were away. I tried not to notice the privileged position of Julian vis-a-vis the children of the chauffeur. But you don't have to reassure anybody like John to be playful with his wife. We were riding the limousine back to London, christ the camera and sound men were still with us, and I asked John if I could kiss his wife. No answer. Their handgrip tightened I think. Silence. Yoko: "I liked that outfit you wore at the Klein's party." — Jill: "Really, were you more attracted to me then?" — Silence. Yoko: "I don't like to make it with celebrities." Silence. Yoko: "I like to be paid." — John changes a white t-shirt for the

Yoko yellow grapefruit shirt for the BBC interview it's supposed to be about Yoko's book. I'm amazed. He's a woman I said. And I notice his hands have that slight soft fleshy look of my first male lover from Liverpool. Yoko smiles and she doesn't do that often "that's right you see, John is a woman and I am a lesbian." She's getting better in her feints and dodges. John says both boys and girls have always liked him, and he and Yoko will have a homosexual experience when they're 90. I sing them a couple of my foolish childhood songs and John harmonizes on the one that goes on about brushing those tears from your *eyes* and trying to realize that the ache in my heart is for you-*ou*. I have to pee again suddenly, and urgently, and John tells the chauffeur to find a fence or a hydrant or hedge or something but Dan says hold on we're *almost* there and we were. And at the studio I know I think I was still doing my best for Yoko by attacking the set just after the warm-up before the audience arrived to sort of command the interviewer to change the setting so that Yoko was in the middle instead of on the outside although my sympathy was wearing thin and my motives were exhausting themselves they did it anyhow but it didn't matter too much because the interviewers are really mostly still keen about John and his old Beatles problems and John can't help himself he wants the show too and Yoko is left her inscrutable oriental poise not too successfully obscuring all the anger and frustration of Japanese and American and English woman-hood combined if as I interpret it she would but see it so it would be a help to being people and selves together as people, selves, if that's important besides I like to think it is. At cocktails in a studio following the interview I go after my own wasp type and I really mean it, a man even, and Dan and John both ask me if I scored. That's a word even a chauvinist like me doesn't use. Anyway I didn't. Score. So they drove me to an address I designated on their way home and walked downstairs to the bar and began necking immediately. I guess she had liked me from a woman's meeting a Sue 18 from Sheffield she was awfully pretty and nice and sexually sweet for a faceless young body, do you think Shaw is right that youth is wasted on the young?

—*August 5, 1971*

Zelda, Zelda, Zelda

In October 1936 Zelda still had grand plans about her spiritual mission to mankind, but she was not permitted to talk about them. Zelda was crazy again. Scott said she now claims to be in direct contact with Christ, William the Conqueror, Mary Stuart, Apollo, and all the stock paraphernalia of insane-asylum jokes. On April 23 1930 Zelda first entered a hospital and it was on the outskirts of Paris and it was called *Mal*maison. She was speaking or raving of her great love for Madame Egorava, her ballet teacher. At Prangins in Switzerland she was diagnosed by Dr Oscar Forel as a schizophrenic, and not simply a neurotic or hysterical woman. X enjoyed seeing Y fixed in his or her error, as we call any faith that is not ours. The official invalidation of Zelda Fitzgerald had begun. She was 30 years old. She said herself she didn't seem to know anything appropriate for a person of 30. Writing to Scott she said At any rate one thing had been achieved and that was that she was thoroughly and completely humiliated and broken if that was what he wanted. According to Zelda's biographer Nancy Milford, Scott was trapped in his alcoholism as Zelda was in madness and exzema and he avoided coming to terms with it by placing the blame on Zelda. According to the preface to Zelda's only completed novel *Save Me the Waltz* the preface written by a man Harry T. Moore says Hemingway saw that in the Fitzgerald family the wife continually interfered with her husband's work because she was jealous of it. No question. In the winter of '28–'29 Zelda began writing the first in a series of short stories that dealt with the lives of six young women and without exception the stories were published under both Fitzgeralds' names and the sixth story "A Millionaire's Girl" was published by the *Sat. Eve. Post* and although it was Zelda's story Scott's name alone was signed to it since the *Post* had wired him that they would pay four thou for the story if Zelda's name was omitted. In 1925 a story written by Zelda with Scott's climax and revision won two stars in O'Brien's short story collection for that year but Zelda received no credit for having written it and it was published under Scott's name alone. Scott had once written of Zelda that she danced exceptionally well, drew cleverly but hastily, and had a startling facility with words, which she used only in love letters. In 1920 George Jean Nathan magazine editor discovered Zelda's diaries and made an offer for them but Scott said he could not permit him to publish them since he had gained a lot of inspiration from them and wanted to use parts of them in his own novels and short stories (. . . Zelda apparently offered no resistance). Milford's conclusion was that he drew ruthlessly on the letters and diaries with no sign of disapproval from Zelda and that Scott somehow possessed a right to Zelda's life as his raw material and indeed of course he had already noted that he married the heroine of his novels. Carl van Vechten a kindly man said Zelda tore up the pavements with sly remarks . . . She didn't actually write them down, Scott did, but she said them. It was a long decade and someplace in there Zelda came of age and got mad and decided to become a somebody in her own right but she had no money. What had our mothers been doing then that they had no wealth to leave us? Powdering their noses? Looking in at shop windows? Flaunting in the sun at Monte Carlo? If only Mrs S. and her mother and her mother before her had learnt the great art of making money and had left their money, like their fathers and their grandfathers before them, to found fellowships and lectureships and prizes and scholarships appropriated to the use of their own sex . . . So saith Virginia Woolf whose aunt one Mary Beton once died by a fall from her horse in Bombay leaving Virginia a small legacy news of which reached Virginia about the same time the act was passed that gave the votes to women, a coincidence remarked on by Virginia in this way: Of the two — the vote and the money — the money, I own, seemed infinitely the more important. The key to Virginia's independence. The key to Zelda's became her insanity for of money she had none and knew not how to acquire any for what money she earned and she did earn some in '22–'23 or so by her stories belonged to her husband by custom if not by law by then the law may have altered but certainly not the customs which are the foundations of the law. Scott would ask Zelda what would she do if she had to earn her own living and Zelda would reply that she'd studied the ballet and she'd try to get a place in the Follies. Or the movies. And if she wasn't successful, she'd try to write. But in order to become a ballet dancer she had to study on Scott's money which he used in part to keep her in place by saying she had no right to complain as long as she was materially cared for. It seems even that Zelda's original decision to begin studying the ballet in 1927 evolved out of her anger fear jealousy of Scott's involvement with one Lois Moran Hollywood actress whom Scott would uphold in an argument with Zelda as at least a girl who did something with herself, something that required not only talent but effort — a reproach to Zelda that was a clear complaint against the very dependency upon him that he had cultivated as a naturalborn congenital chauvinist. She was his darling girl. What was he to her? By 1930 a drag I surmise. Her letters to him from the bin are loving and despairing and accusing at once or by turns. Mostly she seems to be saying "without hope or youth or money I sit constantly wishing I were dead." Her soul had magnified the lord and he had regarded the low estate of his handmaiden. His was the power and the money and the influence. In a hundred years, thought Virginia Woolf in 1929, women will have ceased to be the protected sex and will take part in all the activities and exertions that were once denied them. As a model for contemporary American woman Zelda was an unsuccessful Joan. She was immolated alive in the top floor of a wooden old loonbin in 1948 and not so gloriously at the stake. She burned up just like Joyce's daughter Lucia who was also declared by Dr Oscar Forel at the same institution Prangins in 1932 two years after Zelda to be schizophrenic and not merely a neurotic or hysterical woman. Nobody has honored Lucia with a biography. You can scrape what you will from Ellmann's brilliant biography of her father. We don't really know why Lucia "gave up dancing . . . no physical stamina . . . her thoughts jumbled during the next two years toward panic." But we know that her mother Joyce's wife Nora had no *apparent* ambition. What was Lucia's? The parallels between Zelda and Lucia stagger me. Milford: Upon occasion she (Zelda) would break off abruptly for no apparent reason and make plays on words which had no meaning the doctors could fathom . . . Scott rarely had trouble following her . . . Her earliest letters to him at 18 or 19 were marked by a smiliar lack of conventional continuity and were full of sudden turns. Ellmann. Joyce had a remarkable capacity to follow her (Lucia's) swift jumps of thought which baffled other people conpletely. — What're the customs of entanglement when everything is confused. Every girl marries her father and then promptly transforms him into her mother. In bygone days, before the facts of parentage were known, the Earth was thought of as mother and husbandless, sufficient herself for all her childbearing, or vaguely fertilised by the dead spirits of men buried in her bosom. Every human being can and does enact with hisher own body the double role of the child and the mother. The bride cedes to the man the privilege of penetrating the mother's body in a real sense. Those bygone days before the facts of parentage were known are of course not only the early days of the species when as explained by Engels the tribal social structure of group marriage certified the position of the woman as the only clear parent of the child but the days of each of our individual childhoods as well when our origins seemed remote and mysterious and inexplicable until defined by the literal emergence of the father in the modern family. The origin of individuality. Of the hero out of the chorus and all that. The women are now stuck with the habits of centuries of male psychology and they we must and will play it out to its Logos conclusion when all will become as it were one again in the beginning when a bisexual being was born of an egg or according to Oken who also found out about it also the first wo(man) developed in a uterus much larger than the human one which was the sea and all but now on our journey back to the beginning naturally first the women can and will claim the fruits of their submission out of the debris of our technological civilization by approaching all the hitherto forbidden sacred promontories of Mt Athos where just a few decades ago even Jane Harrison herself was not permitted to set foot. For Zelda we can cry and cry because she was courageous far beyond the written word and she broke her head on the bridge leading from the old civilization to the next and she never really knew she was right. Scott was playing out his inherited male role and he had a more evolved creature on his hands than either of them knew what to do with or about in the cultural context in which they grew up. By 1926 or so by the time Zelda had not unhappily fulfilled her social obligation as bride wife and mother she was ready for her own individuation and the culture basically would have none of it. You might say then that she commenced leading her wrong life to the hilt until 1930 when she was about 30 herself and her head erupted out of the pressures of contradiction into the incredible resolution often called schizophrenia. The most terrifying and hazardous means of achieving it of all the known human exploits. Zelda went over the edge into the other world. In order for a new organization of matter and energy to be formed an old one must always be dissolved and others violated or disrupted in some way. As a merely incipient feminist she threatened the continuity of family life. Indeed. And she knew it. Writing to Scott she said his presentation of the situation was poetic, even if it had no bearing on the truth: Your working to preserve the family and my working to get away from it. And on another occasion "a woman must be a goddess to direct her own life and a goddess is one who manages to keep her purposes aloof from a woman's ordinary lot." Yet one whole half of her head never gave up her conditioned and realistic dependence on daddy Scott. One interpreation I offer of her frantic intensive four years training to become the world's foremost ballet dancer in her late 20s is her reaction to the threat of losing Scott to a rival (Lois Moran) who represents the possible loss of a dubious income which Zelda might hope to win for herself in an independent career. In any event she had no chance, for her first incarceration in 1930 imder care of Dr Oscar Forel at the very moment when she felt ready for exposure on the stage (and in fact she had been offered a position in a ballet company in Naples that she did not take for some unexplained reason) established a pattern of humiliation and submission and adjustment to the very conflicted situation that drove her there in the first place. "Part of Forel's cure had been a somewhat mysterious 're-education' of Zelda in terms of her role as wife of Scott." Scott and Forel naturally conspired to terminate Zelda's ballet ambitions. It's true no doubt that dancing at her age was not the medium exactly in which to realize her truly heroic ambition but as she cosmically sighed from the bin nobody much less Forel could suggest an alternative and she had after all suppressed her writing to make life with Scott more bearable. She wrote Dr Forel . . . And if you do cure me what is going to happen to all the bitterness and unhappiness in my heart . . . It seems to me a sort of castration, but since I am powerless I suppose I will have to submit tho' I am neither young enough nor credulous enough to think that you can manufacture out of nothing something to replace the song I had. In 1931 after a year and three months "treatment" Zelda was released from Prangins and her case summarized as a "reaction to her feelings of inferiority (primarily toward her husband)" and she was stated to have had amibitons which were "self-deceptions" and which "caused difficulties between the couple." The conspiracy between Scott and Forel — the husband and the psychiatrist — is the classic one of our times of maintaining paternal authority in the face of any feminist revolt through the vast overwhelming intimidation of institutional prerogative. I hope Phyllis Chesler gets her book out soon because she has collected enough significant evidence to terminate the psychiatric profession as an unlawful means of coercing women to stay in their place.

The invalidation of women like Zelda who "break through" by the most perilous exploration in the world, the voyage back in time in consciousness to recover the paradise of lost dimensions of being, is extensive, and condoned by a society that presently as ever has everything at stake in preventing such revelations to be confirmed. Shortly before her death Zelda asked a visitor if he didn't believe in revelations, saying "I know! I've had them! I have been dead and seen another world and come back again alive to this one." But each time she came back her means of communication, any means to realize her vision, to say what she had seen, to report her voyage back at home base, like the astronauts, was frustrated in relation to her only conceivable means of economic subsistence. With Scott's death she was liberated and I imagine she spent a few peaceful years with mother but propriety dictated modesty in her work and I think she mostly painted and what she painted was flowers.

Her final seizure as indicated by Milford was set off by the visit of this young man interested primarily in Scott who somehow slipped and informed Zelda of Scott's last infidelity Sheilah Graham who had been Scott's secret replacement while Zelda endured the confinement that in the end confirmed their separation. Correction about the painting. She worked also during those six years she lived with her mother on *Caesar's Things* never completed I would like very much to see from reading Milford's judgment of it I wouldn't be surprised at a piece of writing quite outside the mainstream of American fiction standardized as acceptable and sometimes great (i.e., a "masterpiece" by Fitzgerald) by the male literary establishment and related to that "other" tradition of late Joyce and late Woolf and continuous Stein and always the crazies of France. In her assessment of Zelda's work Milford throughout her biography affirms the judgment of male history as set forth say in the infuriating preface to *Save Me the Waltz* in which this Harry Moore establishes a claim for interest in Zelda's book as a contribution to an understanding of her husband he says her book "stands out as unique because of the intense interest readers have today in the life and works of F. Scott Fitzgerald" and further he concedes that her book is "a literary curio" since "she had at least a surface ability to write, as she had at least a surface ability to paint and dance in ballet." Really. If we could obtain *Caesar's Things* (Can we?) I feel certain we'd find Zelda the genius. *Save Me the Waltz* is absolutely substantial and brilliant but still conventional. Milford describes *Caesar's Things* as a difficult novel to read and to understand not only because it is fragmentary and at time incoherent, but because of the peculiarity of Zelda's grammar, her piling of image upon image, her displacement of conventional syntax."— ! — Scott once said possibly she would have been a genius if they had never met. Zelda once put a double lock on the door to her room where she wrote because Scott said he would destroy her book. Scott once accused her of going crazy and calling it genius. It doesn't matter too much about the genius bit. What is certain is that Zelda by going crazy did cease to be a femme a homme and became a total individuated person although she was never permitted to believe it until she was too broken to be able to seriously assert it in the world of credentials and accomplishment and that was when both her daddy the Judge and her other daddy the Great Writer were dead as Virginia

Woolf once said something to the effect that she would never have been able to do what she did had her father been alive. Last week I suggested a possible cause of her periodic seizures which she too thought of as illnesses, tho' suspected, like Zelda, something divine in them, in another form of the male-female conflict much milder than Zelda's because of her financial independence and Leonard's unabashed enthusiasm for her work and her confidence as a cultivated aristocrat. In *A Room of One's Own* Woolf reviews the history of the position of women in and out of fiction and constructs a little case study of what she imagines would have happened had Shakespeare had a wonderfully gifted sister in the 16th century. Someone should be working on the histories of all the sisters. Did Mozart really have a sister? Did Michaelangelo? Did Marx and Engels? Does Engelbert Humpledinct? Does it matter? Yes. My informant Snowshoe No. 22 wrote that she found out just last year about a sister of Thoreau. In England I heard about the sister Alice of William and Henry James and I just obtained her diaries, edited by a man. The imaginary talented sister of Shakespeare as Woolf pictured her ended up in the 16th century exactly as Zelda did in ours. Possibly Virginia thought we had really progressed since she herself was enjoying a certain advantage. Things have progressed but the woman of Virginia's accomplishment and recognition is still the exception. Zelda hovers between Virginia and the imaginary sister of Shakespeare who killed herself before she did a thing because nobody would let her do anything not even be an actress and the actor-manager Nick Greene who had told her no woman could possibly be an actress had taken pity on her and made her pregnant. But see now this description fits Zelda: Reviewing the story of Shakespeare's sister it seemed to Virginia that "any woman born with a great gift in the 16th century would certainly have gone crazed, shot herself, or ended her days in some lonely cottage outside the village, half witch, half wizard, feared and mocked at. For it needs little skill in psychology to be sure that a highly gifted girl who had tried to use her gift for poetry would have been so thwarted and hindered by other people, so tortured and pulled asunder by her own contrary instincts, that she must have lost her health and sanity to a certainty." Zelda is no novelty in 1971 either. Zelda the wife mother daughter sister is still a relic of the law of chastity that dictated anonymity to women right through the 19th century and tolerates her publicity in the present only under the greatest duress.

—August 26, 1971

Serial Monogamy with Raisins & Honey

Zelda the wife mother daughter sister is still a relic of the law of chastity that dictated anonymity to women right through the 19th century and tolerates her publicity in the present only under the greatest duress. Check out all media for the evidence. Bella becomes Bellacose for a heading in *Time* and her beauty — if you agree we're all beautiful — is suppressed in the disfigurement of three photo caricatures. Ann-Margret becomes successful or something more than a twit or a tramp or whatever she once was made out to be and her success is celebrated by a photo as a glamorous aging cosmetic witch. Christina Ford invited the managing editor of *Life* to tea and for that honor was repaid with an invitation to write about her theories as an anti-feminist. Carol Burnett was advertised under a photo of herself in clown drag or possibly as a model for powder and phony lashes in huge caption as the very happy wife of Mrs Joe Hamilton alias (in subletters) Carol Burnett in case America didn't realize that only a very happy housewife could also be a successful tv personality — on the side. Or by patronage of a very happy husband. The first woman to cross the Atlantic alone in a sloop is honored with a paragraph and no picture and I can't even remember her name. Germaine is saucy and available and we know about that. Gloria is beautiful and a very nice person and they'd like you to think that's all because they put her down for the one thing she does and likes to do and that is writing which is the substance in any event of her public position. Kate is a wonderful lesbian and they discredited her shortly after they glorified her and in fact used her as she would say as the first stick to beat the women's movement with. The image *Time* used to advertise Viva on the occasion of the publication of her book was in profile at full term pregnancy. Jackie Kennedy was toothpaste glamor in her husband's life and respected by dignified images in her husband's death and afterward she became the first traitor of the land. Diane Arbus is dead and now I know all about her. Elnora Coleman is dead and she was black and nobody will ever know about her. Sylvia Plath is dead and she's a best seller. Janis Joplin is dead and I suppose they think it served her right. I don't need to tell you what they'll do with a lesbian. If a lesbian isn't a whore and she isn't a married mother what is she? For openers she has to be ugly because a lesbian got to be a lesbian over the disappointment of not being able to obtain a man. A sort of rebellious spinster. Another way of putting it is as a question what happens to the virgin who doesn't marry or whore if she isn't a nun? There's a card game called Old Maid that's still popular I suppose. There's no social category for the reconstructed virgin or lesbian, who retains her sexuality. That's what she's clinically diagnosed as criminal and perverse. From time as long as anyone remembers a women either belonged to a man or she paid her dues in any modern form of the temple prostitute or she relinquished her sexuality. Such as it ever was. It's the revolution in our century recognizing the sexuality of the woman whose hysterical disorders were observed (and induced) in the European clinics as displacements of sexual energy which has caused the corresponding social revolution of active and famous women. Meaning women who cease to be merely passive objects and observers and become actors or prime movers and as such name their names on the stage of history. This is an awkward time. The old prejudices are still operative in an old structure that's breaking apart at the seams. The bulk of men and women remain unconscious of the invisible civilization which is displacing the one in which they are still imprisoned. The media people as regards women are making the wildest compromises. Many media people I presume know what is happeneing. Many are as unconscious as the masses they imagine they are serving. Between the two the results are pathetic or diabolical and occasionally courageous and mostly confusing. What are the people to think? What is *mother* doing on television? They don't really know yet. But they do comprehend the double message at the subliminal level transmitted by the ambivalence of the media them-selves. Certainly at the subliminal level they'll be assured that the business of men is still the order of the day when they see that even Gloria the new queen of women by media pronouncement is granted some 10 minutes or so on nationwide network on the day of the women's massive demonstration while two pleasant absolutely harmless and beastly boring chaps are allotted over half the program to discuss their treasure hunting off the coast of I can't remember where.

And at the same subliminal level they'll be aware that the woman doesn't yet present herself herself. They see that the woman is appearing by license or permission of the man. Thus to appear at all she must win his approval. And what makes her commendable? Whatever it is, the talent or public function of the women, she has to fit one of those sexual categories as well. Married mother or modern whore. The first is chaste and is not so likely to appear, for chastity and anonymity means the same thing and a woman who becomes exposed is a woman named and a woman thus named and exposed is no longer chaste which is simply the historical position of woman as subsumed under the name and perogative of the male as envoy and captor and legatee. The second, the whore, and we have some pretty high class ones now, is the woman people would naturally say well she wouldn't be doing this anyway if she wasn't a loose woman and of course they're usually right and since the old prejudices are very strong it's a way of discounting the new sexually mobile woman, if that she really is. It may be serial monogamy with raisins and brown sugar. I don't know.

I just know that hardly any woman in the media can seem to get a straight deal yet. The sexuality of women is still as much in question as her apparent freedom. The Masters & Johnson Whorehouse is an interesting point in case. In Leticia Kent's interview in *Vogue* you can see by her determined questions how the Masters & Johnson couple are super-sanctified pimps who take on the men by reference from an authority — the church or the psychiatrist — and supply the women for the men as "therapeutic" surrogates. Going back a bit, still the best understood public woman by far is the performer or entertainer who has survived all sorts of Christian and Victorian slander and repression from b.c. onwards to win a piece of bread in some acceptable form of the sublimated temple prostitute. Her true origins are by now clothed even in the respectability of the art forms acting and dancing. The woman is still much more hard pressed as a professional musician. It was and remains the body that counts. In this century for the first time in the history of professional dancing women attained to an autonomous prestigious position by asserting themselves as creators in a medium still regarded at large as pure body and now by the way and I can't resist this and now right in America where this logically happened the women have been suppressed temporarily — dethroned if you will — almost singled handed by the persistent concentration week after week on male dancers and choreographers by an undeniably powerful critic imported some time ago from Europe where the classical male-dominated ballet continues to reign, for royalty was basically a king and the king sponsored the ballet and the king recreates his retinue whereever he goes. I'm still talking about Zelda if you haven't noticed. Zelda is an encyclopaedia of the Western sexual tragedy. She played all the parts and they never added up to a whole. I don't think she would have struggled so hard at the ballet if she'd known its history in relation to her own sex. Or she would've found her way to the Denishawn people who encouraged women to be more organic and individually creative, following the example of Ruth (St Denis) herself, who was coming out of the still young exciting tradition of such as Isadora and Loie Fuller. The American indigenous dance was a matriarchal affair. All the men were gay and all the women were amazons of some sort — determined beautiful ambitious idealistic educated independent plainswomen and coastal pioneers. Lesbians too I always thought. Although they married for the show of it. Anyway Zelda's model had to be a Pavlova. She might never have heard of the Denishawn outfit. And her mother sent her as a child to a ballet school like the rest of us. Also at that time it was not established that an outstanding dancer in the American tradition could be acclaimed as an international hero. The glory of Nijinsky and Pavlova was patented thru the long authority of the ballet. The paternal puritanical rigorously exacting and virtuosic requirements of the ballet in which the student is continuously judged by the loftiest unattainable standards has always seemed to me one of our most exquisite cultivated insanities.

—*September 2, 1971*

Anybody Dying of Love

It was the foolhardiness of the adventure that made it so appealing. Nothing is quite true and this isn't quite true either. I woke up six days ago 3 a.m. and decided to cancel the summit meeting in the woods. I was about to do something moderately terrible again and not hire anybody to protect people from myself. God forces me to think abominations that I might experience Her grace. We don't even have those magnificent attitudes of not giving a damn anymore. Except when I'm going someplace with Gregory. I have a feeling a lot of people love me and nobody loves me but I think Gregory loves me so when we're driving crosstown in his mg saying preposterous things on our way to LaGuardia for an outlandish event in Syracuse I experience that fatuous luxury of not giving a damn. Even when we see overhead a flock of thick black felt birds flying with capes of solid chrome. Contra quam est nota natura. We've come to an impasse. We can't disagree on anything. I took a lesbian nation friend to dinner who said she only likes lesbians. I said well Gregory is a lesbian. She said she could tell when she saw the moustache and also that she'd be very embarrassed to appear in my column which made Gregory say it's good for you and she said thanks I hope your penis falls off in the kitchen. She kept commenting on her remarks and then commenting on the comments to her remarks. A straight one who does this said also my column is definitely a problem. It certainly is. The only time I need to use quotation marks are when the words I write are mine. You have to have a grand strategy to cope with all the hostilities and your own excesspools and spillikins. Already four hours of sleep aren't enough for a gemini chemistry to maintain herself through the first one woman exhibition in America in a museum by the wife of a Beatle and another night of only four again and up before dawn for a flight from Syracuse to Albany where she decides to hitchhike south because her van is being driven from the city to the woods by a friend and stands at the NY thruway entrance an hour in a cold windy drizzle before a somewhat scary slob picks her up and deposits her too far from another friend who eventually comes anyway to make sure she gets to her own Woodloo of Woman who are she is convinced determined to understand their own lesbianism by talking about it nothing more. My popular position now is Martha Shelley's that I won't be straight until all of you are gay. Susan B. says she feels apologetic whenever she leaves me and I forget to say how abjectly apologetic I felt for so many centuries over being gay and not even being able to apologize for it in case they should find out you had something to be apologetic for. In Syracuse Rosalyn Drexler said Jill how did you get to be so free. Huh. The husbands and brothers of the women of historical days could not, we are told, have allowed their women to rave upon the mountains. No and that's why the women went off by themselves to rave and they did. Rosalyn also said all my old happenings seemed to be flying apart. I didn't know I was Dionysus then. Dionysus is unique in the frequency with which he is defeated bound imprisoned routed and even destroyed, and in the number of times he must be rescued. Rosalyn held my hand going up in the press plane at LaGuardia and I complained when we landed she didn't hold my hand on the way down so she said it was because she felt absolutely safe and didn't want to call my attention to the landing. We were supposed to number 69 on the Mohawk charter but I could've brought my son for the last minute empties like Charlotte Moorman didn't make it and appeared later at the museum having paid her own way including a full fare for her cello and I had suggested to Brian Hirst that Richard could write up the event for his school paper but I should've just said I was bringing an assistant like Gregory did. I had to sit very close against Gregory's assistant in the mg. I met him the night before at a Guggenheim opening where I stood both of them up when a beautiful young woman stepped rightout of a Renoir and into my arms once again an angel appeared to resolve the problem of being in a threatening area at one level paranoia is the only intelligent response to the world. I fell in love for the whole night. Anybody dying of love these days should go down in history. I think I was in love with Gloria for a week in August when I even composed a letter I didn't send asking at the end if she'd like to have lunch or lust after having said a lot of incredible calculated garbage concerning what any of us were supposed to do now that everybody had been informed by *Newsweek* that she was the one sought by us all. I didn't have to do anything much. Brenda won't claim the credit for it but it was she who suggested a gay-straight consciousness raising affair and notified me that Gloria had said to count her in. And I said let's wait till Susan S. returns from Europe and I thought if we could get Jane Fonda and maybe Jackie Kennedy and a royalty or two and of course Kate would come, and Anselma, and Phyllis, and we could bring everybody up to my forest and provide a lot of rope and a case of rum that I'd have the makings of my most exquisite disaster to date and we did. The passivity of Dionysus may in part be associated with the fact that so many myths take place in childhood, but he is at all ages unable to cope with Hera and reacts to any threatening gesture she makes with panic or paralysis or both. There's a masochistic sensuality about these tales — a voluptuous savoring of degradation and disintegration. In Syracuse I saved myself up for the summit the next day so all I could manage was a dashing flying exit down the ramp at the airport for the camera men who were also making a movie of us on the plane (David shielded his face the way criminals do) and innumerable suggestions to Rosalyn and a May Ann alternately that we spend the night together in our hotel and repeated attempts to ascertain the cost of the whole venture to the Lennons and refusing to run with the pack when John & Yoko made a lightning brief appearance scuttling like rabbit between rooms it was a hard day's night clip all after One Beatle and asking the director at the press conference if they planned to have another exhibition by a woman (he said art was art whether by man or woman) and asking Yoko & John if they planned more cocktails and hors d'oeuvres and dinner for us and Yoko if she'd grant me a personal audience and Yoko & John if they'd please send me all their records as promised to play on my new machine I need some records and changing into a seethru black shirt in some bookstacks during the luncheon. At the conference Gregory said I'm going back to the hotel before I get on the plane and Rosalyn said yes you *should* use your room. Yoko made a speech thanking us for coming and saying many people question why we do an art show in a museum when people are starving and the world is in such crisis. She told us the world is now divided into two classes: those who can communicate and those who can't. John said his statement was that he agreed and they kissed. The museum is lots of Yoko's work and I think it's quite a nice show. As late as the 17th century monarchs owned so little furniture that they had to travel from palace to palace with wagonloads of plates and bedspreads, of carpets and tapestries. The telescope piece was my favorite. Looking thru a telescope positioned on a balcony you can see the words evidently printed about 25 yards across the gallery on a wall "Please look at me. I am so small." Above the words is an oval mirror. Rosalyn said it was such a sad piece so I cried a little. Rosalyn is very perceptive. I don't know if I really wanted to go to bed with her or not. She's larger than anybody I've been to bed with and that might be interesting. Anyway I reminded her she used to make passes at me regularly, including putting her hands on my bare breasts once in a doorway on East Broadway. Certainly I like older people. My first lover was 52 and my second was 65. Why is everybody so young now. I have a feeling a lot of people love me and nobody loves me but on the plane Rosalyn said she and Sheindi love me so when it's all over maybe there'll be a few old friends and we'll sit in rocking chairs the most impressively numinous temples are caverns of twilight reminiscing of the tattoos we had with our names on them that fell off. It's pride and presumption that precede a fall. Kate said the weekend was such a catastrophe, that what was supposed to happen could never happen, that they just belong to a different sorority, that's all. I should've brought Yoko from Syracuse to complete the problem. She might've enjoyed hitchhiking with me in the rain outside Albany too. This a.m. I woke before the lesbian contingent that stayed and awakened Kate to whisper like boarding school over the difficulty of names. She doesn't know what to do about names either. Nobody has a clear view, we can console ourselves. Gregory's the only person who doesn't give a damn. We're into the silliest human affairs. It's so ridiculous. And we think it's so important. That's what Kate thought too this morning after I said hey look at the rain and the leaves driven down to the Bach but last night she was storming at me how I had a nerve getting only three hours sleep and crying in the sink and challenging people so heavyhanded getting them all uptight and scaring them when there was such important work to do and all these people had come and the opportunity was gone forever and like that until I smashed a bottle of pickles to stop the assault and said later in the aftermath at least a couple of old friends know how mushy and feminine and ridiculous I am and how necessary it is in order to attract attention, to dazzle at all costs, to be disapproved of by serious people and quoted by the foolish. Anyway I was convinced it was all my fault & I had done everything wrong but Jane said you have to be perfect to do everything wrong. Glorious a perfectly proper person. I never met such a nice perfectly proper person. She's a very nice properly person. Dionysus represents not so much irrationality as the liberation of natural emotions from the tyrannies of ideology and culture. At Syracuse John in the press conference said he's always been a radical because he was always in trouble. Fate offers us misfortunes worthy of our characters. The world is hemophiliac. David wasn't ecstatic to see that his ice tray contribution to Yoko's Water Piece wasn't labeled or even filled with water. He thought if John Cage had sent it in they would've filled it with water. John Cage probably sent nothing or wasn't asked since he didn't accept the gift Yoko offered him a Box of Smile a few months ago although I accepted the same gift and I wasn't asked either. I was included however in the newspaper press release collection brochure passed out by the hostess on the plane with a controversial couple of paragraphs I wrote about Yoko in 1961. Charlotte showed me an original of this clipping out of a manila folder she was carrying. Charlotte was Yoko's roommate at that time and she managed that concert which was Yoko's uptown debut. Charlotte said in that piece of Yoko's she sat on a toilet making weird sounds with the cello. I'm glad Yoko found a use for this old review I wrote because she remains determined to be hurt that I shouldn't have included it in my book while it happened that a piece I wrote from London in 1968 including some mention of a performance by John did get into the book. We fought over this & other worldshaking matters for an hour on the phone long before Syracuse so I didn't understand why she said she and John loved me too. In Syracuse

David remarked you're on such a down trip Jill, just because you don't like Yoko there's no need to extend it to the food and everything. I said I like Yoko but she isn't very nice to people. David said she can afford not to be. I said that makes me like her even better. And I didn't have a very strong sense of sisterhood that day. She's getting off the best way she knows. From washington Snowshoe wrote her theory on karma is that whatever you get thru in this life you don't have to repeat and anything you settled in previous lives you don't have to worry about this time regardless of how many others are hung up on it. She thinks we all knew each other before in greece the return of the amazons & children of the dawn and everything we were but last time we made it starting from the top the aristocracy and this time we have to make it from down below, add that & understanding of how does it feel to be on your own and level out elitism even though we're obviously still beloved of the goddesses and gods whom many lack. Nobody's credentials as a radical are impeccable. For the woman woods party I really wanted Garbo Harlow Hepburn Dietrich Smith Sayre Plath Monroe Joplin etc. — Garbo is okay cause she's alive and well and she won't sue. We know Janis was gay, and some lesbian sisters are certain they could've saved her. Maricla said the meeting sounds very elitist Jill and I said absolutely. Further transformations also run true to the hero myth. Oedipus could think of nothing worse than a base origin. Dionysus represents an essentially masochistic solution. The Angry Mother is the Straight Mother. The challenge from her son creates her counter-attack and revenge. Now a Gay Woman who is still Straight in her head is also an Angry Mother. The selfdestruct of Dionysus the DaughterSon is a way of dissolving the boundaries in distress. Kate says I don't know my own influence and a soft pitch here and there would have a proper effect. Kate's pretty heavy herself. She's almost as demanding as I am. She just asked me how to spell cunnilingus. The party was a huge success because we became friends and Jane came and so did Susan S. who is eloquent even if conservative and '50s an original hero of mine I wanted very much to introduce to Gloria Kate Anselma Brenda etc., and I danced with Phyllis who's warm and squeezy and has the best rap going about the old and new amazons, and Anselma cried a little, and Susan B. was exhausted, and Brenda I hope left the meeting to go directly to the White House with Gloria. Now's the time since her old man is in Paris on business. Seeing a kindred shape we swoon away. As for Dionysus in the end it is almost as if the defeats and persecutions were the important part of the story — they are often dwelled upon more fully than his triumphs. And even if a lot of people love him and nobody loves him there's always in one lifetime or another a Geoff Hendricks in a long beard and old denims in a Syracuse dining room writing a dedication in your new record book beginning this is a kind of love letter for I love you in a deep kind of way although we have never talked with each other until recently there has been some very basic kind of vibration communication . . . and Dionysus felt that way too and loves him back and that's the way the world will end even with a whimper and even if our greatest talent as with the greeks remains our facility for mutual destruction . . . And the rest of this is the story by Kate.

—October 14, 1971

from a letter in progress . . . and any reasonably intelligent monkey in the world now who doesn't know that all women are lesbians, let alone Janis Joplin . . . I suppose you saw the objection in *The Voice* letters asking me to substantiate my statement. I wish I could say I sacked out with Janis but you know I never met her even. The first question is why anybody would want such a statement substantiated and the second is the one all philosophers always got stuck on how do you substantiate anything at all other than your own experience which for everybody else is hearsay, thus all information is hearsay, including our own birth; certainly when you hear someone say they're heterosexual you only know that by hearsay, even when you see a woman with a belly full of baby if you still believe in the virgin birth. Anyway before and after she looks obviously pregnant, even if you don't believe in the virgin, her heterosexuality, and his, remains a mystery, in same words known only by hearsay. I want to go on about this letter from an irritated reader cause it reveals the core prejudice against lesbians and lesbianism, and for anyone who doubts this I'd ask them to translate the reader's request for proof as to Janis's gayness into a similar request for proof as to her interest in men, or in painted porches or spangles and velvets and southern comfort — I mean even if you hadn't *seen* Janis riding or wearing and drinking these things would you challenge her interest in them? Why is it more upsetting that she might love her own sex as well? And why do we have to wait till people are dead before we add this particular interest to the rest of the list? Why am I asking the question when we know it's because you're still better dead than red and also ready. And the subject believes it too. Even James Baldwin believes it, and I say that that from having seen a few months ago Baldwin's response on the Cavett show to Cavett's last and loaded question as to how he Baldwin felt about Eldridge Cleaver's attitude toward him. Baldwin as would be expected deflected an excellent opportunity to come out in a politically more significant medium than in his own fiction by converting the question into a conundrum or a collusion in the general social conspiracy to pretend that loving your own sex doesn't exist. If you don't admit it it doesn't exist. As Gregory says I have a habit of stubbornly believing everything and it's one of my numerous devices for being difficult. When I heard from at least three sources during this year that Janis liked women I naturally believed it and I don't need to add (so why am I) that the socalled straight woman doesn't want to believe it for in not believing it she can continue to imagine that it's best to be straight. Especially as concerns the stars. So to satisfy the incredulous attitudes of the straight I offer herewith the expanded dull story of one of my visits to a gay bar in San Francisco where the bartender, a woman, gave me the unsolicited information that Janis frequented that bar, and others, and, when I raised my eye creases for more, the condescending remark that Janis was a liberated person. In other parlance a swinger.

Also, aroused by this reader's letter, I contacted one Sookie Stambler who is writing a biography of Janis. Sookie contributes some high level hearsay concerning three women who were at one time or another Janis's lovers and who can't be identified because they aren't dead. Better more pedestrian hearsay is that the gay liberation front on the coast was angry at Janis for not coming out. It isn't clear whether they made serious attempts to contact her or not. Movement people spasmodically make efforts to reach the famous closet gays (active but not declared, that is) in hopes of a broader coalition and a deeper thrust at public opinion. Interrelated hearsay is that Janis trashed her women, and every woman who was ever gay yet straight in her head knows what that means and how the only way most of us could stop trashing our own sex was by a confrontation made possible through the united interests of gay and feminist consciousness. Anybody could hazard the speculation that Janis's self-destructive habits and personal difficulties revolved around a confusion of sexual identity and a conflict between herself as woman and as artist at war with society for not being all woman insomuch as she was independent and aggressive and stylistically farout, and that though all her instincts were right on, the only corroboration she had was from the freakedout radical rock world which is basically male, and chauvinist to the Kore. Both straights and guys. The latter perhaps being the worst in their straight heads.

I see Janis as a victim like the rest of us, but super isolated by her fame and thus an assumed uniqueness in her troubles. Unique as an artist and a personality yes, but in the substratum of vital needs, no. And every woman can now begin to see her difficulties against the big social fabric of male authority and repression. This is the service of the gay and feminist revolutions. And they never reached Janis. If they had she might not've been such an exciting artist, but she might easily have felt a whole lot better about herself. When you mention someone like Janis now in certain company the company scoffs at the stars but stars are people too and pretty soon maybe the stars will begin telling their stories like it really is. Janis could only scream about it in the symbolic transformation of her work. And as to being gay, as soon as she was dead, practically, a drag queen on the coast called Goldie Glitters dropped the news in a gay rag Gay Sunshine and that's how the news is distorted as a scandal — when the subject herself was unable, by self and social prohibition, to proudly claim the fact in her own words. The trouble was that she couldn't be proud. Sookie quotes a short passage from Janis's "Mama I Got Them Old Cosmic Blues" which may be the closest she got to coming out by declaration: They ain't gonna love you any better/And they ain't gonna love you right/So you better dig it now/It don't make any difference. — Not only could it not make any difference but it could be a lot worse with women when the woman retains that low estimation of herself bequeathed by the social structure. Two women together with a low opinion of themselves can trash each other real bad. And from all the hearsay that's where Janis was at. Adumbrating hearsay: the whole world being hearsay, the information the world accepts and rejects is always political; that is, whose information will the judge accept to further whose interests? Gay people notoriously like to believe everybody is gay, the same as the straights view the world as straight and everything else an aberration. The political nature of the gay persuasion is naturally to enlarge our constituency for healthier free access to our own objects of affection and sexual satisfaction. The revolution is to erode the exclusive prerogative of the straight in us. Hereforth I refuse to believe without substantiation the news that anybody is straight and since I'm not interested in access to anybody's bedroom particularly I'll remain suspicious and incredulous. I hope you'll believe that I saw Janis's painted porsche last week a couple of hours north of here in a foreign car fixit place. "They" said that the paint job costs as much as the car and they "thought" it done by Peter Max. It's owned by Albert Grossman and when I said it was a pity a woman didn't have it they said perhaps Grossman's wife drives it around . . . If you believe any of this you've joined the mighty company of existence by hearsay . . .

—*October 28, 1971*

Movement Schmoovement

Snowshoe: what with everything that's going on a letter probably is
in order since my new woman of the week is from seattle and I'd
rather splat out a letter than compose a piece if you still don't mind
or believe in living free as you said might include here a small
adjustment to another type of intrusion into your wilderness as well
as an exercise in suspending belief when you're reading along and
think hey she wouldn't write that in a letter it's true I'm still not free
enough here to splat out a piece the way I liberally compose a letter
what with everything going on I wonder if my new woman of the
week from seattle is like your new genderless folk out there and if so
we're coming soon. I never made it north of Mendocino. The last
time I was seriously impressed by a woman was in fact in a tiny
ghosttown Caspar five miles up from Mendocino spent about 10
days with a head amazon over six feet high and she was great too
and now this Denby aged 19 also stands over six feet but as a de facto
mesomorph meaning she hasn't stopped growing yet so you might
say she's trying to become an ectomorph which was the incredibly
gangling gawky majestic & flying hair broomsticky look of my friend
back in Caspar. Denby wouldn't ever look that way tho even if she
did grow skinnier into her 190 pounds. She's a round one really. A
smiling pumpkin head. Ruddy all american outdoors perfect teeth
pale blue smart eyes sandy short straight hair wholesome is the word
people use she told me. The other day on a talking gig in new jersey
the women afterward brought in the problem subject of elitism in
the movement and someone said well we do proceed by models
from model to model as it works and I described my new model is
a triumph of size and cool. She makes some sort of immediate sense
& according to Jane who sent her on to me to help reclaim my
camper broke apart last week on a northern turnpike enroute another
talk gig she doesn't have a paranoid sense of privacy so I'm safe for
a day and I was writing all this while she cut up some cabbage and
celery for salad speaking of what you said ah but there's other places
& times & distances & fugitive presents and you and another survivor
snowshoe walking the creek throwing a big branch in watching it

on its majestic way downstream with an escort of sunken leaves
going down too swirling on the bottom . . . it was for me also that
way walking along an eastern stream here one early afternoon with
Denby bubbling under her beaver black top hat and huge inside her
gray vest and carrying her napsack and a heavy tin box of tools we
were hitchhiking out of a remote little acre thru the dead and dying
rusty brown orange hills I felt very happy like we were sisterberry
finns & whitewashed fences forever on the road to noplace
particular . . . immediate sense . . . and throwing our gear into the
back of a light blue truck for a short windy hop to a lonesome
corner . . . and stopping at the wire to a cow enclosure where Denby
approached with a declaration of sweetheart and tramping on told
me how the cows don't like the machines and miss the human hand
and how back home she sometimes took a drink directly off the teat
if she was playing hard near a pasture and got thirsty and also how
she and her pals had a few milk fights . . . and parking our gear for
an on-coming car trying to decide who should be in front and if
one should sit down and who looked more like a girl and what to
remove each time she took off the top hat and me my shades and
once my jacket and joked about the rest I know it must sound like
city innocence in rural paradise to you all this but I have to explain
in order to purge myself of the polluted politics that recently
congested my head and lungs. Your letters predict my immediate
future it seems. The college gigs are okay cause I make a formal
exhibition and sound as authoritative as the situation demands and
even bask a little in the illusion of my own heroism created by a
modest amount of adulation and then it's time to split and that's easy
politics. For the rest, the heavy numbers in the city, of which Ti-
Grace Atkinson if you know who she is was a charter casualty, I
might invoke a nice oldfashioned Huxley line "in some cases man's
dreadful inhumanity to man has been inspired by the love of cruelty
for its own horrible and fascinating sake" to describe my final
impression of movement politics. Movement Schmoovement. There
were only a few encounters and this last one I knew it was all over
when I threw a handful of crackers at the leader and like every
reprimanded child went to bigger and better worse things. Z-gad, as

Denby would say, I'm being swallowed by a boa-constrictor. Anyway for sure if you're having fun you're not having a movement and I like to have fun so I've decided to refuse myself the dubious political pleasure of causing someone and then myself to hurt by walking into a living space of another person and acting as if they're in another century, or have a culture that we don't have. The first phase ended in reform and was succeeded by reaction. I said to Phyllis the culture is behind me and she said it's against you, not behind you. Mixing oil and water. Three straights who talk and act straight. One gay who talks somewhat straight and acts all gay. One gay who talks all gay and acts gay and a little straight. One straight who talks all gay and acts mostly straight. Two gays what talk and act all gay. The new term I heard in jersey is fuzzies for those straights thinking about having "Lesbian Experience." Did you ever hear the Yeats line about how things are torn down and built again and those that build again are gay? Anyway I guess Jane was my true ally and we probably felt like doomed conspirators at the end of some futile crusade. Higher consciousness may be moving to the country and not talking to anybody or it could be moving to chinatown and trashing everybody. Or at least assuming an air of helplessness involving fraudulent appeals for direction thru a show of ignorance. I'm sure someone can invent appropriate other possibilities as well. Anyhow I let them off the hook by exhibiting my distress. A good model doesn't throw crackers or try to blow their nose in aluminum tinfoil. So like what you wrote for me too that politics we cannot handle on any level at the moment and agree for the most part that the only true social interaction will come when we bring it from the inside out and that it won't work from all these platforms erected outside, and I'd add that as women we're not going to discover what our differences are until we become human since as one of these leaders has noted women have internalized the disesteem in which they are held, despising both themselves & each other so I refuse now to go anyplace where my name might be added to the casualty list they call a movement. Wherever Ti-Grace is I'm with her and I reaffirm that I constitute a movement totally myself complete period. If we're going to be casualties I prefer the type Denby sustained a couple of years ago a car rammed her motorcycle. She's philosophical about it and takes good care of herself and still rides bikes. I think the accident broke her leg in nine places so she limps slightly but improves all the time. I wondered and didn't ask if there was any connection between the accident and her height. She laments her present six foot one total and the stop her parents put to her growth when she was 13 and they convinced her that the six foot ten the doctors predicted as her outcome was not suitable for getting along in life. The top hat is perfect. When I first saw her I was really happy. She's huge and huggy and funny and together and dependable and considers herself quite lucky since she wasn't raised to buy her clothes at J. Jacobs but to coach a football team and build a house and stuff like that. She was her father's number one son she says. Though recently returning home to visit she was put out a lot when he introduced her to a friend as my son Lindsay and she had to explain that she didn't like that a bit since she's gotten her head together as a woman now she knows a woman can be a woman and build houses and coach football teams too. We talked about heroes awhile. Her big one was Vince Lombardi. I told her I collected photos of Gary Cooper a long time back. You had to pick a star then and put them in a scrapbook and Shirley Temple was unthinkable. I asked her about reading too. She loved *Lord of the Rings* and regardless of the chauvinism in it no matter what anybody says she's not willing to stop loving the things she loves just because she's developed a higher consciousness. My son Richard loves the *Lord of the Rings* too. Once last year we went on a difficult hunt around where he lives for Bored of the Rings. I've made the inevitable switch so you must be thinking uh she wouldn't write this or this way in a letter it's true but maybe someday I'll pretend I'm writing a real letter and then send it as a piece or vice reversa. I'm putting you the cider your letter Denby and Jane together and pitching it all against the dire blackness and ill humor of the politics of women at war with themselves. The immensity of Denby was a moment of truth. The combined images turned my head. Sitting on my speaker in the white work suit and black clodboots laced to the knees explaining my broken motor and how she didn't have the proper tools to fix it. Deep in a sling chair laughing over

how it's good to play that game "use the alphabet & tell me
everything I am." Arriving late in a foggy moonless night towing the
camper and steaming the tires of Phyllis's buick stuck on the wet
leaves in the last stretch of driveway. Playing the Chambers brothers
full up to blasting any barn away. Noticing a remarkable pale green
bug in the rocks below the door sill. The entire expedition I rambled
on about the sisterberry mutt & mutt or jeff & jeff team going
hopefully noplace and not waiting for any godope either but being
gorgeous outsized girl marvel bums on the bounty. If this was a letter
I might add that I think the clincher that made me realize I've been
unseasonably heavy was when standing on my head Denby came
over and drew a funny face in purple ink on my stomach it's time
again to be irresponsible and irrelevant and irreverent and fuck
civilization and movements . . . from wherever I am in the dead leafy
season . . .

    L., Jill.

—*November 11, 1971*

The Genius I've Squandered in Bed

I want some old violins old wine old people old buildings and some young ones homesick for infinity. Goodmorning, I responded politely, altho when I turned around I saw nothing. I am very busy finding out what people mean by what they say I used to be interested in what they were what they looked like I am now interested in what they say. Please remember your own lines. I make them up, I don't have to remember them. I know, she says, you're operating on about ten levels at once writing two books and two pieces and three letters and two lists and this record book with everything neatly organized all over the room and she went about organizing her part of the chaos. I'm going out to get a fresh air of breath. The ice is still forming a ceiling over the stream. The men are still going up in trees on ropes with saws and mutilating the branches. The rest still looks like a postcard whatever isn't white is black and the white makes the black look blacker or the black white whiter. There's a nuclear family in that car with the woman driving. We talk about our mothers sometimes. Marsha always used to forgive hers because she was right and she M. was wrong and now she's permanently disgusted. Jane says she's her mother's posthumous child. She was born 20 years after she died. Mine shut herself up in an impregnable silence. I'll marry myself to the mozart basson concerto. These Elusivian mysteries. Marsha never mentioned a father. Jane's had a widow's peak and that's all she remembers except for gray eyes maybe and he came around once or twice like visiting royalty and invaded the mythological vacuum her mother created to explain and insure his absence. He is familiar to all of us and not a very interesting or important person. I like to talk about my grandmother's boarder. His name was Mr Shoemaker and he was a drunkard but he walked straight and sober through her living room to go upstairs to his bedroom and out the same way is what he amounted to. Ecce hobo. Marsha's mother took in some boarders, the italians had stinky feet and the germans burned holes in the furniture. Anyway we're all mutant forms — happy products of the failure of the nuclear family. I meet this tree and embrace it and put my arms around it as if it was an old-fashioned woman. Y. wanted to know if I really thought all men were unredeemable, after all they've done some pretty interesting things, like say einstein . . . and I said E equals mother cunt squared, his particular relativity was a wife who left his boxlunch outside the study door every day. The author of totem & taboo himself frankly acknowledged that he didn't know where the actual arena of the drama he sketched could've taken place. None of our mothers were much into the old and new testicles either. Or they reacted a lot in the margins and stuff. Mine was a heathen she said although she sent me to be baptized when I was eight and made me go to some strawberry festival at a community type church place and sent me off to a high episcopalian establishment where they confirmed me and left the rest up to me. I went to confession once. They gave me a small booklet of sins and I chose ten. I never confess although I don't keep secrets either. Jane's mother actually was somewhat religious, but not pious. She was into the rationalists c.s. eliot and t.s. lewis and lewis's science fiction too rather than the books of the common prayer. Before she died my grandmother was trying to find out something about all of it. She wrote out a prayer on a scrap of paper for instance. What did I say yesterday about my grandmother opening the tops of the bottles for me? Wouldju please remember my lines too? I make them up sometimes, I shouldn't have to remember them. I'm busy finding out what other people say or mean by what they say I used to be interested in the looks of them and who they were I am now interested in what they say. In new definitions perhaps especially. Penis envy is the envy of a man with a little penis for the bigger penis of another man. A feminist is a woman who wants a better deal from her old man. Aggression is when a cannibal eats another person and he isn't hungry. A victorian phallic mother is a woman who comes after you with an enema bag. She moves rhythmically to the accompaniment of her own daydreams. The idea that pleasure could be an end in itself is so startling and so threatening to the stricture of our society that the mere possibility is denied. Flying still seems a drastic means of traveling. I'm going out for a fresh of breath air. I go skid on the ice and mail a letter to suzi and to rolling stone. I said to rolling stone why don't they print a photo of a female rock star with a nude man in the background. Or a male rock star with the same. Like say mick jagger with a depressed anonymous naked man in the background. And also how do they come off covering the women on their scene exclusively by men. And why can't they call their rag the male rolling stone. I'm a real revolutionary. I write lines and letters and books and pieces and lists and records and even copy down some ladys room graffiti: "I like grils." The next person crossed that out and said "you mean girls don't you?" And a third person said "what about us grills?" When you think of all the genius I've squandered in bed. I need a movement omelet. I need a bee exterminator. I need a gazebo. I need a superficial excursion. I needed to know if she was really serious about pretending to be ignorant about not being in business. Or I needed the line about richard's question about her seriousness and pretending and ignorance and being in business or not seemed irrelevant to the monopoly game itself. She remembers when she went through her thimble stage. I was fond of the boat or the shoe. I like to talk about the games sometimes. The best was a square board that came with a few sticks and a bunch of small wooden doughnuts combining which — the board sticks and doughnuts — you could play about 75 different games. The other best was a rubber cup and a rubber disc and two dice and for each player a string with a colored wooden ball at the end and I don't remember what happened then. I played marbles on the rug too. And asked my grandmother to open the bottle tops. She was the butch I guess. She had arthritis but she could open bottle tops. I couldn't do a thing like that. I could read and play ball and marbles and toy soldiers and cops and robbers and climb trees but I couldn't do any knots or screws or plugs or wires or anything like that. I suppose I had my revolutions all mixed up to begin with. Next time I'll contrive to be ordered to do what I really want. But it won't be mechanics, even so. Jane said she thought I was just playing the dumb femme, not fixing the light. So she wouldn't fix it. Then she fixed it. Then Marsha fixed the other one. Then I said Marsha must be a mechanical genius because she seems to do everything and she replied that wasn't true, that I was just subnormal. I'm going out for the fresh air. I need the air and the picturepostcard

black and white snow escape. I want some old violins old wine old
people old buildings and some young ones homesick for infinity.
—*January 27, 1972*

Lesbian Mothers Ltd.

I left off mentioning going to a lesbian mothers panel last week and don't know if I'm up to it now. I've been retreating into history. I've been retreating. I've been into people like this one-eyed queen who personally led 10 thousand troops in battle against some roman governor of Egypt. Well I shared a panel presentation with two other women at the Firehouse sometime in February. I didn't think the whole audience was mothers and they weren't. I asked those who weren't if they were thinking of becoming lesbian mothers. Suddenly I wasn't sure why I was there. The other sounds good. It's easy recommending things you don't practically know anything about. My approach to life is completely historical. A wholesome and lofty attitude. Anyhow many women now are "coming out" for the first or second time after the aberration of a conventional marriage and a child or two and are faced with angry ex-husbands and parents and in-laws and poverty and the legal apparatus for taking their children away and the guilt of renouncing motherhood if they feel they *want* to give up their children or *have* to give up their children and the problems of living arrangements if they keep them, including most significantly the psychology of come-out in relation to the children. The legal problems for lesbian mothers who want to keep their children are critical. The law doesn't recognize the lesbian as a fit mother. Thus any father who has the desire and the means can take his child into custody away from a lesbian mother. A threat which retards the gay revolution by keeping the woman a closet case. And which by the same token retards the evolution of finer mothers in the suppression of the affirmation of sexual identity. Certainly I was a younger women at such war with my sex role and without knowing it that I wasn't a fit mother by anybody's standards including my own and I had to let my children go to become myself. Certainly in any case none of us were told what a drastic drag it was to be a mother. I mean motherhood was a soft fuzzy edge tinted photo of the young ageless beautiful cosmically fulfilled mother with her cooing dentyne baby on the cover of oneathem ladies magazines.

Two women spoke first and they were very much into being

mothers. I had had a hazy idea we would all be getting together to celebrate the end of motherhood or something. But here were two women and quite a few more who were proud mothers who were interested in sharing new ways of getting along as mothers bringing up their children with their female lovers and partners. Certainly I've advocated the lesbian communal household with its advantages of multiple parents of the children. I know I've heard about these households the past year or two and always think that I didn't really believe that, but I never thought it through and it was always the thing to do, especially if you didn't know what else to do and your mother thought you should go to a shrink. So I became a sort of a pseudo mother. I thought there were more mothers like that around. I mean mothers not archetypically the mothers, who somehow became mothers for a brief time. I am really a perennial daughter.

Here is some history I relate to from Helen Diner's *Mothers and Amazons:*

> "In time and reality, the Amazon kingdoms not only comprise an extremist end of matriarchy but also are a beginning and a purpose in themselves. Roaming daughter realms, they markedly differ from the serenely tolerant mother clan as old as mankind, which pacifically exiled a young upstart manhood by exogamy. In the mother clan, there was a constant progression of great mother begetting more great mothers. Amazons, however, reproduced the daughter type, which practically skips a generation and is something altogether different. They were conquerors, horse tamers, and huntresses who gave birth to children but did not nurse or rear them. They were an extreme, feminist wing of a young human race, whose other extreme wing consisted of the stringent patriarchies."

By many accounts the Amazons did rear their daughters. By certain accounts the Amazons played a crucial historical role in the long bloody transition from the matriarchies to the patriarchies. Diner's sources are excellent but her conclusions are vague. No doubt we are presently at a juncture in history in which the Amazons return to perform a similar function as the transition is reversed.

Anyway me and my mother were daughter types and probably my mother's mother was more like the mother in the procession of great mothers begetting more great mothers. If that itself isn't a patriarchal fiction. Maybe the three of us were a squad of roaming daughters. The eldest did settle in one place and make the soup for her daughter and her granddaughter and grow up to be a shapeless old woman, so I think that's why I see her as the great mother type. My mother had no more business being a mother than I did without an Amazon community to support ourselves. Our time hasn't come yet. Our time has come. It's doubtless very satisfying to feel that we understand and approve the course of the grand drama of history. This is not the sort of thing the women at the lesbian mothers panel were interested in hearing about, about the antidiluvean queens who're colonizing the world, like this woman whose car I'm driving in right now it's smoking and smelling and its upholstery is a ceiling of black tattered holes and she says it has a '56 transmission and a '65 engine. I suppose she's all primed to vanish into the higher beatitudes. The women who were at the panel are dealing with the law and the kitchen table. The first two women who spoke each live with a lesbian lover and a child. One was very knowledgeable about the law and the problems. I haven't thought much about all of this. Although a feminist lawyer advised me and carried on for me last fall over the vaguely defined crisis of my son and his father who seemed embarrassed over the possibility of his son being identified as my son too and other complications like hanging up on me and refusing to let me see him or my daughter and creating an either-or situation in which it seemed my son had to leave his house totally, be disowned as they used to say, or stay there and have nothing whatever to do with me.

I had endless circular conversations with my feminist lawyer in which we were unable to resolve any action because I wanted to have my son and not eat him too as it were. I mean I didn't want custody and I wanted friendly communications including such events as being able to take him to a Lennon lawn party without having to abduct him for the occasion, which I did.

—*March 4, 1972*

The Myth of Motherhood

The subject of lesbian mothers seems very central to the matriarchal revolution. Lesbian motherhood was the form of the original Amazon communities. Women are again doing the natural thing, but without a woman's law to support the doing. "One of the most shocking lapses of morality, in the patriarchal view, is manifested in the birth of fatherless babies. Throughout the patriarchal age women have suffered outrageously for this breach of male property rights, and their unfortunate babies have suffered even worse. Yet the only thing wrong with fatherless families, so deplored by present-day sociologists, is not that they are fatherless but that the mothers do not have the support and approval of society. In a normal, well-regulated, woman-centered society, this would not be the case. The father is not at all necessary to a child's happiness and development, the voluminous writings on the subject by government and related social agencies notwithstanding. For many millenia, in many parts of the world, women did, and still do, bring up very fine children without the help of men." (E. G. Davis, *The First Sex*.) Breach of male property rights. That's the fundamental issue. Patrilineal inheritance. I wish I wanted to change my name. The women must recreate our own legal system and a primary way of doing it is to begin with the names. My son is abdicating his father's name and sometimes assuming mine. But mine is my father's. But he didn't really exist. But who has a real mother's name? We have to invent them. A woman recently used her mother's first name to make Sarachild for her new last name. Some women are using their middle names for their last names. Some women just their first names or any other single invented name. Name consciousness is a sign of the general feminist consciousness of a male legal system under which women are prime property. Under this system women are accorded certain rights and protection by handing themselves over to the institution called marriage by which the system is maintained. Slaves on a plantation received immunity from hostile external elements. The owner might pick up a gun if anyone threatened his slaves, i.e., Straw Dogs. The Government directly rewards the proper couple by permitting them to pool their income tax and make one return. Here are a couple of statements made by NOW last fall "endorsing lesbianism as a feminist issue."

> "Married women are denied equality under laws that decree men as head of the household, but a wife is nonetheless allowed some legal protection. A lesbian, however, who shares her home with another woman — regardless of her income or responsibilities — foregoes all the economic and legal compensations granted to the married woman, including tax deductions, insurance benefits, inheritance rights, etc . . . This prejudice against the lesbian is manifested in the courts as well. Whereas most divorced women are conceded the right to their children, a lesbian is automatically presumed unfit for motherhood, and can have her children taken from her."

The fault underlying the law is that a lesbian's prime commitment is to another woman. It's illegal in other words not to be in prime relationship to the male who defines the law by this very involvement. The rights of the father to the mother. A way of putting it to understand the position of the lesbian is that the mother has no rights to the mother. I think it's significant that in my case my son aligned himself with me in the classic revolt against the father, and my daughter as it looks right now is a captive in her father's house. Communications reached an all-time low during the past year when her father decided I was even more unsavory and disreputable than he thought I was when I merely rejected him as my domestic playmate. Certainly his daughter is more useful around the house than his son. Still, I recognize an important bond of identity now well established between my daughter and her step-mother. Still, there's no reason except for an angry male why she can't have a relationship with me as well. The law stands behind this angry man and his successful attempt to influence his daughter and discredit me as a friend and sister. Through the law or the threat of the law, every man stands between the natural bond of mothers and daughters and sisters. I mean this in the broad communal sense. Since a couple of basic revelations I experienced a few years ago I would no longer wish to posses a child or person in the sense that society encourages and commands its members to do so in the marriage contract by which as I said and we know the women and by extension her children are prime property. At that time in fact *psychically* I let my children go. I didn't think I could communicate this act of dispossession or catharsis to the panel of lesbian mothers last month at the Firehouse. We all seemed mutually disoriented. I listened to the first woman describe her situation living happily with a female lover and her (their) child and her commitment to changing the law, and I listened to the second woman describe a similar situation, and I realized as they were talking that they were involved in the nuclear family model without the father. I didn't think it was very revolutionary but I didn't mind either.

Or I did. Somewhat. The straight model of ownership in the scheme of oedipally focused children and a projecting pair of parents is the target of gay revolution. I mean I didn't want to take issue or find fault with the particular solutions of these women, but we take positions and develop theories or ideologies to alter and/or destroy the very conditions that predicate any of our individual solutions, which remain problematic. The nuclear family was a male creation. The women originally had no need for such a mono-focused arrangement from the point of view of *identity* since there was never any doubt in a woman's mind who her child was. The woman-centered family was a community of multiple parents. It was the crisis of identity for the male which caused the rather desperate expedient of making a woman captive by contract in marriage. By this device the male thought to secure his position by establishing uncontestable paternal identity. All of present culture is a grand interlocking structure for ensuring these identity rights asserted by the male. The rights of the father to the mother. Private property was an essential development in the early phases of the patriarchal revolution. *Particular* ownership. *Particular* egos. *Particular* identities. Individual problems and solutions. Capitalistic competitive free enterprise. Monopolies and corporate powers. Alienation and representation. Authority and *heir*archy. Parental chauvinism and child oppression. Ownership and individual isolated responsibilities. These are the characteristics of the heterosexual institution. All interdependent and mutually reinforcing patterns which are products and perpetrations of the disease called man. The myth of motherhood will be the first thing to go. Many women will stand up and say that being a mother in a ticky tacky box looking after her possessions is an abnormal unhealthy situation. That oedipal attachments are absurd and unnatural. That we may be the *instruments* of creations, but we have no right to own and dominate our products after we provide the nourishments of the abjectly dependent stage. That no woman can become herself in service to dependents for whom she is the sole source of guidance and well being. That women like men have become slaves to the fabrication of parental superiority. That women and children exist in a similar category of oppression.

For parental chauvinism is an invention of the father. This was one of my basic revelations of a few years ago. I realized I'd been acting like a "parent." I'd say rather I was very schizie. One half of me was that internalized social father. The other half the instinctive communal non-authoritarian mother. My kids would scramble all over me and everything and I wouldn't give a damn and then I couldn't control things when I had to or I'd flash on the restraints of big society out there and discipline etc., and I'd freak out into a huge contradiction. Anyway I really thought kids were a special category of mobile vegetable. I didn't see them as intelligences. My true freak-out occurred when I realized that kids including infants came knowing everything. Cosmic oceanic intelligence. That through education and coercion we as adults had moved into progressive states of specialized and highly operable ignorance. I developed a great respect and attitude of pupil toward the child not yet fucked up and I no longer wished to possess any or at least be responsible for them in the only isolated way in which the patriarchal system punishes both women and children. Women's rights will be women's law. The information for women for the matriarchal revolution is available in the underground press. Here was a recent note in *The Furies*, a lesbian/feminist monthly from washington, d.c.

"In San Francisco, the Lesbian Mother Union is meeting

weekly. The group got together last summer after the Los Angeles Gay Women's conference, where they had attended a workshop for Lesbian mothers. They are working on a program to be presented to the Family Service Agency. The Union wants the professionals to come through with legal aid as well a legal and psychological research. Since Lesbians are not considered to be fit mothers in this society, their children are always taken away from them in custody cases. The Lesbian Mother's Union hopes to gain solid ammunition from mental health professionals and research before it tries to bring forward a test case in the courts."

Challenging the law as it is may be the only present recourse for change. Ultimately there will be a new legal system and it will be a woman's system because the woman *is* parent prime.

—*March 16, 1972*

Stein: Affectionately Obscene Poetry

In history one does not mention dahlias mushrooms or hortensias. Letter from Carol who saying it is pleasing to see that G.S. interests you and invades the dreams of your friend Jane. G.S. is indeed someone in whom to be interested as is Natalie Barney (*L'Amazone*) who was at one time the lover of Romaine Brooks who painted a portrait of Lady Una Troubridge who was the lover of Radclyffe Hall who depicted a good number of these people in *The Well of Loneliness*. They are all of these people extremely interesting but only one was a genius and that of course was Gertrude who is most truly "the mother of us all." I was drunk the other night (Carol goes on) and someone began to talk about Rilke's Duino Elegies and I in my drunken state heard it as do we know Elegies and I thought this was a rather schoolmarmish thing for Rilke to write and then I began to think that it sounded quite Gertrude Steiny... Do we know Elegies and if we do know Elegies how well do we know Elgies do we. And that's the end of that story. G.S. was for a while very much opposed to commas. At the most she said a comma is a poor period that it lets you stop and take a breath but if you want to take a breath. Endeth the quote know yourself that you want to take a breath. Endeth the quote from C's letter. I have thought a good deal about commas myself. I have not thought a good deal about commas. Knowing myself whether I want to take a breath I'll use the comma and if not not. Gertrude Stein has always interested me but never so much as recently. Two years ago it occurred to me that there must be some intimate connection between her stylistic obscurities and her domestic lesbian arrangement. Unknown to me Edmund Wilson made a similar speculation in the '30s. The origin of the speculation might've been the same for him as for me and that was the sudden availability of Q.E.D. or "Things as They Are" published posthumously in a limited edition of 500. I saw one of these in san diego winter of '70 and was amazed to read a perfectly coherent Stein, more conventional even than the autobiography of ABT in which by the way there is an embarrassed reference to the early Q.E.D. meaning quod erat demonstrandum or what has been proved. I think it was her first formal literary enterprise. The story of an emotional entanglement between three young american women who travelled abroad in the summers. The lesbian nature of the involvement was made quite explicit. Conventional as it is except for its content it has a completely unorthodox conclusion. It doesn't conclude. Thus the early title what has been proved.

There is no real linear progression of the story either. The characters do go from one place to another in historical time but they never solve anything, they keep encountering each other in variations of the same problem. I think it concerns a period in Stein's life before she settled in Paris as a young woman in Baltimore in love with another young woman in a possibly unrequited romance. Stein never deviated from her sexual identity as lesbian but she did opt to establish herself exclusively through the formal aspect of her medium as an innovator. In "Portraits and Repetition" she said I said in Lucy Church Amiably that women and children change, I said if men have not changed women and children have. But it really is of no importance even if this is true. The thing that is important is the way that portraits of men and women and children are written, by written I mean made. And by made I mean felt. So she said. Her brother Leo once complained of one of her portraits that her description and the portrait failed to correspond at all. Her brother incidentally became such an impediment to her progress and confidence, offering nothing but discouragement, that she never saw him again but once after he left the house in Paris, having been replaced by the steadfast support of her friend and lover Alice Toklas. The brother represented naturally the male establishment, and as a floundering male he had extra good reason for discouraging his sister. "Nothing could solve his problem of being an intricate engine racing at top speed, but producing nothing." Thinking of Leo as maledom these two statements by Robert Bridgman (*Gertrude Stein in Pieces*) makes perfect personal/ political and literary sense to me: "She had now cast her lot with values that were not necessarily capable of being rationally communicated." And "Because this position was the basis of her independence she could not afford to have him undermine it." I mean I believe these values and this position were both personal and literary and it was essential to protect both from the threat of male disapproval. The dissociation between literary expression and personal life and something called objective observation could be viewed as a political necessity which was the occasion of genius. In other words the necessity of obscurity was the mother of invention. She recalled her excitement when she discovered that the words she used were not descriptive and indeed often had nothing whatever to do with the thing being represented. As Bridgman writes, "Her prose was irritating because it communicated too little too clearly, or it said too much too obscurely." And, "She created several unreadable styles." Although her obscurity grew out of the suppression of lesbian subject matter, she did become at the same time explicit about her sexuality in the context of her obscurities, contradictory as that may sound. Every so often she comes perilously close to saying something. Really though in the poem "Lifting Belly" and the long prose/poem "Sonatina Followed by Another" she makes obvious references to her intimate life with Alice. "Pussy said I was to wake her in an hour and a half if it didn't rain. It is still raining what should I do," Somehow she found a way. She was unable ultimately to dissemble. Considering this direct autobiographical nature of so much of her writing it is clear she is the only upfront lesbian writer of quality and reputation prior to our time. Stein constantly undermined the content of her work while reasserting it in the same devious guise of her innovative practices.

Bridgman says that after 20 years of enigmatic utterances, Gertrude Stein at last chose to speak in a voice of singular clarity. She was 58 years old. He refers to the autobiography of Alice Toklas. I don't agree entirely with his judgment of Edmund Wilson's precocious observation linking her obscurities with her sexuality. He says "Both of Wilson's opinions seem to me to have been correct (he means a later amendment Wilson made that I don't understand). Lesbian sentiments contributed to Gertrude Stein's stylistic impenetrability, although Wilson did initially exaggerate their importance as an influence." I think their importance can't be exaggerated enough. If you were not impenetrable you had to write novels, and practically nobody did that either. In any case it was Stein's ultimate inability to lie that distinguishes her from those who did write in the novel form. It isn't fair to Stein to mention a writer of her quality in the same breath with Radclyffe Hall, but the comparison is worth considering from the point of view of lesbian identity. Hall's book for all its fame is still a piece of sentimental embarrassing realism. But quality aside, who was Radclyffe Hall. If she wasn't Radclyffe Hall she was a third unknown identity behind the pen name behind the fictional character of Stephen Gordon. I don't think it matters that much. The important thing is she had to write a fiction, and a tragic one at that. I think if I'd read *The Well of Loneliness* when I should have I might never've fallen into bed with my first woman. It's a dreary discouraging role-playing story. *The Sheik* was no better. But what was there. The only available Stein was what we continue to have in such recent selections as this penguin book edited by one Patricia Meyerowitz who was the woman last fall contesting Virgil Thomson's outspoken knowledge of Gertrude Stein's sexuality in the *New York Review of Books*. I've quoted Ms Meyerowitz's objections and Thomson's reply before. But at that time I hadn't seen or noticed the refutation to Meyerowitz in Alice Toklas herself, in Toklas's *What Is Remembered*. She refers to the painful joke of Gertrude's about her being an old maid mermaid (the phrase the Meyerowitz quoted to use in part as proof that the two women were celebate in relation to each other) and goes on to indicate that that well might have been the base but that she is now happily gathering wild vilolets. It's a wonderful pointed if metaphorically obscure passage. Anyway it's all the Meyerowitzs who remain(ed) incredulous over lesbian identity who help to keep us from our own. The unavailability of Stein's work has been a chief factor in the conspiracy. Not only was Stein not hiding behind pseudonyms or fiction but what there was of it in her work was a celebration of lesbianism! Affectionately obscene poetry is not apologetic. Djuna Barnes's *Nightwood* is superior literature but for her too the lesbian subject besides being remote in the novel form is tragic and melancholic and bizarre. Contrast Barnes with Stein who said I like loving. I like mostly all the ways anyone can have of having loving feeling in them. Slowly it has come to be in me that any way of being a loving one is interesting and not unpleasant to me. — If she was unable to assert herself politically she was at least very grandly positive about her private life.

And for all its tearjerking tragedy and stereotyped presentation of role-playing lesbianism and its embarrassment as literature *The Well of Loneliness* has a few startling rudimentary political assertions: "Stephen would again and again go over those last heartrending days with Barbara and Jamie, railing against the outrageous injustice that had led to their tragic and miserable ending. She would clench her hands in a kind of fury. How long was this persecution to continue? How long would God sit still and endure this insult offered to His creation? How long tolerate the preposterous statement that *inversion*" (my italics) "was not a part of nature? For since it existed what else could it be? All things that existed were a part of nature!" Radclyffe Hall wasn't so bad. She had a bad time of it like most lesbians and she had to do what we used to call pouring your heart out and many lesbians, if not encouraged to go on by the story, have identified with it. Hall herself was not totally discouraged, like Stein she never deviated from her sexual identity as lesbian, and like Stein and Romaine Brooks and Ida Rubinstein and a number of others she made a long satisfying relationship with one other woman, the one Carol mentioned — Lady Una Troubridge. Speaking of the conspiracy against identity, as regards the painter Romaine Brooks, a number of us last year picked up *The Times* one Sunday to read with great astonishment that this woman most of us had never heard of had just died at the age of 96 and we could now go and see some of her paintings in a small retrospective at the Whitney. In that posthumous article she was identified as a lesbian, and her paintings many of them described as lesbian portraits. Brooks belongs to some fugitive continental elite society of lesbians that flourished particularly in the '20s.

—May 4, 1972

Call It A Day & A Day It Was

She said she didn't think it was politically correct to get done by a dog. I don't like these dog conversations. I don't like dogs. I think they were discussing a love between the species workshop. We have all we can manage getting it straight between ourselves. All they agreed on was that males will stick it in the wall. Two worker types saw my virgin badge this morning and said they didn't believe it. I said it was true. Of course I am. And I'm celebrating finishing my book and I'm not trapped by fame, I enjoy it. I wonder if my mother knows. *MS* wouldn't print this photo of me by Sahm which is childish and intelligent and flattering what else do you want from a photo. What else did she say I said she was? Who said easy times come hard for me and oh mydarling oh well. I lost my record book in schraffts but I found out about elevators in the same half hour. I'm sitting waiting for Dione eating pretzels watching a woman walk right into an open trap and the door close after her I knew she knew to walk in because the light was on over the trap and I remembered how I used to do this myself just as unconcernedly walk in and let myself be carried upwards someplace by this large box and I thought as the light went off and the woman went up what would I do if the box stopped between floors I saw myself screaming but silently as in a dream and I realized at once it wasn't an elevator problem but a room problem in 1965 I was locked in a room I had never been locked in a room before except that time before I was born so I never thought of rooms or elevators as traps and now I don't like to be locked either in or out of a place and it really is a room problem I remembered sitting there in rockefeller center waiting for Dione eating pretzels watching another woman walk right into the open trap and the door close after her I knew. You remember that e.e. cummings title the enormous room. That's the world I guess and we're locked in so I don't know what I'm worried about. Only a vagina has real teeth. Somebody said the beards on men's faces are the pubes of medusa. I've heard the pubic hair of women referred to as the beard of allah. We saw hercules in the desert last night. I let carol drink out of my taurus cup cuz she's a taurus too. carol came up with sk dunn who named her daughter after carol's mother which may be why I always introduce carol as carol dunn which is really sk's father's name and somehow it all makes sense since carol was sk's first lover, I don't mean her father but carol mullins the taurus whose mother has the same name as sk's daughter. I was named after a british movie actress. Jane was named after a heroine in a novel her mother was reading. I'm glad carol and sk are still friends. I'm still friends with sk too. I met her on my mother's birthday two years ago and I lost my wallet with my british passport and my birth certificate all my mother's names when we went dancing. I lost my wallet when carol and sk came up the other day too. Then I found it. I lost everything my mother gave me. I lost my record book in schraffts the day I understood elevators because schraffts is the place my mother always took me for lunch when we came to the city to buy my new tweed winter coat at lord & taylor's and my patent leather shoes for easter at best's. It's all about rooms. And photos. I suppose Sahm is my mother too. She takes wonderful photos, just the way my mother saw me in her candid brownie shots. I lost all of them in 1960-something whenever I was evicted from washington heights and I lost my wedding ring under a car and the city threw out the babybook along with my grandmother's old persian rug. I felt terrible about the photos. The woman I loved said I cried just like a baby. I had a right to, it was the thing my mother and me liked to do best besides play pick up sticks and double solitaire, lie in bed on a lazy sunday and look at the photos and have her explain them again every time including the first three the day she had me, she said, three almost identical shots in the arms of a british nurse, my favorite was in the arms of a british steward on the s.s. george washington. She always said I lost everything she gave me. What else did she say I said she was. When you move you find out what you've been losing and what you've been hanging on to. I have a photo of my first boyfriend but not my first two women. It doesn't matter, to him I was a virgin. We're organizing a virgins international conference. First we might have an international apology conference. Experimental conditioning. Everybody will spend five days apologizing and never do it again. I hope everybody comes and then we can all be friends. We could have a big margemellow roast. Jane said to Bertha so don't you agree an army of lovers can't get out of bed and Bertha replied she didn't realize there was a tactical problem. After the revolution you're so busy getting things organized you don't have a chance to go to bed. Jane said maybe we should postpone the revolution. Bertha: Let's not take the fun out of revolution. Pleasure is the energy principle. Who said schizophrenics can have an orgasm looking at a blank wall. When virginia woolf went crazy she thought the birds were speaking in greek. When I was crazy they locked me in a room and I didn't have an orgasm and my mother came to see me and showed me a photo of her grandchildren. I do have one thing left and that's the blue and yellow ski sweater she knit when I was 19 and went to vermont to learn how to ski. That's all. I think I packed it last week. I can't lose Sahm's photos because she's a professional. But when carol and sk came up sk ript off a few others and said she'd bring them back but she won't. I like the whole photo business but I told Sahm I'm really tired of my ego and have to split for europe soon. The ego the voice the record book the book the rooms the photos the revolution everything. Jane thought I lost the record book at schraffts because of the voice and I said well that's true if the voice is my mother and I guess it is. Anyway I reclaimed it by taxi this morning the longhair driving held up norman o. brown's life against death and asked me if I read it it happened to be the book I was reading in 1965 when I went crazy and I began to remember that time before I was born and the book is done and we met at schraffts to talk about it and about the photos and the rooms and Dione went up and down the trap three times and then I supplied the explanation and she didn't disagree. It takes being locked in a room to realize how dangerous a moving box is. The arms are numb and the sun don't shine. Did I ever say I was a schraffts coffee girl once for eight months, or nine, well I was. I wore a black dress and a hairnet and lipstick and stockings and I was a very good girl. I don't know when I began to go bad. Possibly when I found myself unexpectedly pregnant. It wasn't easy being pregnant and a virgin. When mary maxworthy unexpectedly found herself pregnant gertrude stein said simply that mary "had something happen to her that surprised everyone who knew her." It's all true. Even sk used to say that her daughter jesse who's named after carol's mother was her mother. I never understood sk's arrangement, it was just the first of its kind I'd seen, the father in one room and the daughter in another and sk in the middle with her procession of lovers and ex lovers turned into friends or back into lovers again for all I know I know it's reassuring to have a visit from her with carol mullins the day after she said bernie got up in the morning after over a year I think they've been together and said in her iowa drawl well I think it's time to call it a day and went and bought a big duffle and packed up and made a plane reservation for iowa and went to the airport accompanied by sk and I suppose sk's father and daughter and maybe carol mullins anyway I thought she was supposed to feel terrible so I was glad to see carol but sk was smiling and saying this bernie woman is fantastic, she just gets up and says it's time to call it a day and a day it was and we're all movin' on and that's all. Well aren't you going to do something about it. About what. She came and ript off a few of my photos, that's what. Speaking of photos the last time I saw Ti-Grace that amazing photo of herself just married at 17 in full white drag that used to hang on her wall in an oval frame under a cracked glass was on the floor leaning against the wall and without the glass. I said hey what's going on. She said she's buying some darts and getting it ready to use as a dart board. She's a woman of pronouncements. What else did she say I said she was. I don't know. I declare this done. I just remember sk one day two summers ago thrusting her hand through a glass pane and for hands this winter I bought and lost four identical pairs of red woolen hunter's gloves and borrowed jane's black ones and accidentally left them at her house when the winter was over which means I really know what I'm doing and that's all I have to say. Burn this and memorize yourself.

—*June 8, 1972*

Hordes of Dykes and Faggots

Some are saying this year Gay Liberation is a Sexist Plot. Others that this is the Year of the Lesbian. It looks like both to me. I don't like marching up sixth avenue with the men but I do like the sense I get of an expanding population of lesbians. Women are coming out all over and meeting across the country and forming possibly as many organizations as there are individuals. In the Sheep Meadow I met two Anarchist Amazons from Boston. In Berkeley there's Amazon Graphics. In Washington the Furies Collective. In New York lesbians are reconstituting D.O.B. and theres' Radicalesbians and Radishes and Lesbians International and the Lavender Whales and a group of Radical Virgins who may be hymen chauvinists in which case many lesbians eager to join will be disappointed. I wear my virgin sheriff badge and remain optimistic. Along the march about 30th street June 25 the third perennial Christopher Street Gay Liberation March I shared a few paces with our great white baby father Dr Spock who checked out the badge but seemed unable to react to the word virgin. I followed up his determination not to notice with a statement for his Peoples Party Campaign to the effect that women don't like to be fucked by men any more and in fact never did. He seemed disoriented. I asked him what he was doing on the march. He said someone invited him, I think it was the Gay Vietnam Veterans Against the war. A young man approached the father and shook his hand and said Dr Spock I was in one of your classes at Western Reserve. A carful of lesbians pulled up on a side street and yelled out the windows Dr Spock Dr Spock Dr Spock Dr Spock . . . where's your wife? I asked him about his wife too. Tell me about your wife. He said we-l-l-l . . . she put me through medical school . . . and my internship . . . and she did volunteer work . . . and . . . — And I asked where is she now. Flat on her back he replied. Oh. And I ran up ahead to join my friends. I told the carful of lesbians I thought he had just come out but I wasn't sure. I don't really care. But anything can happen. J. Edgar Hoover left his house and his money and his dogs to another bachelor man. The men are keeping up with their own. Except for Robin Hood I don't know who the men've been claiming but for the women it's been a big year. December 4 the *New York Post* informed us via an Oxford University investigator that Joan of Arc had "a very intense friendship with a girl called Haivette." The investigator of course concluded that "Joan was immature and in fact somewhat of a prude — she overreacted emotionally to the camp prostitutes, often going after them with the flat of her sword." I imagine there's a Society of St Joan somewhere this year. It's all over the place actually. We're just modernizing Joan with an Amazon army. The important discovery this year for women must be the resurrection of the Amazons. Lesbian Nation is Amazon Culture. Amazon Graphics. Amazon Motors. Amazon Electrics. Amazon Moving & Storage. Amazon Museum. Amazon Milk Products. Amazon Press. Amazon Television. Amazon Government! — Sisters Incorporated. The return of the Amazons. For me the discovery came first in Helen Diner's book of the '30s *Mothers and Amazons*. I always knew about Amazons. Everybody knows about Amazons. Amazons were these tall powerful mythological strong women and it was never a good thing to be called. It was a bad name and they were mythological besides. Now suddenly it's the best thing you can think of, the ideal figure, the one you aspire to become, and she was a real historical character known at one time to've inhabited at least regions of South America and areas around the Black Sea if not all over the world. I met a woman last week I'm certain was once an Amazon Queen. I meet them frequently now. I know they existed because after I read the Diner book I checked out some reputable male sources like Plutarch and *Time* magazine. *Time* reported findings of Amazon civilization in South America. Plutarch describes in detail the invasion and occupation of Attica by certain Amazons retaliating against the rape and seizure of one of their Queens by Theseus.

This is the score we are returning to settle. The rape of our mothers. Mothers & Amazons. And very shortly we'll be marching only with the women. The romance of Gay Liberation is basically over. The family romance of the brothers and the sisters. For the favoritism of the parents toward the sons has become manifest. The activist Gay males have revealed their own complicity in the bargain by pursuing the status awaiting them as the prodigal perverted sons.

In New York there is practically no organizational alliance left between Gay Males and Lesbians. The Lesbians actually initiated their withdrawal two years ago by walking out of GLF. Significantly at that time neither the men nor the women were able to avail themselves of any clear feminist analysis. Some of the literature was written and out, especially two key essays, one by Ti-Grace Atkinson and one by Roxanne Dunbar, published in *Notes from The Second Year*, but only a handful of lesbian women had put their understanding of gay oppression together with an understanding of their oppression as women. I call this a fusion of a gay head and a feminist head. Most of us came to feminism through gay liberation. I suppose a number of feminists are now struggling to find a gay head after coming out through the movement and discovering that the world doesn't like their being gay any more than the world likes them as women. That is if they take being gay more seriously than a night or a brief affair to satisfy their curiosity. Seriously usually meaning falling in love. And by falling in love becoming more vulnerable to the social forces by which their relationship is threatened. One curious development this year was a retreat from feminist consciousness by one public feminist discovering her lesbianism by falling in love with a "person." Central to feminist analysis is the revelation of people as female and male. What this woman was doing was denying this revelation under the pressure of her own taboo against lesbianism by trying to slash at the political ground gained by the revolutionary lesbian position reducing her choice to that personal private place from which we all came. These feminists have the horrors over something called an ideological seduction. The line is supposed to go something like you have to go to bed with me because you oppress me by sleeping with the enemy meaning the man. I never witnessed a lesbian actually behaving like this but I suppose occasionally some do and if so so what. The persuasion of the man within his heterosexist institution is no less ideological. The person approach to love and sex leaves the lesbian exactly where she always was, without any political identity. The person approach is post-revolutionary idealism, ignoring the pervasive male ideology by which our choices are governed. If your love choice could as well be a man as a woman then it might as well be a man unless you're willing to struggle into gay consciousness. In other words as a "person" your identity remains male. I think all of us want to be people but we're living in the sacrificial generations. There's no way to become people until we establish our identity as women. Although our tactics may be questionable our analysis is perfectly correct. Every time anyone succeeds in convincing anybody that a personal choice is a purely private one we've lost a little ground won in the battle to keep the male position exposed for what it is and in so doing illustrating the necessity of our own. By the male position I mean the absolute however obscured political nature of the heterosexual persuasion in its control over women. Politics begins in bed. For some reason nobody clearly understands the politics of women and men continue to involve the formation of role dichotomies of domination and submission. The peer politics of women in relation to each other is the definition we're opposing to the male tendency towards authority and heirarchy. The men like to control both women and each other in their shifting pyramid of social disasters. The women unconsciously continue to collaborate in their own submission in the plan. During this year of backlash especially the more astute males have been employing whatever women they can find who are willing by their unconsciousness to be the instruments of oppressing their sisters. The front women. They're right out there every day, in all the media. The women who'll betray their own sex for a piece of the pyramid. The women who may not even know that they're doing it.

A woman in *The Times* for example launching her review of the novel *Patience and Sarah* by Isabel Miller with the sentence "In an age when Lesbianism has become a political rallying cry, it sometimes requires conscious reminders that it is essentially a private affair." Not realizing perhaps that as a private affair we were all brutalized. Nor that in that one sentence she sums up the case for the male position. The women Patience and Sarah, modeled after two women who did get it together in the early 19th century, were certainly a private affair ("their love was a thing apart"), the story of their difficulty in managing to escape and make a life together is the story of their oppression as women and the necessity of believing in their feelings against the one public (political) position by which they had to choose either complete isolation and privacy or condemnation as criminals or whatever lesbians were called then. The novel is not explicitly political, it's a love narrative, but any reader should know that the couple was some rare exception and that their solution was costly. I could list and illustrate many examples of backlash by women in the press. Done by women or by men it's a male inspired backlash insomuch as the men remain in control of the media. Its most disconcerting and perhaps least detectable form is in the reviews and reports of Gay activist males who are also being used by the straight men to continue to oppress women by attempting to co-opt their revolution. Reports by gay males exploit the sexual porn aspects or the life style aspects of their movement including an emphasis on the least threatening and most entertaining form of male homosexuality — the male caricature of the male created artificial image of the woman whom we painfully claim as our own in such martyred calamities as Marilyn Monroe. The male transvestite may make an amusing and instructive parody, but he also insults women by participating, never mind exaggerating, in the dress by which many women are still forced to express their inferior or degraded part in the role dichotomy of aggressive/masculine and passive/feminine. As Flaming Faggot Kenneth Pitchford put it " . . . faggots are seen as being a potentially useful tool to reinforce the very gender stereotypes that women are defying." Pitchford analyzes the media popularity of faggots this way: "A lot of straight men get reassurance to see us as wretched capitalist ghouls (*Boys in the Band*) as silly queens (Warhol), or as masochists (*LA Plays*). After all, neither the transvestite nor the masochist are any threat to the straight men; both seek a dominant masculinist to complete the sexist molecule of reciprocal role stereotyping, and a straight masculinist could easily (and in some cases, preferably) supply this lack without, himself, having to alter a single assumption about the value of power dominance or the inferiority of women."

In the name of the new movement of faggot militants who first define themselves as oppressors of women and who make their first order of business the struggle against their own sexism Pitchford and others I don't know except Jim Fouratt refused to march up sixth avenue June 25 protesting the Gay Liberation Movement "as a male-supremacist, male-dominated abomination." Handouts of Pitchford's 88 reasons why he refused "to march up sixth avenue for a third time in pursuit of that sexist illusion, Gay Liberation," were being distributed along the way. I was conflicted myself but as I indicated the sense of lesbian expansion and solidarity compensated somewhat for walking with the men. I haven't cheered or chanted like that since a boarding school soccer game. Not even in the march last year. Crossing 59th street into the park it was really grand. We were into the lesbian version of give me that old time religion and calling up all historical lesbians who amounts to Sappho and such stand-bys as Gertrude & Alice and Christina of Sweden and Mata Hari and such contemporary dead luminaries as Janis and Diana (Oughton) and Sylvia (Plath) and such live ones as Ti-Grace and Betty and Bella and Gloria and Greta etc. in the refrain that goes If It Was Good Enough For So & So It's Good Enough For Me. It would've been nice to have had Dr Joyce Brothers along with the great white father Spock. It would've been good to have had all those feminists who are falling in love with their best friends. And all those closet dykes of NOW. All those women who still see the lesbian as a "woman apart." As a public feminist said to me recently we got all this mail from women thanking us for printing that piece (that personal affair between two women) saying they've had similar experiences and now they know they're not alone and *they're not lesbians* (emphasis mine). As though some women are lesbians and some aren't and it's forgotten that most *all* women are socialized out of their feelings for other women. But if the feminists won't join our marches they can't keep us away from theirs. And when the lesbians take it over it'll become a celebration as well as a complaint. We're not gay we're angry as Pitchford says, but wherever we collect as one without straights we have a good time, and I mean without any kind of man, and you can see straight women at all woman parties and dances beginning to let go and feel like it's really okay to have a good time and then you can see the shape of the future Amazon Nation. The big dance this year the night before the march was a few hundred angry ecstatic abandoned Amazons from the fabulous nations of virgins galloping from the edges of oceans in purple sashes and ostrich plume helmets and armynavy store parachute boots. These annual festivals celebrating the return of the Amazons. Galactic landscapes and subterranean labyrinths and ancient hillsides of reclining Sphinx. Sphinx on parade. Sphinx Memorial on Capitol Hill. Sphinx Dutch Cleanser. Sphinx on george washington bridge. Martha Washington National Holiday. Every Day. I asked Nath at Sheeps Meadow looking down the sloping hill at the hordes of dykes and faggots entering the meadow from the street how many would she estimate and she said . . . oh, I think 200,000 for a minimum. As for the faggots I have a lot more to say about the demise of Gay Liberation and the new incipient ideological coalition between Feminist/Lesbians and Revolutionary Effeminists or Faggots who refuse participation in the reformist Gay Rights movement seeking acceptance within the (male) system by attempts to legalize homosexuality. If you look above in this piece you can see a place where I strayed from developing this subject by branching into the problematic feminist aspect of the lesbian issue after saying "significantly at that time neither the men nor the women were able to avail themselves of any clear feminist analysis." I plan to develop it next week. As to the march the real extra support of lesbians Sunday came from flaming faggots at home or on the sidelines, not from Dr Spock or Tinkerbell.

—June 29, 1972

Their Inappropriate Manhood

Last week as I said I strayed from completing some report on the emergence of revolutionary effeminism which I think is important for women to perceive and for men to join. The effeminists unlike their brothers of gay liberation are not expecting women to participate in any of their meetings or marches or city hall protests. I don't think they're into meetings or marches or protests although they were protesting the christopher street gay liberation march this year handing out leaflets of kenneth pitchford's 88 reasons for refusing to march among them that gay liberation is a sexist plot between gay and straight men to keep women and faggots in their places and that the only time he went to a dance at the GAA firehouse the light show included stag movies one of which showed a nude woman being raped by a nude man and that all the new gay syndicate wants to do is to climb up with straight men on the backs of women as in ancient greece and that the gay male leaders of gay liberation have written for screw and gay and two of them are also in fact partowners with the main man straight sadmasculinist al goldstein who allowed screw to carry advertisements for films showing the rape by their fathers of girls not yet 10 years old and that the men of gay liberation make the playing of roles in the sexual act the central question of their lives using gutter phrases butch and femme to calssify and objectify them when any faggot knows that the focal reality of his life is the bitter lack of any tenderness in men gay or straight, any gentleness, any willingness to cooperate rather than compete, any sincere consideration or concern for others, rather than the same monotonously repeated self-preoccupation with ripping off another orgasm from "our" despised and nameless faggot bodies and that marching is boring anyway are a few of the 88 reasons. I think what the effeminists are doing primarily is consciousness raising in small groups and developing an effeminist analysis which acknowledges sexism as the root cause of all oppression. Such an analysis from men has been long forthcoming. The gay books to date excepting that by dennis altman have been an accounting of actions by gay militants and the politics of the movement and personal statements about coming out and new studies and interpretation of homosexual oppression. In other words books and essays dealing only in gay consciousness which without being completed by a feminist consciousness remains just as straight as straight in its apologetic demand to be approved and accepted by straight sexist society. Gay liberation has defined itself as an oppressed minority rather than as a movement for revolutionary social change. Gay liberation from the start was associated with every left cause in the identification with other oppressed minorities. In common with the left gay liberation identified the enemy as the white ruling class with the emphasis on the white ruling class male. The effeminists have correctly located the enemy within themselves. I can't say the enemy isn't within me too, I mean it's a world-wide problem, the difference between me and the man being one of birth and from there of consciousness. I could sit across from pitchford for an hour or so to discuss these things and know that he agrees he's my enemy for we were all brought up that way. Thus there isn't much to say except ideology and to wonder what that would mean in any organizational sense and I don't think much. Nor do they.

The best they can do is to say as does pitchford that it should not be their purpose as revolutionary effeminists to get feminists to regard them as certifiable non-male-supremacists — a typically masculinist notion and quite impossible anyway and in so saying acknowledging their task which is to eliminate themselves. These are potentially the men whose coming Valerie Solanas predicted when she summarily and casually provided men with their mission in life as the men's auxiliary to *S.C.U.M* — "those men who are working to eliminate themselves . . . faggots who by their shimmering, flaming example, encourage other men to de-man themselves . . ." A fine point to consider is that the rhetorical vision of effeminists includes eliminating the manhood from themselves rather than themselves. Valerie was very advanced. I don't know how it's possible to be walking around as things are as a man and eliminate yourself as a man but one thing can be done and that is to comprehend the necessity of it. There are apparently a few practical things that can be done too. These things could be called taking on the burden of reparations for other men. The project that seems to most interest pitchford is faggot child care centers. He says he tends to bond with other men who like to take care of babies which is in his self interest since he has a three year old kid whom he looks after 50 per cent to slightly less than 50 per cent of the time and occasionally slightly more. He says they're convinced faggots will never be free until women are free and that they've discovered that their task is to rejoice in their condemned qualities of effeminacy and to support defend and promote effeminism in all men everywhere by any means necessary. I knew when I first heard of the effeminists four months ago that here were the first authentic western male revolutionaries. The first men to confess the inappropriateness of their manhood and to withdraw the classic male demand of support from the female. The effeminists are not saying any more to women teach me and help me to be this and that and you understand I can talk to you other men are so insensitive I need you etc. never mind the rest of it in the forms of whores and secretaries. Besides that however and mainly it's what they're saying about themselves that makes sense. Sometimes a male overtly defending his sexism comes on to me like challenging so what are you going to do reverse things and be strong as the men implying I guess that things would be just as bad but with the other sex on top and I say no I'm not going to be strong like men but strong like a woman which is something else entirely but strong nevertheless and that doesn't mean affirming the masculine principle in ourselves either since I don't think there is such a principle except that which we learn from the male culture in any case the female principle by itself is strong enough. The female principle is a double X and that's complete. The male principle is an X and a Y and according to the geneticists something is missing. If it's the female principle which is missing it could account for the evolutionary imbalance that has taken place in which the male principle has overrun us itself and the world. I've heard that the only male east or west of the rhone valley who understands and admits this is tagore of india.

So that makes tagore and the revolutionary effeminists. Why marcuse and philip slater and norman brown continue to lag behind

I can guess only that they have good wives without whose services they wouldn't be marcuse slater and brown. Anyway if these three can't put it down we can understand why no other man can. I mean put it down on paper, assuming they understand the problem. I'm still naive enough to think it's remarkable nevertheless that not one of these deep thinking social critics and historians of the human psyche hasn't cut through all the crap to the sexist core of the social catastrophe they're trying to illuminate. They're still basically actually into their own savior psychology of the good guys and the bad guys for example in marcuse's contemporary marxism the bad guys are the corporate stockholders who oppress *him*, the workers being defined of course always as other men. As feminists and effeminists point out: every time feminism has risen men have figured out some way to co-opt it, like making the basic contradiction workers instead of women. Women were beginning to say women of the world arise and marx was saying workers of the world arise. Women were beginning to say the same thing the turn of the century and freud came along to say women should be accepting their lot. Now we still have socialism and psychology and we have other diversions like population and ecology not to mention the war. Women marching for peace are seriously misguided. The man can keep women very busy worrying about war and peace. To stop this particular war in any case would be like stuffing some kleenex in one hole of a dam that's collapsing from arizona to maine and on around the rest of the globe back to arizona. But I don't want to talk about the war (war is a mere symptom). The class analysis behind socialism is always useful but it continues to deceive both women and men and with more serious consequences women. Classism and racism are subvariants of sexism and to accept this you have to comprehend history and biology and by history now I mean all that history that predates male recorded history which is just about all up until this time that has been available to us and by biology I mean some investigation into those precultural forms of ourselves in which we can locate the origins of sexism in the reproductive adjustments certain animals must've made to their catastrophic environments and so forth.

I don't have any answers and I don't know that anybody does

but we don't need to know specifically which means to have answers since we can know through our cellular memories and by knowing this way we know all we need to know which is that sexism (or the predisposition to it) is rooted in some historical biological evolutionary process and classism and racism and ageism are very late variations attending cultural developments. So history and biology are the same study ultimately. Each of us contains the total history. This is what leary used to rave about as the high priest of psychedelics. The psychedelic revolution itself being another diversion. I mean the cellular memory of the high priest having remained outstandingly male. I used to say whatever happened to lisa lieberman? I think she was alcoholic and I'm not sure what else since she was really sort of working for the high priest but I ask the question because I know she made a lot of noise and she was a woman and I wonder if she had some other cellular promptings we should hear about. The voice of this woman is lost in a chapter in a book by leary whose male worthies were a lot less alcoholic except for a nameless nun. The point of all this detection and exposure has overrun us itself and the world. As pitchford puts it in this essay of his From sexual liberation to revolutionary effeminism he said to be shockingly blunt, it is the male principle in human beings that has brought us historically to the verge of extinction and he goes on if we are to survive it will be because the female principle, once omnipotent in pre-history, is returned to power so that our warped existence can be set right again after being awry for 10,000 years and he concludes this great work — the worldwide anti-gender revolution that is already underway — is obviously a matter of women seizing power and he wonders whether men can ever come to be considered partisans of that revolution and I doubt it myself in any concrete sense unless it's by way of such current effeminist activities as educating other men into struggling against their sexism and creating their faggot child care centers and at least ideologically affirming their support of women. Here's an essay by steven dansky called God, Freud, Daddy And Us Faggots in a publication called *faggotry* in which dansky (an early gay male polemicist) says that many faggots have left the gay liberation movement because even the most radical and militant factions have made a one-sided attack against sexism. He goes on faggots have left gay liberation because they have seen male supremacy as the root from which all other oppressions branch . . . "We will not have our freedom on the backs of women . . . We are what is feared most: effeminists . . . Men who are struggling to become unmanly, men who oppose the hierarchy and ideology of a masculine fascism that requires the domination of one person by another, of one sex, race, or class by another. We will become gentle but strong faggots who will fight their oppression in militant ways, faggots who are vulnerable to each other, able to cry, but not passive or paralyzed in our struggle to change." End-quote. I guess a lot of people might want to know why revolutionary effeminists call themselves faggots. It was over this word that I first heard from pitchford. He wrote to me june 12 he was surprised that I had recently addressed two of my columns to a man and that the man was identified as a faggot. These were two columns written as letters to vince aleti who had referred to a column of his in a rock magazine as a faggot column and somehow I knew because of his reference and others or probably more likely just by what's in the air that the word like dyke had acquired some positive currency and I used it that way without knowing there was a movement which is what pitchford was writing to inform me about. He said they had split from the whole gay movement some time ago because of its outrageous anti-womanism and its sexism in general and he criticized the exclusive use of GAA spokesmen in *the voice* who among other things apparently use their names to hard sell sadomasochistic porn movies that degrade women and faggots and such and he included his journal called *the flaming faggots*. This is what he says about the word faggot and he's quoting from a leaflet out of florida: Through the process of consciousness raising we have discovered that most of us have always been bothered by the word gay. We felt it trivialized us: we're not gay, we're angry. We also noticed how women in daughters of bilitis and those splitting from glf (because of its anti-womanism) were both reaffirming their right to the single proud word, Lesbian, to describe themselves, even though this had once been used abusively against them. We disliked the two-word phrase gay men. It made clowns of us; male homosexual was hard to keep saying over and over. Then we learned that the word faggot originated from our persecution in the middle ages: when a woman was to be burned as a witch, men accused of homosexuality were bound together in bundles, mixed in with bundles of kindling wood (faggots) at the feet of the witch, and set on fire "to kindle a flame foul enough for a witch to burn in." So the enemy has known all along the danger in strong women and gentle men, has known that both present the same threat to masculine domination. That is why we have decided to embrace faggot as *our* one word description, complete with a piece of our buried history unearthed, and accept it positively as a tool to cut through our last ties to 'passing' — those of us who were in the privileged position of having such an option. We call ourselves faggots in the name of jacques demolay, in the name of bernard de vado, tortured by fire applied to the soles of the feet to such an extent that a few days afterwards the bones of his heels dropped out, in the name of 19 brothers from perigord tortured and starved for six months running, in the name of all nameless brothers still tortured in mental hospitals and in psychiatrists' offices by aversion therapy, shock treatment, apomorphine, and succinylcholine. We are flaming with the fire of final revolution. We are not ashamed of being faggots. We are proud. Endquote of the quote. I'm giving out this report so as not to be misunderstood myself and because the media thus far has not made the information available and I think as I said that the movement is important for women to perceive and for men to join. I don't like pitchford saying that just as black liberation emerged to the left of civil rights movement and radical feminism has emerged to the left of women's liberation so our movement of faggot militants is beginning to be heard to the left of gay liberation by so saying he omits in typical sexist fashion the first movement actually to be heard left of gay liberation and that was radicalesbians (although he mentions that many lesbians have already split) who by the way should also be considered as left of women's liberation and radical feminism so long as we're into this lefter than thou talk. Nonetheless these faggot militants have assimilated feminist literature and are somehow welding it to their own history as faggots for an effeminist analysis which should if it's completely consistent whatever that is or at least honest emerge in its actions at the service of women in the Solanas spirit of self elimination and the reinstitution of the female principle. This account of a historical conspiracy of faggots called knights templar to seize power makes me nervous. Written by pitchford in his journal as a proud account of faggot history it seems inconsistent with what he says elsewhere about the necessity of the return to power of the woman. Other bits of history I find more inspiring, like his reminder that the reformist gays . . . are always harking back to periclean greece without realizing (or do they?) that until the dominance of christianity faggotry was always at least tolerated if not glorified precisely because it was the instrument which the historical patriarch used to overthrow the prehistoric gynocratic matriarchy . . . The first male rebellion against female rule was possibly one of brothers homosexually bonded against a matriarch. The parallel to contemporary gay liberation as a male movement should be clear. As many papers and magazines testify in reports and editorials and reviews the gay men whether consciously or not are in collusion with their straight brothers to continue the oppression of women and the men's auxillary.

—*July 6, 1972*

athens, or thereabouts: I thought athens was blue until I took off my glasses and then it was yellow and white like other coastal cities and not very good looking although I didn't put any stock in my judgments since I was slumping from not sleeping in the back of the cab it was two in the afternoon but for me it was seven in the morning in new york and the last time I'd slept was 24 hours ago. So I went to this king minos hotel and flaked off at three and woke up wide awake at two in the morning took a bath did my exercises read my greek history book and played with the buttons around my bed by accident I rang for the maid and didn't know how to turn it off so I ordered some coffee and juice when she came and developed the idea of watching the sun rise from the acropolis. The city of athens is really all about the acropolis which was the original city it's amazing I think that the monument of a city is its original city in the form of an enormous fortified hill from which you can see everything that came after it. I don't think I really knew the acropolis was a hill until I saw the thing rising out of the boxes and terraces of the flatlands of a modern city the image of the parthenon out of countless reproductions taking shape of reality way up there against the sky I started out of my slump in the back of the cab and thought maybe the trip was worthwhile after all. I suppose it looks like the first glimpse of the manhattan skyline to a european who doesn't expect to see any indians. I suppose it was like landing in london and seeing the buckingham palace which looked like the 42nd street library. I suppose it was a genuine greek experience and it was certainly more impressive than the view of mont blanc from the plane flying south out of geneva. What was impressive about geneva was the metal check in the terminal depot waiting for the continuation of the flight to athens in new york the check was pretty uneventful I took off my belt and virgin badge and neck piece and passed through an electric eye of some sort and waited while these men at a table searched my stuff bags for the weapons or whatever it was I needed for bailing out and collecting ransom they didn't find it and my friends waved me happily onto the plane expecting a good cut of the take I guess anyway in geneva it was nice being suspected of skyjacking! A swiss dyke in a red dress got me in a big brown booth with a swinging door and felt me up and even grabbed me at the crotch it was a whole interesting introduction to switzerland I felt very special and criminal and wished they suspected me more. Already bertha had told me to watch out for the stewardesses jill on twa they're all queer and I didn't think much of it until after geneva when I began to notice and sure enough this french stewardess with arched eyebrows strapped herself into my empty row for the takeoff and told me how sexy it was in cairo where she was going and other obvious invitations I thought if I wasn't so tired I'd just go on to cairo and forget about athens if she'd only do something about her lipstick. I used up the rest of my energy to overlook it. Anyway I had a good time at kennedy biting jane's white soft muscular appropriate legs and thinking up this poem. A woman gets wet like the ocean/ A man turns to stone like a stiff I haven't written a poem in years. A woman wrote to me that there are only fragments of sappho because no woman is an island and I thought that was a strange remark. I think it's even stranger that our one historical dyke was a greek considering what we're supposed to know about greece and how the greek men are now I wonder how different they could possibly have been then. I don't know why no woman isn't an island but the reason there are only fragments of sappho is that the men in another time and along the way found it necessary to abolish any competition to their own image the way a new dictator comes along and buries the images of his predecessors except in the case of sappho and any other women we should know about the process involved the two sexes over a number of millennia. I saw the clue to the fate of this one in a 1911 encyclopedia under the entry for sappho it said her reputation in ancient times rivaled that of homer's. I brought homer into athens by the way. I was wearing the eyes of greece and jane's brother's t-shirt and carrying the odiad & the illysey and unpurturd about not being a classycest as leticia used to say I have a prenatal classy education and that's all you need to realize how the avars and the slavs devastated the balkans and the visigoths seized all the byzantine possessions and the barbarians reached an understanding with the persians who sent an army into chalkidona and the people of constantinople were terrified and the last greek tribes arriving poured violently into the greek peninsula conquering the acheans and destroying the fortified acropolises and killing the kings and seizing the achean treasures, and everything. I'm still very tired. I went out to ekali a surburb to see gail and charoula who know lyn and the holy spirit and others and slept from 3 to 6 p.m. and from midnite to noon and from 3 p.m. to 7 and thought I'd straighten myself out by sleeping again at 2 a.m. but then I woke up at 6 so what can you do it's still all fucked up and so is the food. For food jane said tell them not to soak everything in oil so I did first thing in the hotel I told the maid to bring the coffee and juice without oil please and that was fine and then I ordered breakfast down in the lobby at 5 (a.m.) and said to put the eggs in water not oil and they did but the milk was caky and curdling and the coffee was french and the toast tasted like steamed olive trees or something or so I imagined anyway I knew the food scene would be hopeless and they wouldn't have any amerikan mayonnaise I should've brought homer and mayonnaise. All I really want to do is go to the country and grow carrots and draw pictures. It's such an ordeal seeing the rest of the world. Seeing how the citystates of the kings gave way to the oligarchies and the democracies an such. And the plumbing doesn't even work, like gail said don't flush the toilet with any paper in it you know they had excellent plumbing in crete in 12000 b.c. and now the toilets won't even take paper. And everything reminds me of everything else. So I might as well be where all the other things are. Walking out this house in ekali I thought I was in new hampshire. Walking down this road into a fishing village I thought it was cadaquez. Coming back to ekali from the fishing village I looked up at the stars and said the stars are the same as in the states. Driving into athens from the airport I thought it could be havana. Looking out over the city from the acropolis I thought it was just like los angeles spread all over the place for miles and with these dry brown stony hills growing clumps of green or it was just like san francisco except that they didn't put the houses on hills here but they do have the saronic gulf of the aegean which could be the san francisco bay of the pacific I liked flying into athens over its gulf which is green not blue and trying to imagine all its ancient traders and pirates and invaders although I couldn't possibly I was too sleepy but I rarely do see what isn't there the way that song goes that's supposed I think to make you feel all misty and ghosty and did those feet in ancient times walk upon england's mountains green I get that feeling on st patricks day on fifth avenue hearing the bagpipes that's all. So I didn't expect anything from the acropolis. After all I'm not even greek. I don't know why the english are so excited about the greeks. I'm beginning to think I should be getting into some of my own mythology too like some old celtic goddesses maybe instead of fooling around thinking I have some remote connection with artemis and athene and atlantis and all these dark oliveskin black-eyed beauties from the south. Anyway as I said I didn't expect anything from this big old hill of the greeks. I just thought it would be great to see the sun rise before all the people came to the world's most famous international tourist trap. That's the way I did it at stonehenge. I saw stonehenge silhouetting itself at 5 a.m. in the mist on the amesbury plain and almost managed to see what wasn't there and that was druids. So thinking of my stonehenge success I walked toward the acropolis in the early morning light of athens after that 5 a.m. breakfast in the lobby of the hotel and stopped in the village below the hill for an hour to read my book. Was the virgin mary assumed or did she ascend. I'd decided on my way that the acropolis at odd hours was probably like central park and I wasn't any more anxious to be raped by the greeks than by the amerikans who at least don't come right up and grab you when you're minding your business going someplace in public in open daylight it was worse than mexico city where as phisby said of somebody she knew she had an ulcer by the time she got there wherever she was going just from ignoring them I guess they're all from the same race of latin barbarians and the women are invisible although I needn't have worried about the acropolis since if I'd gone as far as the gate I would've found out that you couldn't get in until 7:30 and by that time the international tourists like yourself would be keeping you plenty of company. I suppose it's ironic too that one should have to be thinking of rape on the way to the great temple of the virgin the parthenon but that could be just the point, in ancient times apparently it was the first object of the invading tribes (i.e., tourists) to secure for themselves the protection of the local goddess. And I wasn't wearing my virgin badge. Although in new york I was very cocky or rather cunty walking out of the cleaners the morning of departure the cleaner asked me where are you going and I said athens and he smiled and said how nice and still smiling but you'd better take off that badge or you won't have a good time and I replied without thinking listen I have a *very* good time — with women, and didn't wait to check out the reaction. I wonder sometimes if we can afford to go on not being charming. Or how productive it is to retaliate. Or why I wonder about any of it when all you're doing is approaching the sanctuary of athena parthenos in all its doric majesty which is a hot hill of marble rubble and 46 columns intact or restored and the ruins of six powerful maidens in long flowing chitons holding up with their heads the roof of the southwestern porch of a place called the erechtheum off to one side of the parthenon. I couldn't see the original athena by phidias who apparently was 39 feet high and wearing a helmet adorned with a sphinx and two winged horses and carrying in her right hand a winged nike or goddess of victory six and a half feet high and in her left her shield the outside and inside surfaces covered with reliefs depicting the battles of the giants against the gods and of the amazons against the athenians I couldn't see it but I could speculate what was going on in this part of the world besides what they say in the books when the chiefs according to the books were men and the deity was a woman although it isn't insignificant that the erechtheum was so called after the ancient king erechteus who was supposedly born on the acropolis and raised by the goddess and enjoyed her special protection and was considered the ancestral father of the athenians he was represented by phidias in the form of a coiled serpent beneath the feet of the goddess but even more significant I think that the god poseidon was also honored in the temple somehow because of the great struggle that took place between him and athene for the possession of attica the olympian gods pronounced athene the winner for she had made the athenians a present of a plant until then unknown but the spot where the contest occurred was deemed to be holy and the dispute was sculpturally represented on the west pediment and so forth anyway what I'm saying and remembering is that the presence of the god at all and in that form of the struggle which took place say around 1700 to 1600 b.c. is the clue to the apparent paradox of a male chief and a female deity was undoubtedly the compromise settlement offered by men to appease the slowly vanishing matriarchies which survived only in the symbol of a deity to which the men could appeal for protection and for clemency in their crimes and assuage their guilt in seizing political power from the woman much the way the christian religion intelligently introduced the virgin after centuries of pagan resistance to the christ although the dispute still goes on like in england you have christ church and in france the cathedral of our lady which is the vestigial pagan or athenian tribute to the original great mother cult which certainly preceded such aids and comforts as athena who was in a sense a plastic token survivor which may be why I couldn't actually see her at 7:30 in the morning anywhere near or inside the ruins of the temples or around the marble rubble. So much for the acropolis of athens. It was nice seeing the real thing in columns. I liked looking down at the restored theatre the south side of the hill and seeing an actor enter and speak to a woman up in the seats cleaning with a huge broom. I didn't like the flea market or the modern agora the tourist trade in chintzy souvenirs below the hill forming part of the village which looks just like france. I liked a whole lot driving to rafina that fishing village to eat cod squid shrimp & octopus at a table right on the water watching the boats come in from the islands. I'm directly south of leningrad and I don't know what to do next. I never know why I'm here rather than there especially when as I said everything reminds me of everything else. I do like thinking about history for example I keep trying to remember what isadora said about the acropolis I think she and her family camped out in sight of the hill at that time the city was a village stretching out into barren plains and they didn't have any water it was a funny story but anyway there's that famous photo of her in her desperate black at her most romantic arms outstretched amidst the columns which is what I mean about this madness of the english for the greeks and it's still going on. Everybody knows that most of the parthenon is up in the british museum. That elgin fellow just went right up on the hill with a bunch of workmen and walked off with everything they could stagger off with. I think it's worth another war. The wars men make are never over anything more serious and what are they stealing anyway if it isn't the woman. Spolia and praeda are spoils and booty and if you get enough of spolia and praeda you have gloria. Theodosius divided his emprie between his sons honorius and arcadius and the first took the west england spain france italy africa and the second took the east the balkans asia and egypt. I'm still very tired. But I'm beginning to wake up. I remember something else about athene that she was an olympian meaning a male creation and really very similar in her function to the christian mary, athene being to zeus what the christ became to mary, the head of zeus equated to the virgin womb of mary, the god giving birth to himself in both cases in different guises, and that the great mother cults exposed by jane harrison were pre-olympian naturally, and here's some neat history that around a.d. 450 when the byzantine empire through theodosius became christian the temple of the acropolis at athens became a christian church! Later on when the turks took over I think it was converted into a harem. Later on a venetian bomb hit the place and 28 columns came crashing down and this doge francesco morosini who did it wanted to take the whole west pediment depicting the dispute between athene & poseidon back to venice with him as a trophy of his great deed. I think I may stay in greece a few centuries to find out what happens next. I think what I really like best about traveling is writing about it. The illysey of gullibles travels.

—*July 27, 1972*

Strage Degli Innocenti

june 17 a note in my record book written in athens should I go to florence or venice or rome or cadaquez or london or paris or all of them or stay and go to delphi and marathon and eleusis and mycenae and santorini and rhodes and lesbos or do that and also the rest or what. I was waiting outside american xpress for susan who was waiting for me in madrid so I went to myconos and delos and flew directly to london to see the rest of the parthenon at the british museum where certain of the heads originally belonging to their bodies are in places like the louvre or copenhagen or for that matter back in athens somewhere so you can find a real reason for going places by following it all up. Some people know exactly where they're going and why. The quest for the lost atlantis has inspired an immense literature. The classical schoolers laughed at schliemann when he set out for troy with homer in one hand and a spade in the other. I think now I've evolved two fairly precise reasons for going anywhere one is to find the appropriate location for an annual nervous breakdown and the other is to practice not losing vital documents and to manage to experience the former while succeeding at the latter since the loss of any said document in a foreign city tends to produce a terror and anxiety that exceeds the emotional quota for a nervous break-down. Anyway the improvisation and ingenuity entailed in the satisfying realization of these two projects constitutes a whole art form which I should add includes some expectation of being saved just when all hope has been lost. Flying, for example, is the ultimate act of trust. Thus any time your crisis is clearly peaking you know you can get on a plane and feel saved if nothing more pedestrian like people is available and by so doing too you can reasonably expect that you've created the possibility of another crisis just by flying into more trouble of a strange place weird customs language barriers tourist claustrophobias money freakouts directional dilemmas health problems time lags time leaps time laminations and generalized hatred of amerikans who themselves could care less. One project is conserva-tive, the other liberal kamikaze. A person executing both successfully will be seen disintegrating in a huge square amidst the pigeons or on some cathedral steps or in an airport or a restaurant anyplace will do so long as you're raving disheveled hysterical dissociated or simply languishing and dissolving in a pool of your own making it doesn't matter but at the same time you must have all your effects intact on your person or about you well organized and immediately handy including your address book which you can lose as soon as you get home. Not that my address book mattered terribly much on this particular trip. For example arriving rome one person I called who'd been described as "an admirer in rome" was this anna maria marinelli pellegrino who had become unreachable since she had moved from the number given and her husband's first name was unknown to me and there are countless pellegrinos in the roman directory. Also arriving venice I expected to locate mark di suvero but I had two german addresses under his name and for venice it just said studio. I expected actually to see his steel beams crisscrossing the grand canal and a crane in the middle of the piazza although sheindi had told me that all he was doing was saving the city. In that case of course anybody would know who he was. I stepped off the plane and went up to the first italian I saw and said do you know where I can find mark di suvero but they never heard of him nor did anybody else in the entire city including the peggy guggenheim gallery so I decided I must have the wrong city and maybe he was saving germany. You may think by the way just because I said so that I flew directly to london from athens but I didn't I wasn't going to fly north and then south again simply to spend more time in the air although I don't know why not. Anyway it's common form for composers of historical romances to insist that their stories are really true. Any merely corroborative detail is intended to give artistic verisimilitude to an otherwise bald and unconvincing narrative. Sometimes gertrude floundered around without a subject but we know that's no longer necessary. The subjects abound, the problem is how to undermine them by making them increasingly important in diminishing perm-utations, always maintaining absolute fidelity to fact. Atlantis stands for a vanished civilization, not just a buried building. There's no limit to the number of new sentences that can be produced. It may not be so much the new sentences that count as the constant alteration of impressions. S(he) who understands me finally recognizes my propositions as senseless. But as to impressions I remember saying as prelude to what I plan to say now that the view of mont blanc from the plane flying out of geneva was unimpressive and that was to create an unlikely contrasting intermediary link between the parthenon and the sexy metal check at geneva airport but flying back the other way from venice to paris over the alps the pilot instructed us to look again and this time it was fantastic and I wrote down in my book right away it's the alps that make the world worthwhile which is not to say that I wasn't impressed the first time I was but not so much since my mind's image was parthenon and nothing else measured up even the reality of it and besides I wasn't yet flying in order to be saved but more important I was more involved in using the image as a sentence vehicle than as a report from the wilderness which is still the idea and why even the slightest alteration of impression serves to expedite the generation of new sentences which in turn change our lives. After athens I took to flying from city to city, or just as accurately from airport to airport. If you're not gonna stay a long time in a place you might as well stay a day. I am now in a position to make sweeping and unqualified generalizations about everyplace in europe except austria hungary germany belgium denmark sweden norway yugoslavia russia china alaska & australia. The italians like to paint ceilings. The italians never heard of their own pope joan. The italian (and the greek) drivers don't just tailgate, they piggyback. And so on about italy. About england I take almost all if it back concerning old lord elgin I should've known or remembered that he bought his marbles from the turks to save them from exposure theft and mutilation (so it said on a plaque in the museum) or at least so that innocents from abroad in a later time could travel from one country to another to find the various remains. The hercules by the way is magnificent if you like that sort of thing. If you don't he's missing his hands and feet. In athens while I was there four people died by lightning. In delos I died by sweating. In grease I saved myself and got back at the natives at the same time when leaving this island myconos I boarded their little boat to be motored out to their big boat I wanted to go back to piraeus early on this apollo instead of the naias on which I had gone and for which I had a return ticket I climbed up the plank & ladder to the apollo they wouldn't let me on (the apollo and the naias are two different companies they said) and I had to climb back down into the little boat to return to shore and wait for the naias so safely motoring away I gave the arm the hand and the mouth to all those greek ossifers up on deck there of the apollo and wished for leto to lurch out of her cave on delos and hurl a tidal wave at them. I've heard they'll kill you if you're caught giving them the hand which as a gesture is merely a thrust of the arm with a cocked hand fingers spread like meaning stop and which has something to do with their mothers. I suppose all their mothers are virgins and they think everybody they fuck isn't their mother. Anyway myconos and delos were difficult but not traumatic and that meant that some other place or places was required to fulfill the purpose of the trip. The chosen town manifested itself as rome at least as a point of origin or watershed the taxi man for a start didn't put his flag down and charged 500 liras for a few blocks to a hotel in which the room was a hot box on a street that sounded like an endless motorcade of tanks and mack trucks relieved by squads of scooters and racing fiats and the men in the post office resisted all my attempts to explain that I wanted to send my letter special delivery as well as express and rome just generally is oppressive with culture and catholicism I was overwhelmed by st. peter's and griped by claustrophobia descending into the sistine chapel I walked in one door and right out the other noting the hordes of art appreciation groups pointing and gesticulating at the ceiling and the pity was being repaired and anna maria marinelli pellegrino my admirer was not to be found and I felt like the strage degli innocenti in those tapestries was the only thing I stopped to look at along the miles of galleries leading to the chapel and I saw two donkeys trotting very fast on the way to the vatican or I hallucinated that and so altogether I was well prepared by the next morning at the airport for a series of exquisite frustrations beginning with standing by mistake in a line all of europe in the summer is a line for an hour in the wrong building I was at alitalia international instead of national then squabbling fiercely with another taxi man who wouldn't put his flag down I said I'd call the police then waiting in line for a ticket to venezia venice to you and me and being told I couldn't buy the ticket here and then another line to buy it and to be told I had to wait in still another line to change the traveler's checks which I did while raving disheveled hysterical dissociated my pants falling down my plane was due to leave in five minutes I couldn't even find the entrance dock I don't know how I made it but I did and I didn't lose any vital documents either so rome was a crashing success and I was ready to take on venice. I meant to stop in florence but I flew over it by mistake. I've complained that everything reminded me of everything else well venice is definitely different. I was very pleased for instance to step off the plane and right into a boat instead of a bus for the ride to the city. I was just as pleased to be deposited right at the palace of the doge at the great piazza of san marco after polo which is what we used to call di suvero whom as I said I expected to immediately find. I walked past the continuous dinner music of strings and accordion thinking if I was crazy I'd think it was just for me. Well I walked and walked and took more boats and even gondolas and couldn't locate di suvero or a hotel and the heat rising from the canals was a steady boil so venice was working out very well too and by early evening things were critical. It's easy to see why aschenbach died in venice. There's too many pigeons and unnecessary columns. As I was experiencing my crisis I thought it was too bad they don't provide at least a female tadzio for an amerikan lesbian. Everybody knows that death in venice for aschenbach was worth it. Tadzio or no I expected to be saved and I was. Saved by Sattis. Sattis was a tourist displacement place and they sent me instantly around the corner to a cool fine room in a hotel called casanova just off the piazza where I think I captured venice for one second before leaving I was sitting there the pigeons were flying the bells ringing the orchestra playing it was all very european and decadent and busy like a bosch or a breughel I felt treated and totaled and still together in my various effects. The remedy for my next flight was alcohol. Helplessly they entrusted their safe passage to the air to carry them whither it would. The novelty on air france was lunch in an orange plastic brief case. In paris after one night at the esmerelda I was saved sort of by a waitress in a café who didn't understand me but who was leaning into my lap trying to help me which meant finding a phone number for twa in a pile of directories and I was saved by one ms odile wable at the twa place on champs elysee she gave me a free trip to london somehow and passage to new york for much less than the extraordinary amount of bread they want for flying back sooner than you said you would and I suppose I was saved by a certain andrew we know from home who saw me at a café on st germain and said he'd been at the ocean and all the doors had opened and he'd been having esp for two months and later he left a big bunch of flowers at the esmerelda and I didn't have time to stay and say anything more. I thought I should do something useful for humankind and go and interview a famous person but I didn't do that either. I think the first thing jane said in new york was that everybody has a miserable time in europe and nobody admits it. The thing is there's nothing wrong with a miserable time so long as it conforms to certain aesthetic expectorations of novelty or improvisatory ingenuity and you don't exceed your emotional quota by losing anything you don't really need like your address book.

—*August 3, 1972*

The March of the Real Women

It was common report or it was generally believed or I heard it said that something or other something. I went to a meeting which I almost never do and I had a good time and tried to claim the credit for doing everything wrong again. I went to this same meeting two weeks before and distinguished myself by sitting in a corner and pretending to be invisible. The irkstwhile expresident of now and then ordered me from the back of her head not to write about it so I won't. These meetings every tuesday over at the illogical seminary on 20th and ninth have concerned the august 25 strike and march of women and this last meeting could perhaps be characterized as a struggle to determine what we mean by women. Ostensibly it was a parliamentary battle over the speakers. The truth of the matter was out near the end when a particularly disagreeable disgrumpled 50ish member of our own sex I think said passionately *we want real women speaking*, and other things like you people have your own gay liberation day etc, although this woman was not representative in her style of the other straights there or anyplace else necessarily she does I believe typify the entire right wing of feminism which doggedly resists the logical outcome of the struggle against the patriarchy. The great confrontation within the movement continues to be that between the straights and the lesbians. A reliable source tells me that at this date 60 per cent of the radical feminist organization has come out and the rest remain predictably defensive and deprecatory. Another organization of feminists is by point of order either lesbian or celibate. The evidence is overwhelmingly that it is not gay women who are becoming straight. The violence and ardour of this next to last meeting before the march was paradigmatic of the intensity of the issue within the movement. Many straight women translate their personal problem into a movement rhetoric that goes something like but we can't alarm all those women out there across amerika especially the women we want to know about feminism who don't know about it yet and they'll all be saying see I told you so they were right the woman's movement really is a bunch of lesbians. This attitude belongs to the well known standard conservative media approach to public taste and opinion geared to maintaining the status quo which no matter how you look at it is patriarchal. For example at the meeting the expresident I mentioned jackie ceballos stood and made an impassioned plea for a speaker or speakers who would look (*look*) conservative enough to appeal to all those women out there, whoever they are. Her remark set me thinking about another great split which to my knowledge hasn't been articulated in feminist analysis and that is the split in amerika that originated in the '50s and culminated in the '60s dividing the country into straights and freaks in the most general sense crossing color sex age and class lines. The best known agents of this revolution were the psychedelic drugs. As recently as 1970 I for one regarded people as open or closed by virtue of natural or induced freakouts and imagined that the key to survival was an unqualified expansion of consciousness. Now if you weld the counterculture onto feminism or vice versa I think it can be seen that right wing and reformist feminism is represented by women who like their old culture men never turned on tuned in and dropped out or did any of those things thought to be subversive of the continuation of sanity and order. A number of feminists beginning at least with valerie solanis have noted the ironies of the sexual revolution what that meant for women in its updated counter-culture form: more and better women to fuck by the new pleasure oriented freaks. The counterculture may be at heart a new mystique of masculine aggression, and a lot of those turned on tuned in dropt out women may still be hauling pots in the kitchens of the wonderful free communes, but sexist considerations aside (if that's possible), there remains the phenomenon of mind expansion and concomitant revolutionary attitudes by which women as well as men can be distinguished from each other in what leary has called the struggle of the flower people against the metal men. Not that the flower people are supposed to be struggling. A subsplit within the counter-culture occurred with the campus activists and now the whole movement seems confused by the generalized public co-option of the various styles which once indicated who was what. Anyway as to feminism I hazard my own statistics that old culture women or women you'd call straight in the straight freak dichotomy are overwhelmingly the women we also call straight in the straight lesbian confrontation and that the counterculture women within feminism are those who were lesbian to begin with and or those who were and remain the most amenable to the idea of discovering the superior pleasures of lesbian sex. That's a gross generalization. There are many freaky straights and many straight freaks and indeterminate combinations thereof. I guess off and on radical women like to think of themselves as swingers or something. I don't know what those women are doing if they're not yet turned on to feminism. I imagine that by now even if they're not aligned with feminist organizations they've absorbed the reformist feminist lines and they have their old men *help*ing them haul those pots in the kitchens. I think it's fair to say that freaky straights seriously in the feminist movement don't stay sexually straight for very long. I don't think these women would say any more as a couple of them did two years ago in some feminist essay we don't carry with us, as part of our movement baggage, an understanding of homosexual technique . . . (!) I mentioned something called a straight freak above and I'm not sure what that is. There are some old dyke heads around, dykes who still think they're queer, i.e. different, dykes who still think you have to work with men, dykes who still think their lifestyle is a bedroom issue or that they're a special interest group whose interests are secondary to that of straight feminists, dykes who might deep down rather be straight themselves in other words who still think they're queer and have to explain and apologize and all that. It's the difficulty of dykes assuming their own vanguard position that divide the dykes and threaten to undermine certain major important confrontations with the straight feminists. The feminists always trot out that line about sexual orientation and how it isn't supposed to matter and of course it isn't but it very much does right now in this pre and post stage of human liberation (I mean when we are humanly liberated sexual orientation *won't* matter) especially since almost all the feminists complaints and demands revolve around their heterosexuality whether they say so or not. Thus their sexual orientation matters a lot. This is a difficult challenge for the dykes who naturally see themselves as much more than sexual women and who're sensitive already to the use of their own word as a discriminatory practice to describe a woman as nothing more than sexual. Thus the dykes have to say both things at once. That sexuality absolutely is at the core of the feminist revolution, and that the revolution also transcends our particular sexualities in the sense that our erotic life should be a component in the life of a totally functioning satisfied woman. But when that happen we'll all be a woman since you are who you sleep with and to continue sleeping with the man is to remain only half a woman and a half a woman is not the ideal functioning satisfied woman. Anyway the present local politics of interdyke struggle is a reality in the ongoing conflict with the straight women.

The meeting I went to was as I see it a major victory for the feminist/lesbian approach to feminism, it was an uproarious and horrendous and hilarious evening at the end of which both dykes and straights were astonished that we had somehow managed to nominate and elect at least five upfront lesbians as speakers for the march and two others we think might be and one who isn't upfront and one who's pending, this was at least a dramatic reversal of one of the first marches when as martha shelley tells it she had to storm the mikes (by kate's permission who was speaking) to speak for lesbians that year they didn't even elect a *token*. The substruggle of the dykes surfaced at the end of the meeting last tuesday. Ostensibly a few personalities were involved and the issue seemed to be the disagreement between dyke separatists and dyke collaborators meaning dykes who work with men at GAA. I suspect the conflict is a lot deeper and that this particular disagreement is symptomatic of that difficulty I mentioned of moving into our own vanguard position. To any old dyke head the token situation is still the proper place. Whatever the conflict it was actually two dykes at the end who initiated the move to reverse everything and eliminate speakers altogether. For myself I don't think it's all that important whether you have speakers or not but clearly in this case to eliminate them would have meant a setback to a critical feminist/lesbian victory. Everybody was screaming and out of order. I yelled sour grapes. Someone yelled fuck the democratic process, let's have a queen. Some woman was yelling at me that it was all my fault, that this sort of thing happened whenever I came. And the dykes as I said were turning against themselves in some weird political myopia that only the inside inside might be able to understand as sue schneider said when she came out of the closet she heard the door slam behind her, meaning I think that a lot of dykes didn't hear the noise. So anyhow a vote was called and I thought that was it that all was lost but I was wrong and a clear majority voted to keep the speakers. Before that when this woman was carrying on and accusing us of coming in a bloc which we did although I said I came as myself which was also true and anyway what is the straight faction if it isn't a bloc even if they don't admit that most of their issues (abortion prostitution sterilization contraception child care marriage and divorce) are heterosexual issues it seems ironic to me they should be accusing us of wanting to know if the candidates were "gay" especially since so many "gay" women are themselves "experts" on heterosexual issues, like marriage and divorce, both as "gay" and "straight" women, and since so many "gay" women are centrally involved in these very heterosexual projects like abortion again as sue schneider said one half to more women working on the abortion project in new york are dykes who help with counseling and putting up women from all over and she thinks moreover that if we dyke-otted the women's movement it would fall apart in two days. As to the march this should be the first year of clarity for lesbians who constitute the revolutionary pivot of the feminist revolution until this time trapped as token between gay males and straight women that's sort of what I really wanted to say to that woman at the meeting that lesbians are fucking really tired of being tokens and of many feminists not declaring their own conversion and telling like it is how the entire straight feminist movement is sexually confused sick celibate furious at men unable to be fucked by men any more unwilling and scared and discovering the (still criminal) pleasures of love and sex with their sisters. Like when're they gonna start telling their stories. As to maintaining a conservative stance and softplaying to all the sisters "out there" in middle amerika I could quote phyllis chesler here saying women, including many feminists, respond more positively to those projects which ease the burdens of the female status quo rather than to those projects which attempt to redefine or abolish the status quo. Easing the burdens of motherhood and supporting abortion reform are essential tasks, yet both imply a continuation of a powerless female responsible for children and for birth control. Endquote. The feminists in amerika are still not recognizing their most powerful force for change in their most independent aggressive and sexually alive women. A strong feminist in london told me right off that the lesbians there are in the vanguard of the movement and this was a woman who lives with a husband and a child. The only feminist who has asserted herself in this manner in this country is ti-grace atkinson who has apparently been so well treated by the movement that she is now supporting the mafia. People like midge decter I dunno they're so far out in left (or right) field that at this stage of revolution in a city like new york at least you wonder if they ever saw the ball at all. She's one of those who never considered sexuality without a man ever not even with an asparagus or a rhubarb. So what do these women think when they know that most of the women marching in the women's march august 25 are the dangerous dykes of that great original broadeyed sunken race called women. A logistically very easy and tactically correct maneuver. We're not coming to take over as sue said we're coming to get your attention for awhile. She said in missouri they used to say we'd have to hit the mule over the head with a two by four to get their attention so you could talk to them. I don't care about marches or meetings or any of it. I don't care what the straight women think unless they agree with us we're oppressed and we want woman power and revolution should be fun or we should forget it. The Cistercians, or somebody, is Coming! A Torrential Rain often accompanies a Major Eruption. Then we go away to the country and say after the butterfly is formed it must rest and realize its being as a butterfly.

—*August 24, 1972*

Writing into the Sunset

So I laid out in the sun in a chaste lounge and burned my cleavage
and thought if I didn't decide to stay there it was only because I had
failed to leave. I mean rather if I *did* decide to stay there and the
mistake and the correction alike are purely aesthetic. I've come to
realize that only one thing is worth bothering about: becoming
beautiful. It certainly is best not to do anything. I heard that two
dykes holding hands at a business meeting were accused of having
an orgasm. Oh these straight ones with their vibrators and their
alarm clocks. Oh all we need is a nice enormous sunny sumptuous
studio and a lot of exciting work to do and to just go there and do
it and not talk to anybody and to evolve some complicated strategems
for keeping everybody in the dark. Oh I remember being at the
christopher street gay liberation day march last year and a nice young
woman asking me what would I do when nobody paid any attention
to me any more and I thought about all the years I'd gone unnoticed
while I enjoyed my reading and writing and I said well I guess I
would just go on enjoying my reading and writing. Oh and then too
if you were never beautiful you get better looking as you get older.
Oh and none of it matters. You have to go through what you go
through to be where you are. A charter to commit the crime once
more. I dreamt I gave birth to a baby in a canoe. I dreamt I put my
arms around kate who said she'd lost weight and was lying in bed on
the set of somebody's play. I went to see kate at the dugout to set
straight the old *time* magazine story since I was thinking about media
distortion which seemed important and so does a field of crickets
and wild strawberries. All my cross and troubles go to the door with
thee. A friend says there's no help for it but to stop writing stop
publishing and go into a coma. It's just very suspect if you do anything
at all. And look what happened to bella. She's been hired as an
informant. I didn't dream about bella but I saw her before the defeat
and she made me cry so I guess she was hurting a lot. I wouldn't run
unless there was a reasonable expectation of winning but sometimes
a damaged duck is forced to run. Ceremonial cannibalism is found
in many parts of the world. The desire to obtain the qualities of the

dead person. People talk about it different ways. People respond more to publicity than to good work. People don't think about public people as regular people. People think that the work of a public person is the person and it is but it isn't too. It isn't, I found out, when I'm exhausted and an attractive enthusiastic young woman says I don't remember her from last week on the street someplace and when I do remember that I don't remember her name and it's true I don't but I want to be friendly but I'm exhausted and she's saying but I've been reading you for seven or eight years . . . so clearly my image of exhaustion and amnesia and mere politeness wasn't measuring up to my work in her mind's expectation I really wanted to say look I'm not the person who writes those things and I know that's true but I didn't and it isn't. Anyway I'm evolving some new personae. In only a few days I managed to be florence o'connor and bertha harris and professor sadie von masloch and occasionally just jill. I like being florence and that's well established so far as I'm concerned but bertha harris and sadie von masloch were an exciting new investigation into the possibilities of multiple identity. I'd rather that everybody just automatically loved me but we know that if you do anything it's optimistic to think you can do anything right. If you join or make a group in order to do something you're accused of being elitist and if you don't join or make a group you're accused of being an individualist. (Jane o'wyatt says a group is elitist when it forms and democratic when it dissolves.) If you do both you're accused of not being able to make up your mind. If you go away it's a copout. If you're sick you're not healthy and if you die you deserved it. I could be bragging or complaining or apologizing. It seems irrelevant in any case to the momentary position of the stars. Any uninhibited display of egotism devolves into the heroic quest for the cancellation of the self. Anyway I'm not a star, I'm an asteroid. I went next door for an oatmeal cookie with marshmellow stuffing. I passed a man who asked for a pen to write a message on his mailbox and who wanted to know if I was me and I said sometimes why not I have nothing to hide. I became famous when I went crazy and I went crazy because I stopped smoking cigarettes and before that I was a cigarette smoking ignominous cricket of the arts and that's the entire truth so kelp me odd. I have letters sometimes from people think I just sprang fullgrown out of the head of athena as soon as the world lesbian was breathed outside the closet. I had a letter from a woman saying my writing and star trip is ripping this lesbian (her) off and so far as she's concerned I'm a middle class bitch who makes money writing in a totally pig paper as a spokeswomen for Lesbians and that my ego satisfaction is killing her which makes me the enemy and that my writing style shows my middle class self indulgence which I try to pass off as a women's language or beginnings of a new women's culture. It hadn't occurred to me to pass anything off but it's a thought. It has often occurred to me that I may be stranded between the literati who can't stand my subject and the subject who is traditionally opposed to the pretensions of the literati. Blessed be the Christians and all their ways and works/Cursed by the Infidels, Hereticks, & Turks. A mixture of blood between the immigrants and the local aristocracy was inevitable. There's no mistake or correction but if there were they'd be purely aesthetic. I've come to realize that there is only one thing worth bothering about: becoming beautiful. Or what was it marilyn monroe said: I don't want to make money, I just want to be wonderful. I went to a party where lots of women were wearing red shirts and suddenly I was standing with two women one of whom I didn't know addressed me smiling saying so you have breasts jill johnston and that's all susan brownmiller has ever had to say to me. I don't know whether it meant she thought I personally didn't have breasts or if lesbians generally aren't supposed to have any or possibly she was just making a pass at me or what but it could be that women as well as men are deeply threatened by a female who doesn't expose her breasts very often and paradoxically who appears to be flaunting herself. I went to the party as professor sadie von masloch who had come in from the department of cunilinguistics at Transylvania Institute of Technology the only college of science and engineering for women to speak on equality in education at the women's rally august 25 on fortyfirst street after the march. My speechwriter was martha shelley. My outfit was london black gabardine deep cleavage circa 1968. My assistant was lyn kupferman. My photographer was susan rennie. My politics are impractically pure and sue schneider said they don't expect stars to act like revolutionaries. For sanity sake cancel yr next ego trip. Or make sure yr original fictitious speaker will conclude her 19th century romantic tragedy in north carolina in time to speak for herself. I prefer looking like a butch fatale. It makes things easier. Already I've been accused in the papers of not being a lesbian and I'm mobilizing a squad of revolutionary lawyers to sue. I'm serious about that too. The papers and publishers are always conferring with their lawyers over such items as whether so & so might sue if it's merely implied that they might be homosexual the reason behind it all being that such attributions affect a person's livelihood so I have every right to sue and I have many witnesses to vouch for my good standing as a woman loving woman. Anyway I risked further mis-representation for an evening. I risked everything in fact just by doing something. I'm not the person who writes these columns so that doesn't have to count. I don't know what the lower class elitists want me to do, I don't want to learn auto mechanics, and I can't work up an interest in plumbing or electricity, and I don't see why I should be a waitress or a cashier when people are paying me to move words around. As for representing Lesbians I don't represent Lesbians I represent myself, and sometimes other Lesbians or just others like my work and what I say and I know that because they tell me they do, and besides I'm a prerevolutionary lesbian village voice writer, I came out the winter of 1969 a few months before the stonewall riots and before that I was famous for being crazy and before stonewall and even feminism which I'd never heard of I signed two contracts for books because people asked me to because I did something called writing. Anyway I'm not famous except on special days and then I enjoy it. I would rather have spoken on education at the rally as jill or even as florence than as sadie von masloch. We say outrageous things with great pleasure. We do what we have to do and then see where we are. A charter to commit the crime once more. I dreamt I gave birth to a baby in a canoe. I dreamt I put my arms around kate and I went to see her to set straight the old *time* magazine story. The maneuvering of *time* was a masterpiece of premeditated murder. In august 1970 they put kate on the cover. In november 1970 they printed the news she was a "bisexual" as a belated confession as it were. I met kate that november only a few days before that panel at columbia organized by women's and gay liberation there at which she came out and I was one who was pressing her and I was unaware of the complexity of the problem. I was involved in my own complexities coming out. I said to her why are you posing as straight in the media and she just answered because she couldn't jeopardize the woman's movement and we went to a bar and had a drink and she made me cry and I went to california that week because everybody was making me cry anyway and I wrote in a farewell column that I was a luxury that the women's movement could not yet afford and I didn't know how true it was and still is apparently even among lesbians I'm a luxurious writer passing off a middle class self indulgence as a women's language or beginnings of a new women's culture. Actually I'm not middle class at all, I'm a british bastard, and there's a long tradition of aristocracy in the line of british bastardy, so that could account for all my errudishin and disarming dishonesty and pretensions in general. I'm working up a character analysis with the help of good friends like jane and bertha harris. Difficult but not evil, timid and aggressive, vague and demanding, unstable but never nasty and so forth. Remembering that the main thing is becoming beautiful becoming beautiful I laid out in the sun in a chaste lounge and burned my cleavage and thought if I didn't decide to stay there it was only because I had failed to leave and I've mentioned already the aesthetic importance of making a mistake if it sounds good and you can press your advantage with an equally interesting correction. The mistake *time* made over kate was not a beautiful one. They made her look crosseyed and weird on the cover and they wouldn't print the news that she was "bisexual" in august in that issue because it was scandalous and two months later in november they used it as scandal in a not unsuccessful attempt to discredit her as a leader in the movement, making it look as she says as if she'd just been chased out of her closet when in fact in august when they interviewed her originally she had told them everything about her life. For somebody who likes to do things it must've seemed as if the gig was up. Only last week in fact kate says she was walking along in the march august 25 and a young girl on a bike stopped and said are you kate millett well I thought your book was very pretentious so it's clear the original mistake however aesthetic and instructive was in just doing something. The whole business is rotten to the encore. One day you receive a hate letter and the next day a raggedy ann doll and you go and buy a bmw and go writing off into the sunset in yr middle class indulgence clutching yr doll and yr cleavage striking a beautiful purple pose and thundering forth yr metrical incantations for the benefit of the crickets and wild strawberries it could actually be the life and perfecting those complicated stratagems for keeping people in the dark I suspended my disbelief a long time ago expending prodigious amounts of energy we thrash erratically toward innovation. Literature is a defense against the attacks of life and the other defense against things in general is silence as we muster strength for a fresh leap forward. The diabolical aspect of the women's movement is its indictment of any action by which it is generated. The individual in any case was always in trouble, the individual in amerika as elsewhere risks ostracism loneliness grave self doubt and perhaps incarceration. And then if you do something as a group you risk the collective fascism of the group mind and vote. Whatever it is the counsel for the defense could begin by pointing out that she is not attempting to prove the contrary of what the prosecution has asserted, in other words we might as well do everything. Then whatever you do you could say that it isn't really you doing it, or you could say it isn't you and make yr disguise just as transparent and then claim you wanted to present a transparent disguise so that anybody could see you were merely pretending not to be you in case you thought otherwise and so on. As sadie von masloch I was standing in actually for bertha harris whose existence is still in question. I wouldn't mind being bertha harris but the one I was speaking for really does exist and if it weren't for her 19th century tragic romance in north carolina I wouldn't have been sadie von masloch either. Actually I was bertha and sadie and florence and martha and sue and jane and jill and the flying circus and everything and why aren't you mad at me too. The identification of all of them is fairly certain but there's some question as to which is which actually it was bertha who called from north carolina to say she thought it was wonderful and beautiful and it was martha who invented sadie von masloch who wore her last black london gabardine cleavage which she burned in the sun on the lounge and it was jill who nominated bertha after sue had made the speech saying we should have a dyke on the podium for equal education and florence who enthusiastically recommended bertha just recently employed by richmond on staten island to come up from the south as an upfront dyke in the women's studies program although nobody had ever heard of her she was instantly elected and that is the story of bertha harris and the last triumph of dykedom. The end of the story of kate and *time* was that kate was being ordered to speak out of both sides of her mouth at once, by gay liberation to come out, by women's liberation to shut up, and *time* made up everybody's mind by using the information that women's liberation wanted hushed up using it against them and against an individual which for women's liberation could've been seen as just one of their new chief indians biting the dust but to tie it all up by a neatly contrived coincidence of middle class indulgence in all our suspensions of disbelief it was bertha harris in november 1970 after *time* did their job who sent a telegram to kate reading time's not love's fool.

—September 7, 1972

Fanatica Femina Fatiloqua

I want to be too embarrassed to say how much I've thrown the ching lately to find out what I know already. I wanted to talk about nothing just to feel myself on course. When enough such verbiage had accumulated I could feel ready for some aggressive recapitulation and the revolution would be apparent. I said to Jane is there a revolution or are we making it up and she said we're trying to make it up. But we don't have to do much or anything or do we have to pick up the cues, I dunno. Hey Zorina, you missed yer cue. But she'll do something else backstage. The message is that we're all on course even when we miss the cue. The continuum is the course and the revolution is now. I guess the cue is some sort of reminder like a scouts mark on a tree trailing the forest. According to certain astrologers I think we don't have to do or perceive anything since everything happens the way it was ordained by stellar systems. The ching somehow lines itself up that way. A medium between me and the stars in case I can't see the stars myself. We used to say it's in the stars as a serious cliché. Saying it that way we didn't have to take it seriously although using the phrase or not didn't affect knowing that if it happens it might as well. If it might as well then there's nothing to worry about. One of the queens was telling Alice that she had to run as fast as possible to remain in the same place. The plan is there and we're doing all this effort, running. Or writin and talkin. *Spectre* by the white revolutionary lesbians in ann arbor stopped after six issues. They say 20 more *Spectres* won't change anythin — only people DOIN stuff — actin on what's already there . . . We're gonna keep fightin, but now in a more real way. Is talkin and writin an action? Of course talkin and writin is an action. I was having an inspiration while she was discussing the cigarettes and the worcestershire sauce. Wouldn't it be fun to run for mayor as a lark? Madame butterfly and all that. And so this brings us to other things. I'm drunk and waxing eggplant. I feel alright except for my mind. Remnants of old habits and trials of new possibilities. Everything is getting ready again to begin. The country is devastating. The two seasons are locked in invisible battle. One day in the city on fifth avenue Rochelle Owens passed by and came up to me and said hello and that was very nice even though she said she thought I was too much into greek myth and I said listen I don't know anything about greek myth but I know it's important. The old greeks knew about the seasons for instance, the revolution occurring right now, the combat between the forces of light and the forces of darkness, and how they could master these changes by noting their regularity and marking off the passage of time accordingly, how the cycle is manifested in peoples and nations calling for social transformations and they had those dionysian resurrection dramas which found their way into the christian ritual and dogma. The Mother, the Daughter, and the Holy Boast. The reconstruction of history is the springtime of woman's resolution to an attenuated conflict. The lady had a most checquered career alternating between a whole series of love affairs and virtual imprisonment by her husband in convents. She had beautiful eyes but she couldn't see. I just read a biography of Mary Wollstonecraft and had to feel awful about a woman who saw as much as she did at a hopeless time. She got herself all together too as an independent person writing for a living then got herself all mixed up in men and babies and died some gruesome death in childbirth. I had a dream that richard had breasts and jane said that's an interesting solution. I had another about a red sports car and that wasn't so interesting. Jane had the best involving finding a manuscript of Gertrude Stein which had never been published which we all liked. Lynn and Maricla prepared it for publication by soaking letters and words in egg batter and rolling them in bread crumbs and pan frying them. The edition that Jane made was rubber letters about a foot tall. The book was a room piled high with grey rubber letters. You know the story of G.S. and T.S. Eliot. Eliot and Gertrude Stein had a solemn conversation mostly about split infinitives and other grammatical solecisms and why Gertrude Stein used them. Eliot said if he printed anything of Gertrude Stein's in the *Criterion* it would have to be her very latest thing.

So she began to write a portrait of T.S. Eliot and called it the fifteenth of November, that being the day she wrote it so there could be no doubt but that it was her latest thing. It was all about wool is wool and silk is silk or wool is woolen and silk is silken. She sent it to T.S. Eliot and he accepted it but naturally he did not print it. Gertrude Stein was delighted when later she was told that Eliot had said in cambridge that the work of Gertrude Stein was very fine but not for us. I found out recently that a rose is a rose etc. originally was not written beginning with the article "A" and in fact rose was a woman. I found out that Mabel Dodge's career stretched from Gertrude Stein to D.H. Lawrence, from buffalo to florence to taos, through four husbands and an indeterminable number of male and female lovers. I found out also that in 1898 Gertrude Stein spoke before a group of baltimore women on the subject The value of college education for women and that her ideas were based on the just published book by Charlotte Perkins Gilman, *Women and Economics*. According to Richard Bridgman not only did Gertrude Stein dismiss contemporary marital arrangements, but she also asserted the greater force and purity of sexuality in the independent woman.

"She was unmistakably seeking to validate her own condition." Fanatica femina! Fanaticism is a fine thing, meaning excessive zeal, to be very much for what one is. There is only one way to be very much for what one is in a society which remains determined not to like it and that is to be fanatical. When we get it all straightened out we may be more relaxed about it but we could still be excessively zealous in being very much for who we are. Note the excessive and ancient zeal of the heterosexist cause. What I think is that the wives of rock stars before they send anti-lesbian literature to influential newspapers should find out something about lesbian/feminist political theory and analysis and consider the fact that influential newspapers are delighted to print unsympathetic material about lesbians by the wives of rock stars and any other woman-divisive stuff they can get their hands on. No amerikan feminist in her right mind would attempt to incriminate her sisters in a male publication. The criticism of straightness by lesbian/feminist thinkers is a political stance and strikes at the heart of collaboration with the enemy. It is, in effect, not a criticism of any private woman or private pleasure but of the institution by which woman remain oppressed. If people can't separate these things and put them together as well and then separate them again and put them together to see the personal/political sense of it all then what can we do, there was an especially ferocious straight woman a few months ago at a meeting and Jane said we just have to turn her around and point her at the enemy. Anything suitable is so necessary. Constructing your greenhouse and talking to the plants you like. Wanting to be too embarrassed to say how much you've thrown the ching lately to find out what you know already. That whatever the wives say or the papers print it doesn't matter nothing can stop the revolution since the stars and the seasons are making it happen anyway. I don't know a thing about astrology but I believe in it totally. I said to somebody last week on the phone I feel terrible and they said they felt terrible too and so did all the other taureans because we're just now moving into the new aquarian age and aquarius is opposed to taurus. Oh fine, I said, you mean we have to feel lousy now for 2000 years. They said no we're just in the transition. The transition is over. I got up the day I threw Revolution (Molting) and wrote straight on for 15 hours and cleaned the barn and ran on the road and stood on my head and ironed my pants and answered my mail and threw out the berries and the pits and called up washington and said we were on our way. On your own day You are believed. Supreme success . . . Political revolutions are extremely grave matters. They should be undertaken only under stress of direst necessity, when there is no other way out . . . Times change, and with them their demands. Thus the seasons change in the course of the year. In the world cycle also there are spring and autumn in the life of peoples and nations, and these call for social transformations. In the country in the dense silence in the bleak brown wasteland of empty trees crowded with tiny bulges getting ready to be leaves you can feel this terrific conflict going on and this time this year I know it's me. The ching is just a dead old book and I change all the genders and I don't know why a dead old chinese book in the wrong gender is giving off such vital cues. One day it was so vital as to be paralyzing. It happened in the morning and I regretted doing it instantly it was Splitting Apart and I really didn't feel that way, I felt fine, but it said terrible things like inferior people were pushing themselves up and crowding out superior people and nothing whatever should be undertaken and one should absolutely not go anyplace and things like that. I then called up anybody I could think of to try to determine who was preparing to do me in and also I spent a very energetic day dispensing duties and details and being righteous in other words. I tried to erase the reading by throwing another and got Youthful Folly which in effect chastised me for questioning the oracle. So I waited a suitable length and threw a last time and was relieved to find out that I had the inner truth and some possession in great measure and I left for the city. Ten minutes on the road and the state pigs pulled me over and kept us there an hour searching every inch and crevice and compartment of the vehicle and calling on their microphones to remote capitols for information concerning papers and identities & such and at last writing out a ticket for going thru a stop sign. I had plenty possession in great measure. Before all that happened I called Danny he was one of the people I called and said listen are you getting ready to do me in over my book and he said look you have a lot of indian clubs in the air, it could be anything. So I thought about *every*thing and I couldn't come up with a road scene involving a particularly gestapo oriented state pig. But then, being on course what can we do to stop what we're doing except stopping when stopping is part of the course. You have to read Elizabeth Gould Davis's *The First Sex* — *The Aquarian Age* upon whose threshold we now stand, will be "inimical to man," as Macrobius prophesied in the early days of the Piscean Age. The "new morality" of the Aquarian youth of our days perhaps bespeaks a return to matriarchal mores too long suppressed by the materialistic patriarchal values that have prevailed for the past 2000 years in the Occidental world. The Aquarian Age of the next 2000 years will see an end to patriarchal Christianity and a return to goddess worship and to the peaceful social progress that distinguished the Taurian Age of four millennia ago.

—*April 13, 1972*

In conjunction with the philosophy of revolutionary effeminism I present this brilliant piece of iconoclastic genetics and philogyny by a west coast male, jerry cobb. He calls the piece Philogyny and he sent it to me about a month ago: Philogyny: A Concept Worth Developing:

The so-called "men's liberation movement," or just plain "men's movement," has met with considerable criticism from feminists and effeminists alike in the brief span of its existence. These criticisms include the suspicion that we are merely a knee-jerk reaction to women's liberation, a "me-too" way for the lonely straight politicos to spend the evenings their wives or "old ladies" are away at their own small groups . . . a way for us to lessen the guilt of being the oppressor class in everybody else's book . . . a way for us to learn the proper rhetoric in order to "update" our monogamies and "sensitize" our conversations with and energy rip-offs of women who would otherwise be getting their lives together. Men's groups have been ctiticized as being ways for us to hang on to our male privilege by "reforming" our attitudes and coopting feminism in order to be able to say, "Not us! We're the good guys. We're getting our own shit together!"

This, of course, is precisely what women and gay effeminists fear most; that men's groups are just another form of male bonding, which has *always* oppressed them. Men calling each other "brother" and giving each other support as they rap down how "oppressed" they've been all their lives, how they realize they've been shitty to their "sisters" in the past, but now that they're "getting in touch with their feelings" they're going to be soft-spoken gentle chauvinists.

All this solidifies our victim's fears about "men getting it together," an occurrence which has led to their abuse, rape, and/or death in the past. Only this time, "male consciousness" is tantamount to cheating the executioner.

Men in small groups have been saying "right on" to *almost* any feminist analysis while *exempting themselves* by soft selling themselves as "exceptional men." This, they think, will get them laid more and better while being "politically correct" at the same time. I have personally seen in my own conscienceness-raising group, men leave to fuck over women as soon as the group had taught them enough "liberated raps" to make it as particularly slick pigs in the "real world," getting out of c-r before they started to have any self-doubts. No wonder women don't trust men to "liberate themselves!"

Some men hope to "deal with their gayness" so that they might become androgynous and rip off men sexually as well as women. (See "Fellini Satyricon: The Ultimate Straight Male Rip-Off, or: Men's Liberation at Its Best," also "Androgyny and Male Supremacy," both in the May, 1971, *The Effeminist*.) Variations of this theme presently seem to be the ultimate goal in the more "vanguard" men's circles.

But none of these approaches tackle the real roots of sexism. Straight and gay men are still organizing around their *maleness*, an approach doomed to failure because, apart from it missing the point, it forces us to be relativistic ("We have fewer privileges than so&so"), it forces us to try to discover an "oppression" of our very own, to believe it's all "society's" fault, or our upbringing, or childhood trauma plus pig media that makes us the sexists we are. We believe that maybe "coming out" will cure us of our misogyny, or perhaps celibacy until we think of something nicer is "the answer."

In any case, the men's movement has always operated out of the premise that men are products of socialization and are themselves, innocent victims of an external "male supremacy."

There is another analysis which may smack of pre-destination and hopelessness, but these feelings are male defenses which keep us from facing the truth, and have no place in an honest men's movement.

The dictionary defines *philogyny* as "a fondness or respect for women." I think that the opposite of misogyny, woman-*hating*, can be put more strongly than that. This word/concept sprang into my mind before I ever thought of looking it up to see if it existed. My concept of it would be closer to "an acceptance of and devotion to things female, and the recognition of the primacy of femaleness." A philogynist, therefore, wants nothing short of a restoration of humankind's original Matriarchy in whatever form the women who pull it off choose, *even if that means our own destruction*. If males organize around this concept of actively aiding, on our own, women into separatist revolution (and it is in the species' interest to do so), we will have gone a long way toward solving the contradictions previously stated. Insofar as there are millions of openly declared misogynists in the world, we must not be apologetic about embracing philogyny. This is really why we joined the men's movement in the first place: not out of a love for masculinity, which we *know* is reactionary, but out of awe and respect for the women's movement. By coming together not as males but as anti-misogynists, as lovers of the Female Principle (this is *not* to be confused with heterosexism!) we do not preclude our communistic ideals, our collectivism, male friendship, or gay love based on our common beliefs, nor do we become passive self-pitiers who only wait for the end while contemplating suicide. We become dynamically aligned with, although separate from the forces of cataclysmic change; the true Sexual Revolution. There is some not insubstantial evidence to support the theory that maleness in general and human maleness in particular is a geologically recent genetic accident. Many myths (racial memories) relate the splitting off of men from women. (The early Semitic patriarchs, realizing the danger to male supremacy inherent in such memories, reversed their Adam and Eve myth to have Adam *give birth* to Eve, through his *rib* no less, a patent absurdity!) In *The First Sex*, Elizabeth Gould Davis describes how the ancient Greeks, as they became progressively more patriarchal, transformed the gender of their goddesses while attempting to retain their original powers. This brought about the ludicrous situation where Zeus originally a female *gives birth* to Athene from his head, another perversion of nature.

The one thing these myths all have in common is the memory that one sex came first, and existed without the need of the other until something *internal* happened.

Many "primitive" cultures practice male mutilation apparently in order to imitate the female so as to regain men's lost humanity. Frequently in male puberty rites the penis is gouged lengthwise to create a male vulva, or lacerated to produce male menstruation. In some societies the fathers take to birth stools during these ceremonies and act out mock labor while their naked sons, painted blood red, jump from under the writhing father's skirt in simulated birth, a vain attempt to prove that men are creators of their own kind, and a marvelous insight into the inadequacy men feel over their biological role in the species. Circumcision is itself a modified form of penis mutilation designed to make the male less offensive in the eyes of the Great Goddess, the original god of all peoples everywhere (See *The First Sex*).

Certainly the Y chromosome which makes us male is a damaged X, the female chromosome. I used to think that "Y&X" were arbitrary designations which would have been served equally well by "A&B" or "1&2," but not so. Under the microscope chromosomes actually look like Xs and Ys, and a Y is obviously an X with a leg broken off or severely crippled. The Y chromosome is more susceptible to various congenital defects such as color blindness and hemophilia, although in misogynist culture we prefer to interpret this male weakness by females for being the "carriers." Occasionally males are born with a double Y chromosome and these individuals have been shown to be born killers incapable of warmth or gentleness because they are much farther removed from the ideal female XX, making them "super men." As all other genetic factors in these individuals remain the same, we may take this as further proof of the undesirability of the Y chromosome or male factor.

Throughout the animal "kingdom" the pattern persists; the male of any species is the sexual adjunct to the female, an anomaly whose only purpose is the production of sperm. How, then, could female have ever existed without them?

One hint is the fact that the male mutation was not universal among life forms on earth. As we go down the evolutionary scale, and hence closer to the oldest established life forms, sex differentiation becomes less common. Here we find "sexual" creatures who reproduce by mitosis or budding (hence, by definition, these animals are all *females*, as only females may give birth by whatever means); "hermaphroditic" animals which fuse briefly to exchange chromosomal material, *both* individuals of who later reproduce by various

161

means (again, all females); "advanced hermaphrodites" such as the earth-worms (annelida) where each animal produces both sperm and ova, and after cross-fertilization *both* give birth; as well as certain maverick species such as the Artemia "sea monkeys" who reproduce at least five different ways, certain shrimp which begin life as females and *mutate later* into males; and crustaceans such as Daphnia ("water fleas") which are all parthenogenic (capable of "virgin birth") female *until times of genetic disaster* (temperature change, solar radiation, mineral imbalances in the water, etc.) when males appear among the offspring. These fuck the females to again produce parthenogenic females. (Sexist biologists claim this proves that "sexual" reproduction is favored in nature to produce genetic change in offspring, in Daphnia's case, they claim, this produces immunity adaptations to the altered environment. I propose that the environmental disaster *incapacitated* the female's normal parthenogenic powers, while already developing young ones were genetically *damaged* into *freaks* (males whose purpose was merely to "re-charge" the females into repro-duction as a stop-gap measure, for the post-disaster *female young are indistinguishable* from the pre-disaster Daphnia, meaning there was nothing "defective" or genetically "inadaptive" in the pure female that the male had to "fix," merely that cataclysmic circumstances had temporarily rendered adults partially infertile. Young Daphnia which were in the reproductive stage when the disaster struck grow to reproduce normally (without males) *even if the radical environment persists*, proving the basic soundness and adaptability of the all-female system. The male mutants, of course, die out once parthenogenesis resumes, and no new ones are produced barring new cataclysmic event.

All this goes to show that dual sexuality is by no means nature's only way, and that there may well have been one or several primeval genetic disasters which introduced among the "higher" animals (which are more susceptible to gene damage due to greater complexity) the freak occurrence we call maleness. In some phylla the mutation didn't "take" because the original females later regained their fertility, rendering the new males "obsolete" and useless; in some the mutation was eventually assimilated into the individual creating hermaphroditism where separate "males" would be genetically intolerable; while in other Phylla, most notably the very complex Chordata, the genetic disaster *permanently* disabled the original females, simultaneously creating mutant males who became indispensable for procreative purposes. Undoubtedly other mutations were produced as well, but these must have been infertile or sexually incompatible with the female and therefore were selected out. Males, on the other hand, retaining one undamaged chromosome were adaptive regarding the now damaged female. (Could females have been originally XXX? This would explain what males are "filling in for," as well as explain the nature of the damage to the female. Perhaps parthenogenesis requires an additional X chromosome?)

Among many species of animals the male is portrayed to us by the misogynists as being the more "beautiful" gender. The peacocks' feathers, the mallards' plumage, the lion's mane, and mooses' antlers come to mind. And yet what are these characteristics but mutations which may seem frightening to the females who are the norm? The colors of the peacock cannot appear very beautiful to the totally color-blind peahen. In fact, in all these cases where male zoologists and animal behaviorists tell us the female of a given species is "hypnotized" by the male's colorful display, both male and female are in actuality color-blind. More likely these females are grossed out and half paralyzed with fear by this perversion of her own body type which she must fuck in order to perpetuate the species. The males of most species, regardless of how subjectively "beautiful" they may appear to us, are treated as disdainful sex objects at times of oestrous, and repulsed as disgusting monsters at all other times. The male moose, for example, is a loner all year, fighting with other lone males being his only non-sexual contact with his kind, while the females live out a complex communal existence as they must have before the genetic disaster. In the spiders (the only other animals besides Man who practice rape) the mutant male is incredibly tiny compared to the female, and is a total sexual adjunct to the true (female) species. He just fucks, but she does all the spidery thing like spinning webs. Ants and bees, for millions of years earth's most highly advanced beings (they may have had a common ancestor) treat their male mutants rather harshly. The queen alone is capable of producing specialized offspring so different from each other as to seem separate species, yet she does this from the sperm collected during her one fuck with the drones (those very few males hatched specifically for this purpose) on her "maiden flight." (Ant queens sprout temporary wings for this occasion, lending credence to the common-ancestor-with-the-bees theory.) From this supply she then mothers a tribe of neuter females frequently numbering in the hundreds of thousands. This takes years, but the queen does it all from her single supply of sperm. Perhaps these intelligent animals went to these biological extremes in order to get rid of the quarrelsome drones in short order, because on completion of the "maiden flight" the drones, their duty done, are killed on the spot or driven from the hive/nest. Not being complete organisms, they die quickly on their own. Evidently these animals only partially lost their parthenogenic powers when the males first appeared (which was well after the establishment of their respective societies, judging from the complete lack of social roles developed for the males) and although now obliged to fuck with them, the males are definitely unwanted in the all-female culture.

Examples of despised males in the animal world could go on and on, but the point is this: *the female of any species is what that species is*: the male being only a regrettable accident in those species that were unfortunate enough to produce them. If you wish to know what praying mantises are, look at the female (who, as everyone knows, eats her mate immediately after fucking him). To find out what lions are like, look to the female: and to understand the nature of humanity, LEARN FROM THE WOMEN! To point to baboons or other pack animals where females are physically subjected by the males is not to prove that males "always were and always will be," or that they are "naturally superior." It only proves that they are naturally dominating, slavemaster-mentalitied brutes wherever they have occurred as the physically stronger mutant. AND THIS HOLDS FOR H. SAPIENS.

Men, as genetically incomplete females, have sought to pervert nature since prehistoric times by assuming sexual superiority by suppressing their gut knowledge that *women are the species*. At first men tried to regain their missing humanity by (rightly) worshipping women in the form of universal female dieties, then by imitating them in rituals to gain a semblance of equality, and finally by declaring themselves superior to women and ascribing all their traditionally male neuroses to women, and taking naturally female traits, culture, and inventions as their own (See Valerie Solanis's *S.C.U.M. Manifesto*).

But men, having mainly developed only the left hemisphere of the brain (See It Ain't Me Babe article) established a totally one-sided culture. Having been denied his biological creativeness (even our breasts are vestigal, not to mention our inverted genitalia), man *had* to invent a mania for technology (See *The Dialectics of Sex* by Shulamith Firestone). This, too, began as an imitation of women's culture which had already invented agriculture, music, carpentry, religion, philosophy, government, language, art, astrology, animal "husbandry" and domestication, weaving, etc., while the mutant men were still banished from the women's villages as uncivilized meat-eating hunters (See *The First Sex*). Yet men were able to separate invention from ethics, and set into motion the chain of soulless scientific discoveries that has culminated in the development of thermonuclear warfare. Not that many of his toys haven't been useful and fun, but the death-oriented inventions far outnumber the more whimsical ones.

In his never-ending quest to "master" nature, against which he holds the gripe of his general inferiority, man has sewn the seeds of his own destruction. I am not again speaking of H-bombs, but of the recent "discoveries" in the field of genetics, among them the fact that *women are basically parthenogenic*! In fact, even a pin prick in a human egg will begin it dividing sperm or no sperm (See "Cloning: A Recycling? Or An Answer to Copulation?" by Michela Griffo in May 1972 issue of *The Furies*). Without its full human complement of 46 chromosomes, however (sex cells have only 23), the ovum will not develop into a complete fetus, but *any* 46 will do the job! A woman may remove her egg's nucleus and surgically implant a nucleus from any cell in her body (hair, inside of cheek, etc.) and give birth to a "carbon copy" of herself (cloning), or she *may implant another woman's egg nucleus into her own* (23 plus 23) *and have their baby*, always pure female, always a unique individual! Further work in this field will produce true genetic engineering, a technique which at first will be used as a way of selecting out birth defects, then as a way of choosing desired physical characteristics, then perhaps as a means of restoring the female body to its former parthenogenic capabilities. Finally, exogenesis, or "test tube babies," will be perfected, thereby freeing women from the tyranny of their biology, perhaps the final step in human evolution.

Given a feminist revolution (or counter-revolution, as Elizabeth Gould Davis calls it) whereby these tools will be in women's hands, I can foresee no reason for the continued production of human males. Stripped of their stud role, without even taking into account women's natural repugnance for the male abomination (see Simone de Beauvoir's *The Second Sex*), men will have even less purpose than the drones of the ants and bees. Why should the "trunk of the species" keep these troublesome, murderous beasts around any longer than need be? Perhaps a few might be kept as relics, reminders, zoo specimens, or side-show freaks, but this is not for us to decide, and this line of pursuit only keeps us from dealing with the immediate contradictions.

As philogynists, we must do everything within our power to make sure women seize control of these tools once developed. We must aid the feminist/lesbian revolution in every way we can, starting by staying the fuck out of their way. We must support the research into genetics while plotting the demise of the men who develop it, lest they surgically rape women by cloning *themselves* in woman's body (the ultimate male perversion; a thousand identical Nixons or Hitlers!). We must, along with Revolutionary Effeminists and Faggots (See "Flaming Faggots Manifesto" by Kenneth Pitchford in *Double-F Journal* or as reprinted on the back page of *Brother No. 3*) *de-man ourselves,* not to gain favor of women, but as a way of being at least half human for the interim.

Just as we know that sexism is the root of all other oppressive "isms," so we must realize that maleness is the root of sexism. Just as the Vietnamese war was no "mistake," but the inevitable result of U.S. imperialism, we must face the fact that sexism is just as predictable an outgrowth of maleness. As long as there are men there will be male supremacy, however subtle.

Contemporary misogynists such as Zwillingsbruder in Berkeley, a gay male supremacist group, will call us "tiny men," pathetic masochists, or "pussy-whipped fatalists," yet as potential members of Valerie Solanis's predicted "Mens' Auxiliary to *S.C.U.M.*," we welcome the chance to help set things aright, to help undo the damage of 10,000 years of male oppression, to take on reparations for it by de-manning ourselves, by working toward and rejoicing in the "second coming" of the Female Principle.

We may not, as individual males, live to see the last generation of our kind, or even the Revolution that will bring it about, but as Revolutionary Philogynists we recognize the damage our gender has done, will fight against its continuance while we live, and when the end is in sight, we will proudly recognize that as one of the last generations of men we will have served a noble purpose. In the meantime, there's 10,000 years of work to undo!

—September 14, 1972

Could I Have a Light

There may seem to be nothing to say but as an imprisoned young frenchwoman said in desperation I'm writing you all the same, as you would toss a bottle into the sea. I rediscovered the trees and the river and perhaps my confidence too. I may try to postpone the revolution until the leaves have turned. I want to be completely different from yesterday or the day before. I want to be overcome by a sense of infinite consequences. I want to be a total object, complete with missing parts. I want to play the guitar and sing somewhat. I want some balloon therapy and summore white berries on red stems and lavender unopened flowers in an oldfashioned glass. I want to be more than just a grown girl who identifies with classical heroines and automobiles. I want to be a progressed planet that moved out tomorrow. I'm very disconcerted by appearing to be writing what is going to happen next. We're all here, what's the phone ringing for. I was writing about richard and saying I didn't know where he was right now at which almost moment he called me up and said where've you been I lost you and now as I'm writing I have him on a plane for seattle so I suppose he'll be doing that too. I'm writing into the sunset and into the future as well. I don't know what it does to settle the past except to settle the past but you don't have to write about things to know they're about to happen and that doesn't mean we know it until after they happen and then after the fact we say oh I knew that was going to happen and so we did although it seems impossible to acknowledge it unless you're employed as a medium who also settles the past for people possibly to establish their credentials as acrobats of time and my ribbon is running dry and I think I'm evolving a plan and one of my selves will let me know what it is before long. In trude nothing is as unusual or provocative as it may appear. I won't send you flowers because you're going away and because certain gestures are intimidating. If I write about nothing nothing will happen. Any kind of local sensationalism could be our daily fare. Any kind of going up the mountain in my boots in the rain to plant three amazon solution balloons after iwo jima. Any kind of trees which are mortally beautiful and I have a glass in a rose and the yellow wall is tumbling into an electric blue and my visitors have not yet come forward to say what our last conversation was about. We were however sitting on some pebbles by the crick river when somebody said her last words were could I have a light and I think that was edna st vincent millay tiger tiger burning blake and oh my froze and oh my fiends it gives a lovely when these things happen in litterature everything is different I'm not concerned. I had two martinis at gregory's with four black olives. I had one cup of coffee at gloria's with two drops of saccharine. I had three irish whiskeys at susan's with nothing and nothing. I had one large orgasm at jane's with plenty of kisses and kats. Oh pussy kat I wish I could send you to summer camp. Oh I'm sending richard to seattle and they said I could prove he was born by just writing it down and having your neighborhood pharmacist agree with you for 50 cents by doing something called a notary public. Oh it's wonderful we can invent the past by writing it down too. The tangled mess of documentation upon which the cases for our real existence rests. True fidelity is that of ideas. As soon as you say it it is. It's real even if she's making it up you know what I mean it doesn't matter what's true any more it's all true. The troop of what you say is what really masters and the only impittance of tiqueneck is that wean you say it biddy you haven't sage it. So mach for finnegan and other runny nosed geniuses. If I write about something something will surely happen. I'm not clear on the purpose of settling the past unless we go back to invent it but I'm not keen on writing myself into the future either. Color me. Blow me a bubble. Brig me a turned leaf. Be my transceptor and remitter. Be my disconcertion and infinite consequences. I want to be completely different from yesterday or the day before and I don't want to do something new like go to an orgy. I was casually invited to an orgy while eating in a restaurant and I didn't want to and I had a letter from a woman in ohio inviting me to a swingers thing and I don't see the point of even saying it except as an excuse to note I'd rather make love to myself in a trunk in the desert and that doesn't mean I don't find lots of women attractive and I don't think it means I can't say so just because I appear to be married I just think orgies are confusing I picture it very abstractly romantically with botticelli's graces gliding under waterfalls if they touched me lightly licorice & lazuli I suppose it will happen now and it's heavy flashes of previous lives otherwise why would we say it if not to invent them by merely remembering them I was casually invited. I was writing last week on friday that day about women and men and violence in the streets and what to do or not to do about it and that very evening I experienced violence on the streets and I almost never do I've lived in new york city for hundreds of years and I have eyes all around my head as soon as the night sets and true to my mother's earliest instructions I never pass a man on a lonely street I make deviations and detours even circles and backtracks and trapdoors and hatches and shafts and spirals and smokescreens I make my way thru the obstacle course of the male sex but last friday that evening three women we knew were out on the street one was screaming one was slumping against the brick wall one was leaning over the one slumping and it happened because the one screaming encountered the two black men who insulted her who then knocked off her glasses and her jaw and who then smashed the one we saw slumping against the brick wall in the face her face was all blood we called the emergency the police came she had a concussion and three women chased the black men they couldn't find them I was writing. If you write about nothing nothing will happen. What can be accomplished by noting that in 1120 the white ship of Henry II went down with his only son, his illegitimate daughter, and a niece. On this point the present witnesses agree and abound: that whereas once in our schooldays we would register and regurgitate this information as pure information including six subjects we now pay attention and read carefully his only son knowing very well that such a sentence would never read his only daughter and in this way we write ourselves into the future by reinventing the past. My visitors bought soap bubbles and balloons sue and mary and mary said she heard the voices of several different people coming thru the print and sue made a drawing that was finished when her hand was tired and mary said sue was still a child and we smiled and I thought her first toys were probably crosses and relics and rosaries and she's very good at catching bats too. I was pleased to arrive and find a bat flying around a room not having written about bats recently or ever I know nothing about bats except that they're black and they like your hair and I'm settling the clear past. Any kind of local sensationalism. Another week of sterling tragedy. I cowered in the kitchen and the classical heroine chased him or her away we thought back up the chimney and we went to sleep. I woke up at three and yelled for the heroine whose armor was a headband and whose weapon was a white paper shopping bag. I was suffocating under a blanket and wanted to know if my choice was to suffocate or to emerge and have a bat in my hair. I didn't have to do either because the heroine caught the bat in her white paper shopping bag and took her outside to the mortally beautiful trees. There may be nothing to say but as the imprisoned young frenchwoman said in desperation I'm writing you all the same, as you would toss a bottle into the sea.

—September 28, 1972

Dyke Nationalism & Heterosexutility

Reading this bit out of voices from women's liberation, an anthology published 1970, I interpreted it first as a lesbian and then realized straights would make the same interpretation from their point of view and in fact that it was probably written by a straight I deduced from a parenthetical remark about hard-ons and clubs and being dragged by the hair and grovellings at the feet anyway the bit I mentioned is as follows: ". . . should leadership be retained by forces of but limited vision, the revolution must be cut tragically short of its full potential, for commitment to the lesser goals such as a pseudo-vanguard does envision will turn against the revolution at the very moment it stands poised to overreach them." The parenthetical remark is not irrelevant so I'll quote that too. "If you, brother, can't get a hard-on for a woman who doesn't grovel at your feet, that's *your* hangup; and sister, if you can't turn on to a man who won't club you and drag you off by the hair, that's yours. Keep your hangups the hell out of this revolution." One might pose these statements of heterosexutility against comments that read ". . . concealed beneath shabby plots and platitudinous melodramas of her fiction is a devastating analysis of the nature of heterosexuality and its implication for the liberation of women" to spell out the sexual biases at the heart of the dichotomy in the movement. It seemed necessary to establish the sexual orientation of the author of my first quote (lilith's manifesto) to indicate whose limited revolutionary vision was in question. The feminists per se continue to launch a polemic of sexual improvement and a denunciation of the feminist/lesbian solution, alluded to in such phrases as a commitment to lesser goals, a phrase likewise conjured by lesbians to compass the feminist position, which seems to us without a vision of total independence from the male to be indeed a commitment to lesser goals. The argument bears a(nother) predictable resemblance to the great issue within the black movement dividing the blacks between integrationists and black nationalists. The blacks, meaning black males, are way ahead of the women. The media for example has yet to print any proposal or proclamation of women for a separate (amazon) state. The degree to which both blacks and women have been colonized, as groups and as individuals, is the index to understanding the two extreme positions and all accomodations thereof. At the same time the current positions presuppose the possibility of changes in consciousness wrought by the respective revolutions. The extent of black nationalism next to the small underground voice of dyke nationalism, the comparable direction in the women's movement, can be accounted for by the relative absolute intactness of black identity maintained in amerika by the ghetto experience and preserved I surmise by a racial memory not nearly so far removed in time from its origins as that of women, whose identity has been contained and co-opted for a few thousand years at the least. Women have been totally colonized, we haven't had the ghetto experience like the blacks, a whole language etc., that binds you together, and the enslavement of women is not a phenomenon limited to any specific time and place. Thus it isn't surprising that the major most visible most vocal platform of the woman's movement continues to be that of integration into the male power structure through the various cries of equality. Comparing the token status of blacks to that of women and considering that comparison in relation to the population differential it doesn't require much imagination to see how completely the male standard operates to contain the woman's movement on a demand rather than a seizure basis. I could pursue the analogies between the black and the woman's movements, but I want to get off here some items I've been collecting pertaining to the lesbian/straight conflict within women's liberation, primarily indicating the resistance of socalled straight women both to the lesbian experience and to the lesbian experience as a political position. Many women want the "Lesbian Experience" but that's apart from and related to the fear and resistance of it that's been implanted by a profound social prejudice in a homo-erotic culture, the male homosexual brotherhood. The love of the oppressed for itself still seems a dire extremity.

Recently a prominent feminist told me "we want to sweep the lesbian issue under the rug." I didn't think to say I suppose you'd like to sweep the black issue under the rug too. The movement abounds in surprises and contradictions and the only liberated comments I've seen recently came out of a *sunday times* book review by one helen vendler who teaches in boston and writes books about yeats and wallace stevens anyway in the *times* she was reviewing a $75 biographical dictionary called *notable amerikan women, 1607–1950,* and writing along like this: 'Like the euphemisms about nervous afflictions, euphemisms about sexual relations abound in these biographies. Only sluts and adventuresses like Lola Montez or Maria Monk or Victoria Woodhull, ladies of unconcealedly scandalous life, are said to have lovers. Other ladies (Edna St Vincent Millay, for instance) have 'friends' or men who 'propose marriage to them . . .' The euphemisms about Lesbianism are perhaps in many cases unavoidable, since one hesitates to invoke the word 'Lesbian' or to imply sexual relations when often none took place. However, there is many a lady in these pages who has a 'close friend' with whom she 'shares a life,' who becomes 'closely attached' to 'an attractive woman several years her junior,' who writes 'a long series of deeply affectionate letters,' who finds a helper who 'devotes her life to her older, more talented friend,' and so on. The trouble with all this is that it implies that sex is absent from the lives of these women, while covertly recognizing the quasi-marital nature (and therefore the sexual base) of these living arrangements. Even when explicit Lesbianism, including sexual relations, is demonstrated in standard biographies (as in Bridgman's recent book on Gertrude Stein), *Notable American Women* shies away from the fact: Alice B. Toklas is said to have served Gertrude Stein as 'confidante, typist, critic, and finally, as nurse.' The inference is that ladies only want confidantes, typists and, finally, nurses, when as everybody knows they want lovers like everyone else. The euphemism in Stein's case is made the more useless by an appended sentence referring to Hemingway's 'not so subtle hints about the nature of the relationship between the Misses Stein and Toklas'.'' Did the *times* know what they were getting that week or were they aggressively making reparations for their didion article. Vendler refers to Robert Bridgman's book on Stein (*Gertrude Stein in Pieces*), a book by the way which does much to deliver Stein from the scandal of the critical conspiracy of silence over her sexuality by analyzing in detail every aspect of Stein's life as it related to her work without due emphasis on one aspect or another, thus integrating her sexuality as one essential component in her life with the matter-of-fact respect traditionally accorded any straight person of letters. Those "not so subtle hints about the nature of the relationship" quoted by Vendler are the polite euphemisms for the virulent and still unquestioned prejudice. Vendler's allusion to "a long series of deeply affectionate letters" passed between "close friends" reminds me of a passage in a fine book I read recently about Gabrielle Russier, the french woman who suicided shortly after her imprisonment and retreat to a sanatorium over her celebrated affair with her 16 year old male student. The author remarks: ". . . her prison friendship with Muriel was a curious one. In a way, this girl, who was 18, seems to have become a nonsexual substitute for Christian . . . when they were parted Gabrielle wrote her letters that seem oddly intense . . . described as 'poetic' the letters were pedantic, flowery, romantic." Why nonsexual. Would the author so automatically say nonsexual if the "substitute" had been a male? Isn't it just as fanciful to say nonsexual as sexual where no concrete evidence exists, as I assume in this case it didn't? The clue in any event to the author's (and society's) problem is in this statement pertaining to Gabrielle's treatment in prison: ". . . because her hair was cut very short, like a boy's, the most spiteful of the prisoners put the word around that she was a lesbian. Odious comments and remarks were made in her presence." Here are three related statements by amerikan feminists, this first appearing in an essay in the current *massachusetts review* by cynthia griffin wolff called stereotypes of women in literature.

>". . . in addition to their sex-linked inadqeuacy, ambitious women were often portrayed as sexually perverse. Sue Bridehead is not a lesbian, but she is certainly frigid. Hermione and Gudrun (in Lawrence's *Women in Love*) are sexual grotesques. Even George Eliot's heroines tend to channel their sexual forces into unhealthy directions until they have recognized and accepted the essentially domestic quality of their talents. The notion that a liberated woman must be sexually

aberrant is, of course, still with us: and female intellectuals are labeled promiscuous or lesbian according to the fantasies of the accuser."

This second is in the same review and it's a letter addressed to carrington by j.j. wilson in answer to the publication *Carrington: letters and extracts from her diaries*, chosen and with an introduction by David Garnett. j.j. wilson writes:

". . . would a woman editor have dwelled quite as much on your sexual 'problem' . . . ? I can guarantee that she would not have used the evidence that you had deep attachments to your women friends, that you hated your period that you adored your brother, that you loved a man who couldn't wouldn't ball you, that you married a man you didn't love, that you loved some men you didn't marry, and that you often felt guilty for spoiling the joy in a relationship, to declare you 'an unconscious lesbian'"(!)

Do we have to rely on the men (Bridgman, Virgil Thomson, etc.) to identify our lesbians? Can we continue to rely on the women to be the chief guardians of the closet. How long will it be impossible for me to relay the casual information (gossip, if prohibitive) relayed to me by susan sontag about simone de beauvoir? Why should any information about anybody be damaging? And so on. My third example by an amerikan feminist is from a bookpamphlet *sisters in struggle 1848–1920* by debby woodroofe:

"During the day, each would take her turn watching Stanton's five children while the other wrote. Their relationship was one of deep sisterhood. Unsympathetic historicans have been unable to understand the sisterly feelings of suffragists such as Stanton and Anthony and cannot refrain from speculating that this prowoman impulse must have passed over into lesbianism. They refer to Stanton as a 'spouse surrogate' for the unmarried Anthony. Feminists today, rediscovering sisterhood with other women, reject the arrogance of the male historians whose ideology made closeness into scandal and demanded the isolation of women from each other."

A feminist from the beginning with at least a more diplomatic if not enlightened line about lesbianism told me recently she wanted to write an essay called susan b. anthony was a lesbian but she couldn't locate any concrete evidence. The deterred author is gloria steinem and I think her original diplomacy has more recently been contaiminated by some political understanding (horrors) of the lesbian position I don't really know but I'm always optimistic. I told her in turn that I'm currently more tolerant of the straight woman problem and she said tolerant? The feminist newspapers excepting of course the lesbian tags are not noteworthy exceptions to the general straight woman problem. Here's a reference to steinem and the straight media in a recent issue of *off our backs*: "there was also the inference that Gloria had joined forces with a radical lesbian faction of the women's movement and planned to turn women's liberation into Amazon Nation." I'll have to ask her. I really think she's still an Integrationist, but I'm looking forward to a personal/political rapprochement between the two objectives. I don't see why we can't maintain one extreme objective which incorporates aspects of the "other" positions or at least while listening attentively to maneuver ourselves into intelligent debate. One chief obstacle to a dialogue right now is that lesbians are so vastly outnumbered and still so discriminated against by society at large that lesbians are righteously (and rightfully) inflamed by the slightest off remark by a straight woman who by definition retains the position of privilege in the ranks of women as things stand now. I have more evidence and more everything on the subject and no more time this week . . .

—*October 12, 1972*

R. D. Laing: The Misteek of Sighcosis

All that is certain about "mental illness" is that some people assert that other people have it. (Morton Schatzman)

Not since approaching Richard Alpert in '69 have I felt it furthered me to see "the great man." Approaching R. D. Laing last week was for me something of an exercise temporarily discarding a new frame of consciousness for an earlier one still very much with me but not so visible or accessible. Thus I approached with a certain ambivalence. I should've seen the man in '69 when I was in london and made inquiries and went out to kingsley hall and let it go at that. He seemed as unavailable as the queen. It was just as well. Had I located him I think I would've been prostrating myself as a sort of "patient" and my mission essentially was a lonely one, I spent a week in a fancy hotel reading oedipus rex and dissolving in the bathtub and then bought an old black ford prefec and went traveling into myself into the heart of france accompanied part of the time by a very young british boy who made the big trek to india and acted as my "great man." We were certainly always into some great man or other. The addition of Laing to my roster was a fairly recent one. It must've been '67 that a fellow in new york put *The Divided Self* into my hands, and that was the year that *The Politics of Experience* had become available in this country. I didn't read *The Divided Self* at that time and I resisted reading *The Politics of Experience* because it was written by a psychiatrist. I didn't have to wonder what a psychiatrist could possibly offer me at that time. So far as I was concerned the entire profession was a shuck and the sooner western civilization had done with it the better. And I didn't think so because I was a woman, I had not then linked the profession with the patriarchal status quo, I thought so because I had been personally brutalized by it, and although I respected other people's judgments of themselves being helped by going to somebody's office, I didn't think *any* of these doctors in offices could be trusted when the chips were down, I mean I knew they were all in collusion with the hospital-prison system. I had witnessed the entire system in its operations at every level and I knew. The primary function of the profession was (is) to help people "adjust" to their roles in the self denying hierarchical structures of this scarcity oriented work-pressed society and to lock them up if they couldn't. Helping was to help people function better. A person was thought to be "breaking down" when it was observed that they weren't functioning. Other expressions, of violence and withdrawal and apparent unintelligibility, were naturally viewed as acts of defiance accompanying the inability to function and threatening the social order (represented in the authority of the psychiatrist) and requiring punitive corrective measures to maintain the general level of fear and terror at the possibility of one's own individual deviation. The attainment of true individuality through therapy was either a thing of the past or the privilege of the rich or a rare misunderstanding of certain deeply concerned people like carl jung who in any case had an unusual historical grasp of prototypical figures of deliverence in the dramas of rebirth; but this is a mystical tradition to which the psychiatric profession never laid claim, outside of such exceptions as jung the profession emerged as the guardian and the beneficiary of the state. An army of medical bureaucrats. Here and there a stray individual who had suffered who happened to have the same credentials. Such a one was wilhelm reich too, one driven mad if not by his own perceptions by the opposition to them within and without the profession. In scotland in the '50s another such a one was emerging and this was Ronald Laing from a poor middle class family in glasgow. By the mid-'60s Laing was in london at the center of a revolutionary group of ex-"psychiatrists" developing the communal idea of their vision at this place called kingsley hall in a working class section of london a place where people could go and freak out or "go down" as Mary Barnes put it anyway to *have* this experience that the psychiatric profession cum society has been so determined to prevent people from having. This was 1965. As Joseph Berke the amerikan trained doctor who "assisted" Mary Barnes put it "Ronnie and his friends and colleagues very much wanted to get a house in which they could live and personally provide an efficient life support system for one or two people who would be undergoing a psychosis 'trip'" and as he said of himself ". . . to *stop* acting towards others as taskmaster for some agency of institutionalized brutality." 1965. A pivotal year for the mind of the western world. It isn't insignificant that while Laing and his associates were launching their freakout center in london the psychedelic movement in amerika was going into full bloom. People like me just happened to be in the wrong place. It was one thing to go off the end on an acid trip but it was still quite another to go on one of those unpremeditated journeys identified as madness. What was happening in the west in the '60s was an unprecedented convergence of two traditions: drugs and madness. The one was elucidating the other and together constituting the first widespread challenge to the civilized insanity of western rationalism. A number of individuals had made the proper connection between the psychedelics and states of madness or so-called schizophrenia, but this was not popular information, and if you made it yourself it seemed the wildest supposition, thus Laing's *The Politics of Experience* was the first official news linking the two experiences although he never actually says so in the book it's clear that the model for his revolutionary view of madness is the psyche-delic one, transposing as he did the psychedelic terminology (guides, trips etc) onto the madness experience and coming up with an apocalyptic vision comparable to the great pronouncements of high priest timothy leary regarding the purgative effects of the psyche-delics. Popularly a good fullranging acid junket was considered an induced "psychosis." A year ago I wrote that having read *The Politics of Experience* again recently I was disappointed that Laing wasn't explicit about the source of his revelation and transposition. It was either in high priest or the politics of ecstasy that leary described his meeting and tripping with laing in millbrook and later in london and in 1969 richard alpert told me about flying to london and triping with laing so I concluded that laing must've been protecting himself professionally by coming on as the high priest of madness without any direct personal infirmation as to how he got there and I determined to ask him why. Any Laingophile can find a logical continuity between his earlier books *The Divided Self* and *Self and Others* written in the late '50s and *The Politics of Experience* written roughly from '61 to '64 although not available here until '67. Yet the break between the books is such a before and after affair that you *know* the transition must've been another modernday crucifixion and conversion number. The question was was the man revolutionizing the profession or was he just going round the bend or what. The profession itself reacted with predictable hysteria and dismissal. As Laing said on the cavett show november 9 95 per cent of professors of psychology in this country declared that he was a dangerous lunatic at large. The threat to the profession was perfectly expressed in a book published last year called *R. D. Laing & Anti-Psychiatry* which sums up the range of agreement with and antagonism toward Laing's positions and pronouncements. A respectable member of the profession one Theodore Lidz for openers said he had relatively little quarrel with *The Divided Self.* While he considered the book a different type of approach than he would use, he thought it a "brilliant work" that "held out the promise of a really great mind in our profession." He went on, "*Politics of Experience,* on the other hand, is a wild and whirling commentary that demonstrates little grasp of the reality of human development." Within a few years it appeared Laing had turned traitor to the profession. How had this happened? How had a brilliant young scotsman obviously on his way as an important figure *within* the profession been so foolish as to turn his back on an already considerable reputation by writing a crazy book like *The Politics of Experience?* Why is the profession still so threatened? This same fellow Lidz I think provides the answer, saying things like "the idea of breaking down distinctions between doctor and patient doesn't appeal to me at all." Or "I was upset at first when I found that Laing was writing for a general public rather than for a professional audience." Or "I think *The Politics of Experience* is doing a real disservice to a number of people who take it very seriously. I am speaking of the notion that it is good to be schizophrenic, or that one should force himself into a psychotic experience." There you have the three central expressions of the problem: A man anxious to maintain his role as doctor will be just as anxious to withhold the "secrets" of the profession from the public and that includes the necessity at all costs of upholding the notion that there is actually something called schizophrenia. A doctor needs a patient to complete his identity, I'm reminded of genet's judge pleading with the thief to go on being a thief, and a doctor needs his profession to institutionalize and legitimize that identity, and the profession needs a terminology to label those objects, the patients, through whom they've established their identity in the superior authoritative half of the bargain. I've observed before and so does one of Laing's colleagues in this collection of essays I mentioned the name-calling nature of the psychiatric text-books. And I've experienced this situation that Joseph Berke refers to: If his "patients" claim they are not ill they challenge his pretensions . . . mental patients can find themselves in a special bind. To get out of the hospital, or to ease their life within it, they must show acceptance of the place accorded them, and the place accorded them is to support the occupational role of those who appear to force this bargain. Endquote. Most "patients" have been successfully brainwashed into a career as patients. Those who haven't and who become temporarily trapped by the profession may view themselves like the blacks as political prisoners and indeed they are. In 1965 for no reason other than that I had gone out of my mind (or into it) I was locked into a gray walled dungeon with no way out and shot full of paraldyhyde and 1000 mcs of thorazine and locked into a cell within the dungeon a room containing a peestained mattress and the dents of bludgeoning heads and trussed up to a bed and laced up into a straightjacket and left to die for the night I did and I've never been the same since I'm just beginning to get in touch with the phobia I acquired in one night's time an elevator problem is the least of it and I stand as witness for thousands like me for whom *The Politics of Experience* came like a belated vindication against our censure and invalidation by the Modern Inquisition. I've written in this paper before that people like me were leaning out of our disaster areas waiting for *any* parchment of evidence to verify our trips, just to indicate that we had actually been someplace, never mind that we saw something interesting where we went and that there might be some value in it. The total invalidation of the "inner journey" by the psychiatric profession was a damnation from which few were lucky enough to recover. And you couldn't expect any help from your friends, who believed in the profession. They'd be "kind" to you as a "sick person" but they weren't about to find anything interesting about your trip, much less think you'd actually been anyplace, except to the bin, which was a legitimate enough place to go since they helped to send you there. It is then in the continued spirit of the refusal to respect *other* people's experiences and these same *other* people's *assessment* of their experiences that the critics of Laing have the exquisite gall to go right on trying to tell us all what's good for us, i.e., in this *R. D. Laing & Anti-Psychiatry* book:

> "Bright young schizophrenics, like bright young people generally, are interested in reading about their condition. From the vast and varied selection of literature available to them, they appear to show a marked preference for a book called *The Politics of Experience.* The authors, like other members of the 'square' older generation, are of the opinion that they know what is best, and that this book is not good for these patients."(!)

The authors are miriam siegler, humphrey osmond, and harriet mann. The authors would still be telling us what's best for us.

> "Laing's psychedelic model is its implication that schizophrenics will benefit from being seen as persons embarked on a voyage of self-discovery. It would be closer to the truth to see most of them as voyagers who have been shanghaied, for unknown reasons, on to a ship which never reaches port."

Exactly. But not for the reasons provided by the authors, who note the voluntary aspect of psychedelic voyages as compared to the spontaneous nature of the psychotic episode, concluding that any involuntary trip (uncontrolled, unplanned) is necessarily bad, like being "shanghaied . . . on a ship which never reaches port." For one thing it's quite rare, in fact as I see it apochryphal, that anybody on a voyage, whether shanghaied or not, doesn't come back, it's impossible really to go anyplace you can't get back from, I'm not completely certain about this, I just don't know anybody who didn't "come back." (I just read this bit of corroboration in David Cooper's *Death of the Family*: "I have never known one person who did not go fully into his particular madness and come out of it within about ten days, given a certain lack of interference in the guise of treatment.") At one time a few centuries ago in europe mad people were herded onto ships of fools and these ships of course never did reach port, and this is not a bad description of contemporary psychiatric practices by which innocent people abroad in their minds are deterred (or "shanghaied" if you will) from reaching port by coercive detours to familiar dumping grounds of social neurotic adaption. My own cliché for this experience has been that my trips were aborted until I did it myself and went the whole way round and back to port in my own good time and without significant interference from those who like to tell people where to go and how to do it, and the port I reached then naturally was precisely the place these people are determined to prevent you from arriving at. I mean the port of some semblance of detachment from the great civilized neurosis of normalcy. Cooper says what we all have to do in our first-world context is to liberate ourselves personally by a Madness Revolution and I agree. He says we can perhaps talk about "madness," which is the genocidal and suicidal irrationality of the capitalist mode of governing people, and "Madness," which is the individual tentative on the part of actual, identifiable people to make themselves ungoverned and ungovernable — not by undisciplined spontaneity, but by a systematic reformation of our lives that refuses aprioristic systematization but moves through phases of destructuring, unconditioning, de-educating, and de-familializing ourselves, so that we at last get on familiar but unfamilial terms with ourselves and are then ready to restructure ourselves in a manner that refuses all personal taboos and consequently revolutionizes the whole society. Speaking of Cooper and his book *The Death of the Family* I recommend the current flick *Wednesday's Child* in which we can see all of our parents in caricature in their collusive authoritative madness which society calls sanity. These parents "know what's best" for their child, and this child is torn apart by her need to become herself and to satisfy her parent's expectations at the same time. It's an understatement to say that the tradition of Laing and his colleagues stresses that civilization impedes the development of human potential. As Berke puts it we're up against a whole society which is systematically driving its members mad. I would go further and say that most all of us are mad practically from the start, and by mad I mean what Cooper means, that madness cultivated in every family to ensure the proper functioning of its offspring, and that madness which is the effective uncoupling of our inner and outer realities with a persistent valuation placed on the outer such that our inner worlds recede and shrivel up and petrify in forgotten ruins beneath a one-dimensional reality of consciousness devoted to a grasp of concrete things and objective facts and goals and principles. We are, as Laing wrote in *The Politics of Experience*, socially conditioned to regard total immersion in outer space and time as normal and healthy. Thus the madness with a capital M that Cooper refers to is this fantastic eruption at some later stage of living of that forgotten inner world, I suppose a kind of convulsive involuntary natural effort of the organism to reunite the inner and the outer by grandly retreating from the familiar outer and embarking dangerously on a voyage through the regions of the lost interior, regions traditionally accessible to people identified as crazy visionary artists, say. A well-known passage in Laing's own visionary work reads "We respect the voyager, the explorer, the climber, the space man. It makes far more sense to me as valid project — indeed, as a desperately and urgently required project for our time — to explore the inner space and time of consciousness." *Humanity is estranged from its authentic possibilities.* — The reason the psychiatric profession proper finds Laing's *The Politics of Experience* so detestable is that in this work Laing was closing the gap between Self and Other (Patient and Psychiatrist) and identifying his original schizoid model of his early clinical work as the norm of human existence. Split between inner and outer, split between body and mind, split between spirit and matter, split between form and content, split between experience and behavior, and so on. As he remarked wryly on the cavett show after cavett asked if anyone here could define schizophrenia and nathan kline the Inquisitor (director of rockland state) said it was a split between feeling and thinking and behaving this description applies to most people he meets, most psychiatrists for instance. The word schizophrenia is applied indiscriminately to most anything. Laing and his associates deny that there is any such thing as schizophrenia, except as a term of personal and social invalidation. "I emphasize that schizophrenia is a term rather than a condition, and this is an important part of our work, showing how people are invalidated in their own life styles, their life experience, by having this term applied to them" (Berke). The label is a social fact and the social fact a *political event*. The person labeled is one of Them. There's Us and there's Them. The Self and the Other. The Other is the Enemy. In any interpersonal theory of psychiatry the person who gets to be deemed mad is the loser in the hide and seek games that people play as the Self and the Other. Laing is the first hero of the psychiatric profession, he gets the molten medal of honor for finding himself in the Other, and by so doing exposing the profoundly schizoid nature of the profession itself. By now I've read the early "brilliant" book *The Divided Self* and you can see how refractory the young scotsman was even then, applying as he did a Sartrean existential–phenomenological method to demonstrate the *intelligibility* of madness states, and further of perceiving the individuals held prisoner in the hospitals he attended in relation to the world around them, both at home and in the hospital setting, and not in that clinical abstract isolation by which people are instantly typed as the Other and imagined to be suffering from purely *individual* disorders. Even so, it makes me very nervous to read such a book. That Divided Self is still the Doctor and the Patient. Only a Divided Self could be so authoritative on the subject. But he was still thinking about Us. That one or the other of those two selves was you or me they were talking about, they were talking about us behind our backs again, writing us up as clinical studies for "professional audiences." Anyway the author of a work I first saw in '67 in the form of a Divided Self which I couldn't read who followed that up one year later with a work that entered the mainstream of the subversive psychedelic literature of the '60s seemed a strange man and I wanted to meet him. It didn't matter by the way that *The Divided Self* was written and printed in the late '50s. We don't all keep up with everybody's chronologies. Then when I knew the chronology better I still wanted to know how he got to *The Politics of Experience*, and why he was still hiding, in a sense. I heard he was coming to amerika for a talk tour so I arranged with difficulty to go see the man the nice woman working on his tour was afraid I'd challenge his manhood or something by bringing up a subject as irrelevant as women's liberation. She kept saying he was in very good shape. I thought he could take care of himself in any case. Better than I could take of myself. I mean it costs you something to go and see any "great man" these days. Especially any great man who claims to be one of us. I went at the ungodly sunday morning hour of 10 to room 608 at the algonquin and expressed my ambivalence as soon as I walked in the door. I'd seen him the night before at hunter college and I said so and I said it was difficult to imagine a woman sitting before such a big audience with that kind of confidence and authority and commanding that sort of ultimate attention. Any woman, that is, who isn't a "performer" in an entertainment medium. His wife, Jutta, agreed readily and he didn't say anything but he wasn't hostile either. I liked them both and made myself comfortable right away by talking about myself. I wondered suddenly what my *real* motivation was for going, and was I just presenting my credentials as a true crazy to establish a peer identity if that was possible or was I after all this time since '65 attempting to prostrate myself as a "patient" and if so was the algonquin early on a sunday morning the proper place and time for a cure. I don't know. But we got into ourselves and I had a good time and I did find out what I wanted to know basically about the morphology of *The Politics of Experience*. He said he first tripped in '60, which makes sense, and he wrote P of E between '61 and '64, and he tripped with both leary and alpert in london on different occasions in '65, and in answer to my suspicions concerning professional protection he said he was and is one of about 18 medical people in the british isles who are authorized officially by the home office to do as they will with the psychedelics and that this authority has given him a certain significant pivotal function as a buffer between the kids and the government. At some point when we were fairly deep into it, into ourselves, he said he always was peculiar. I said well the scotch are peculiar and later I told jane who said that was scotch chauvinism and that's okay I know my name is scotch and laing said yes it is. Anyway he qualified what he meant by peculiar by telling me he always was able to get into himself. I'm not sure that's how he put it. I knew what he meant. Like he could induce himself into that other world and bring himself back. If you can dig that. And he reminded me in case I didn't know which I didn't really that in *Self and Others* (also a late '50s book) he put forward the case of a 34-year-old woman in a kind of death trip lasting five months after the birth of her third child as an example of an experience of psychic disintegration and rebirth that later became the very heart of *The Politics of Experience*. "She went out of this world into another world where she was enveloped in a tapestry of symbols." — "She came back from that world of the dead and unreality, to this world of the living, in flashes of realization. She came back in the spring, after the strangest winter of her life." — These were not the remarks of any conventional doctor judge. And in fact in his commentary on the case he includes this prophetic thought: I have alluded elsewhere to the possibility that what we call psychosis may be sometimes a natural process of healing. (A view for which I claim no priority.) Possibly this was a key case, or experience, for the later visionary. I suppose the turning point was '60 and that first chemical trip. All things combined there's not such an illogical transition. What he tentatively suggested in *Self and Others* is merely realized or unfolded and evolved in *The Politics of Experience* in which he moves simultaneously into social criticism and a mystique of psychosis asserting in effect that the very states of mind that society in its delegates of psychiatrists had condemned and consigned to its jungles of justice were in reality states of grace visited on any one of us normally fucked up schizoid individuals passing by chance into forbidden territory. "No age in the history of humanity has perhaps so lost touch with this natural *healing* process that implicates *some* of the people whom we label schizophrenic. No age has so devalued it, no age has imposed such prohibitions and deterrences against it, as our own. Instead of the mental hospital, a sort of reservicing factory for human breakdowns, we need a place where people who have traveled further and, consequently, may be more lost than psychiatrists and other sane people, can find their way *further* into inner space and time, and back again." Such became the place called kingsley hall, opened in '65. At the algonquin I told Laing and his wife I went out to kingsley hall in june '69 and was quite depressed by the place and wondered what if anything went on there. They told me people very often walked in there under the impression that nothing was going on and in fact something very much was but it wasn't immediately visible. Even so, the physical structure was extremely dismal, a huge brick mausoleum of a place with a barren cavernous interior and broken windows stuffed with rags. I remember a glimpse of some big suffering christian paintings in a huge room. I was offered some undrinkable brew by a fellow who talked simultaneously about mathematics a girl friend and witchcraft and bore a heavy crucifix on a hairy chest. I saw two other people waft in and out and I left within a half hour. The paintings were Mary Barnes's paintings and the fellow was John Woods, who appears in Mary's book (*Two Accounts of a Journey Through Madness*, with Joseph Berke). I think Mary was still there when I stopped by. The place closed a year later in '70. This book by Mary Barnes and Joseph Berke is a fantastic document. The way Mary put it she had come to the place where she could "go down" to before she was born and grow up again — to come up again straight. She said it was all about coming to know what she wanted. The "right" thing had always been what someone else wanted of her. For his part Berke said Mary was the right person at the right place at the right time. As soon as he got to kingsley hall he realized that the best way to learn about psychosis would be to help Mary "do her things." Berke played the part of "good mommie" to the regressing 45-year-old woman who successfully embodied the thesis of Laing and his friends that psychosis is a potentially enriching experience if allowed to proceed full cycle, through disintegration and reintegration, or death and rebirth. Berke comments that Barnes had elected herself to the position of head guinea pig, but the nature of the experiment had been determined by *her*, that she had her "trip" all worked out for years before she ever heard of laing or berke or the rest of them. One of Laing's projects in new york this month was a showing of a movie called Asylum made at the quarters they acquired after kingsley hall shut down. A young woman by name Julia appears to be on a trip similar to Mary's. On channel 13 after the showing the interviewer asked Laing what happened to Julia and Laing said the last he saw her she was on the continent and seemed fine and was married. I forgot to ask in turn whether he thought she was fine because she was married or what. But we did talk about feminism. I said he shouldn't say "women's lib" in amerika, supposing he said "black lib" or "black libbers" and he took note of the correction. I know he has a heavy early marxist lenin engels trotsky socialist orientation to the world and he grasped immediately the concept of "men as a class" whether this was his first introduction to the idea I don't know but he said after a few moments' pause he thought he would have to agree that sex discrimination historically preceded class distinctions in structured hierarchies. That was all, except when we were getting ready to leave I said the tour woman was afraid of my seeing him, maybe she thought I'd appear like solanas at the door with a rod at which he pantomimed the result of this kind of entrance screaming and falling backward onto the couch and clutching his balls. Suzi Gablik was there by then and she asked him to repeat the performance and he did. That wasn't all actually. I recommended Philip Slater's *The Glory of Hera* he wrote it down promptly in his record book similar to mine only bigger and he recommended a fat paperback he flashed at me *Malleus Maleficarum* concerning women and the Inquisition he said a *woman* should write this and I wrote it down in my record book similar to his only smaller. I wondered if I felt an affinity because we're both scotch and peculiar or because we've read a lot of the same types of things or because he's just a nice bloke and I like myself okay too or what. But I didn't forget my ambivalence and resentment at knocking on his door in the first place. I said in fact that I resented his credentials. He said but you have your certificate of insanity. Yeah but I want *both*. And what could he say. I mean I'm still quoting these authorities. I want to know when I get to be my own authority. For a year I worked on my crazy book surrounded by dozens of three by fours of typewritten quotes by the authorities not the least of whom was Laing and I abandoned the project to write my political book and when I start in with the crazy book again I'm promising myself not to look at a threebyfour. It isn't just the world out there that's reluctant to grant any person their own authority, it's the world inside yourself and a part of that world for me is the internalized Inquisitor of the hospital system who indicated by the most elaborate punitive modern machinery that if I thought I wasn't much of anybody before my "experience" I could be certain that what I had become was a total non person in a non environment of my own non making. The internalized Other. I don't romanticize the crazy trip any more than Laing and his people do and this is a big misunderstanding. The thing is although it isn't the perfect solution to anything, it *is* a *way* and it's a way we need to know a lot more about and I'd even hazard the thought that when we have a body of literature descriptive of the "inner journey" comparable to what we have in space and mountain and jungle and underwater exploration that we'll be a civilization on its way to recovering a lost unity of inner and outer. I mean that that would be an indication. There is something called schizophrenia and it means brokenhearted. Much of the misunderstanding concerning the word and a state or states to which it's supposed to refer has arisen over its unfortunate association with the similarly derived word: schizoid. If the latter indicates the *split* nature of all our normal functioning lives of civilized sanity, schizophrenia means to me the cataclysmic brokenhearted experience of fragmentation and disintegration of those normal processes in some weird counterdynamic of a *fusion* of all those dualities. Laing has been criticized for encouraging people to plunge into their madness and of course he does but he doesn't romanticize the state at the same time. He says madness is an understandable reaction, not a proper adjustment to the world. He's surprised actually that more people aren't screaming and having the creeps in the world we live in. He says madness is *potential* liberation and renewal. The point is that we don't even know how liberating it is yet because a shizoid culture naturally validates only its schizoid members and punishes both voluntary *and* involuntary efforts of certain of its members to (re) integrate themselves. "This process could have a central function in a truly sane society." Those who had

been there would help others to get there and to be there and to go
through there and to come back and to assist others and so on. For,
as many who've been there have said and written (including people
like Zelda Fitzgerald by the way), the sudden unexpected and
unprepared-for plunge into the forgotten ruins of the inner world
can cause great terror and confusion between inner and outer realities
and cause others to panic and take police action of some sort in
response to the "peculiar" behavior of their friends or relatives. I
suppose at some moment of exit or re-entry the moon travelers
experience this (con)fusion between this world and the other. They
might at that point wonder where they are. They've been trained for
the other world, they know what to expect, and they have plenty of
guides pressing buttons down in this world, and they have all these
back-up systems, but re-rentry is a terrific burn for the ship and I
can imagine it's a wild moment for the mind too. Burning and fusion
are the same thing. The first indication I had in '65 that I was going
someplace was a slight burn in my foot. You may think the analogy
is far-fetched, but I had a friend gene swenson who went on an
intergalactic journey in his own space ship, I've forgotten the details,
but I know he went, possibly the reason nobody believed him was
that it wasn't written up in the papers. The splashdown occurred on
the roof of his tenement on 4th street and the recovery operation
team was the local precinct police and the check-up took place at
the hospital. I suppose the astronauts get the psychological test
treatment too. And you remember originally they were locked up in
a trailer or something on the carrier after the frogmen pulled them
out of the water. The analogy breaks down at the point where you
might say gene was on a more dangerous trip since he had to
improvise his own guide and preparation system. I remember him
for example bending intently over my radio one afternoon listening
for "number signals." As for preparation there was none. The trips
were a little on the sayonara side. He did come back however. He
came back three times, and after the third time the Medical Inquisition Recovery Team and all the rest of their frogmen had at last
convinced the guy that he was a "case." He was ready then to take
their tranquilizers forever and get a nice nine to five job filing

something and wear a suit and a tie and go to a shrink very often regularly to keep himself straight. The last thing that happened was he biologically died in a carcrash in kansas with his mother. At 35 he was still going back to kansas to see his crazy parents who were never his most avid supporters. I'm sure I wasn't the only one who kept saying don't go back home gene, there's even that famous book title you can't go home again, but who were we but an extended family still telling him what not to do. I don't have any idea what the complex dynamic fuel system was that launched gene on his trips, who could ever know what that is, much less the chief passenger, but I do know that his life situation was basically untenable to himself and that a journey to "other regions" was in order and that as a one way ticket to bellevue he became a two-time loser every trip he took. No credibility anywhere. One day he came over to my loft with ann wilson who brought a taperecorder and a cardboard mobile of the galaxy she strung up from the ceiling the idea being gene was going to recount his journey but we got into kansas and the family instead somehow and somebody said what's that got to do with the big trip and I said oh it's all the same thing but I didn't know what I was talking about and even if I did we didn't know what to do really. We didn't know what to do about ourselves. The journey solution was no big deal if you couldn't come back and seriously change the conditions of the place you found it necessary to leave. No roles for the mad. The point of black elk of the oglala sioux is that the "illness" of black elk as a young boy, his passage into the ancestral realm of the dead, actually *qualified* him for his future assumption of the role of healer of the tribe. Who else in fact could "make whole" if not the one who had "been there" if by whole we mean the (re)unification of all our past presents and futures. By contrast the artauds in wasichu land are a weird breed of outcast, tormented by the keepers of real time and real place. And if the old indians could read and witness some of our stumbling efforts to recover ourselves I wonder what they'd make of it, i.e., a passage like this out of david cooper's *Psychiatry and Anti-Psychiatry* ('67): I shall concentrate on afterdeath experiences within the biological life span. These occur in so-called psychosis, in experience called mystical, in dreams, and in certain drug states. Also they can occur, rarely, in certain waking states where the person is not engaged in any of the four types of experiences that I have expressed above in a hateful language of categorization. — Maybe this is what we have to go through in order to get back there. I don't mind cooper myself since he's been there personally. When in fact all these doctors go there and the personal testimonies begin to replace the clinical studies, the patients liberating their doctors as it were, the self recognizing self in other, we'll have the makings of some authentic initiation ceremonials into our cosmic heritage as members of the primeval slime. Whatever you say about leary he's a true madman, he's one who did it, he forfeited his earned rights to the rewards of a mad culture, he can't come back any more than gene could, but he created something of a role for himself out of the credentials he had, out of *that credibility*, his experience as a professional in matters of the psyche in fact was not only a credit but a certain sort of preparation as a successful navigator of his own trips. Problems of control. Problems of navigation over an eight hour period however not being the same as for three weeks or five months. The thing is in a sense that we're not able to realize yet that the profession through these fellows did remain intact. A bunch of doctors of psychology went 'round the bend not too long (about 10 years after) the momentous invention of acid in that laboratory in switzerland, an event that put them in touch with the ancient religious traditions of the profession, that is, with its potential shamanistic functions of exorcism and deliverance, long predating its modern police function as guardian of the state. Laing's analogies between the Inquisition and the Modern Psychiatric Profession should be well taken. It was a bit spooky to see a medieval Inquisitor facing a modern shaman as it were, on the cavett show no less. It wasn't hard to catch who was who. The one a kind of transmigrated viennese patriarch (nathan kline), the other a scotch mystic, the two in the middle (cavett and rollo may) ordinary confused men of our times, may's big line is that society is crumbling (oh dear oh dear, and his jowls quiver a little, like a disbelieving old maid aunt), cavett hopping around for answers in front of his not too well concealed layers of masks, as I saw it quite threatened by the scotch mystic whom he sensed rightly to be capable of penetrating those layers, and who was as Laing told me a few days later probably relieved and appreciative that Laing didn't take advantage of the vulnerability. Anyway the classic antagonists being Laing and kline. Laing:

> ". . . who sets the computer . . . who controls the system that determines who needs treatment . . . sometimes the patient thinks the psychiatrist needs treatment and then the psychiatrist takes account of this as proof of how much treatment the patient needs . . . who is to administer treatment . . . who is the transgressor? . . . who is out of line . . . and out of place . . . who should get back to their corner and stay there . . . should we give treatment to the president (those who are really *at* it [applause] or to those who drop out and say I'm checking out, and I'm not coming back) . . . who would be giving 'Tranquilizers' to whom in the days of the witches . . . 100,000 women a year killed . . ."

And up kline with his medieval reflexes: "Many of these women were self confessed witches. Today we would view these people as mentally ill." It went on like that and it was all very clear. We exchanged some remarks about the man at the algonquin, I said he's a scary character. Jutta (Laing's wife) said he was extremely threatening, Laing said you have to back off from these guys, I said yeah but I think anyway he's more threatening to women and we dropped it. Laing was never an inmate at rockland state, but he makes the proper historical connections. And he didn't let the impotency question raised by cavett into the hands of the inquisitor. He took charge of it right off. Q: Can the startling rise of the women's movement be responsible for male impotence? A: It was said in the old days that men's penises had disappeared and sometimes other people couldn't see them either and this was called *bewitchment* and the *Hunt* is still going on . . . to blame women for our own ineffectualness. Agreement by rollo may (society is crumbling anyway) and change the subject. End topic. I wasn't ready to get into the women aspect of the whole crazy question and the profession etc. I was trying to restrict myself to sorting out the males, in so doing the level of my ramblings is post-revolutionary, as though we're all people again and nobody takes count that these people we're talking about are in fact males. There are two healing traditions in the west and one of them is female and that was wiped out and that was actually the tradition of the witch. Certainly the witches were the midwives and had charge of all matters concerning women and childbirth. The professions are presently mightily confused. What is thought by many to be a psychiatric profession is in reality a law enforcement agency. Hospital treatment is exclusively moral. To frame the activities within a medical model a trial is called an "examination" and a judgment a "diagnosis" and a sentence a "disposition" and a correction "treatment." The lost true profession is the ceremonial deliverance of childbirth and all true doctors are midwives. The grave of the self opens and a child is born again. Birth and death are the same event. The "inner journey" is in reality a return to the labyrinth of the womb or tomb. "The process of entering into *the other* world from this world, and returning to *this* world from the other world, is as natural as death and giving birth or being born" (Laing). We might thus understand better the great (con)fusion that may occur at moments of exit and entry. The burning up of the ship. The demolition of the boundaries between self and other. The re-entry into mother. The movie played backward. The splash-down on the roof of a tenement. The launching pad at carnavarel. The carnival of comings and goings. All this and purgatory too. The death-in-life situation of the normal dead(ly) civilized condition is a desperate clinging to life in fear of the death that has already happened countless times. *The Dreadful Has Already Happened.* It's a memory problem. We've been sleeping for centuries. How do we get lost and become ourselves at the same time. To be both separate and the same. To be at once the mother and not the mother. To become one's own mother. Pure Mind. "In certain forms of 'psychotic' experience there is, at the height of the experience, a pure anoia in which the 'outside' becomes continuous with itself through the 'inside' so that all sense of self is lost" (Cooper). The terror of the loss of self. The madness of it. The birth of our selves from our false selves, our social selves. As Mary Barnes says, we go from false self, to madness, to sanity. The dire extremity of madness as a last ditch solution. The burning up of the masks. A little egg of a self inside a box inside a box inside. The chinese boxes. The dissolution of their walls. Going further back down to the Void. The Matrix. The Chaos. "Human societies in diverse times and places have relied upon a method of 'psychotherapy' which western man has forgotten and suppressed: the return to Chaos" (Schatzman). There is now a new (old) male tradition of therapeutic ritual rebirth, the gravedigger and the midwife, in one, the assistant at the delivery, the old men at their own tribal initiation ceremonial pushing their members through some surrogate male legs. To become their own mothers. To come. To deny the mother. The question now I think is what about the mothers. What about feminism. The delivery of Mary Barnes by a male midwife is really something. And I think Laing and his associates have been all along particularly sympathetic to women, but that doesn't mean they would encourage or even permit the (re)emergence of the female healing tradition proper. In all their writings to date their feminist consciousness is totally marginal. They know about the sorry state of women but their political understanding of the world stops with socialism. It isn't fair, at the same time, to criticize their early writings on feminist grounds, if most of us here were not exposed to feminism before '68 or '69 why should they have been and what can the males do with it anyhow. What in any case can this handful of crazy doctors do. I blurted across the hotel room to laing's wife Why didn't YOU go to Ceylon? Last year Laing spent two months in a monastery in ceylon in intensive mind training. The doctors have been going east too. *Orientation is knowing where the orient is.* The control mastery of the yogin. The craft of dying in the tibetan book of the dead. The males wandering into their sanctity. Over the dead bodies of women. The womb traffic is heavy. I didn't have to argue with Laing and his wife, who did in fact go to ceylon to visit, and Laing demonstrated her reception there, the monks would shake her hand, with body and glance averted. I said the same thing goes on here and he replied well at least they're up front about it there. Behind every great woman is a man, uh rather a woman.

Most of those accused of being witches were women . . . the whole campaign against witches was permeated with the spirit of aversion toward women. Civitas dei. Civitas diaboli. The law enforcement agency of the Inquisition in its older form of the Church and its new form of the Modern Psychiatric Profession is primarily an agency to keep women in their place and exterminate them if they can't. The office procedures represent the initial stages. The hospitals the final solution. I didn't mention that gene swenson was homosexual. He had an Inquisition installed in his Head. By the sights of family and state he was a Bad One. He had a normal false self system that occasionally just crumbled. Being pedestrian about it they say he'd be labeled insane because he would be seen as trying to escape from "crazy" or disturbing relationships (read "society") and that was true and he went to the orient too, he was very involved in chinese characters and confusions. "One is even tempted to ponder on the daring hypothesis that in the 'psychotic' families the identified schizophrenic patient member by his psychotic episode is trying to break free of an alienated system and is, therefore, in some sense less 'ill' or at least less alienated than the 'normal' offspring of the 'normal' families. In so far as he enters a mental hospital, however, his desperate attempt to liberate himself would seem to fail in terms of his deficiency in the necessary social tactics and strategy" (Cooper). Problems of control. Moving from false self to madness to sanity. A midwife at this point in civilization seems imperative. It's a mother problem all the way around. The bad mother is rampant in the Laing and Esterson book *Sanity, Madness and the Family*. There's no analysis of how she got that way. That's why I recommended Philip Slater's *The Glory of Hera* because I think he's one contemporary writer (male that is) dealing with the hopeless position of the mother in the family, and state. I also think Laing is finding out something about feminism and that eventually the orient and the new therapy and the new sexual politics are going to merge into a comprehensive political-psychological theory and counter consciousness that will be a more effective subversive deviation from the patriarchal authoritative hierarchical law enforcement reality oriented materialistic sexually repressive fucked up culture in which we live. I can see the

Laing people for instance getting together with the radical therapists in amerika, a sexually mixed group which puts out a rag called *rough times* (originally called the *Radical Therapist*) there's quite a bit of heavy sexual political consciousness. In a paperback collection of theirs called *The Radical Therapist* there's quite a few essays by feminists, including Mary Barnes (feminist?). In an Editorial Judith Brown says Male supremacist behavior in psychiatry and psychology is perceived by radical feminists as one of the single largest enemies of women's interests. Maybe the two groups are blending already. Berke and Schatzman are in the book too. I don't know. A Madness Revolution. Berke:

> "The reason why most psychiatrists are unable to communicate with people who have entered the deeper levels of regression is that they do not utilize their own enormous reservoirs of primitive emotion to make contact with such individuals. They try to force the other to speak in rational modalities long after he or she has decided to declaim in an 'irrational' tongue. And I do not mean by irrational unintelligible. I am referring to the language of the infant, the melodies of primary feeling, which are, in themselves, quite comprehensible."

A stray case of normality!

—*November 30, 1972*

Delitism, Stardumb, & Leadershit

On Saturday December 16 beginning 9:30 a.m. at McMillan Theatre of Columbia University 116th st. and Broadway will commence a conference for women only called A Feminist Lesbian Dialogue: Is the Sexual Political? — This is an unpaid political announcement. I thought up the idea a few centuries ago and then asked a couple of columbia women if they'd help launch the thing and locate the spaces for it and we met over orange juice & vodka one sunday at noon at max's which wasn't officially open and then we called a meeting which caused instant widespread agitation and dissatisfaction since the entire dyke community coast to coast was not invited. I think basically there was a misunderstanding as to the nature of the meeting that we were meeting to confer when in reality we intended to meet to organize. The intention itself it seems is always suspect in these situations. That is, who intended what, and by what prerogative, and for whom, or on whose behalf. The main thing is that when a group forms it's elitist and when it dissolves it's democratic. Since elitism is worse than the plague anyone involved in a group is asking for lots of trouble from the more indeterminate group at large until the group shows signs of internal disintegration which was true of our group immediately. I don't like groups myself. I prefer being lost in china without a friend to being found in a room with a group. I like the illusion that I'm not accountable to anybody but myself for whatever I decide to do, for example being permanently lost in china, and I feel bound and gagged by the consensus reality of a group. Nonetheless I thought this feminist lesbian thing was extremely important and that I should submit to being bound and gagged for a couple of months while the group decided all manner of things including the size and color and quality of its paper cups. That's for the dance in the evening. There is a dance and it begins at 8 and I don't even know what particular place on campus it's been designated to happen. That's how much I have to do with it by now. The group took over totally. The group isn't even a true group any more. A true group is defined by its membership boundaries. Whether it's a group of a certain permanency with a title and officials or a group like ours which was constituted for a specific function. The boundaries of this group dissolved and that was my intention. There's only one group I feel I belong to really and that's the group called women. I feel I have more in common with women than with frogs or grasshoppers or men. If I was seriously upset being lost in china I'd go looking for my bowl of soup at a nunnery. The women there may be nuns, but they're still my political peer group. I mean it doesn't matter what these women do with their bods, whether they do anything or not, since we have so much in common politically and we have the same basic equipment by which in fact we came to be identified as women who by virtue of this very equipment constitute that political group. After all, this was the revelation of feminism. We always knew we weren't frogs, but it was never clear that we weren't men. We were all one group and we were called *man kind*. Some women are beginning to wonder now if we don't actually have more in common with such specious as crustaceans than with men. That may be an idle thought, but crustaceans and women alike are not given to erecting skyscrapers. Crustaceans and skyscrapers aside, we are now eager to delineate the boundaries of the group called women by the maintenance of a collective deviant identity as it were as it were as it was. Anyway I couldn't see organizing a conference with the entire group, it just isn't practical. I'm not a practical person particularly but I have some rudimentary knowledge of organization procedure required in the selection of paper cups. I dislike meetings for purposes other than parties and I knew dimly that a meeting of 40 or 100 women or so to determine such items as cups or any other apparently serious matters would enlarge the scope of our involvement to unbearable durations. Sadly however there is yet in our society no authentic authority in a spontaneous group. There is therefore a certain tacit permission accorded any organizational group under the auspices of its known establishments, i.e. NOW, or Radical Feminists, which is currently organizing a conference on Marriage. Any ad hoc alliance is automatically elitist. It's an insult to choose yer own friends. I don't know how important all of this is. I have a rather theatrical orientation to life. In my theatre days I received numerous invitations from people to attend their events or whatever they called them. Somebody obviously would have an idea for doing something and then often as not they would ask other people to collaborate on it and then finally they would invite the population at large to come and observe and/or participate in the results. We could have hundreds of these conferences. The reaction from certain elements of the dyke community seemed to be that this was the only conference in the world that there ever was or would be. Not only is this not the ultimate conference but its actual occurrence will be as illusory as every other insomuch as the feminist/lesbian revolution is an ongoing conference and that any particular conference merely represents a kind of formal acknowledgment of a general consciousness. The theatre parallel may be insensitive, considering the global moral issues that seem to be at stake, and the emotional investment in revolution, in which context an event is more than an evening's entertainment, an event concerning issues about which each of us is an expert. The leadership problem in the movement may be second to none, and it's related to the credibility of static or spontaneous groups. As would be expected most more or less permanent (static) groups defer to an elected leadership. Such groups, having a hierarchial structural affinity with the basic institutions of oppression, are well qualified to attack these very institutions with social and legislative reform. The leadership problem is mobilized around the conflict between the essential ideological rejection of authority and the necessity of getting things done, as well as all psychological vestiges of conditioned dependencies on authoritative leadership. The praxis of the woman's movement has devolved upon process as opposed to product, on collectivism as distinct from hierarchic forms of engagement. The consciousness raising group is a leaderless structure par excellence. These structures and the revelation of feminism, that we have a common problem and that is in being women, make sensible reflections of each other. The anxiety generated over any incipient leadership springs I think from the threat such leadership may be seen to pose to our common political condition which transcends our old individual sense of wothlessness. That is, leadership threatens our solidarity by triggering old responses of worthlessness in relation to the very real oppression of static appointed elected assumed leadership in the real world of male authority. At the bottom the problem in all the worlds is distinguishing between authentic and inauthentic authority. The authority of any authority person in the world in which we grew up is granted by arbitrary social definition rather than on the basis of any real expertise that a person may possess. As Adrienne Rich says in this essay I just read in the *New York Review of Books* ". . . authority derives from a person's status — father, teacher, boss, lawgiver — rather than from his personal qualities." She's talking about the family and the patriarchy, and she makes the all important point that the sacredness of this institution — "sacred in the sense that it is heresy to question its value — relieves the titular head of it from any real necessity to justify his behavior." It has been in fact by *this* system that we all came to feminism as worthless individuals militantly aligned against authority. Thus the failure to distinguish between spontaneous leadership and static authority is an understandable one. Some feminists, specifically two lesbian/feminists that I know of, Martha Shelley and Rita Mae Brown, have tried to define the difference between stardom and leadership without projecting the possible conditions of leadership. Besides that, a star is not necessarily not a leader and vice versa, although the distinction they've brought to attention is a valuable consideration. Anyway inherent in the distrust of leadership is the automatic association of leadership with domination. No doubt the central characteristic of authentic leadership is the relinquishing of the impulse to dominate others, but this is not a quality of leadership to which we've been exposed. To lead and not to dominate seem like contradictions in terms. Yet the women's movement has been productive. I mentioned the reform type organizations, and I'm not disparaging them either. To move against the enemy utilizing the familiar organizational arrangements of the enemy is not an ineffective strategy. It's one front, rear guard or whatever. But there've been other kinds of products in the movement and I think these are the source of the greatest agony. Given as we are to process primarily, when it looks like there may be a product, the perpetrators become deviants to the tacit or overtly acknowledged leaderless underpinning of the movement. Thus one might be attempting to lead and to deny that one is doing so at the same time. A product somehow always involves identity and identity can mean status and prestige and status and prestige accruing to any particular women make other women feel worthless (again). Because the word reaches *other* women through the media and the media is male and the male media creates *stars*. A star is a certain type of appointed authority. A given position. A constant identity achieved by a particular recognized accomplishment. Another static assumed situation in other words. I need hardly mention the continuous crisis in the woman's movement between the individuals and the group over the publication of every woman's book. Possibly the most feared product of all. The next conference should be called Power Money and Fame in the woman's movement, subtitled Confessions of Some Amerikan Woman Eaters. Anyhow the worst thing about a book is that it's a solo operation, an indenfensible crime. It's also a class trip, it means you finished high school and your parents were skilled laborers and you weren't born in the tennessee appalachians. But I have more to say about this dilemma another time. I want to go on making my pointless abstractions about leadership. I can't be very specific because I don't know myself how to define or identify authentic authority, I suspect in fact that if we could we'd be making a familiar brief for the old legitimate types of authority and I think we desperately need some revolutionary forms of assertion that slip in and out of process like an eel that might suddenly and unaccountably *know* a way upstream that hadn't occurred to the others who follow along for an hour or two until that particular mission is accomplished. A person who's a source of energy and initiative in a project might be considered a natural leader and that might mean for an hour. Sometimes it's a rare minute. And it isn't necessarily Charisma. We are very often taken in by non productive charisma, in the vacuum between static authority and spontaneous leadership. All organizations tend to move in the direction of closure — hierarchical forms which transmit information through channels that run in a linear direction, from head to mass. Revolutionary structures stop short in their own linear direction, from head to toe. Chinese revolutions getting stuck at levels of static leadership. Heads or heroes replacing old heads. Positional authority replaced by charismatic authority. When the charisma fails the tendency is to regress into authoritarian modes of directing energy. A proper leader does not lead. I follow the thought of somebody because it interests me. I lead myself to china to get lost. I follow myself one day to columbia to talk about lesbian feminism. I submit to being bound and gagged for a couple of months while the group decides all manner of things including the size color & quality of its paper cups. I watch while the group takes over. I become a part of an elitist spontaneous group which shows almost immediate signs of internal disintegration. I watch while my own original idea turns into the bidding of a finally enormous group. I watch myself sometimes try to control events. I watch others on other days try to control the same or other events. I hear reports of widespread agitation and dissatisfaction. I look forward to being an irresponsible individual again, not accountable to anybody but myself.

—*December 14, 1972*

Mary Kissmas & A Hippy Nude Year

there is no god and mary was his mother. the steam was coming off the roofs and i thot we were on fire. she couldn't undertaker anything, too much light darkens the mind. there's some tactical insignificance about doing anything but living. what somebody found was incontrovertible evidence that it all means zero. that phrase predicts the pattern of our ruin. what it is that one becomes is *that* that that is that it is. certain movements we make can be distinguished clearly as being simian or reptillian or piscine or bovine. soap bubbles and the forces which mould them. people only pay attention to what they've discovered for themselves. i knew i had gangrene or leprosy of the legs and one night we remembered a childhood disease called impetigo so i rushed to the doctor who said it was poison sumac or oak or allergy related and i wasn't suppurating but giving off the serum of the cells. i applied the yellow stuff out of a one half ounce of cortisone or mycolog creme nystatin ceocymin sulfate gramidcidin triamcinolone acetonide in an aqueous perfumed vanishing cream base with polysorbate 60 alcohol aluminum hydroxide concentrated wet gel titanium dioxide glyceryl monostearate polyethylene glycol simethicone sorbic acid propylene gycol ethylenediamine hydrochloride white petroleum polyoxyethylene fatty alcohol ether methylparaben propylparaben and sorbitol solution and wrapped my legs in paper towels held together with scotch tape and went on living. we went to eat at the boston union oyster house and saw this creepy adventure flick called deliverance. i went to the 46th street docks to see gregory go away on the cristoforo colombo and eat champagne and drink fish on cracker and meet gregory's mother's stockbroker and watch the helen mcallister tugboat push them all out to harbor. i went to princeton and purchase to talk about my former life. i distribute my body in different parts of space. i internalize a series of unanswered questions as a builtin mystification abt my elemental identity. i regard a neat bundle of wood for a desk divider. i swear at the ice on the driveway. i summarize the five months of my death state. i make numerous complaints about my feelings. i decide to modify my part into a more likeable character. i try to clear away the rubble of understanding. see that it doesn't happen again. i produce a new explanation and pray to make it improbable, each of us cld rediscover the possibility of doubting our origins despire and in spit of being well brought up. i hazard being original one day and say oh i'm making a living being bad. check that. check that. it's like we're in this summer camp without adequate supervision. we do exactly what we please and then right it up as well. i practice detachment. i don't read the papers. i note the visitation of two cows and a black horse . . . a promising practitioner of naturalism. in her posthumpus ascent to lasting literairy esteam she still contrives to dismay her readers in approxmire the same protortion that she impraxis them. in 1893 alibaba was robbed by one of his 40 thieves. on page 144 of *orlando* virginia woolf says orlando professed great enjoyment in the society of her own sex, and leave it to the gentlemen to prove, as they are very fond of doing, that this is impossible, which is almost as political as i wished to be today. get yer flexible flyers and we can go belly woppin together. mary kissmas & a hippy nude year. the most unforgivable character i met in new england recently was one virginia fuller tucker mcilvain perkins aged 64 born 1909 the third of three sisters who stood on her head on television in 1944 and was pronounced legally sane by the state supreme court and whose mother said she didn't have any imagination and who was knitting lots of red & white santaclaus stockings formerly of scaneateles says the best way to pass the time is to waste it. she's done so many things besides standing on her head on television i axed her what was the most important thing she does and she said circulate. whenin aye was a kiddling. like my good bedst friend. she's a very shellfish person. i blamed jane for my leg disease or jane's mother who caused jane's face to brake out in a disfigurement the day after she told her she looked pretty and what a nice girlfriend her brother had how she washes the dishes and everything i analiced dis way dat her mother was running a straight trip around her and if she was pretty that meant she too could be straight like her brother's girlfriend and wash the dishes and everything so right away she developed a facial disease to make sure she wouldn't have to be pretty and straight and i caught it on my legs where it turned into poison oak or sumac so i wouldn't have to be straight either and i showed it to everybody i could in order to gift the impersian of being permanently unattractive. those very dangers most dreaded can themselves be encompassed to forestall their actual occurrence. it is notwithstempting by meassures long and limited. venit ut vinceret. she was not educated to be a mother like her mother and like all other mothers who were educated not to be themselves but to be like mothers. a disease is a defense or a deflection. what one should note here is the invention of a discipline of disintegration. she spent another night with a terrible storm raging in her head. she said there was a white cat in a white cadillac with two black people looking out the window. she said a friend of hers was being held against his will in a chinese cookie factory. she says she meets herself coming out of the center she's moving toward. she says she gets tong tied in the face of all this glibness. she says she didn't say this at all and i'm making it all up and that it's extremely unamiable nonsense and i'm a selfindulgent abuser of langwedge and she (?) (writes) i have often resented yr articles for their sloppiness and unintelligibility which she attributes to my frustration and anger not being able to write like a "nice girl" and i throw ketchup bottles in restaurants too and i'm throwing a massive electrickoolaidacidtest for feminists and the oknoid state is the normal state of the well-conditioned endlessly obedient citizen and it requires a good deal of patience and hardwork to be exquisitely sloppy and immortally unintelligable. magna cum cura. potentissimus audacissimus messissimuss. electra is alone/ on the coast of france tonight/ she never writes. by being loved one is placed under an unsolicited obligation. to be eaten doesn't necessarily mean to lose one's identity. jonah remained very much himself even within the belly of the whale. i throw last year's rainbow scarf over my red and black chequered lumber jacket over a striped vertical candycane shirt over a red and black horizontal striped undershirt. i walk into midmorning mist my shoelaces trailing snakes in the wet grass. i've never been impressed with catatonia as a lifestyle. i experience confusion and express bemuddlement. i exercise creative modesty based on exhibitionism. i argue in order to have the pleasure of triumphing over me. i interiorize these contradictory signal systems. i stop and see two three four men in orange in kayaks rushing down the river as if they're in a hurry. i tell jane i'm going to tell everybody she cut a vertical for a bookcase three inches too short. and she castrated her cat too. and she hates her brother. and she was reading orwell's the clergyman's daughter and she said only a man could say a woman has monstrous breasts. that's zs polliptical as i wisht to be tomorrow. i sd to gregory on the cristoforo columbo gregory you look really good today if i was straight i might even find you attractive but then what would i do with a faggot and his mother's stockbroker claimed i dismissed the line as soon as i said it but i didn't i was so pleased i repeated it and repeated it so i could remember it so i could speak it abroad long before the sentence is executed, even before the legal process has been instituted, something terrible has been done to the accused who is now happily by then in lisbon or turkey or venice now finally we may be able to begin to say what it is. what somebody found was incontrovertible evidence that it all means zero. all that aside, trust in god, she will provide. she's a pretty good carpenter but you can't ask her to come and make bookcases for you. she's not the one who is here who is not all there. she is the one who risks meeting the lunatic in herself. she is the one who resorts to inappropriate types of rationality to defend her positions. she is the one who jumps out at you in a new england hotel and says she's virginia fuller tucker mcilvain perkins circa 1909. she is the one in a sterile room saying you have oak or sumac or an allergy related mother disease. she is the one who is nine years old who says her name is now a jennifer harris instead of whatever it was the day before whatever was the name of her father. mary kissms. what it is that one becomes is *that* that that is that it is. certain movements we make can be distinguished clearly as bovine, say. i dreamt a fabulous muscular woman was crouching ten yards behind an enormous brown & white dappled cow seated like a dog facing a hurdle and that the fabulous woman took off as tho in a race and sprang onto the back of the cow and somersaulted twice and sat upright on the haunches of the cow who took off in turn for the hurdle knocking down a board in the jump after which the woman was seen striding off in her tall muscular legs. i was still using cortisone and paper towels and scotch tape so it wasn't me. and all i wanted to do for a week was to go with jennifer to bunky parker's birthday party. there's some tactical insignificance about doing anything but living. soap bubbles and the forces that mold them, as i mentioned a long whirwind ago . . . ceux qui parlent de revolution . . . sans se referer explicitement a la vie quotidienne . . . ont dans la bouche un cadavre!

—December 21, 1972

The Comingest Womanifesto

(paper delivered at the Feminist Lesbian Dialogue at Columbia U., Dec. 16, here slightly altered and amplified)

first or second off i'm into thinking weird all in these difference places in fact in as many places as we are women and so i ask myself when i meet this one or that one i ask where is them politically sexually & where is one in relation to this one or me or where am i now sexually politically since i'm not the me i was yesterday or last year and where are we going or am i already ahead of myself or behind and is somebody else slightly behind or ahead of that and if not then what or what anything i mean how should we behave and where should we think or what are we permitted to assume much less concerning anybody else their total life their total past who are they who am i who am i to them to become if anything & so on like is the one i'm talking to about to sleep with a woman for the first time in which case would i cause her not to if i accused her of oppressing me by being the kind of a woman who sleeps with the man and if she does anyway will she then be terrified to think she might be thought a lesbian and if so should we condemn her for thinking what we were all brought up all these centuries to actually think altho we now think we're so smart just because a few of us now know that it not only isn't bad but it's great in fact it's the best and that that when you ponder it makes us the Ultimate Feminists etc. i mean we think we're really hot shit and we are and so what is that gonna do for us when so many women are still so scared the question is do we want more of us or do we want to just go around saying what hot shit we are and how you straight women are lousing us up just to make sure they'll go on doing it and if so how long would it take before the women called lesbians reemerge as a special interest group and how long after that before you can't say the word lesbian at all any more as if there *is* such a thing as a lesbian the boggler being the more i say it the more i feel it doesn't exist since so many women now actually are lesbians and you wouldn't hear anybody anymore say well huff

huff this woman must be a lesbian because she hated her father and her mother was a bitch or whatever they say along those lines or she got to be a lesbian harumph because she had a terrible first sexual experience with a man and all that you wouldn't hear that except in these clinical psychiatric journals anyway even tho from this new point of view there may be no such thing as a lesbian any more and besides which we know now that all lesbians are women i have to go on saying it to make sure anybody knows i'm defining myself politically as a woman committed woman and the word feminist to me doesn't totally convey that idea since so many feminists advocate a change in our situation in relation to the man rather than the devotion of our energies to our own kind to women i have to ask does this make us enemies when we are all potentially dedicated to ourselves and when we believe in feminist issues per se i.e., abortion reform and when we are in a sense each of us all the women we ever were including straight possibly just yesterday or last year or the last time i slept with a man two years ago or four years before that in a tenement on houston street with two kids still thinking i was straight and i was even tho i was in love with a woman i still am that woman i am all the women i ever was which is all the women of the world in transition i become more completely a lesbian or woman committed woman as the centuries pass and more of me becomes me or the me i think it's such hot shit to be which it is by which i mean a woman the more i sleep with myself and eat myself and write myself and breathe myself the more woman i become i become the woman myself i am who i sleep with it doesn't mean you're not a lesbian if you never slept with a woman before if you consider the person you sleep with the most is yourself and that's you a woman from this point of view we all are lesbians right from the start altho what we are and what we think or say we are can be altogether different things it doesn't matter even by the sights of advanced ideology you can't demand that people be where they're not yet ready to be even if you say all persuasive and important listen a woman committed to herself meaning a woman as combined image of mother daughter and sister was is absolutely at odds with society which has been in the

modern western world organized around the principle of heterosexuality which in effect means the prime commitment of woman
to man who is committed to himself or saying it another way if
you say what i really mean when i say you're oppressing me when
you sleep with the man is that you're giving something so vital to
the man is the same as withholding it from me your daughter your
sister or how in effect you go to bed with my brother by paying
him more attention you deprive me in proportion as you do so is
all very good logic possibly especially when we can say furthermore
look you who have for centuries given your best services to your
sons what in the end have the sons done for us if not to persuade
us or coerce us to serve more sons okay and go on and say and
look around you do you see any lesbians becoming straight and so
on no matter what we say however i'm convinced we can't very
well demand what anybody isn't ready to give who may in fact be
ready to change tomorrow or next year who may know a lot more
in advance of her current opportunities or her present practical
situation or emotional readiness or who may be putting her life in
order to make big changes we don't know about anyway who
probably won't be significantly impressed by anything so much as
the example of our own togetherness all of which doesn't alter it's
true the social fact that the very women we wait for continue to
hurt us by damning us or ignoring us or hating us or tolerating us
or condescending us for loving ourselves or oppressing us by
objectifying us as potential Lesbian Experiences or projecting onto
us the sexism and puritanism and chauvinism of their own expectations of all they've known in relation to the man we won't stop
them from doing this by accusing them of it or by objectifying
them in turn by say making any woman a princess or an all purpose
mommie or even necessarily by carrying on about how when you
saw me at that party and said so you have breasts what you meant
was so you're a woman after all like a guy saying to a faggot in a
locker room you really do have balls as though a lesbian or woman
committed women is less than a woman or somehow a male for
liking other women the way males do supposedly and thus being
less a woman not being a woman in the sisterhood of man

pandering females or when you say oh i happen to love a woman now but i could as well have a relationship with a man if he were the right sort of person as tho we were not all *persons* before the *feminists* taught us we were women in the sense of being a political class in which case what you're really saying is if the right sort of *man* came along or when you say if all else fails we'll try loving our sisters as if your sister was a last resort and even if you do think you mean just sex i translate it to mean loving your sisters which means sex and *every*thing i still know the truth is demonstrable only by example and the only way to proceed historically is to respect personal places places even we feel are detaining us or delaying us or deterring us we respect them nevertheless for being the places any woman is capable of being the way we respect a wasp for being a wasp we don't condemn a wasp for being the type of animal who would string us if she could i don't want to pursue the example the example that concerns me here is the assertion of our own logic and model in this way enough women by a few centuries time will become the hot shit we think we are to make a viable amazon nation or tribe or tribes of women capable of sustaining themselves independently of the male specious we have to remind ourselves that in 1972 in amerika we are a fugitive band who can't afford to isolate ourselves from the woman in the middle who in any case remains a potentially total ally or the woman we are gradually becoming as we become more of ourselves as we leave more of our straight selves of ourselves behind ourselves we gradually become ourselves all the women we ever were we are ourselves still the woman in the middle it doesn't make any sense to be our own enemy and if we don't see common cause with feminists feminists are not likely to see it with us either especially when it's so easy to find reason by offense to say we'll have nothing to do with you when it's still so scary to proclaim the ligitimacy of an identity so recently criminal or sick or sinful we must therefore as i see it take all the chances and risk being the ones to continue being hurt and insulted by exposing our thought as the logic of the feminist/ lesbian position and exposing our selves as the models of the revolution by realizing we are each and all all the women of the world in transition and not placing ourselves thus above and beyond or ahead but directly in the center as the moving force of our collective conscience.

—*December 28, 1972*

The Red Baroness in America

these are some stories of women. i intend to adhere to the subject. the mood is both strong and vulnerable, tentative and expansive. (not) all the parts can be moved. i planned originally to share some stories of my cars. and other peoples cars. the best car story i remember from eighth grade was by harriet beecher stowe who said the automobile would divide humanity into two classes: the quick and the dead. my friends indicate that i'm so one i should be the other and that's because my present vehicle was made by the germans. i now drive instead of just going from one place to another. i don't drive and daydream any more. i don't know if the germans imagined their juggernauts hurling 75 or 80 mph on country amerikan winding roads, possibly all they had in mind was a normal cruising speed of 90 or 100 or so on their own hiways, but whatever the conditions the product they've turned out says drive me. esther tells me that's no excuse. she didn't explain for what. i suppose for risking my life. i don't take it lightly myself. i take my new career as a racing driver seriously. i approach the launching pad with intent to speed and nothing else. i pass everything else that moves on four wheels at double dispatch. i don't even *see* the things that don't move. all i care about is passing everything that moves and breaking my own speed records for arriving anyplace including any aimless trip whatsoever. i take adverse conditions into account too. i made it one night from hartford to new jersey in one hour and a half in a blinding rain storm even though i had to pause or slow down momentarily while a vw bug in front of me went into a wild spin and a half and i paused extra to admire its trajectory across the three lanes spinning like a top in each lane and miraculously escaping bodily contact with three other onrushing vehicles and ending up dead still facing in the right direction in the emergency pullover lane. i've already bragged about my three hour and 15 minute record maiden trip from washington d.c. to manhattan. i have no intention of repeating the trip just to outdo myself. i'm just writing about cars. these are some stories of cars. i intend to adhere to the subject. the mood is free and confined, regular and irregular, rectangular and unmanageable. i planned originally to share some stories of women. everything which is necessary is in her. and what is not in her is not necessary. she was turning in circles and saying the whole world is moving. she represents herself as a sphere. the news was beginning to spread. there were more friends, more flowers, more cars! she was invited to write a column in a city newspaper called the brakes. she wanted to call it just motor. i mean motor. the word motor sums up everything you need to know about cars. i don't use fancy words like engine. i would however toss dymaxion around in architectural company. the same thing over & over & over again. how important the third over is. the important thing about my life & times right now is its quality of risk and speed. i haven't been so fast since i played right wing soccer. a study in contrasts is what it's all about. the way one might enjoy taking up soccer after playing croquet every year until you were 13. i've been driving tinlizzards since i sat on somebody's lap to steer their heap when i was nine so i deserved something dangerous and foolish and impractical at 15. i was brought up on gingham and seersucker. the last allaround washnwear type thing i had for a vehicle was that rectangular underpowered dinosaur they call a vw camper which made it across wyoming at an all time high of 25 mph. other outstanding features of my great house on wheels were its motor spattering oil capacities and its ability to turn over on any bridge on which the wind was above breeze warnings and its general reliability under stress on remote turnpikes for just breaking apart. i had one fine trip in this house. i parked it for a week on an island off maine overlooking some reefs and seaweed and holed up inside to write very comfortably as though i'd discovered the allpurpose self reflecting box with a window on the ocean of the world. when i wasn't doing that i was struggling on the outside with my feet touching the ground with this survival equipment by hudson's called coleman's, these frightening lanterns and stoves. the lantern i busted immediately and presented the remains to a friend. the stove i gave away to the stranger who relieved me of the house one day on a local street i accepted the first comer for whatever he seemed to have in his pocket. i told him it was a famous house because it had appeared in *esquire*. that seemed to really turn him on. i wished him luck in his camper phase. we all have these camper phases even if you don't actually get one. everybody likes to get into somebody else's and rummage around checking out the compartments. the reason i liked it all originally was for its compartments. i didn't enquire into its efficiency or anything like that. this german number i have now is efficient completely by chance. that is, i had no idea i was obtaining the darling of amerikan afficionados in european models. it's not that i didn't know it would be faster, *anything* would be faster, nor that i didn't know it would be more reliable than a rambler pickup, but nobody told me it was a racing car favorite of the nazis. the model by the way is a bmw 2002 stands for bavarian motor works and i feel exempt from any responsibility of collusion with an unpopular nation state since i never did know where bavaria was and for some time i thought the b stood for british. the reason i thought of it at all was that three or two years ago i happened to see this exquisite backside of a medium small orange number parked on a west side street and it occurred to me right then that i'd get one. i jumped out of whatever tinlizzard i had at the time and found its identifying insignia. i'd never heard of it. a bmw. a british motor wench i surmised. anyway the romance was all visual. the only thing i like better now visually is anything else german with a lot of chrome. i really dig chrome. and in 5000 years when i'm finished with my creditors i'll have this one painted the silver blue metal flake job. oh lord wonchu buy me — a mercedes benz . . . my friends all drive porches, i must make amends. oh lord wonchu provide me with a mechanic for free. for anyone considering seriously becoming a racing car driver i have to offer this inside information that an 8000 mile check on a small bavarian affair costs $135. which may be nothing to nazis and nebuchadnezzars but for myself i can't reconcile that sort of price of a tuneup to the $50 i once paid outright for a '51 pontiac that i'm still sentimental about. i can't believe i abandoned that one on the street just because of its radiator. it wasn't even a motor problem. i don't remember what was wrong with its radiator. i remember getting after a suitable interval an allamerikan prone sprawl of a desoto that wouldn't go in reverse and which i abandoned within three weeks. i remember hearing a story about a car that would *only* go in reverse.

i know lots of car stories. i know lots of car and women stories. all the cars in the world are driven by people. all the people in the world are women, except some of them are men, whose mothers permitted them to make them. the mood is soft and dynamic, relaxed and concentrated. (not) all the parts can be moved. i suppose if it were possible the hiway engineers would've constructed some special bypasses over around or under their tunnels for women. i heard that a woman mining engineer in colorado won her case for entering a tunnel. apparently they don't permit women in tunnels out there, possibly here too except for driving, and i for one go through them very fast. i timed myself last week in the new haven tunnel it was a five second run. it's more exciting to pass everybody in a tunnel too. and there's no excuse as esther said. and esther wouldn't drive with me. once rosalyn said she wouldn't drive with me either but she didn't remember why. i've only destroyed one car and that was my mother's. i've never hit an animal. i've only knocked two people down and it was all their fault. and i have only one speeding ticket in my german racer. i suppose they know i'm out practicing. I don't know why they got me that one time. i was doing 80 at 2 a.m. on the meritt and this pleasant pig who probably didn't know who i was pulled me over and said did you know you were doing 80 ma'am. of course i knew i was doing 80. what'd he think i'd be doing at 2 a.m. on the merritt parkway. he apologized and punished me at the same time, so undoubtedly he was confused. not all of them i'll have to admit are so charmingly ambivalent. most of them in fact actually are on the lookout for these ex favorites of the nazis and they cruise up and down everywhere just especially to hunt us down. the only times anybody ever stopped me in my house was for having long hair and/or when my son was in the passenger seat. my son by the way was instrumental in the purchase of that house. the fact is that one year i was homeless and very upset about it and richard who was nine and driving along in a tinlizzard for an outing said casually why don't you get one of those things with a box in the back and i thought he meant a trailer, i'd always associated campers exclusively with trailers, so i didn't take it seriously for a year until when i was on the coast and saw zillions of these boxes that sort of went with the driving equipment and thought that was for me, i had no intention of retiring into a trailer at the age of 15. trailers and retired nuclear disasters were the same thing. anyway so i had my camper phase. during my truly big trip, a three month junket to the coast and back, i slept in it a total of three nights. when you have a car that you *can't* sleep in nobody wants you to stay in their regular plumbing and electrified houses and when you *do* have one they're quite eager for some reason to put you up, so the true benefits deriving from a camper are those of increased and unlimited visitation rights, something to consider if you prefer squatting in other peoples houses the way all the women i know do. there's a history of good luck with cars in my family. my grandmother never owned one. my second cousin eddie had a fine ford with a rumble seat. and my mother made her first fortune driving a model-t when a rich man's son oscar somebody piled his motorcycle up on her running board ramming the handlebars into her head causing her to sustain a concussion for which the rich father of the son paid my mother 10 grand in those times was a fantastic sum and she became an adventurer by taking a boat to europe. she didn't drive again for dozens of years. the only other story i remember about the early days was being compelled to go for sunday afternoon drives with my grandmother in martha and elsie's black chrysler and reading the funnies and throwing up. i never thought i was destined for the racetracks. except for eddie's rumble seat i didn't take cars seriously at all. there was nothing to it then anyway. there weren't any japs or germans. there weren't any rpms and the word handling was unknown. the thing about a foreign efficient car is that it *handles*. i told jane all about my car history so that when i acquired this current juggernaut she used it against me and acted as though i didn't deserve having something that *handled* or something that had such an overqualified motor that a number of its incidental details were fucked up in a royal way like when a certain type of person sat in the car it wouldn't start or a certain type of other person got in the car the key would get stuck in a door so you couldn't put it in the starter and stuff like that and in fact she didn't think i was *capable* of *handling* this fabulous piece of machinery as a mechanic put it and that's because she happens to be a true car freak and that's because she owned a morgan. i always thought a morgan was a horse but now i know better. i know a *lot* better. i can't identify them on the road, but i display an interest in them and i intend to get one when *esquire* or the vw outfit people come across for that photo i posed for they didn't tell me was going to be an ad for those lousy campers it looked as if i had nothing better to do than to advertise what a wonderful house i was leading in my life when in reality it was a minor miracle i'd survived to have the photo taken at all. the vw people wouldn't recompense me a cent for all my broken down motors or the mental cruelty i experienced as a snail being a sort of beast of burden carrying all these compartments around. kaput. i'm paying everybody back by being a terror on the roads. and they'll never get a picture of me. i go too fast. i take other drivers on too but basically i'm practicing to be faster than myself. i don't like to pick up challenges by strangers but i've noticed i can't very well ignore certain dudes who think their crummy dirty dent chrome dodge is a match for any german. the thing is there isn't a dude under 70 who won't start driving with his prick as soon as he registers that a *woman* is on his ass and then he turns into a goddamn bombardier. but it's a solo flight most of the way. i go too fast for most anybody to determine *what* sex (if any) is causing the wind and they assume it's a male anyway unless otherwise proven and if they do see anything i suppose it's a longhair marine so essentially after all they're pretty polite and move over and make as much room as possible as soon as they hear the blast and recognize a nazi racing-car driven by longhair marine. okay i've taken care of some car tales and some women too. i didn't say i had a very important sexual experience in my camper, so i guess it was worth it. the most exciting thing is to think of anything, then you don't have to do it. i never expect anything to materialize anyway so i have basically a good time. the components exist in a peculiar idiosyncratic space. and i experience the other stories as my own so that in effect i can imagine i've done everything. the most impressive car story i ever heard was from lois hart who told me she had her nervous breakdown in a '51 chevy. i wouldn't ever forget it. the way things shake down currently is that jane got a saab and esther drives a vw squareback and gregory leaves his mg in garages to go abroad on boats and phyllis b. totalled her bug two weeks ago and bertha's is in north carolina and i saw the ex old man of an ex lover of mine in a bentley one day and i saw her mother in a taxi and sheindi says she's getting a learners permit and richard wants a license next year and rosalyn probably still doesn't drive and i don't know what my mother has and ingrid said her favorite job was a '51 chrysler and the only other human i know who has a bmw 2002 is brenda hyphenated and i take it back i forgot so does simone and the wheels i want next is a bavaria four door six cylinder sedan maroon with folding wings and a rocket fuel jet propelled engine for short trips to the moon whenever i'm in the mood.

—*January 11, 1973*

As Anybody Lay Dying

some woman at a party said her mother said when you grow up you'll have all the things i never had and then i'll hate you for it. some other woman said she was living her mother's dreams and another woman said her mother never had any dreams. her mother stopped dreaming when she was five. i'm not certain i want to tell any other mother stories. i wanted to tell about st mary's or about my life on the bowery or about conversations with straight women who want to know about good sex or is there anything that isn't about the mothers. the hero is in the habit of relating all that has gone before for the benefit of the beloved whoever that might be. i wanted to go on about my cars too but then i read that a. huxley said there was only one new sin invented since the original seven deadly and that was speed and also i received a religious card from two people in new jersey saying they were giving a mass for me and further i received two letters about cars from two different women each signing their letters lake circumspect when all along i thought there was only one and that she was in denver although now i recall an original correspondent identifying herself as lake circumspect from someplace in michigan who then appeared to be moving around from there to boston or connecticut to denver and even new york since one of them introduced herself to me at b. & c.'s one time and i thought she was the one and only lake circumspect alias ellie sometimes the thing being it seems really unlikely there'd be more than one lake circumspect in the world and writing about cars somehow so so what i had a neat note from a woman in brooklyn enclosing two color photos of her cars one of herself in an old stingray and the other of her current bug painted abstract inflationist or stuffed expressionist but i don't feel like going on about cars this week anyhow, very much. for almost 17 years she said nothing memorable and all went well. when communication is established there's nothing more to be said. here's a dialogue of the future: a: i'll make some toast if you turn on the tube. b: i don't want any toast but i'll turn on the tube. a: okay i'll go and make my toast and you turn on the tube. b: okay you go and make your toast and i'll turn on the tube. a: okay. b: would you bring me an apple. i think i should write a play. & make up all my myriads of drifting minds into one. it's those pauses that's our undoing. the moment matters, but so does the century. so we could proceed with everything. the idea is to construct an excuse for not going on and then use that as a rationale for doing so. is there anything, then, we can actually point to, if all this is generally true. red socks. wine suede gloves. gorgonzola. hot cider & brandy. no monopoly (anywhere). a plaid flannel shirt. a little girl in the park. a teddy bear in a gingham suit. a *mother*. i had a mother who didn't cook or keep house but who knitted sweaters caps and mittens and made a gingham suit for my teddy bear. we discussed our mothers as knitters one day. the item i liked the best since i never lost it until i gave it to richard was a ski sweater yellow and royal blue and jane said her mother knit a ski sweater that was maroon and white with reindeer on it for her male cousin and she knit her some mittens that were red with two gray stripes on the cuff and her initials and one time she knit one of those things that go around your neck under your coat to connect both you mittens so you wouldn't lose them. i doubt that this is the most interesting thing about our mothers but it's easier than most of the other stuff. i suppose it was my mother's idea for example that i go to the local ballet school when i was eight and climax my studies by performing with a bunch of other little girls in a cold gymnasium in a forget-me-not costume. and that isn't so bad considering what some mothers do like wendy wonderful told jane her mother dressed her up for kindergarten as the fairy princess. the whole mother bit seems to be a big idea. i had a dydee doll and a raggedy ann and all but they didn't turn me into a mother because i never developed any overwhelming sense of what was best for them. i didn't send them to school and i didn't take very good care of them. i didn't mistreat them either. i was bigger but there didn't seem to be any satisfaction in taking advantage of them. i guess i didn't lay much value on size per se. i guess i remained my own kid. i guess that's really where it's at. the mother bit is just an idea. i was particularly thinking this not long ago when jane was getting off some rap about how everybody suddenly appeared to her to be such a baby. she said everybody's such a baby. i just see babies walking around on the street, with these boxes, doing all these funny things, wearing all these clothes. babies driving trucks (did i tell you about this guy in the cab of an enormous truck at a traffic light playing a harmonica.) babies carrying big boxes and wearing funny clothes. babies pressing the buttons for elevators and staring at the floor (& they're afraid to look up to look at the ceiling or anything — that's why i dig tourists staring at the skyscrapers). babies jaywalking, and carrying coffee back to the office, delivering things to each other. babies looking at a window of big ceramic frogs. — it's funny. babies in the subway playing games about staring at other babies, and some don't look away. some scribble on the cars and the posters. there's other babies who're adults. the adult babies make posters with the letter printing in white and the background in black so the bad babies can't write on them. and there's the babies at the toll booths who take their time giving you a token when the train is sitting in the station. and these old babies on the buses who stare at you and want you to give them their seat. and pregnant babies who don't stare at you and usually get the seat. and puerto rican babies hanging out on their stoops, and on and on about babies. i got into her rap and could really see it. i had mostly regarded the presidents and senators that way. now i see that we're all implicated but we don't know it so the best we can do is cultivate attractive symptoms. i went to see eva hesse her sculpture at the guggenheim and i was very upset and i wondered if i would've been so upset or upset at all if eva wasn't dead or if i saw the work and didn't know she was dead and if i would've thought the work was that beautiful if she was still alive. it was thinking about eva made me want to write about my life on the bowery. i lived at 119 and she lived diagonally across the street and i didn't know she was making all these beautiful things. i didn't know her personally to speak of at all. i saw her on the bus a couple of times. i knew she was a friend of sol's. i knew she was at a party i went to when she was dying but i didn't see her and i was told her face was blue. i heard a lot about how she was dying and i remember seeing her work on the cover of art forum the very month she died and thinking that's what happens they wait until a woman puts her head in an oven or something and then they say she was pretty good.

i remembered meeting her before she lived on the bowery and she seemed to be just the wife of this artist i went to review his work in a loft on fifth avenue and i thought to myself she was very good-looking but that's all i remember. now i read in the guggenheim catalog that "the most painful notations (in her notebooks) record the central trauma of individuation provoked by the death of the artist's father in the summer of '66 and the rupture with her husband which peaked at this time as well, events without which, I believe, Eva Hesse's art might have remained an effort primarily of local interest" and yesterday a woman i know in new jersey told me she thinks she knew eva as a little girl in washington heights and there was something tragic about her and she couldn't recall what and suddenly she remembered it was about her mother having died. not that eva was acting tragically necessarily. it's just that anybody without a mother was supposed to be tragic. anyway i was trying to put a few pieces together to make a fuzzy picture. i thought that if those surgeons couldn't do anything for her head she should go to new mexico and lie in the sun and i never trusted those people anyway. but then i thought well if you're dying and making great art of the sort where "the voice no longer speaks to us, but beyond us" and it's possible that your computerized karma has set you on this course of being capable of making great art only in the process of dying too young and painfully then the sun and new mexico or any other smart healthy idea remains pretty superfluous and still somewhere in the realm of thinking you might know what's best for somebody. so i sort of cried at her show of great sculpture at the guggenheim. i was walking down the spiral ramp away from it all and i looked back i noticed there was this guy in a reddish beard and a plaid shirt and he looked very upset too but the other people were examining the work the way people do ordinarily and i wondered if i was upset because i knew her or what. now i think it has something to do with the bowery. there may've been any number of dispossessed females up and down the bowery around that time. i didn't see how she could live across the street from her ex just for openers. i couldn't see any of it for any of us. yet we were doing it and making a whole life out of it and i liked my loft and its masonite floor better than any other dump i ever crashed in and i think actually we were getting ourselves together after a great assortment of personal disasters. so i don't know. my newest idea is that the slight memory of eva and the big sight of her sculpture and my knowledge of her life and the recollection of the sainted bums on the bowery and their goddam guilt inducing afflictions got me feeling like a really heroic gesture was going on across the street that i didn't know about and now i'm sorry and i don't know why. and now that i've found my subject i'm quitting this time around anyway.

—*January 25, 1973*

Great Expectorations

tuesday jan. 23 i got on a united flight 769 at newark to go to grand rapids. going to grand rapids was like going to timbuctoo or kalamazoo. it's the sort of place you've always known about and you don't know why, i suppose it has something to do with the name, the name stuck in your mind back when you studied the really important places in geography such as boston or raleigh for being capitals or tobacco centers or something and you just happened to remember places like kalamazoo or tallahassee because they sounded very weird. grand rapids doesn't sound very weird or anything but i can't think of any reason i might know about it except for its name. it's a mythical city like the others. i was actually supposed to be going to this place called allendale to do a talk thing at some obscure college and the woman who invited me was supposed to pick me up and drive me there from the grand rapids airport. i like airports a lot and i'm afraid of strangers so i told this woman on the phone from new york that i'd be arriving at grand rapids at 6 p.m. when in reality my plane was arriving at 3.30, that way i could enjoy myself in the airport and finish my book and find out about grand rapids and observe all the other anonymous strangers. frankly i prefer total strangers to the kind of strangers who expect to make your acquaintance. i like to address them in a familiar offhand way about the time of day or the price of eggs and see what happens. the trouble is in most places in the country you're not sup*posed* to strike up a conversation with strangers, so usually they look at you funny as if they think you're crazy or they look right through you pretending they didn't hear you or they say one thing very short and snappy making it clear they're not interested in associating with strangers. i don't mind too much though. i like to just look around, and overlisten conversations if i can. the first thing i did in the airport at grand rapids i asked the waitress behind the counter in the coffee shop why grand rapids was grand and if they had a rapids here. her name was lorna doone and she didn't know but she asked me about my accent. she thought i had a new york accent. she said that after i told her i came in from new york. that was the extent of our conversation. i started talking to a woman across the counter and she wasn't unfriendly particularly but i stopped because a teenage woman was whispering about me to her mother or her aunt or somebody and i got paranoid, that's why strangers don't talk to each other, the tradition is carried on by the children and the younger people and they're not very inhibited about letting the offenders of the tradition know that it isn't done. i had a good time anyway. i went into the bar and sucked on a couple of martinis and overheard some fragments of a few gruesome stories by a small crowd of rubber-neck business jerks sitting next to me at a round table. i wrote down whatever i heard. i go to the people for my stories. a while ago in new york a black woman asked me if i went out among the people and i said right away that i was the people myself and i could tell by the tone of her voice that she thought i was playing with her mind or something and i wish i'd told her that i really do go to the people, at least whenever i happen to be among them. for example on one of my numerous flights from airport to airport this trip around i happened to be sitting next to this type who interested me for some reason, possibly because of his raspberry tweed jacket and his tie that had all these colors running together, more probably because of what he had inside this case he was carrying which he opened up on his lap, it looked like a folded up shovel and there was some other hard indeterminate object and a lot of papers and letters and stuff, and then he started using a calculator and i was more interested than ever so i started in a conversation and i practically *inter*viewed the guy right on the plane. i wanted to hate him naturally, but i found it very difficult, he was totally sincere about everything he said. he was apparently completely happy about being a sales promotion representative or whatever he called it exactly. he was beaming about it in fact and he wasn't threatened in the least by my hostile questions. he said sales and products is what makes the world go round and after a while i got to believing it myself. he said he had one objective in life. what was that, i asked breathlessly. to be the best sales representative he knew how to be he said. and he has a son in college who's going into the same thing. and he has a daughter who thinks she's going to be a nurse. and what does your wife do i asked, as if i didn't know. and then at one point i asked him what his wife might be doing at this very moment and he consulted his watch and said well right now she'd be serving lunch to his son who'd be home from school. i felt then as though i almost hated him and i asked a lot of hostile questions about his products and his attitudes toward them in order to press my advantage but he came off with flying colors. he said certainly he believed absolutely in his products, otherwise why would he be selling them. and besides he gets to choose his own products, if he doesn't like something he doesn't have to sell it, he'd like to sell calculators for example because he believes they're something that can do people some good. the main thing is that he intends to excel in his chosen field. he was in fact at that very moment on his way to a meeting in milwaukee at his own expense to learn something new about his field. i had to say to him finally that i didn't understand why we were getting along and i could only imagine it was because he happened to be the same sign as me and i get along with my own sign and it turned out that he actually was not only my sign but only two days away from me. we were getting off the plane by that time and the last thing he said however was that he gets along with most everybody, he was beaming and waving goodbye, so i realized there was no excuse for not hating him and i wondered what was happening to me. i didn't have to wonder too hard. i had the usual quota of horrible revolutionary experiences on this particular trip, so my sales promotion friend was just some freaky unnatural exception. i almost became a "future stewardess" for instance. i got onto this north central plane from chicago to madison wisconsin i believe it was and as i walked back to the lav i noticed a little boy holding a silver pin of some sort that he got from a tall graysuited steward in a moustache standing in the aisle over a black bag at his feet and i wanted to know right away what it was the boy had been given exactly, i found out it was a "future pilot" pin in the form of a cheap wooden pair of wings painted silver so i asked for one immediately and was presented with some *gold* wings that said "future stewardess" on them, i'm not kidding. i said c'mon man, whadya think i am anyway, and i handed them back and got the "future pilot" number. i know there's one thing i'm *not* gonna be in my next life and that's a flying waitress. i don't know about being a pilot, but i like the silver wooden wings. and i told the story wherever i went, to all those strangers who logically expect to make your acquaintance. one thing about being in the air for some reason it isn't totally taboo to talk to strangers and since they're *complete* strangers and you feel pretty certain you'll never see anybody again it's a very satisfying experience to make these short artificial intimate communications with alien creatures who feel the same way about you. i wasn't dying to see this woman who'd invited me out to her college, i had some reason to believe that she had great expectations of me. i think she actually expected me to save her or something, i really do, or at least to fall in love with her, which is the same thing i guess. i didn't know this or suspect it until about the third letter i had from her in which she said she thought she loved me although i might be too tough for her and then i was afraid to go. it gets me how anybody can decide they love somebody or think much of anything else about them when they've never even laid eyes on them. i don't think i even ever thought that way about ingrid bergman. the thing is though that i could tell i really liked this woman, from her letters and poems and everything, and i didn't mind coming along to be outrageous for the revolution on her behalf in the middle of amerika's great wasteland and all, but i can't see being *personally* the object of anybody's expectations in the name of the revolution, i see myself as a medium for transmitting the ideas and that's about all. otherwise i hope to get away from it all and to be transported around from building to building or airport to airport like a visiting sales promotion expert and to be idolized a little bit from a distance and to hear something new about the world. so i was sort of drinking myself to death in the airport there at grand rapids by the time 6 o'clock rolled around and my woman was due to meet me. the culture encourages women to instigate the crimes of passion for which the woman is then condemned. i'm trying not to expect very much from other women myself. i expect a lot from myself but if anybody condemns me i want to be the one to do it. i like to trot out my credentials as a cosmic personality in the hopes of not being considered anything in particular at all. this is close to that old forgotten feeling that you can't stay on the earth for another minute. anyway i guess i have to say i survived grand rapids and allendale and my sponsor and all her friends and i went on to bigger and worse things in madison via chicago and in ann arbor via milwaukee and detroit. i even found out what grand rapids is all about, as i suppose everybody else knows they make furniture there and they go to church a lot, church is a big thing. that's what barbara the poet told me on the drive back to the airport after doing my tricks out at her college. some people say there was a big cloud of literal consciousness repression during the '50s, well i don't see how the world is that much different, it's true that a lot of amerikans have blown their heads out on one thing or another, but anyplace you go in amerika outside of freaksville on a few city streets or deep in the boonies on a clump of god's lost acre you see the same old people in permanents and sears dresses and patent leather pocketbooks hanging on their crewcut beer bellied old men about whom you know damn well they'd *never* talk to a stranger, so i don't see how anything has changed significantly, although sometimes i'm more optimistic i didn't feel optimistic a bit after i was almost arrested for disorderly contact or rather conduct in the grand rapids airport on my way back out of there. i was standing at the north central ticket counter with barbara getting a ticket for chicago and madison and asking the saleswoman how the planes were today, i always do that, as a matter of form i ask if the planes are nice and safe today, it's sort of a superstition i suppose, and they *always* smile a little patronizingly and say yes the planes are fine or something like that, they might even mumble a line about the excellent record of the airlines, anyway they know it's a game and they figure i'm a harmless nut, sometimes i even throw in that they must think i'm crazy, just to vaguely apologize for asking their indulgence; well for some reason this woman in grand rapids was very uptight about my questions concerning the safety of her planes and the more defensive she got naturally the more alarmed i became, especially since i was querying her in particular about the two recent crashes at chicago, where i happened to be landing, and at one point i asked her *why* she was so uptight, i don't remember what she said, she was scribbling out my ticket, and around that moment some pinstriped business dude came up along behind me practically snorting down my neck and saying something like you're holding the rest of us up too which wasn't true and i swore a big mess of stuff at him and also told him to get his fucking dirty feet off my jacket and the woman handed me my change and we walked away all puffy and huffy when i realized i didn't have my ticket. then what happened barbara walked back to get it and the woman told her she couldn't give me a ticket and she was calling the security guards, can you imagine that, i was really floored and wanted to get the hell out of there so i lined up across the way at united who would also take me to chicago, and the men there said yes and smiled the usual bemused smile the planes were fine today, but along came these scary characters in their navy blues and guns and holsters hauling us back to some office, it was maddening and embarrassing and upsetting but i thought i could handle it because i'm very cool with the cops, i really am, and what i did i put on my best wasp new england posture and accent and all and just kept quietly insisting in a tone of injured dignity or something that this man has been extremely *rude*, which he was. of course these security officials were on *his* side all the way, and *he* hadn't even registered a complaint. they kept barking about how he was a "professional man" and when barbara wanted to know what they meant by asking if the official *knew* him the official said "no, but i know his title" but whatever it was his attire made him innocent obviously, and i thought to myself that's how all these business suits in washington get away with their wars, if you're a man in a business suit you can do anything you goddam please, including being rude at ticket counters. anyway the main thing was that "ladies" don't use "four letter words" in kent county michigan. the fact is i guess that i upset the whole airport by being a lady and yelling at this dude that he should go home and fuck his fucking father and that's how i almost got arrested in the middle of amerika's great wasteland of churches and furniture and whatnot. i said listen i've never been in kent county michigan before but i'll probably happily never return and in the meantime here's looking at you or some such inanity and i couldn't wait to get out of there. the incident cost me eight bucks in a different air fare and i was pretty shook up. i was waiting for the plane and standing at a phone booth calling the voice with a margarita at my elbow, and that's not allowed in kent county michigan either, old gun and holster came up and said i'd better get that drink back to the bar. i was sure by that time they didn't like the way i looked which happened to be a lot of dull silver studs and rhinestones on a denim number from the london jeans machine place. i suppose when you go out into the land of the bible belt and all its good citizens you should wear something that's considered to be legitimately color coordinated at least. possibly i added a fragment of instant credentials when i acquired my "future pilot" wings on the flight from chicago to madison. anyway my sales promotion friend didn't seem to mind the way i looked. he just commented that i didn't have on a "gown" or anything. that was his idea of being funny. anyway generally it's impossible to look right out in these areas if you want to feel really good about the way you look yourself unless of course you still feel great looking that way everybody else looks and that means being daring in a color coordinated pants suit i would guess. i'm not interested in clothes at all particularly, sometimes i have an "attack" and go out all over the place searching for something i decide i think i really need, otherwise i don't care that much any more, except for my various blue jackets, one day i realized they were all blue, that may be because the whole world is still my boarding school where the navy blue blazer was the most impressive aspect of our uniforms since they were decorated every year with the chevrons and such of our athletic achievements, i donno, what i'm trying to arrive at saying actually is that when people are arrested for the way they look it seems like clothes are something to really think about. i think if i'd been dressed to the nines like any good housekeeper on her way from city to city they wouldn't've cared that much about my four-letter words for which they said they wanted to arrest me. they said that "ladies" don't use "four letter words" but the point probably was that i didn't look like a "lady" in the first place. this whole lady culture is getting me down. the ladies look terrible and i'm not attracted to them any more either. they can't run properly should they be in trouble and they smell of cosmetics and they look all stuffed into somebody else's idea of themselves and they can't tolerate the rest of us. if they'd just *smile* and be friendly. how *can* they be friendly when they look so awful. i told gregory about michigan and he said he doesn't think about the people in michigan, or what they wear, it's all ridiculous, he's given up thinking about it, he just goes out there to do his lecture, then rushes back to play with his trains. he has a set of toy trains. and he's back to wearing suits and ties because he can't stand looking the way everybody else looks. it's pretty confusing. who is everybody exactly. is everybody our friends or is everybody Them. i guess for gregory everybody is our or rather *his* friends and the implication is that *we* all look alike too and going among his friends he has to wear the uniform of Them out there in order to feel different, which may be the way you feel really good about the way you look. there's something in other words about feeling the same and there's something about feeling different too. i like resembling my friends and i like looking different Out There and i like being different from my friends too and very often i wish i looked more like Them. it's all mixed up i think actually. i still prefer my stompers to any other type of shoe since i discovered stompers but i haven't yet succumbed to the street dyke uniform of overalls, i don't care to look shapeless before my time. i didn't want to get into this clothes business at all particularly. i was leading up to my encounter in ann arbor michigan and the ultimate impossibility as i now see it of looking any way at all. before i forget it i have to say right away that it's all very well for gregory to get back into suits and ties but what would i get back into if i was suddenly tired of looking like everybody else who happen in my case to be sensible revolutionary women who dress for comfort and play and mobility and with an invisible or aggressive appearing unavailability to the man. some dykes for example are monochromatically invisible, and some are polemically obvious in overalls and baseball bats. or lavender armbands. or visors and leather chaps. i'm sort of kidding. i did meet two incredible women up north a couple of weeks ago however who might be said to've resembled a complete set of dickens bound in cowhide. i watched in amazement as they gathered themselves together to leave. leather chaps. leather boots. leather shirts. leather vests. leather coats. leather gloves. leather hats. leather accessories. leather *every* thing. i've heard they even have leather pillow cases and leather candle holders! i want to visit their leather house and read a leather book on their leather bound toilet. some people do manage to be truly different! the thing is they have a leather business. a lot of leather ingenuity goes into all that packaging. i don't like leather that much but i admire the way they appear to be different both from Them and from Everybody Else. and how they can undoubtedly appear with better credibility out among Them since leather is a valued and somewhat unavailable middle class commodity. and they certainly look unapproachable to the man. the straight women by the way in contrast to dykedom seem to be arrayed around on the streets or wherever like decoys. i wonder often what it is that the straight *feminists* want, since they claim to be fighting the same war, the strategy of the disarmament of rapists or men, rape coming in many seductions as germaine wrote in *playboy* last month, is as serious as i intended to be here, i'm always serious, anyway i wish they'd start wearing overalls and if they did i would too, why should i care about looking shapeless before my time anyway. another good question. and according to the ann arbor auto mechanic dykes i should cut off my hair! that's what i was coming to. a lot of women poured into a room in a building on the university campus on two days notice to view the dyke from new york who in turn was curious to see the fabled stompers of ann arbor who indeed were there. one somewhat femmy woman put her foot in her hair right off by declaring that bed was her own business and a rather fierce dialogue ensued basically over the length of her hair. at last i can tell my wendy wonderful hair story. a year or two back wendy wonderful was at a feminist demonstration where these women on a stage were cutting off their hair, saying that men play with your hair, and wendy yelled from the back why don't you cut off your breasts too, men play with your breasts. i don't know what kind of a political argument that is, but i identify with the hair problem, and i care about my breasts as well, and i don't like to be personally attacked over my own disarmament solutions. at the same time i appreciate the short hair position. i think the position is that some dykes think that femmy women in their long

hair are soliciting male protection as opposed to male assault. i believe
it works both ways and many combinations thereof. not all guys
want to assault and/or protect any particular woman. i don't want to
solicit assault no matter what, i do want the protection they offer
from their own kind and that's why i get along with the cops, who're
not necessarily your ultimate protectors or anything, i know i know,
essentially i don't want anything at all from them except good
manners and better contracts. well it was a hairy scene in ann arbor.
i was beginning to be overwhelmed by new waves of strangers too.
i'd just come in from madison and about 200 women in a chapel, it's
really a strain greeting that many people you don't know who appear
to know *you*. the dykes in madison however were a lot more lesez
faire. i told all my stories and got away with looking exactly the way
i did, or so i assumed since nobody criticized me. i hate to be
criticized. also every month i get pregnant and when it's close to
delivery time i'm very sensitive. nevertheless i told the most critical
of the ann arbor women that i'd consider seriously my use of the
word kid to designate a child. i won't cut off my hair and i won't
stop using the word fuck to coopt male language to throw it back at
them if i have to, that is in every place excepting kent county
michigan. actually i appreciate being challenged on political grounds.
the tyranny of normal consciousness is a certain political smugness
over the rightness of your own current set as well as other types of
consciousnesses and i like to add and subtract effects if the spirit is
willing like i have a new gallows humor laugh and a new way of
saying yes that appeals to me and yesterday i asked jane to cut my
split ends. i just don't like any sort of skinhead fascism. we all went
through that as bobby soxers. the thing is there isn't any consistency
anywhere anyway. it's a joke. the short-hair stompers and overalls
who was criticizing me the most for instance and who was preparing
to leave this house where we'd repaired after the room on the campus,
i asked her as a matter of form was she going to some other house
where perchance of course she lived with her own group of women
or something like that, and she looked me right in the eye and said
no, she lived with a man. — ! see, so nothing makes any sense, or else
everything is all about transition. and when we *arrive*, what will *that*

look like. most of the time i was trying to relax, like a wet sandwich. there i was draping over a chair at some desk behind my aviator blues telling desultory stories in a mellow alcoholic haze of the bloody marys off the last plane trip when one totally sober stomper said Why are you sitting up there in front of us, Why aren't we in a circle? i wanted to say why did you come here, but i said Do It, and they Did It. and we were then in a circle and i continued telling stories and all but i really began to feel like crying, being pregnant and such, and i wanted to be home, and see Everybody Else who looks familiar. one reassuring thing happened however and that was a religious type (i presumed) in femme boots and a leather fringe who came up and shook my hand and said you're a very evolved being, that's the phrase those people use, she seemed a sort of ascetic variation of the frontier chick (that's barbara the poet), whom i had left two days before in grand rapids, and who had also criticized me, for not reading my stuff lovingly enough she'd said. although otherwise she liked me fine, too fine in fact i thought. she told me before i arrived she'd informed her class that i wouldn't be "nice." she was certain i wouldn't be nice. so she expected it. i suspected she really wanted me not to be in order to satisfy some butch fatale expectations of some sort. she herself was more or less just the way i expected to find *her* according to photos and descriptions and poems etc. tall beautiful romantic frontier femme drag earth mother and mother of two beautiful daughters out in the middle of no-wheresville amerika between various impossible worlds. 20 years of a straight marriage done and gone. one daughter off with her own beautiful daughter. the other aged 13 living with her and her transitional mate whom she described as 17 years younger and who wears earrings and femmy clothes, etc. i called the morning i left new york and said i don't stay in houses where there's guys. i don't know why she'd expect me to be any less uptight than all the women of the midwest who're supposed to be in love with her and be uptight because as she wrote they get pissed off at her for living with this man. not that i was dying to jump into bed with her sight unseen or seen or anything at all including being in love which is a state i don't understand too well these days anyway, but i'll tell you i'm not rescuing any woman personally from a man and moreunder i can't even work up a sufficient attraction to do it, i don't think i could do it for the queen, and that's because i look at a woman who's cohabiting with a guy (*especially a faggot* for chrissake), and i see her as a cocksucker in the literal sense of that term and i have instant repulsive reactions like i don't want to be contaminated or something, i'm really serious. i don't even want to say will you teach me to love you and leave you in just one night. i didn't want to be responsible for anything whatsoever except reading my stuff materoffactly the way i do and fielding the same old questions about how women must have as hard a time getting it on together as women and men and such and as i mentioned being idolized a little bit from a distance and hearing something new about the world. as simone said when she got into my german racer the other day and noticed the raggedy ann and the teddy bear why don't you just tell them you're a little girl. but i always think they know that already. i'm going out to get a set of toy trains too. if they're waiting for me to grow up, i'll make sure to stunt my growth. anyway i didn't feel great about not being able to save the beautiful frontier woman of the midwest. it isn't by the way that she hasn't made it with women before either. the way i heard it in fact she did every thing at once at the end of the old straight marriage. feminism women the faggot the works i guess. a couple of women brought her out sexually and she brought them out politically she said. the question is what next. and i didn't have any answers. she's a good feminist, what's she living with a faggot for. i donno. how should i know. she's scared. me too. we were standing by her car in the parking lot waiting for the old man with the keys to go to the airport, here i am way along in my story and i'm still leaving the grand rapids airport!, there was this awkward silence, so i tugged on her scarf a bit and said whatsa matter, and she moved over and i had to hug her and i even sort of kissed her, it was very embarrassing, i'm pretty reticent actually, and she said oh she was gonna say something silly but then she thought better of it. i'm glad. it was bad enough at the airport when i kissed her again, this time goodbye, and she said she wished i'd fallen in love with her. see what i mean? everything is hopeless. shit, the faggot is her woman for the time being so so what, the whold world is living in the time being. at last i was leaving the grand rapids airport and saying goodbye to the woman the whole midwest is in love with. i've never written totally about one of these college junkets before and now i suppose it's becoming my winter odyssey. i want to convey every detail. the color of their hair and the size of their houses. i had an indian dinner in a wonderful house on stilts at the top of many stone steps overlooking lake michigan when the sun was going down. i met a fantastic woman called rachel in the cafeteria of this thomas jefferson college. i met terry the dyke and copied some of her writing out of her journal into mine. i saw ann wehrer from the old days because she met me at the detroit airport and drove me into ann arbor. i met a woman who was unable to tell me her life in a shorter time than it took to live it. i have a letter here from a woman in madison thanking me for the confusion and the excitement i created. i learned about riot control architecture on college campuses. i threw a male student out of a class at that thomas jefferson place by threatening his life with a coke can. i had a very interesting time. i always do. and i'm almost always anxious to leave soon after i get there, in order to see what the next place is like. i don't like either fulfilling or disappointing peoples expectations. i think expectations are old-fashioned. if i expected a tornado tomorrow what would i do about it anyway. nothing neutral and detached and intellectually pertinent ever happens. you always have to be fulfilling and disappointing. your image has preceded you in an absolute riot of expectations. everybody thinks that you and your image are the same thing. they don't even realize that the only thing that actually exists is your image. expectations are all about images. if i expect a tornado tomorrow i form an image of it in my mind. if i don't expect it why should i think about it. my conclusion therefore is that it isn't wise to go anyplace at all. let them come to you and see how you don't actually exist. you sit all alone in a new england winter reading books and playing vivaldi. you try to get more involved in snow shovels and things, be a little bit more outer directed. a very regular life. an outrageous person who leads a routine life. a big irresistible force that leads you toward whatever the future will be. the force of the unexpected moment. if you lead a daily life and it is all yours. last week sk told me there's gotta be an environment where we can relax and assume that we're all god. this is definitely not the environment on the college circuit. being god means not thinking about anything in advance of its happening. being god means not existing. in the meantime if we insist on accepting invitations to places we have to put up with our images. i've learned a great deal about myself that way. not all of it very reassuring. most of it not very good at all in fact. i leave a wave of disappointment behind me and fly away with terrible guilt tremors. the very act of leaving is a disappointment. that's basically why it's wise not to go anyplace. arrivals and departures in themselves are the original expectant forms of fulfillment and disappointment. the first mistake is existence. that's why we worship god. we don't remember how we got here and we know it was a mistake. then we make things worse by moving around creating expectations, unless you travel all the time without going anywhere the way gregory does. staying still is the earthly form of being god, like a tree. or launching yourself into orbit, like a radio satellite. that's how i got to be god a few times, by launching myself into orbit. a snow shovel or a head of lettuce can become holy that way too. of course we *are* in orbit here on earth, but not enough of us know it yet. people haven't read bucky's operating manual for spaceship earth. or they have and they think *bucky* is god. that means they think he exists. we're all under the illusion that we exist, i am too, when i go someplace i have my own expectations. i'll never be god until i stop thinking i exist. all of this explains why people don't mind other people so much when they're dead. existence is very threatening. of course death is disappointing too. the price of arrival. the kind of god who is said to exist is an icon and icons are always crucified. an icon is an image. there's no hope for images. images come and go. god doesn't come and go. god is my unexpected moment. god is not my expectation at all. god is me in the new england winter getting more involved with snow shovels. i think i can perfect my image by staying home. i love going places though. besides by the time you're 88½ you don't have to go anyplace to have bad things happen to you, they're working on your image all the time. i heard that salinger disappeared into a cabin in the woods forever and i suppose what they say about him is he's some sort of crazy recluse. you and i may think that's a good thing to be but other people have other ideas. other people always have ideas, that's the trouble, the whole world is about other people. other people who don't know other people develop ideas about them, so we all have these big ideas about other people. the other people are the strangers i was talking about. strangers everywhere. the strangest experience i ever had at one of these colleges was at this place called albright in reading pennsylvania. for some reason that nobody seemed to understand including me and the people who invited me i was the keynote speaker for this spring arts festival, and the reason it was incomprehensible was that there wasn't a single dyke on the premises that i could determine, and the level of their feminism was cosmopolitan or redbook advice to teenagers, thus there was a kind of mutual embarrassment all the way around and in fact near the end of it my own sense of the un-intelligibility of the occasion was confirmed when a woman told me confidentially that when they heard that this Lesbian was coming to the campus and she was going to *sleep in a dormitory* they went around psst psssting to everybody that they'd better lock their doors, can you imagine that? well that was one place whose expectations were completely satisfied, i didn't get to sleep with anybody. the first thing people think about is sex. that's one reason i liked that woman rachel in the cafeteria at allendale michigan so much, all she wanted was for barbara and me to straighten out her life. i have a letter from barbara in fact saying contrary to all my expectations that my visit was just what she (barbara) needed and she feels like she's getting so strong she's almost a goddess! it's a good thing i left. i'm terrified of goddesses. she rightly i suppose identifies herself as the Mother, who has more *power*. i'd seen her already as the earth mother but i thought that was just a frontier style, women for the festival of life and all that, the women that is who still bake bread and string beads and sew patches on their old mens denims. i know i think a lot of women are confused between their Mother and their Daughter aspects. it hasn't been allowed for one thing for the Daughters to remain the Daughters. i for one had to pretend to be a Mother before i could get to be my Daughter again. some children look like ancient crones and they probably are. i think one of these days we're going to separate the Mothers from the Daughters so we can be clearer about ourselves. i want basically to be with my Daughter clan, with an occasional visit from the powerful Mother, who casts good spells and stuff. i just spoke to danny and i asked him if he was the Son or the Father (i think he's more the Son) and he said he sees himself as the Son being cast a lot in the role of Father. but i don't want to get into that. the thing is sometimes i can't figure out what anybody is supposed to do. in the cafeteria it was very clear. here was a confused desperate Daughter and her Mother and her Daughter had all the answers. that is, we recorded back her own words more or less, we heard her and bounced it back until i supposed she believed her own self. what was happening was she'd been living up in the hills in a clever original house that she herself had built with her boyfriend and now their relationship was so lousy that she was afraid to even go there since he'd smashed some of her sculpture, she's a sculptor too, and was beating her up sometimes like the very night i was due to talk there he beat her up and she couldn't come and so forth, but i suppose she loved the house and the main thing was she felt some responsibility to a project she'd committed herself to on the campus and she didn't know what to do. i'm sure she split. she was living her future already. it takes a while for the images to catch up. the trouble was she couldn't be god where somebody was fucking around with her image that way. she was big and beautiful with strong features and dark eyes and a builders hands. anyway so i got to feel like i helped save somebody. and i didn't have to jump into bed or anything. one reason i flew away from there with those guilt tremors was that i believe inadvertently i turned on a student and promptly ran away from her when i realized what'd happened. there was a neat party at barbara's after i talked and we were all dancing a lot and i forget that for some women if you have bodily contact with another woman in the act of dancing or whatever, it means instant sex or the prospect of some great romance or possibly even a lifelong marriage, who knows, but i got up to dance with this woman and suddenly she was very hot and bothered and saying things like she didn't know whether she was ready for this, and i untangled us immediately, rather tactfully too i thought, and made some excuse for going someplace else, *she* might not've known whether she was ready for it whatever it was but i knew myself. then the next day in that house on stilts at the top of the stone steps overlooking lake michigan she was there and she said suddenly to the assembled company that she was *very* confused and didn't know what to do, she felt like she was ready to come out, so how was i supposed to feel, and what could anybody do. nothing. i'm sure she's come out. she's come out in her mind so she's come out. i don't put much stock in the images at all as i've been saying. the world is mind. and other people have other ideas, etcetera. who cares about other people. nobody does, that's the trouble. then it comes to you that you can do anything as long as it's not you and you refuse to recognize yourself in the street. the whole matter of focusing on the problem is one of the large penalties for having one. the first point to note about biographies is that we assume an individual can really have only one of them. this being guaranteed by the law of physics rather than that of society. physics is images. as terry the dyke said when a woman in her class walked by us everybody's her business. terry was up there on lake michigan too. that's where i copied some stuff out of her journal into mine. i had an embarrassing scene with barbara there too, although it wasn't the end of the world or anything. she arrived and handed me my cheque in an envelope and with it or rather on top of it a pink candy heart that said kiss me. then she tactfully disappeared. she went into the kitchen to find out from her friend ingy what happened when i threw this male student out of ingy's class. while she was gone i was fooling around with the plastic bag of candy hearts and sort of looking for one myself when accidentally one fell on the floor and it said ask me so i gave it to barbara when she came back but i don't think she thought i meant it and i didn't. after all, she's the powerful Mother. i don't mind being attacked by and mauled somehow occasionally by the Mother, but what's the Daughter herself supposed to do. anyway as i'm thinking about it now and tallying up a few experiences with the Mothers i see that oftentimes what's happening is that the Mother is living with her Son, the hermes or the dionysus, the faggot in other words, the one who refused to become the Father, and come the revolution she begins to perceive her Daughter, the persephone, her daughter the dyke, her lost old self, and she goes out looking just the way the myth says she does, but either it's been so long that she's forgotten how to look, or she doesn't look long and hard enough, or something, i dunno, i know i can't do much myself with the old Son there lurking in the background, especially when the old Mother is sort of challenging me in this ultimate way like that if i don't come across me myself in person she the Mother will then feel justified in giving up the pursuit of her Daughter in order to linger on with the Son. you know what i mean? i could give two other examples of this contemporary drama, but i wouldn't want other persons living or dead to misunderstand what i'm trying to say. it happens always in different guises. i'm just beginning to catch the pattern. the last time it happened the Mother was very explicit and demanding. i thought she was kidding. the trouble was we Daughters were challenging this Mother to death ourselves. it was a mutual mistake. she was coming on to the Daughters, and maybe even another Mother or two, i don't really know who's what truthfully, and she had the Son back at the old homestead. it sounds like grendel and beowulf somehow, i don't know why. anyway it was hopeless, i was enjoying myself with another Daughter, and i wasn't going to save her from the Son anyhow for sure, and she was pretty angry about it in the end, even though we managed to present her with the ultimate Daughter, a seven foot amazon princess, that was hopeless too, since the amazon princess had her own Daughter, and between the lot of us in the end she could feel universally justified in keeping a *harem* of goddam Sons, for all i knew, or cared. i cared, but it's still too much about images. expectation. arrivals and departures. i'm vowing to make small decisions that're in opposition to the existing order of things. snow shovels and such. it doesn't matter whether you go anyplace or not. the best thing that happened to me this trip around was ending up in albany late at night with just enough cash for a motel, the fine absurdity of going to albany because there wasn't a plane into new york and you just wanted to be in

the state of new york so you take whatever they have and that means you don't know *what's* going to happen to you tomorrow . . .
—*February 15, 1973*

Time Wounds All Heals

i'm bored with the michigan wisconsin story and i'm already in england where i've promised myself to be by the time anybody reads this. the winter odyssey is over. it's all about books and bells from here on in. the story has been told many times. some parts of it may be true. the sequence is unconscious and the unconscious is the most orderly place of all. nice play, shakespeare. amnesia is a social event. i'm reactivating the father investigation and other cocoons. there's a girl called rosemary i haven't met yet. and a boy called arthur. and some other nights of the squaretable i presume. the romance family is not necessarily an invention. in any case the feminist project is to recover possession of the paternal titles. see *sleuth* with olivier and michael caine and substitute for caine a girl. *sleuth* is a fabulous flick. the sleuth is the grail quester or so i read it. the british are the masters of this modern detective story. the problem is how to take the bull by the udders. the bull or minos or olivier is first found by the quester at the center of a maze constructed of tall hedges just outside the palace or manor house where he is recording a new episode in his detective story on his tape recorder. he's a famous author of such novels. he's at the center of his prize possession, his woman, whom we never see. minos's palace at cnossus was a complex of rooms, ante-rooms, halls, and corridors in which a country visitor might easily lose his way. according to some historians the labyrinth was so called from the labyris, or double-headed axe, a familiar emblem of cretan sovereignty, shaped like a waxing and waning moon joined together back to back and symbolizing the creative as well as the destructive power of the goddess. according to every feminist's favorite author, elizabeth gould davis, the labyris was symbol of the goddess and of matriarchal rule, not only in crete but among the lycians, lydians, amazons, etruscans, and romans and it's been found in the graves of paleolithic women of europe buried 50,000 years ago. there's a feminist bookstore called labyris just a few months old in new york owned and operated by two women on 33 barrow street. there's a feminist restaurant on 11th street near the docks called mother courage after the revolutionary woman of the brecht play. the women possess their own means of production and nurturance. the women are inside themselves, their own food establishment, and they sit down and talk to you as if they owned the place, which they do, the intestines of the labyrinth of the woman. if you're a woman it's an easy place to go to. an insiders hangout. i don't go to england as an insider exactly. hardly. i don't know what i go as and i don't know what for particularly either. the queen is in good shape, so it can't be the grail. and i don't need any souvenir bells. and i don't need to meet arthur and rosemary, who might not be dying to see their name contaminated by a dishonorable relative. the project actually might boil down to a hunt for the proper sort of derby hat. the hat i might then set up as a still life with a toy tommy gun in metallic blue i bought at a grant superstore place. the bowler hatted man is more like a figure in a book then a human being. that's where the books get thrown in with the bells. my earliest idea of my father was out of a book. the book was called *carillon music and singing towers*. a later idea occurred in a book called *the banquet years* containing a photo of apollinaire in a derby and a moustache. one of his transmogrifications. the one who died young of the spanish influenza. the one who said please doctor i don't want to die, i still have so much to do. the other image was of this one was a head swathed in bandages. at four o'clock in the afternoon of march 17 in the year of 1915 second lieutenant apollinaire was sitting in the trenches reading the lastest *mercure de france* to which he was still sending his regular chronique, la vie anecdotique, when some blood started dripping onto a page from a shrapnel that pierced his helmet over the right temple. i should add the bandage to the tommy gun and the hat. that would be very obvious. the choice of effects is not difficult. it's their juxtaposition that matters. the arrangement of new mysterious associations. the coordination as equally present of a variety of times and places and states of consciousness. the labyrinth could be the bowels of the old man too i guess. to reach the king a visitor is passed from one guide to another to be led thru the maze. the first objective of the young aspirant in *sleuth* is to reach the lord of the manor in the center of his perfectly symmetrical maze of hedges. the game of troy, the siege of troy, was the penetration of the maze to win or capture a maiden, and that is the apparent quest of caine as an unwitting sleuth. the maiden as it turns out is the middleaged wife of the lord of the manor, the famous author of detective stories. the author of course has invited (lured) the lover of his wife to his house. he is the king in the sense that he appears to be the correctly descended englishman. the challenge to his throne is distinctly from an outsider, an upstart, a hairdresser of some italian origin putting on fine airs and manners. he is the traditional hero. the hero sets out on his journey with no clear idea of the task before him. he comes in red sports car and parks in the circular gravel driveway. whither he rides, and why, he does not know, only that the business is important and pressing. he hears the voice of the man who called him, a garble of overtones emanating from the hedged enclosure dictating to himself the new episode in his novel. traditionally in no case was the fisher king a youthful character. that distinction was reserved for his healer, and successor. the main object in the quest of the grail was the restoration to health and vigor of a king suffering from infirmity caused by wounds sickness or old age. the grail stories were medieval romantic evolutions of the ancient fertility rites centering round the death and resurrection of the divine king. one of the fatal symptoms of decay was taken to be an incapacity to satisfy the sexual passions of his wives. the custom of putting divine kings to death at the first symptoms of infirmity prevailed until recently. when he had ceased to be able to reproduce his kind it was time for him to die and to make room for a more vigorous successor. in certains tribes a king even while yet in the prime of health and strength might be attacked at any time by a rival and have to defend his crown in a combat to the death. *sleuth* is a combat to the death. one might assume that the author (olivier) is still hearty, though hardly young, he's certainly intense and energetic, effusive and extravagant in his outpourings, yet the subject of his impotence arises, the pedestrian justification for a domestic tragedy. his wife had been looking elsewhere, and his mistress confided to the hero that he hadn't been able to get it up in a year. the health of the king was always absolutely intrinsic to the state of the land. the king is ailing and so is england. the restoration of the land and the survival of its inhabitants was at stake. this is why the status of the author is made very clear. altogether this is a time of mounting and unendurable distress. the life of his wife has been a perpetual surrender of ease and comfort to the service of others. it's no wonder the two male antagonists are so desperate to have her. even though she remains invisible. one wonders what they do actually want. the grail is still a mystery. the symbols of the great search were the cup and the lance. there was also the sword and the dish. hearts diamonds spades and clubs. the four suits of the tarot. the labyrinth is the form of the detective story. the story is the seasonal wanderings through the landscape of the woman. the ups and downs of the man. the men're hung up on legitimacy, because theirs is so tenuous biologically. i never did go through the proper channels, i attempted to make contact by jumping in a pool. i appreciate however the artifice of the search. famosus ille fabulator. the details of the symbols. the reactivation of the father investigation. the romance family is not necessarily an invention. i lay the derby upside down to achieve the chalice. i lean the toy tommy gun against the chair to signify the sword. i make a reservation for london on boac on washington's birthday. i note that christ was crucified march 25th and resurrected the 27th and the pub date of my book is the 30th. i note that my son's birthday is the 31st. i arrange to travel with susan b. whose best friend in england is named rosemary who will meet us at the airport. i remember that rosemary who went to cambridge to study history is also a british bastard. i am notified by my unconscious that at my age my father was travelling the atlantic by boat to install his goddam bells in all these episcopalian towers. i remind my readers that the belle in the tower is the captive virgin, the maiden (head) at the center of the maze, the garden of even. you remember poseidon built rings within rings of a fortress to protect himself inside at the center with his wife and mistress clito. during the day the king surrounded himself with his friends and bodyguards such that an aspirant to the throne could hardly hope to cut his way through them and strike home. a belle in a tower in the form of a huge hunk of metal is a very permanent fixture. in the movie *sleuth* the expensive effects of the lady in question, her invaluable jewels, are hidden someplace in the wall in a safe, naturally, and the first task of the hero is to locate said safe (it's behind a dartboard, naturally) and then to help the ailing author dynamite the thing, which they do, causing the dartboard to erupt at its center into a gaping smoking perfectly circular hole. from some ancient point of view kindness could be anticipated from a woman only so long as she remained a virgin. the hero (caine) the hairdresser descendant of an italian is an offender of the prime water. he presumes to violate the woman of the palace. the woman herself is a mere plaything, a *femme a homme*, the object of her crazy husband's fantasies, she's all over the house as a windup doll performing acrobatic tricks or pouring tea or smiling approvingly or playing the harpsichord. he touches a button in his pocket and his toys do their tricks. his real woman hasn't been responding correctly, she's been playing around on her own. he wants her back and he wants to murder her, he hates her, his pride is wounded, he's a furious fellow, he's falling apart. the malady of the king is always antecedent to the visit of the hero. in the least contaminated version of the grail story the central figure would be dead and the task of the quester that of restoring him to life (my prime source is jessie l. weston). this of course is precisely what olivier has in mind, and by inducing his victim (savior) to jump through a series of hoops, i mean an elaborate obstacle course or labyrinth of clues and objectives, as a sort of test of his worthiness as it were, even persuading his victim that he actually wishes to be rid of his wife and that he is helping him to have and to keep her by setting up a phony theft of her jewels so that the interloper can maintain her in style through the collection of burglary insurance, he leads him expertly into a scene of mortifying humiliation and a mock murder in which the hero victim savior hairdresser etc. is literally almost scared to death, and following which we witness the amazing revitalization of our author and his household of rejoicing toys all gyrating and laughing and bobbing and sireening at once, the most clamorous being his mockup sailor (sinbad?) his alterego i presume, a mortimer snerdish puppet who laughs and applauds alarmingly. anyway thus endeth the first chapter of the flick, the victory of the incumbent. at some point the two figures begin to merge. i won't give away the rest of the story. the horror of the occasion is by every means magnified and funereally enriched. what we are witnessing is the crucial matter of the possession of the proper woman. such preferences and priorities are not easily and effectively transmitted. the class struggle of the movie may obscure a more fundamental contest between the forces of life and death, of spring and winter, the safeguarding of the cup of plenty, the problems of the broken lance. the class struggle is merely a civilized decadent form of its embodiment. the morality play that is *sleuth* leaves the paternal inheritance in question. the men have outwitted themselves, for both are the losers. the bandage on my head of apollinaire is an essential prop for the play. apollinaire was in love with madeleine, a young girl he met on a train. "The shells were bellowing a love-till-death/ the loves which leave us are sweeter than the rest/ rain, rain, go away and blood will staunch its flow/ the shells were bellowing listen to ours sing/ purple love saluted by those about to die!" in certain versions of the grail the king is wounded, as a punishment for sin, for having conceived a passion for a pagan princess. what one should note here is the invention of a discipline of disintegration. the men of sleuth are properly living and dying in the ginnunga gab, the time of transition as the virgins travel round the world of their mothers reclaiming their paternal titles. la belle dame sans merci hath thee in thrall. the labyrinth of error will be the initiation of the daughters into the wombs of their selves. patient, reliable, uncomplaining. bowing to the inevitable yoke of her sex, she accepts her tasks. she has no idea where to begin. she makes reservations, she reconstructs her virginity, she exposes herself to the media (: scenes from the execution), she collects and disseminates bad news. she advertises feminist restaurants and bookstores. she makes the kind of collage you put up on the wall, she practices being simultaneously overt and mysterious, she exploits her expansive personality and celebrates it in her writing, she assembles the symbols of her death and her future. her farther unknown. usage externe. the bowler hatted man may be the perfect vehicle for anybody's projections. he takes on an increasingly mythological aspect. he has come to represent all men.

he walks around anonymously with his chalice on his head. his mother will serve him his supper. time wounds all heals.

—*February 22, 1973*

There'll Awe Ways Be An England

well i went to england and i didn't see any feminists nor too much of anybody else and i was neurotically famished and rationally cold and determinedly homesick and righteously paranoid but in nine or ten days i figured out the country and that was what i went for so it was an awful and worthwhile trip. the first thing i did i went to sleep for six hours on the top floor of roy jenkins's house on ladbroke square. the next thing i woke up and called george and peter and suzi and charlotte and carolee and i forgot who else but the only person who answered was peter who told me there was an r.d. laing soiree of some sort going on at eight at a paul somebody's house and i should go and i did i left roy jenkins's house on ladbroke square and never returned, much no doubt to the relief of whomever was there who never saw me as i was whisked up the carpeted stairways as though i was a poor relation of one of the cooks or something. anyway i took a cab over to this paul's house and thought how wonderful and clean looking london is and how all its cars are shiny and sleek in their small interesting economical designs, no dirty old crates all over the place, and i came to my first sweeping conclusion about england as i pondered the outstanding fact that none of its taxis are bent out of shape, they're spotless and scratchless and scrupulously immaculate and i decided this must reveal the character of the english in conjunction with their space which compared to ours is relatively small. later george told me this was ridiculous, that the taxis in england are built like trucks and the english are *always* having accidents, they drive around like demons as if they know what they're doing but they don't, and in any case the taxis he would've led me to believe can sustain the onslaught of a sherman tank and come out looking brand new the way they all look. i've never seen an accident in england, and what rosemary told me was that the english are very frightened of touching each other. whether benign or repressed the fact is that it's a lot easier and nicer getting around since the people watch where they're going and are forever politely excusing themselves at any real or imagined contact, and i assume this is because their character has been molded by tight quarters and short distances, the pushy ones left long ago to invade plymouth and boston and cross the rockies and develop a real amerikan sense of arrogant limitlessness etc., which i suppose includes a capacity for grand and gratuitious generalizations based on any fleeting observation and delivered with great confidence at the slightest provocation. nevertheless, i did find out what england is all about. it's all about my father, who died more or less when england did. the english are somewhat dead. amerikans may be brash and crude and ugly in a lot of ways, there's no doubt we're a beastly lot actually, but we are alive, there's no question we're alive, even if we're alive with desperation and delusions and crooked impossible schemes for saving the universe and a greedy consuming materialism and a grubby untidy incestuous belligerance, whatever it is and however unpleasant, we are by comparison with a country like england alarmingly alive. all features great & small. can you imagine for instance that as dead an amerikan as andy w. is up in lights over the title of his flick *trash* at picadilly circus which is like our times square? or what may be equally significant that an amerikan as nervously alive as me arrives in england always possible naively expecting the england of the representation in my new record book in the form of a photo blueprint made by jane of these suffragists around the turn of the century being led away violently by the bobbies outside buckingham palace? i mean that we can't even go someplace, and someplace for that matter which may be quite contented with its demise, without projecting our own agitation and restlessness which we think is being alive. i went quite dead in england anyway, i always catch the spirit. at the laing soiree at paul somebody's house i even exercised a bit of will power and restrained myself by not charging vocally into the excellent silences which at times would overtake the company. the company by the way was a large group of people packed tightly into a living room of a high ceiling, sitting on the floor in curving banks against the walls and facing the master with what i assumed to be a reverent attention awaiting the first utterances. i'm sure it was un-amerikan for me to be there at all, it was certainly unfeminist, and although i respected the silences i did find the opportunity to more or less deplore my own attendance by being no doubt brash and crude and hopelessly undeferential and altogether predictably amerikan. old r.d. was getting off some good stuff too, stuff about the impossibility of relationships and all that should cross all race color age and sex lines and interest absolutely everybody, and i was certainly interested, and i even tossed in some two cents on the subject, i said if you want to know i said something smartassed about how it seems to me that any form of detachment, i.e. zen or yogurt, is another kind of attachment, a very deep comment, but essentially i realized at some point that i'd hate for anybody to think i really wanted to be there, in other words that i might have any intention of becoming an initiate into the london laing circle, a group of sycophants if ever i saw any. i know i'm full of contradictions on a subject like this, going and then trying to deny that one has ever gone, and such, but that's the nature of my involvement in whatever vestiges of admiration i still retain for men, among whom i have to still say i think laing is a pretty good head. i even went out of my way, arising from the london apathy, to go over to his house in belsize park and have tea and cheese cake and admire his 2½ yr. daughter and his beautiful german wife jutta and compliment his style in refusing to take advantage of the authority vested in him at such as these soirees by meandering awkwardly or haltingly in and around his subject without appearing to answer anything. the purpose of my visit may have been however to sort of apologize for my own appearance at the salon by saying that i would consider it humiliating to personally publicly invest any man with that authority etc. etc., it's a hopeless contradiction i suppose. possibly the purpose of the visit was to talk to jutta who's a fine person besides being beautiful, and she didn't make me feel as if i had to convert her to anything, she might actually be satisfied living with the most amenable psycho-analyst of the western world. i don't know. i called joe berke too and he thinks r.d. is a terrific chauvinist (i suppose berke isn't), and tho' he has great respect for him he can't work with him any more, it's impossible he said to be around him without being a sychophant, and all he talks about these days is what he has for breakfast and how many baths he takes a day. there are in fact now in london two sets of communities, freakout houses modeled after the original kingsley hall, and berke is involved in the set that isn't laing's set, in fact i imagine berke and a couple of associates formed a splitoff community, it sounds like the professional jealousies that arose around freud. we are reminded of the brief nature of earthly power and glory. berke of course is an amerikan, in case that makes a difference, and i for one think it does. i wonder if r.d. would've branched out at all, i mean get all involved in therapeutic communities and other extroversions if the amerikans hadn't sped across the atlantic in the first place in search of the english guru of psychology beside whom i'm suddenly imagining they rallied to the cause and rushed to the barricades of one sort or another, always of course respecting those intermittent silences. i have to say by the way about these silences that they're probably the most alive thing in england, these pregnant silences, silences by which we might enliven our own hysterical gatherings. characteristic again of the amerikan space of which perhaps we have too much. always rushing in to fill it all up. terrified no doubt of what might happen if we don't. we might die. yeah. well, i don't know truthfully *how* dead or alive the english are, but one thing is certain and that is it's impossible to get to know them. and i think now that that's the real reason i always go dead there. i want to integrate totally with the situation. i begin speaking a polyglot of english accents as soon as i disembark and very quickly i become as difficult to get to know as the natives. i go to sleep more or less, even after recovering from the time lag trauma. not however until after i've been variously and repeatedly discouraged, learning my lesson anew each time as it were. the day after the laing affair i charged with bright amerikan anticipation out of george's place on dorset square into the gray london winter expecting god knows what and wound up being dizzy as a drunk dog in the mill of foreigners meaning english people on charing cross road walking up to tottenham court in and out of these highly confusing bookstores buying a satchels worth of history and the grail, i thought i was going down or taking off, the disorientation was intense, until i brought myself into order by clugalugging two glasses of milk in a wimpy bar, and began already to feel chastened by the english chill, if only because as an amerikan i expect a lot to happen and suddenly all that's happening is that you're disoriented by streetsful of very polite and remote dead strangers. their avowed impulses are only part of their entire attitude. i have no idea what their attitudes are in the least. but i must admit that the analyses and conclusions i reached were corroborated by one englishman and one amerikan man, and in a sense by rosemary who reiterates that the english are simply repressed. i met colin naylor at the salisbury pub, he's the editor of arts & artists, and he said very cheerily that everything is quiet here, under the table, that it's usually in the form of a nervous breakdown when anybody in this country beings expressing themselves. and it was george (walsh), gregory's friend, who said what i suspected when it occurred to me that england was dead and so was my father, the two events being causally connected somehow, and that was that the individuals in england feel however consciously or un- that their country is a 3rd rate power and that whatever they do won't make a difference particularly, which is why you get that muted or "given up" sensation when you disembark, and that by contrast naturally the amerikans do feel that what we do will make a difference and that's because we live in a greedy aggrandizing imperialist pig world power place, which is what england used to be. the whole place seething with savage enthusiasm. yet i don't imagine for a second that the working classes in england have been affected one way or the other by the alteration in their country's fortunes. i have more to say about that, and this and that. anyone may think i went over in this terrible time of year just for the hell of it but i really had a purpose and the trip was successful because i found out what i wanted to know, no fooling around. other than that, i'll probably continue making these devastating journeys, the fantasy is still very much alive. there'll awe ways be an england. (beware the ideas of march.)

—*March 8, 1973*

Who was Virginia Woolf Afraid Of?

One thing i'd seriously like to know about england is how class conscious they still are. i could read about it possibly. i mentioned it to everybody i talked to practically and no one seemed to have any better idea than me. so that's about all i have to say about it. i've just been routing through quentin bell's book on v. woolf looking for these passages concerning something called "the servant problem" between virginia and her sister vanessa and here it is. it was 1917 or so it seems before the war before 1914 "a surprisingly large number of people could employ . . . one indoor servant. labour was plentiful and girls would accept places for their keep and a pittance. the rich, who might afford a ratio of say six servants to one master, probably found them more efficient than we our mechanical appliances." before the war the woolfs kept two servants, the bells four, according to quentin the minimum for a household in which the wife had a full-time occupation. during the war female labour became scarce because there were good wages to be earned in the factories. but the real problem apparently was a moral one. this is how bell put it: in hyde park gate (virginia's family home), with its army of servants, the situation had been frankly patriarchal. leslie stephen was the head of the house. minny, julia, stella, or vanessa were his deputies and the servants were immediately responsible to them. everyone knew their respective place. the system had the faults and the virtues of bene-volent despotism. during the years between 1904 and 1914 that system began to break down; the stephen sisters lacked the social assurance of their parents; they disliked the servant/mistress relation-ship, but they did not know how to avoid it. paternalism only works when both sides accept it as proper and natural. when it breaks down, injustices may be removed, but the moral situation becomes extremely uncomfortable. mrs bell and mrs woolf looked for, felt for, some other and more equal form of contract between employer and employed. the stephen sisters had become socially conscious, and seemed temperamentally incapable of maintaining the old master-slave standard, yet as bell points out domestic conditions at that time were still so primitive that someone had to be perpetually at work if any sort of comfort or cleanliness was to be kept, and virginia and vanessa both were serious artists. the dilemma was never solved. relations between virginia and the two women who worked for her and leonard for 18 years according to q. bell were exasperatingly ambivalent. bell says "they were part of the household, in a sense a part of the family, but they were also independent human beings, equals with feelings to be respected. Ideally, hopefully, they were friends. but how many of one's friends are there whom one can see daily, who are dependent on one for a livelihood, who hold one's comforts in their hands, and with whom one is never bored or cross? and how hard to base a friendship on a written character, an interview, and no similarity of upbringing, of interests, of educations, or of class." and he went on to say that class today is almost a dirty word, hoping it represents less than it did 50 years ago in english society. i doubt it so long as there's a nobility. i think the death of virginia's father and the move of the four children to bloomsbury where the two boys imported their interesting kinky friends from cambridge for their soirees projected the women at least out of the rigid unconsciously accepted class structuring of their heritage, and they remained exceptional people in this respect as in others, the bene-ficiaries of the structure at its most material as well as its most intellectual, having developed a capacity even to comprehend the injustices of the system by which they benefited. the servants were possibly the most disoriented. bell says in bloomsbury the servants had to deal with neurotic and unusual people who wore the wrong clothes, hung the wrong pictures, held the wrong views, and had the most peculiar friends. in '17 for example vanessa's cook found herself in a position of discussing with her mistress the relationship between one of the guests, who happened to be lytton strachey, and a seductive stable-boy on an adjacent farm. (i wonder that bell didn't question *who* was seductive, why not strachey — because it's always the inferiors, i.e. girls, who're at fault and seductiveness was a fault especially if it crossed class lines.) what bell is incapable of doing in his fine biography is drawing a connection between the patriarchal household situation of virginia's early days that he outlines so well and virginia's burgeoning feminism, which ultimately he views as irresponsible, what with hitler crossing the rhine and invading austria and everything. correctly enough he notes that events in 1938 didn't turn on the Rights of Women but on the Rights of Nations. virginia's second feminist work *three guineas* had just been published, a lot less playful than *a room of one's own*. as a man bell is blind to the war and hitler and his own guys etc. as a manifestation of patriarchal attitudes to which virginia is addressing herself. her book might actually have been seen as very topical. a number of women in fact were enthusiastic. but as bell says her close friends (read men) were silent, or if not silent, critical. maynard keynes for instance declared it a silly argument and not very well written. but bell himself (virginia's nephew by the way in case anybody doesn't know) makes the best male criticism: what really seemed wrong with the book, he says, was the attempt to involve a discussion of women's rights with the far more agonizing and immediate question of what we were to do in order to meet the ever-growing menace of fascism and war. endquote. substitute father, or patriarch, for fascism and war. what indeed were they to do about it, being men and all. i don't know if virginia herself made any ideological connection between class and sex oppression, but there were indications that her sensitivity to the working classes was growing apace with her feminism. by the 1930s in any case the working classes themselves were becoming more conscious. a woman named agnes smith wrote a long eloquent letter to virginia objecting that she'd said nothing about working women in *three guineas* ("of what use was it to suggest that women should refuse to manufacture arms when they were only too glad to have the opportunity to manufacture anything?") and virginia replied that *three guineas* had indeed been addressed explicitly to women in more fortunate social positions. they continued a correspondence off and on until virginia died. virginia was caught in more than one con-tradiction (not the least being her marriage to leonard i suppose). in 1928 radclyffe hall's notorious *the well of loneliness* was seized by the police. the home secretary was pressuring the censors and old radclyffe went into a court case but she was adamant about not wanting anybody to testify on behalf of her book unless they saw fit to say it was a great work of art and to virginia this seemed too large a sacrifice in the cause of liberty. the matter was compromised somehow and virginia did appear to testify, the book being condemned nevertheless at that time. virginia called it a "meritorious dull book" and quentin "a sincere though feeble effort." again however, she was identifying herself with the cause of women. it seems to be incredible in fact that virginia in 1928 in england would have been exposing herself to guilt by association in support of a frank lesbian work, unless she actually thought she'd be promoting the sales and appreciation of her own book *orlando* which was published officially six days after radclyffe hall's court case! quentin remarks that *the well of loneliness* had given virginia's sexual theme in *orlando* topicality, so possibly her motivation was somewhat material; but the lesbianism in *orlando* is highly whimsical and off center and embedded in the most fanciful of historical romances, not nearly upfront enough to seriously incriminate its author. nonetheless, her personal life around that time was adventurous in the extreme. she actually left her old man alone in london to spend a week in france with vita (sackville-west) who was as is wellknown the *subject* of *orlando*. you have to be amused by bell saying she "identified herself with the cause of homosexuality by spending a week in france alone with vita." there was even a quarrel between virginia and leonard before they set out. as to her week she wrote that she'd never laughed so much in her life, or talked so much, and that vita was an angel to her, perpetually sweet tempered, endlessly entertaining, and lovely looking, etc. nobody knows what they did in bed. i don't care. if virginia wasn't a lesbian she wasn't the daughter of leslie stephen. i have to credit bell with this really sensitive observation about it, he said they might've done some bedding together but whatever may've occurred between them of this nature he doubted it was of a kind to excite virginia or satisfy vita but that the point was of no great importance; what was, to her, important was the extent to which she was emotionally involved, the degree to which she was in love. that's pretty good going for her nephew. one might've hoped for as much from the reviewer in *the times* a few months ago who kept stressing the trauma of the george duckworth business. i have to mention by the way something very amusing while in london i saw an ad in the

l. times or some paper for charlotte wolf's book called *love between women* (a mixed bag) published by the gerald duckworth firm. gerald was also virginia's half brother and he published some of her early work. the duckworth fellows were a rude addition to the stephen household, the sons of his second wife julia, who was virginia and vanessa's mother, but there was never any question who the real tyrant was. both julia and stella (duckworth, sister of george and gerald) were sacrificed to his demands, and vanessa was next in line until the sisters inaugurated a survival program on their own behalf. this is the first horror story i quoted out of the bell book: julia loving her (stella) less than she did the others, and loving leslie more, had been willing to sacrifice her and the rest of his convenience, and — what was far worse from stella's point of view — had sacrified herself, so that at length in the great campaign to save her mother from exhaustion, she had been defeated both by leslie and by julia. endquote. when julia died her widower became unbearable apparently. virginia said forinstance that leslie actually told vanessa that "when he was sad, she should be sad; when he was angry, she should weep." virginia, says bell, "who witnessed it all, was consumed with silent indignation: how could her father behave with such brutality and why was it that he reserved these bellowings and screamings for his women? with men his conduct was invariably gentle, considerate, and rational so much that when virginia and her aunt caroline emilia stephen suggested to maitland, his biographer, that leslie was sometimes rather difficult, maitland simply wouldn't believe it. leslie he objected, was the most modest, the most reasonable of men — and so he was with his own sex. but he needed and expected feminine sympathy." — ! after her father's death vanessa dreamed that she had committed a murder. lytton strachey once said of leonard woolf that he was like swift and would kill his wife. i saw an elderly gentleman in london called henry michael howard who knew my father and at one point exclaimed rather wistfully i trust i haven't said anything too rude about your father. we all have little in common except our subject. in 1909 clive (quentin's father) wrote to virginia offering criticism of *the voyage out*: "our views about men and women are doubtless quite different, and the difference doesn't matter much; but to draw such sharp & marked contrasts between the subtle, sensitive, tactful, gracious, delicately perceptive, & perspicacious women, & the obtuse, vulgar, blind, florid, rude, thoughtless, emphatic, indelicate, vain, tyrannical, stupid men, is not only rather absurd, but rather bad art, i think." — not the similar phrase used by keynes criticizing *three guineas*: not very well written. — virginia replied: "your objection, that my prejudice against men makes me didactic not to say priggish, has not quite the same force with me . . . possibly, for psychological reasons which seem to me very interesting, a man, in the present state of the world, is not a very good judge of his sex . . ."

—March 15, 1973

Busted: Illegal Attire in the First Degree

i considered having two cats named after me being the event of the week but now clearly it was being arrested at the 23rd precinct last night after waving at a cop outside the guggenheim and wearing illegal clothes or something. it must be for being bad for over a week. i don't know what town we were in but last week i remember driving late at night to a large house for "coffee and brandy" by invitation of a "very nice lady" who hated all of us and that was seven of us and her daughter didn't like us either. we had coffee brandy grass milk crackers and muffins that stuck to their papers and we watched a movie without the sound except for the comments of the hostess who kept exclaiming that the movie was without its sound or identifying one man or another as some man who had slept in her house and editorializing the movie as tragic and hopeful, it happened to be some original color version of the laing asylum flick that we saw here on channel 13 when r.d. came to raise money for his house, and the father as one of those well meaning and insensitive people like all those people in that "wonderful" book sanity madness and the family well meaning insensitive people who destroy their children. enter daughter. who put on a rolling stone record for us i've got you under my thumb and other appealing numbers. every time some body started giggling her mother made for the kitchen announcing coffee. we giggled about everything. antidote anecdote manicdote nannygoat ankleoat antelope elope elope. they hated us. the mother was talking about transsexualism, i don't know why, i never talk about it myself and i cut the whole thing short in fact by saying it was sacriligious, tampering with nature like that, and her daughter said you can't mean that. i said what do you mean i can't mean that. she was saying i couldn't mean what i mean. there people go again trying to say that you've said something you didn't say or you've said something you didn't say you said or didn't say or don't mean you've said what you meant to say to say. i said i meant what i said. she said how can you say that with a drink in your hand. *drinking* is against nature (i was drinking her mother's drink), clearly equating alcohol with transsexualism — crimes against nature. later on her mother put her to bed. she said so. she came downstairs and sat down relievedly next to her fire and brushed a wisp of beautiful gray hair delicately off her brow and said she'd put her children to bed. the other children i guess were these male freaks who ran her picture projector. the child her daughter is a full bosomed proper lady like herself. have a good time dear but don't go near the water. here's your hurry what's your hat. and we left to leave thank you ever so much for the coffee brandy grass milk crackers and muffins that stick to their papers and the wonderful silent movie. goodnight goodnight. never darken our daughter again. anyway i was arrested last night. and i was just discussing with gregory our habit of not being invited back places. it's something if you can be there at all. i was urged last week to go on to the long john silver radio thing at midnight. bertha said i shouldn't do it it's an awful thing to do so i called the people who'd urged me to do it and said i couldn't do it but they urged me again and said i should do it it would be a good thing to do so i did and i brought bertha and it's a five hour gig into the small dawn but we were ejected in ten minutes i don't know why except i thought he was a hateful person and i told him so possibly that's why. long john nibble or nebish or nebble or something. he said jacqueline susann comes on to his thing all the time, that was supposed to recommend his thing to me. just tell 'em the next time we can't make it, that we're all in various states and degrees. i thought it'd be a relief to attend the big opening of the season at the guggenheim gregory said they were making a very big deal about it and he had the fancy tickets. he has anemia too and he's going to leningrad in june and he wore a black velvet suit with a black bow tie as a date he was a proper couple. i remember very little even now except drinking downtown with jane bertha phyllis charlene & co and leaving them to pick up my date and almost going swimming in the coin pool at the museum i was hanging over the whadyacallit the bannister that round white curving railing that separates you and death with a lovely young woman in white clothes discussing the coins particularly two large copper numbers glistening strange inscriptions and removing our shoes or lower accourtrements to dive in and remove them which she did i put my boots back on but never laced them up properly which is possibly the reason the jock in the blue helmet outside the museum manhandled me into a cop car to go to the 23rd precinct. they did say i was illegally dressed. i shouldn't be walking around as a marine they said. i said i bought it in a public store. why don't they go and arrest the store. why do they let us legally buy these things and then lock us up for it later. why wouldn't they arrest me for wearing women's clothes. an ex marine walking around in women's clothes. i should do it and see what happens. i'll hang my marine jacket in the closet and go out in some wedgies and girdles. jane gave a fine demonstration of a man she saw on third avenue learning to walk in his new wedgies. we went to a restaurant where the bus boys are wearing polka dot ribbons for bowties and garter belts made of black lace around their elbows. these jocks in new york don't know what's happening. they need a little fringe around them helmets. anyway i was glad gregory looked so right in his black velvets and patent leathers. he caught a taxi over to the precinct they wouldn't let him ride in the ambulance. i felt really funny in the car there with these regular cops who wondered themselves what the trouble was and i couldn't inform them any better but there was old ossifer watusi or somebody i can't read his name on the violation paper here, dressed down in civies and pushing me rudely and roughly up the stairs to answer questions in a sickly green room with a large cage in the corner containing about seven black people waiting i presumed for the wagon. i could see that they liked black people too. women marines and black people must be their favorites. lavender panthers unite. say all the things you're gonna do, cause time is running out. it's an interesting exercise in not knowing who you are. i was very contained and sounded perfectly credible to myself. i had apparently done all my damage on the street, waving at the jock an all. he didn't want to hear my virgin of it either. and i didn't tell him. i answered the questions politely and politick. in her time, in her own context, my mother was very bad too. having done whatever she did to deserve me. so here i am mommie and i'm never gonna look prettier. a national tour of personal disappearances is being arranged. the first person to see is martha mitchell. don't say anything, and don't say anything about us not saying anything, and don't say anything about us saying not to say anything, say nothing about us saying anything about not saying anything, say nothing about anything. so there. so it isn't the people who play it as it lays but the people who say it as they see it who make the mistakes who're the bad ones, we'll have to find old martha mitchell and sign er up for the lavender panthers. it was late and i was sober as soon as i walked in the station house. i didn't even lace up my boots properly, i didn't want to call attention to myself by bending over, i didn't want to suggest there was anything wrong with myself except for being illegally attired. i folded my hands below the navel the way i learned to do it at bellevue. i showed them all my documents including a *voice* press pass. well that about did it for ossifer watusi there. i know because we were downstairs in a jiffy and gregory black velvets patent leather his hands folded below the navel told me he'd just been outside phoning the white house to notify the prexy's secretary to call off their dogs and the dog at the desk was taking in calls and glancing up or rather down at us surreptitiously while watusi hovered anxiously two yards to his right. it was the city desk at the times that gregory called actually and a *times* man called night or knight was actually calling in and the dog at the desk was mumbling well you have the power sir and so on and then we left. goodnight goodnight. never darken our dogteam again. deus terrestris et absconditis. because of an increase in the cult of the virgin it isn't advisable to leave yer inner circle and go gallivaunting about into enement territorrid widout yer lapis electrix er vas pellicanicum er excalibur caliburnus er at the lease yer poshun fer indivisibility. seeing how abzurd a certrain pattern of condact is in yerself to others. i'm still considering having two cats named after me being the event of the week. don't say anything and don't say anything about us not saying anything and don't say anything about us saying not to say anything etcetera.

—*May 3, 1973*

Kraut Fishing in Amerika

the unscrambling of omelettes is at best laborious and not likely to improve the taste. i've been foregoing all sorts of tastes in order to run lighter and fly longer and sit still higher. one carrot one celery and five glasses of water becomes a splendid feast. i meant to reply some while back to reception of voluminous materials plus letter regarding animal liberation from connie salamone velmadaughter of majority report. connie asked me if i was still eating hamburgers the dead flesh from oppressed beings at wimpy's in london in other words was i still partaking in the capitalistic amerikan male scheme of fucking bodies and if so i hadn't come full cycle into my beautiful amazon body, my primate female body, in the peaceful world that our present feminist vision advocates she asks will there be women butchers??? i confess i've hardly ever given any political thought to food at all. up at sarah lawrence in trying to define a political lesbian i mentioned that i'm vegetarian for the most part but i don't call myself one since i've never been political about it and the same goes for anything we call ourselves. as soon as i realized what a mother in this society is or how it's defined i ceased saying i was a mother and notified both the younger people who emerged from my stomach that i no longer wished to be called mommie and i don't think i should call them "my son" or "my daughter" either. i mean referring to them this way to anybody, with possessive pride. anyway i have to tell connie i've never had a hamburger at wimpy's. i used to eat hotdogs at nathan's however. and i used to eat something called a regular dinner which as a tenement artist in new york consisted of a cowpaddie of chopped meat garbage and a box of frozen peas or frozen peas and carrots and occasionally something exotic like brussel sprouts, always frozen in a box of course. this is my gourmet column. there was no rational comprehensible reason whatsoever that i can recall for my alteration of eating habits. i was brought up on meat milk fowl eggs potatoes and decimated vegetables like everybody else. but when i went crazy everything changed including eating. that was back in '65, when everybody was going crazy and i presume like me thus unsettling their allamerikan habits. i remember babbling about baby food and declaiming the virtues of eating whatever i goddam pleased and whenever i pleased and being completely balmy up at some psychedelic church walking around like christ herself demanding herb soup, why herb soup, i don't know, i'd never been to any indian yogurt or any organic restaurant and nobody ever mentioned it and i never read anything about it either so i don't know. but i became a different kind of eating person. now i see from connie's materials here that i'm something more or less called a lacto-vegetarian, or an ovo-lacto-vegetarian. if i did away with the milk and eggs i'd be a vegan, and that's the thing to be. chickens are given a lot of hormone crap and from cows milk we get ddt and in any case we're partaking of food from incarcerated brutally treated beings. the case against eating the dead flesh of meat fowl fish is clearer. connie quotes a lot of famous old people like a. schweitzer and his concept of Reverence for Life: respecting the will to live and to progress that's inherent in the various life-forms. or mahotma grandi on ahimsa: the principle of non-killing, non-injuring. how a person should do the least harm to other lives. what i want to know is what you might do about a lot of ants in your house. ant poison? import spiders to eat the ants? import birds to eat the spiders? move to another house? develop a hobby of transporting ants in bottles from indoors to outdoors? right now i'm sharing my desk with some medium sized black ones and they're not exactly contributing to my intellectual experiments. i don't see how it's any less reprehensible catching ants in ant traps than it is lobsters in lobster pots whether you eat them or not. i have to stop eating lobster but i don't know what to do about the ants. i have an insect taboo and in fact all sorts of things going on about animals and plants in my head. yesterday i made a careful semicircular detour of large dimension around a garden snake sunning on a driveway. the day before i had a dream i was putting these cats out the door as fast as they were coming in and in fact when i woke up i heard a cat meowing outside someplace. then one day i was walking on this road and a dog the size of a woodchuck was yapping and baring its fangs at me i saw him as a wolf suddenly and even though i've read farley mowatt's never cry wolf i still think wolves are scary maybe because of laddle rat rotten hut or riding hood to you anyway since i didn't feel like swimming back home in this crick river running parallel to the road where i figured the little dog was lying in wait for me on my return i hitched a ride in a blue truck right past the dog's house and in that way saved my life i thought. before i caught the ride i heard a bird scolding me too, for being so silly no doubt. and as regards this new time of year i'm looking around as if i never saw the color green before, i think i've been living in a book all my life. the leaves are doing this whole unfolding trip and i never saw that either and i never noticed things like a tree with a branch of all these creepy foldy green foetuses in various stages of coming alive with one of their ancestors right there with them that lasted the whole winter hanging by one tendon of its stem, a brown parchment corpse of last years leaf. nature's now also full of things that bite you and i'm watching out. i don't intend to bring any corpses of animals into my place either. connie says a feminist kitchen should be a place where the dead bodies of others do not abound. when you think of it it's a weird thing putting dead bodies into your own and it doesn't go down very easily either. i fell on a big juicy red thigh or flank of some poor cow last week where i was a guest for dinner and it still hasn't come out. i do that sometimes i regress shamelessly at some- body else's house just because it's served up and it reminds you of your old carnivorous days when you threw a slab of bleeding liver into a frying pan or seared a cowpaddie of ground garbage they called round or something and you don't want to come on like a vegetarian either. that's because i haven't been political about it and i've had old associations with vegetarianism as another fanatical sect going around telling everybody that something *else* we all did was bad. besides how were we supposed to get all that protein they said we had to have if we stopped being bad. for all the materials on this subject i suggest contacting connie salamone velmadaughter at 616 6th St., brooklyn new york 11215 but here's an item called common fallacies about protein which says vegetable proteins are higher in biological value than animal proteins and that research from a leading institution for nutritional research in the world the max plank institute in germany showed that many vegetables fruits seeds nuts and grains are excellent sources of complete proteins and that soybeans sunflower seeds sesame seeds almonds potatoes and most fruits and green vegetables contain complete proteins and that you only need one half the amount of proteins if you eat raw vegetable proteins instead of cooked animal proteins and that it's virtually impossible not to get enough protein in your diet provided you have enough to eat of natural unrefined foods and all like that. did you ever wonder asks this pamphlet where the wild horse who builds a magnificent body in a couple of years gets all his proteins and answers why from the grass he eats of course. the thing is that thru cattle beef we're getting our proteins second hand anyway, recycled protein, mixed up with cancer and lockjaw and other animal diseases ("affluent nations have a high consumption of devitalized animal foods . . . containing toxins pathological matter malignancies and cholesterol") and according to another pamphlet it takes 21 lbs of grain protein to produce one lb of animal protein, out of which about 8 to 10 lbs of grain proteins could be eaten directly by people. all of this also is mixed up with the morality of property from an economical and ecological standpoint writes connie the conventional mixed diet requires about $1\frac{2}{3}$ to 2 acres per person for growing food for her and for feeding the animals. but this is a very expensive and wasteful diet, returning perhaps 20 per cent of the food value in the case of milk or eggs, and less than half that in meat. a part-vegetarian diet, still including milk and eggs may require about an acre. but with a total vegetarian (or vegan) diet a single acre can support four, six, or even as many as eight people, according to actual experiments. she goes on as there is only about an acre of farm land per person in the world this places a tremendous moral burden upon the user of animal foods in addition to the usual ethical considerations. i don't know why we shouldn't just go out on our all fours and start eating the grass like other sensible animals. if a horse gets a magnificent body that way then we could too. at this point many people like me ask the leading green question what about the plants and along with what to do about the ants in yr house i still think it's important since we know that plants hurt too. i don't see a satisfactory answer in this material here. if plants hurt too then we should eat only the fallen fruit. a flower shop may be no less cruel than a slaughter house or a chicken farm. in all cases we're alienated from the source of what we get. thus we don't have to think about the pain and murder involved in the commodity we're consuming or sending to a friend to make a hospital room look cheerier. as regards plants and flowers unless you wear them in your hair i guess at least there's one comforting thought and that is you don't wear them for shoes or coats, unless you happen to be in hawaii. i'd like to know if i have to start wearing only sneakers, i know i should get rid of my suede jacket. another of connie's fervently scrawled headlines reads man's cruelties to obtain fur thats not his or hers! there's a society called Beauty Without Cruelty which people joined because a few facts of the barbarous practices that flourish under the protective banner of commerce in the beauty and fashion businesses have convinced them of the need to use alternatives to such products. unluckily for instance for crocodiles alligators snakes lizards and all reptiles their skins command high prices. what about the eskimos by the way. don't they dress up like animals all the year round. or is it a question of them or the animals as to survival. and if so does that justify murder. one of my favorite books was owen chase's *sinking of the whaleship essex* which provided by the way the basic material of melville's *moby dick*. it was 1820 or so and owen chase was a youthful crew member on the whaleship essex out in the middle of the pacific someplace when this great white whale angered by the assaults on him and his gang just came along and sank this goddam boat. well many days later while two surviving lifeboats of starving crewmembers were struggling coastward there was an infamous incident of cannibalism on board one of them. they drew lots to see who they would have to eat and as i recall it was the youngest a 16 yr old who drew the shortest and was therewith dispatched by his mates. i guess the issue there was an old sacrificial one, would they all have to die or could some of them survive by the sacrifice of one. that may be the eskimo principle too. i don't know. i hope never to be in the wilds of alaska or the middle of the pacific in a rowboat. bemeantimes however unfortunately i guess i'll have to deal with the moral problems of sneakers versus virtually any other kind of shoe and the ants sharing my desk and the temptations of lobster and whether to let the cats in or out and how much distance to keep between me and garden snakes and the fear of small dogs and how to go on living on one carrot one celery and five glasses of water. actually i feel great. i recommend a grand fast of one day and a pseudo fast of one more day followed by one carrot one celery one apple one egg maybe a day is probably all anybody about needs. with a little dessert of lawn grass. anyhow it's the best way to run lighter and fly longer and sit still higher.

—*May 17, 1973*

A Fair to Meddling Story

she's grumpy because the sun isn't shining, and she slept two hours longer than she needed to, and the last dream she had made her mad. i was mad myself but i only remember her back in the yellow wooden lawn chair reading facing the stream an up the hill. we go to a great deal of trouble to agree to these misunderstandings. i won't bend over frontwards to engage in speculation of the motivation of others. she said there was a chipmunk on a stone wall scolding her and he was mad at florence the cat too, then she thought he was scolding her jane and reconsidered it and decided he was scolding florence, though maybe she was raking over his hole or something. i had a dream about a hole. it involved a hole a tree and a grey animal. it's a fair to muddling story. this large tree trunk was fallen down and a small animal was jiggling one end of it under the trunk trying to save or right it i guessed. the next scenario was this alley oop grey animal with a mouses head and a fat body coming out from a great square hole it'd dug as big as a small room under that one end of the tree. the animal was a variation of ben who's a fixed male cat i sometimes see as an evolved mouse altho he stalks like a miniature tiger. possibly i was mad because i hate ben doing 100 yard dashes around my head at night. i've forgotten. but the hole was a sunken swimming pool. off and on all some day or other i mentioned pools realizing it was warm but not how warm until officially informed that i had an excuse for doing nothing all day except mentioning pools. the tree was this branch that grows out horizontally so far from its trunk and so fat and with so many of its own branches that it requires a vertical support. i don't see loops of meaning curling in cool blades of grass or anything like that. or polished stones tumbling out of heaven. (sold american). i have straightforward hole tree & animal dreams. i have car and plane and children dreams, guilts, anxieties prophecies wish fulfillments idle speculations and passing the time away. i try catching the "significant" ones to see what they're telling me in case i need to be told and very often we do. what if the papers published only the dream news. headlines: president n. dreams of a worldwide communist conspiracy. anyway everyday a special box for the president who sends out reports thru his dream press secretary. checkers returns to life. pat victim of boston strangler. tricia marries prince charles. julie kills david and runs away with patricia lawford. sammy davis jr. makes irregular advances and these are covertly enjoyed. john dean also sucks and john mitchell serves up his wife as legs and breasts of mutton at a huge dinner celebrating the successful rape of 10,000 cambodian women. the president pushes all the buttons and calls billy graham who rescues the family by flying them out in a plane that's shaped like an amphitheatre and contains a unitarian choir in which his mother sings quaker solo. the dream interpreters on every paper make their comments, i.e., this incident seemingly represents a regression which nevertheless leads forward. the basic headlines every day would say things like the underlying structure of the universe is a double message. or, something to be secured or avoided ultimately or immediately. or, too young to be where i'm goin, too old to go back again. or kentucky fried lilly buds with chives and sour cream. or two or more competing explanations require consideration. i wondered if i had a twin if i'd compete with her and i thought we'd probly sit around and laugh at each other. i want more laughs. it's bad enough tearing up the road on yer new radial tires and making sure you don't hit any raccoons. i didn't hit this raccoon and then this young deer bounded across maybe 15 yards ahead and flit into the woods just like that. these're the animals i like, the ones running wild. i wouldn't ever own an animal, not since i was eight and had a terrier dog that ran away all the time, and i don't understand why pauline and lin keep a toucan in a cage and i don't like seeing ben walk by the window with a snake in his mouth. i don't mind robins looking for worms because that doesn't concern me. i'm very interested in animals at a distance or making signs in dreams. i don't see them as signs during the day particularly, whereas pauline does. a snake crossing her path on the road really means something. to me it means a snake crossing my path on the road. whereas that dream of snakes when i was swimming that made me turn back i interpreted right away as a bunch of wicked women and i've stayed away ever since. things that're the most apparent tend not to be. i'm now hanging out with sophisticated

cultivated dignified considerate and gracious people. i speak of
nothing but good manners. i enjoy shaking hands & enquiring after
peoples health. i make small talk with the redheaded freak who
changed my tires and put the old ones in my trunk. i tell im i've
owned so many crates that i have a second-hand tire mentality and
he smiles and says he does too. i make sure go out and admire the
fairy godneighbor who appears for nothing to tractor down my
crabweeds in his toy red mower. i eat alison's fried yellow lilly buds
that she picked along the road without letting on beforehand that i
knew anything strange was going to happen. i tell jane her barrelful
of cold squash and broccoli and chickpea salad is her most magnificent and i remark the bad taste of people who allude to anybody i
know tell who cooks as alice b.t. that's about it for now and that
doesn't exclude being mad sometimes. biting well and speaking little.
flower in the mouth. small & defective always. anyway looking good.
one coming a long way. one always hoping for the best. farreaching.
high cloud, low lake. crocodile queen. shiny black. blooming tree. all
the gnews that's fit to spring. let us contemplate undazed the extent
of my innocence. and this, our life, exempt from public haunt, finds
tongues in trees, books in the running brooks, sermons in stones,
and good in everything. i'll write to sk and tell er i'm glad she's
better. i'll call maria del drago and enquire after kate. i'll send alice
james to kate and remind jane to send zelda to agnes. i'll write about
ann wilson as a great artist. i'll call up winnie and see if richard is
living in the bronx. i'll give alison my apollinaire and get neal cassady
back from gregory and look for tallulah to give alice. i'll tell alice i'll
never go back to her restaurant unless she tells her boys not to insult
women. i won't give her any more balloons either. i take refuge in
studied ambiguities. enantiodromia. the psychic law of the reversal
of all opposites. to disagree with yr pt of view is to have a side
namely that one that's not yours. they can't get it thru their filter. in
dreams the element of judgment is absent. like pauline told me there
was this tribe called sequoia or something which ran its life according
to its dreams. every morning the family wld arise and somebody
probably the father wld preside and they wld all discuss their dreams
and what they meant for their relationships and the health of the

tribe. pauline says a little auto suggestion before you go to sleep is enough to help you remember. she read a long dream to me in leucadia out of her notebook. the one i wrote down yesterday was a phone fear guilt & paranoia children dream. nothing as easy as a hole tree & animal number. a pont ou nul ne passe. the way it went the phone was out of order meaning it made a collection of noises and the receiver "floated" off the hook and this meant whenever this happened that you'd be "booked on suspicion." of what it was uncertain excepting its kafkaesque clarity and i prepared to be "picked up" and told jane who was off someplace another part of this "exposed" house, i puzzled over the correct clothes and ended up with a silk dark print dress tucked into my pants an walked out to meet the feds or whoever it was who was coming. first there was decoys, peoples i knew from before like j. dunn & s. paxton walking toward me "as in a dream" on a perimeter and impassively, then when they got close enough this fed or some badlooking twirpy guy materialized and clamped something on my wrist led us up away up some stairs we arrived where there were these deformed defected children with bulging eyes one as small as a button that's the end of the dream. i know that day richard called from new york arrived in three days from montana and his voice was garbled in bad connections, and a woman from new hampshire told me her middle daughter jill died at four of pneumonia and she was born brain damaged. the president's dream for tomorrow could read: pres. n. has watergate on the chest. i had a virile pneumonia once too and i spent a week in the hospital and what it was was a pain in the chest from not being able to scream at my husband. in the long run he is not evil, only unfortunate, and wishes to be redeemed himself. terror has been succeeded by a terror infinitely worse. needle at the bottom of the ocean. white swan cools its wings. nobby knees and my teeth hurt and this is friday. freida and otto and henry. many feathers no wings. one in fine clothes. one with good news but a little old. yes he is my son, i keep asking myself where i went wrong. i wish she'd stop sitting with her back in the yellow wooden lawn chair reading facing the stream an up the hill. but i go on fooling in the grass with my feet next to the mailbox. i won't power the mower or use any machines or do anything butch except drive my new radial tires. these cats think nothing of walking around with snakes in their mouths. the only form of reprisal left was moral indignation and that has never won any decisive battles. i was the first to come & i am the last to go. booked on suspicion all the way. she says she apologized to every flower as she picked it. i was quoting my own work, without acknowledgment of course. i appeared naked and asked if i didn't look thin and she said no you're voluptuous and i forgot what the argument was all about. if you need one you can create a real crisis by moving convulsively against an imaginary one. to recapitulate: she was grumpy because the sun wasn't shining, and she slept two hours longer than she needed to, and the last dream she had made her mad. then there was a lot abt animals holes pools trees children food promises to be good and the advisability of publicizing the dreams of national leaders. it's a fair to meddling story. my last word is ben's gone crazy, florence is home in heat, mother cass delivered six kittens, i had some rare steak with rug seasoning, i bought the amelia earhart record and some pipes & drums of scotland, i have no vital preoccupation since my foot is better, i'm still staying far away from the wicked snake women, i still specialize in the impossible, i'm still studying good manners, i still enjoy good orgasm, i'll continue to influence this story from a distance and in the morning those who've been favored with the goddesses nocturnal visitation will tell their experiences. we like the original virgin of ourselves. persephone secunda. principium individuationis!

—*July 19, 1973*

The Yearly Mellowdrama

I had a dream richard stayed in san francisco one day and then split for home. I had a dream two years ago I was traveling up and down highways on the coast in a freighter and richard flew up in the air and landed someplace on his back as a small doll. I didn't have a dream 10 years ago he ended on his back on a road in washington heights his eyes rolled up I ran the other direction it happened to be a nurse on her way to a hospital who hit him and I followed her over with him in her front seat unconscious and richard and me discussed it ever afterwards for six or seven years until one day I said well it was a good way to pay me back for i don't remember what besides having him and he looked at me funny and that was that. I remember his left face was black and blue and swollen for a week and that was all but everything was terrible then. It was clear that we were all living thru an ordeal. I tried to remember yesterday whether richard was hit before or after I was driving myself and hit a schoolkid dashing diagonally out from between cars in the middle of a street but we talked about that forever afterwards too. That was back in 1962 when everybody in rockland county wanted to build themselves an orgone box. I remember yvonne asking me if I was into reich and I suppose I said yes since sally was reading the murder of christ and I was in love with sally and that's the way things go and I still don't have a mind of my own in any case. I was a stroller mommie in washington heights living in an $80 walkup near the river and across the street from the park. I would carry one kid up on my hip and trail the other behind me screaming. I would sit in the park and do all the proper things like talking to another mommie and following the kids with my eyes when they left the sandbox and swinging them on the baby swings and buying them popsicles and picking them up when they cried and putting them down when they didn't and wondering whether my mission in life was supposed to be fulfilled. I don't think I wondered that for a second. I had a dream last week I went to an important interview in heels stockings black velvet dress and my derby. I don't remember too much what I whore then except some shapeless $5 jeans to the park but I did have a red woolen dress to just above the kneecaps and it was around that time that john cage saw me in my red woolen dress at a christmas party and asked me to perform with him and david tudor a number of months hence in a thing of his called music walk and I did and I did it in my red woolen dress and for my noisemakers I brought all the trappings of my wonderful maternal existence a baby bottle a coffee can a blender a frying pan a vacuum an apron a plastic sink an egg beater a beater beater and a toy dog on wheels that barked like a duck when I pulled it along by its string. I had a ladder on stage too. I had all this junk and john and david had only their minimum daily requirement of sophisticated electronic equipment and a handful of three by fours containing the brilliant and elegantly scripted hieroglyphics of instructions from the godhead: the wise decrees of chance and indeterminacy. I had gone to all this trouble too. I had come in fact to a rehearsal with a bunch of about 45 of these cards clutched in my nervous little fist, each one explaining to myself how I should do such and such an action like scrubbing out my baby bottle at a very certain time and for just so long during the course of the 10 specified minutes of the piece, the result of some very fancy calculations involving the tossing of coins and an immaculate collection of topographical transparencies that john called a score, but at the rehearsal I dropped all these cards of instructions in some of my domestic water and the ink was blurred and whatever wasn't blurred was dirty and I said to myself shit why should I bother with these cards anyway I'll just plant my junk around the stage and set my stopwatch so I know when we're beginning and when we're ending and whenever I feel like it I'll go here and there and tinker around with my junk and that's what I did in my red woolen dress. I remember john looking quite skeptically at me just before the performance but he didn't say anything and I didn't tell him how heretical I planned to be either. I suppose at that time if you weren't up in rockland county building yr orgone box you were training to deliver up yr ego to the elements by obeying john cage and I really wanted to and I appreciated the orgone business too but no matter what anybody else said my life was conforming to its own internal chaos, it was out of my control to follow any directions from anywhere, much less from myself, so naturally I experienced my better and better orgasms completely by chance and naturally I couldn't do anything on stage that wasn't basically like my life and that was purely by chance according to the whims of the moment confined to my wonderful maternal existence I didn't have much choice as it were but within that choice or chance I was always dropping my papers in the domestic waters and deciding to do something else because of that or something else. I was trying to remember right now whether I had that ladder on stage because around that time richard had fallen off a ladder at marcia marcus's house or not but I don't know I do know I didn't own a ladder myself so it isn't clear why I insisted on the ladder unless me and my kids were all into hanging and falling off things in which case any elevated property would've been suitable to demonstrate one important aspect of my life and a ladder happened to be handy at the theatre as I said I don't know because I didn't know anything at the time I didn't make any connections whatsoever because I was completely unconscious. I didn't put it all together — me at parties hanging from pipes, richard on the street on his back, richard falling off a ladder, richard climbing rocks and cliffs and daring me to be concerned, winnie falling off a slide on her chin her eyes rolling up and me running in the other direction and me at a party falling into a skylight and losing a black heel to the floor below I don't have to try and remember and although I wasn't making any special connections I knew it was all terrible. I had a call yesterday from richard from caspar california. I'm organizing his trip by remote control. Three weeks ago I said tomorrow you're going to seattle and that next day I drove him to hudson's for 2 shirts one pants one nabsack one shoes no name tapes and I drove him to the airport and bought him a ticket and didn't have time to stop at the park so he could see his friends and bought him some french fries and gave him $55 and put him on a united and called seattle to snowshoe whose brother met him at that end the five hours later the next I heard he was standing on tall swaying ladders making $10 a day picking apples. I told danny that richard was among the last of the junior acid freaks who sit on rocks up at the park around the boathouse getting holes

in their pants and I sent him to the coast to see the world and danny
said if he danny lived on the pacific coast he'd drop acid every day
and sit on the cliff and watch the sun go down. A little man was
walking down eighth street last week yelling Wake Up Wake Up, —
They're Coming. — They're coming, of *course* they're coming,
whoever they are, anybody can see that they're coming and so is the
first frost in new england and the birches are showing in the hills the
yearly mellowdrama and I want some candystriped doctor dentyns
with feet and the thing in the back and there is no greater satisfaction
than in everything so I don't know what was wrong about 1962. I
met rosalyn drexler in washington heights in the park strolling her
kid danny around and I was making $80 a month writing for art
news and I was evicted from my $80 walkup so I could move into
another nice tenement on houston street closer to this woman I'd
fallen madly in love with and whom I was chasing around
unashamedly. I was evicted and the eviction men threw out my
babybook and my grandmother's old persian rug and when I was
packing the remains I lost my wedding ring under my ford I think
and that was a good thing too. This has many little interruptions and
a kiss on both cheeks is not in disorder. All the tender pressing of the
complete expression. All the exaggeration in examination. All this is
that intention and some expectation. It wasn't really clear that we
were living thru such an ordeal. I remember rosalyn yelling at
sherman out her window and I remember rosalyn was said to've
punched sherman in the nose, and I remember rosalyn coming over
to see me with a huge bottle of cheap chianti and I remember her
kid danny beating up richard in the sandbox. I remember the sandbox
thing but I don't know if that really happened I might've dreamed it
and if I did it was because danny was more aggressive than richard
and he probably didn't fall off ladders and I suppose that by now he's
a basketball and track champ and I hope he is and for myself it was
a pleasure putting richard on the plane for seattle carrying a beatup
copy held together by a rubberband of the electrickoolaidacidtest he
received as a gift from an elderly freak in the park. Naturally whenever
the children are involved there is always a little trauma. By remote
control talking on the phone to caspar california I hoped richard

would spend more than one day in san francisco as I dreamed he
wouldn't and he would go to the golden gate and sit around on
some new kinds of rocks in that place there and then san diego and
pauline isn't it amazing he's just 14 and I like the whole thing. The
great fabrication of origins and imitations. Few are called and many
are poisoned. Possibly the new business that began to come into
being after 1962 or sometime is the business of connections as we
gradually lost interest in building orgone boxes in rockland county
and the study of delivering up yr ego to the elements by obeying
john cage we azserted our consciousness in connections just yesterday
a letter from snowshoe saying she hitchhiked back to seattle from
caspar having left richard off there she immediately met a joe
johnston for her traveling companion you know richard has been
using his mother's last name and why 1962? Because as I just this
second realized last week a susan I know told me that a man at the
voice said I been writing for this paper since 1962 and that isn't true
it was 1959 and I did it out of washington heights while everybody
was screaming and looking at the box and eating tuna fish and falling
and getting hit and generally going crazy including being unsuccessfully in love. I could get very involved trying to prove something
and jane is sabotaging the argument with oreos.

—*October 26, 1972*

Resurrection for 40 Cents

and so there is no use going on except that the summers follow one after the other and the fashions go with the seasons. the fashion i observed this summer season was trees and dreams and sacred violations. the queens must die. the friends of the foetus gather to assist at her unhappy emergence. once she is seen i guess the secret is out. in what way does she become actual if not seen (and heard). can she be actual to herself if she doesn't see herself and for that does she need eyes. is her eyes the origin of her consciousness of existing. do her eyes have to see herself being seen in order for her to feel herself alive. and once the secret is out won't she violate herself in order to cease this existing. this sense of multiplying separations? the real question seemed to be could the sacred space be expanded or would we go on seeing ourselves as separate and exclusive and if the former what are the strategies of (re)incorporation. for example when you speak to it do you make it so and is seeing still believing. or is there a critical difference between doing and dreaming you are doing as the social organization suggests or are we always dreaming whatever we're doing since we picture ourselves to ourselves in other words seeing is dreaming and we came out looking. i wanted to know this week if the separation in ourselves between actor and spectator is endemic to life or to organisms with eyes or what. do we become increasingly self conscious or excessive dreamers as the social organization becomes more inclusive as a civilization while augmenting our isolation from each other by losing visual touch with all our contributory functions and living in enforced individual units of which the largest remains only the family. the world is too big to consider. sometimes alone i feel total. i dream all my selves into auto fulfilling facets of each other. i move around from room to room depending on the light. i make preparations for things that don't have to happen. i happen things that have no preparations. i don't have to attend to anything less interesting than my own thoughts. it's difficult not to admire our existing since that's what we're doing. the summers follow one after the other and the fashions of living go with the seasons and i am here now and it's thursday. the only essential activity is expanding the sacred space by doubling into infinities until we stop falling into existence or separations. the secret sharers are thousands of butternut leaves. the family is sexual differentiation and that's too bad. a friend says the definition of culture is sexual differentiation. it's clear which half of the difference felt the most hysteria in respect to its difference and separateness but i have my own sex in mind this week. robert graves said the apollo flight was such a crude way of getting to the moon. they can speak for themselves. the christian solution has come to pass. the projection of the father up to heaven as a divine spirit. good morning, yr omnipotence. i promised myself not to go on with their problems. being so much more outside their original inner space their dreams appear so much more violent. the normal heros. the conjunction of love and war. the fearsome possession of a kept port of entry. the roving penetrating eyes of the male. but i promised. i sat in circles for three days with 13 women of me experiencing multiple duplications in dreams and images and ideas and i came out dead and alive and still looking and not dissatisfied with expanding the space or violating a number of intimacies. women don't waste much time any more getting to sex either but intellectual dissolutions are still so much more comfortable. what's the difference between looking and doing and who's really looking if not ourselves. were we conceived in secrecy. and if that wasn't incestuous how many secret incests (inquests) can we go on pretending we're committing. if it stops being illicit does it stop i mean. alice told me eating is the only sensual thing you can do in public and not be put down for it. i went with a friend to a strange apartment where after a suitable interval i asked the woman of the apartment whose name happened to be jill if she minded if my friend and me made love and she said no not if she could watch but two more women arrived and in the end we committed incest or privacy or secrecy and the violation of intimacy was only partial or a matter of information which is a bridge of sorts. and are literal transgressions necessary at all since the actual looking is still from a distance and i wonder how satisfying the group orgies of the living theatre were to the participants. what other uproarious deceptions would their activities generate or perpetuate. gradually the play fills up with corpses, in her honor it would seem. the friends of the foetus gather to assist at her unhappy emergence. falling into the world she becomes the object of fantastic assault. her present solution is to eject her tormentors from the primal scene and experience herself as her double in infinite regress. for 40 cents you can buy a mexican resurrection plant at judith's store in hartford. it stays forever if you want as a ball of vine the size of a baseball and it stays forever as a flat open spreading green plant if you put its bottom side in a container of water. it resurrects in an hour. judith calls her store the perfect union. these ecstatic unions imply a joyful liberation from sanity. she always went without herself. she fell into some ark on the way in and there was light thru the portholes. she thought her thin arms and sturdy legs were peaceful and exciting. she saw mansions in the sky of lavender doors and gold knockers and thought it was a very corny dream. she pretends if she's not looking at anybody they can't see her either. she lives in a purely symbolic world and magically solves her problems. she knows there's certain conventions they'd all greed upon and she becomes inexpensively happy attending to nothing more interesting than her own thoughts. her own images rendered double or in duplex telegraphy. if 13 women can get into a bubble and be their own reflections i guess the rest of us can too. first we went round the circle exchanging dreams. i remembered some recurrent childhood dreams myself. i remembered running in slow motion away from pursuers who never caught up with me although i was stuck in my running i couldn't go nearly as fast as i wanted to and i was told that's because my large muscles are paralysed while sleeping and dreaming i like physiological explanations altho i thought the stuck running had some important universal psychic significance maybe it does. the most over and over childhood dream i had was being in a secret space locked in with a couple of friends or myself or being locked in under a house in those wideranging three foot high or so spaces surrounded by lattice wood enclosures that many houses used to have and being inside there and then hearing a rumble rumble at first distant and then closer and being witness to a procession of sheep emerging from the ground. i saw charlotte moorman being born last week i ventured into the world of people to the americana hotel and saw charlotte playing the cello in a black gown then put down her cello and walk over to a tall cylinder pail where she climbed to the top and lowered herself in and submerged herself in the water of herself and then came out to resume her life as a cellist or her new life or is it old. it's difficult not to admire relevant action at the proper historical moment. a little girl no more than three appeared on the walkplank outside alice's restaurant as i headed for the door she was right in front of me and i stopped and she said take off your glasses and let me see your eyes and i did and i sort of got down lower and we looked very knowingly or something into each others eyes and then she fondled my neck gear and wanted to know what all the junk was. i wonder if anybody was watching. i'm writing so you can watch so i can see myself being seen in your eyes and i can watch you watching me watch you so we can know each other. i fell in love with the little girl. her request for recognition seems pretty uncomplicated. a more complicated request but no less direct if possibly more urgent came in a mysterious phone call from san diego thereabouts a woman's voice saying hello this is dita, i thought she said dita, i said yes, this is dita sackville-west, yes, do you know who this is, yes i do, well i'm vita sackville-west, i could hear now that it was vita not dita, and after a pause or so after i confirmed i knew who she was and all i asked her what her other name was and she told me and we went on from there. i thought she should go to a medium for more information. she was born in '54 and she doesn't know when vita died and neither do i. she began to be possessed two years ago and all she knew of virginia w. was as a name and she feels suicidal now because she misses virginia a great deal. then i said i couldn't help her and she thought i violated her trust by saying that but i believe her and helping is more than believing if whatever you're being believed about is painful and i'm not equipped to provide more information so i wanted to locate a medium. i said we're all possessed or inhabited it's the condition of existence and i think if one of these beings is clamoring for that much attention we need to know more to see what's going on. maybe we need to project them more outside the center of our new ongoing selves. some people surround you with a civilized atmosphere and they leave you inside of you completely to yrself. for that reason it isn't a bad idea being alone a lot. dreaming all your selves into autofullfilling facets of each other. moving about from room to room depending on the light. making preparations for things that don't have to happen or happening things that have no preparation and attending to the concertos of your own voices and admiring your very existing. a friend asked me if it would be any more significant *dreaming* of living in a town with the same name as the town where your mother was born than actually living in such a town and having noticed the connection which is what i'm doing. i don't think so. or i think it's so. how do we know we're not still in the womb and watching a movie of our life. the real unified life of the dream. i see myself in secret violating the taboo on secrecy for fear of retaliation or fear of paralysis or fear of fear out apart from the others passionately in sex love in wet grass mosquitoes singing critics yellow moon decadent demented delirious dissolute drunk the dying surging of the foetal queens. pagan blood returns! the end of romance. the violence of territorial uncertainties. she removes her crown, falls prostrate on the ground, and speaks in latin phrases. she or the other says she could kill her. she or the other says she will puncture her tires. she or the other hurls a longstem glass somewhat over her left shoulder where it lands intact on the grassy strip between the macadam thud. this was the first war period, a period of fashion without style, of systems with disorder, of reforming everybody which is persecution, and of violence without hope. life is so embarrassing. here all forgotten and set aside — wind scattering leaves over the fields. florence was in heat on the driveway and ben was trying to mount her and beyond on the grass maureen was lying on carol's back and we were watching the doubles out of the window and i had a dream of doris humphrey more redheaded than i remember her and facing herself one version older more shrivelled than i remember the other younger and heartier than i remember and she was speaking attentively to herself although the older version seemed more animated than the younger. choreographing her internal dialogue. i can't recall the year doris died. i know she was appearing to me. alma said exstasy happens face to face with another person and it isn't suppliable by the masses, a long day of feeling your body tell your mind to stop thinking. and thinking and feeling your body and feeling your thinking and thinking your body. and so there is some use going on even as the summers follow one after the other and the fashions go with the seasons and the secrets are always out.

—September 6, 1973

Agnes Martin: Surrender & Solitude

going to see agnes martin in the desert came to seem to me like a pilgrimage and i don't see why not. a pilgrimage is a long, weary journey, as to a shrine. a shrine is a tomb of a saint or other sacred person. none of these words may apply to any contemporary venture, at best perhaps they have exotic unreal connotations, but agnes martin is a spiritual woman and she isn't easy to find. unless you happen to be in los angeles when she's speaking at the pasedena museum, which was just my luck last month while passing down the coast. i was mildly disappointed since i wanted her to be as hard to find as i'd been told she was and i guess the last place i expected to see her first since she disappeared from civilization was in the civilization of a museum. yet i was relieved in a way, just to see that she was alive for one thing, and to have the opportunity to see how she felt about me before i made so bold as to trek into her wilderness with only a one-way advance telegram to recommend my arrival. i was disappointed in general to hear that agnes had been emerging at all, she has in fact made six museum appearances this past year, and she told me she flew to germany recently to negotiate the sale of some prints, it seemed therefore that i'd be visiting somebody who was just very inaccessible and not a recluse from civilization, nonetheless she is basically a recluse and she always has been thus it doesn't matter now any more than before how far you go to see her unless you like to travel and see deserted places. i used to see agnes in her loft on the battery and i don't know if she's any different now than she was then and she left new york in 1967. i think if anybody's different it's me and although i thought she was very special then i doubt that i heard what she had to tell me. i was just awed to be in her presence. i knew she was one of the great women. it was a pleasure finding a great woman in new york city during the terrible time of the '60s during every terrible decade it's a pleasure finding a great woman. a great woman may be a woman more interested in herself than in anything else. one way you knew agnes martin was great was because she lived decisively alone and that this was an active irrevocable choice and because she put very little stock in people at all and another way you knew she was great was because her paintings were. i know agnes would say the work is completely apart from the person and i have no quarrel with that myself but i see the work and the person as inseparable too. my earliest memory of agnes is of her work alone but then a little later on i saw agnes and her work together and in fact i rarely saw them apart since whenever i went to her loft almost always as i remember she showed me her paintings and sometimes her drawings too and so for me agnes was agnes the painter although i understand her detachment. her paintings are not about the world and i suppose her paintings paint themselves and in this sense she has nothing to do with it. i think it was 1964 when i stopped in at the elkon gallery and saw all these six by six foot paintings washed out whites and tans crossed by close vertical and horizontal lines muted and irregularly perfect and i called up dick bellamy and said do you know this woman agnes martin why aren't you showing her i thought at that time that if anybody good was around he was supposed to be showing them but of course he knew her work and he wasn't showing her elkon was anyway that was my introduction to the work of agnes martin. a little later on either by design or accident i was knocking on her door to review her most recent show for art news and that was how i met her. already i thought her paintings were beautiful and i wanted to meet the artist. i wasn't the least bit disappointed but socially possibly i was more awkward than she was so i wonder how we impressed each other. her hair was long then and she had lots of it and when i came in it was all loose and she was busying herself putting it back or up and sort of apologizing for being in some dissarray. i know we had tea and i looked at her paintings but i don't know what else. looking at agnes's paintings with agnes was a quiet concentrated ceremonious ritual. there was a very certain distance she traversed from the point in her loft where the paintings were stashed to the spot right next to the door where she showed them. one by one without any hurry or hesitation she would carry them from one place to another, back and forth, and when she reached the showing place next to the door there would be a certain gesture of hiking the work with her foot under the canvas up into position on the nails sticking out of the wall. then she would sit down next to you and contemplate the work with you and wait as i imagined for you to speak your thoughts. i can't imagine what i ever said if anything. i know we discussed the titles. i think very often she wanted to know if some particular title or other was appropriate but i'm not sure. i liked them all myself. desert. islands. mountain. blue flower. hill. starlight. ocean water. leaf. untitled. i liked them all. i thought i could see what they were even though everything was a graph. i used to say to people there was this painter painting mystical geometries as though nobody else had thought of that. nature paintings ruled by the horizontal line or was it vertical. when she was young she painted the mountains as they were or as we suppose we see them or anyway the way you see them at the washington square outdoor art show. in the desert agnes told me she could see in nature there weren't any *real* verticals or real horizontals and right then she gave up nature. in the desert there weren't any paintings at all. there was a rectangular pit maybe six feet deep and 15 feet from corner to corner next to her little adobe that she said was the foundation for a studio. she abandoned new york and painting both when she left in '67 and now she is beginning to begin again. it isn't altogether clear why she left new york and why she stopped painting but if you heard the story it's the sort of story you accept and understand without any explanations. leaving new york has become as much a ritual exodus as going to new york is a ritual initiation. people said oh agnes martin left in a dodge pickup, and nobody knows where she went, or you'd hear vague reports that she ended up in the new mexican desert. i asked agnes how she ended up there, why she chose cuba, and she said she saw these mountains on this road leading northward into cuba in her minds eye in new york and that was how come. i was amazed to find the place. i sent a telegram as i said but i never made the 6 a.m. bus out of albuquerque that i declared i would, the reason being that jane was flying in from new york and arriving 11 a.m. and i didn't know that till after i sent the telegram and i didn't send another because i didn't want to make any more declarations. anyway about 3 p.m. three women of albuquerque drove us north toward cuba where i enquired in the postoffice if they knew where agnes lived. they said no but a man down the road did. down the road the man's daughter explained carefully and i thought it sounded pretty clear. basically she said there was a gate a dry river bed and a little forest. i don't see gates dry river beds or little forests very often so i heard it all in the singular. i'm still certain she said it that way too. well there were lots of gates and dry river beds and little forests. first you had to drive some few miles out of cuba way off the main drag if you could call the road through cuba that. the gate the man's daughter mentioned was obvious enough, an impressive barbed wire gate the sort you have to get out and unhinge and swing away for the car to pass and then rehinge again. then we were on a soft red clay road. then we crossed the dry river bed. then there was a little forest, midget gnarled trees of some sort. then i expected to see agnes's adobe. but what there was was another gate. i didn't think we should go through it but we did because there wasn't any other place to go in order to reach a dwelling unless you went careening off into the sage and the arroyas, those dry river beds in the form of drastic looking jagged ditches that snake around all over the place through those parts. so we went on and everything began to look like a dry river bed and a forest. i asked one of the albuquerque women what we were driving through actually. she said it was a short grass prairie with incursion of sonoran desert species running into pinon-juniper forest. that sounded good. i liked being there and all too, but the apprehension was mounting, especially when there was not only a third gate but a fork or a choice of going off or on the same road unimpeded by a gate. moreover we had passed the half eaten carcass of a cow right along the side of the road and that seemed to create an adage in my mind that when you see a dead cow you should turn back. besides i had the feeling we were within a clods throw of agnes's adobe but some part of my head said we were going to die in the desert. anyway we were all neurotically consuming a bag of nectarines and i was about to die laughing. i thought i'd never be able to travel in the desert with lucia since we were both particularly dying laughing. i said we should turn back. it was quite a few miles inching back over the soft clay bumpy road and reopening the gates and closing them behind us and wondering where the hell agnes was. back on the macadam we went a half a mile up to a little ranch farm to ask this man and his wife if we'd been on the right series of gates river beds and forests for agnes martin and the man said yes and his wife drew diagrams in the dirt and the man gestured out across the plain and said that's her mesa, right there, as though i should be able to see it and there was a curl of smoke out of a chimney that i was missing. it was clear anyway that we had to go through that third gate where the fork was where we'd turned back so we did it again and we came to a real little sage and juniper forest and there it was a small complex of vehicles and structures that had to be agnes. agnes the classicist. classicism she says is not about people and this work is not about the world. classicists are people that look out with their back to the world. it represents something that isn't possible in the world. it's as unsubjective as possible. the classic is cool. it is cool because it is impersonal and detached. if a person goes walking in the moutains that is not detached and impersonal she's just looking back. to a detached person the complication of the involved life is like chaos. if you don't like the chaos you're a classicist. if you like it you're a romanticist. painting is not about ideas or personal emotion. painting the desert in her head. the horizontal line. there's very few verticals in nature. and there she was as vertical as i remembered her which was only a week ago at the pasadena museum sitting on a chair in the middle of the stage surrounded by an overflow audience her hair short to the ears and still brown and wearing a sort of tangerine velveteen skirt to the floor with a white starched blouse slightly femme flared at the elbows and twisting a white handkerchief in her lap as though it was worry beads and my friend with me said she looked a dead ringer for gertrude stein. picasso said he was impressed by gertrude stein's physical personality and anyone might say the same of agnes martin. she's extremely handsome and she has the most brilliant twinkling blue eyes and her body is full and she's very solidly there yet shy and a little retreating at the same time. she giggles and jokes a lot and laughs at herself and i'd never seen her so solemn and formal. and i'd never seen her in a skirt or any sort of a "blouse." i could see she was on her best behavior, even as though it was sunday school or something. the audience too was reverent and expectant. it was a new aspect of agnes to me, although not one i wouldn't have envisioned. as i said she was for me a spiritual woman and i was awed to be in her presence and i believed whatever she said i knew she was a right person a natural woman a presence of the universe. she made pronouncements and spoke in aphorisms and she was known to go into trances and she proclaimed the future and she had no pretensions about herself except perhaps as a painter which may possibly be the subject of her intimate and abstracted speech that she's given lately in several of these museums. it's called the underlying perfection of life and almost the first thing she says is we are blinded by pride and that living the prideful life we are frustrated and lost that we cannot overcome pride because we ourselves are pride but we can witness the defeat of pride because pride is not real and cannot last. when pride is overcome we feel a sudden joy in living. the best place to witness the defeat of pride is in our work . . . all the time we are working and in itself . . . all the time in your working your self is expressed in your work in everyone's work in the work of the world we eliminate expressions of pride. her speech is 4000 words long she told me, and she memorized the whole thing. she speaks of pride, and pride, and perfection and solitude and fear and helplessness and defeat and disappointment and surrender and discipline and the necessity of all these and the necessity of the defeat of pride. besides knowing why she left new york i wanted to know why she left new york but i had no way of asking. she was glad to see me by the way. she baked an apple pie for the occasion and then when i wasn't on the 6 a.m. bus from albuquerque she was disappointed and ate some of it. i was glad she was glad to see me and i was glad we drove past the dead cow again and found her. i left jane and the three women of albuquerque in the car a discreet distance from her adobe and walked over there and hailed her and she emerged from the door beaming in dark blue work clothes very tanned or desert weathered i thought and that makes her eyes bluer and more sparkly. she was pleased i didn't bring everybody to the door at once because she wanted to change her clothes. she put on a clean shirt and pants and i explained that the three women of albuquerque were going home in case she wondered. but first we all had the apple pie and a french fish soup bouillabaisse with salmon okra and tomatoes. i was very nervous. or very high and nervously attuned to her emanations and expectations. later jane and me agreed we were afraid of her. i couldn't remember being afraid of her before so i decided i'd changed a lot. i must've been more presumptuous about myself before. or not so aware of the extraordinary presence i was in. or we were both crazy and i thought she was my peer. i don't know. i *was* in awe, but less conscious perhaps. there was the most incredible evening in '66 i think it was when i brought five or six people over to her loft and we sat around in a vague circle in a sort of a trance as though it was a seance although nobody mentioned it and there was at one point this great overhead crash i don't know what it was it wasn't thunder and lightning it might've been a skylight on the roof or even her skylight but whatever it was she didn't bat a lash she went right on talking and asking us all what sort of a wall or body of water we imagined in our minds eyes and when we saw the wall or the body of water would we cross it or could we and if so how would we do it she went right on with this exercise testing us i imagined for correct answers anyway as though nothing had happened which is her basic approach to life. nothing happens. no verticals. everything the same. a quiet existence. not much time for other people's problems. lots of time to herself. solitude and loneliness and contentment with one self. the union of opposites without trying to do so. the friend who went with me to the pasedena talk wrote and told me the whole thing seemed much stronger now than it did at the time but what she absolutely remembers about it is that everything she said she also negated completely, and she doesn't know how she did it. she does contradict herself all the time with the most bewildering confidence. she'll say all conventional people spend 90 per cent of their time wondering is it right or wrong. what you do is right, that's it. then she'll be cato the censor and tell you how absolutely wrong you are. she'll tell me one moment that associative thinking is the basis of all our distraction and the next that i'm exceptionally lucid when i'm at the typewriter. she'll tell me i'm very prudish and priggish (and she *knows* i'm a snob), and later on she'll say i shouldn't use four letter words. she'll say she wanted to ask me something although she wasn't into winning anything and then suddenly there's an argument and it seems as though somebody has to win something if we're to proceed to the next. i think she's delighted to see people but her fear of being disappointed by people is intense. she says she talks all the time when people come in order not to know more than she wants to know, she said you mean you realized how mean we all are? she said about people who come to see her believe you me, i run em off if i don't like them, if they're inconsiderate. she said it with a little chuckle. and told about a couple who came and lived off her for two days and the woman ate a peach from their car right in front of her and didn't offer her one. she doesn't know really why people come to see her. i wasn't sure myself, being such a pilgrimage and all. i just know she's important to me. and i was very curious to see how she was living in the desert. and i still wondered why she left new york even though i knew. i didn't know how to ask but she offered a number of hints gratuitously. she said i don't blame people for not being able to see the paintings, goodness knows, i have no idea why i did them myself. she said i had 10 one-man shows and i was discovered in every one of them. finally when i left town i was discovered again — discovered to be missing. she said she didn't know if she had left the world behind or the world had left her. she said she left new york because of remorse. she said that out at the edge of the canyon after we walked out through the sage to see the sunset. i didn't say anything at all. i guess it isn't necessary to clarify everything or anything. the canyon and the sunset were what seemed to matter and that didn't matter either. a glow was on us though and agnes extended what i thought must be the rarest compliment for her. she said everybody who comes is very conventional except me. it was after that that we were walking back to her adobe and she said she wanted to ask me something although she wasn't into winning anything. it was certainly a difficult moment. i knew it would be some sort of political question which would mean she would stop liking me having just said out at the canyon that everybody who comes is very conventional except me. i have no idea what she meant by the question all i can say is it concerned domination and i think whether i hadn't experienced domination or being dominating. i thought possibly she was alluding to women as role players. i had no intention of mentioning the despairing word feminism, agnes was born in 1912 and it doesn't take much ingenuity to see that she's better off in the desert throwing mud at her adobe and polishing her green truck than i am going around meeting hundreds of strange women who might have nothing more in common than electricians and philosophers but who in the name of feminism take issue with your four syllable words so that we can all be the same that is to say feminists, thus i believe i was appropriately evasive and the only remark i remember is agnes saying her sister says she believes in men women children and dogs and we left it at that although that wasn't the end of it. the thing is in any case one remains modest and gives honor to the sage who stands outside the affairs of the world. out around her adobe she pointed out the loco weed. which drives horses crazy she said. she explained how you make adobe mud bricks by filling up four rectangular sections of these open wooden frames with the mud stuff and then leaving them out to dry or bake in the sun. she talked about animals having thoughts and how she doesn't keep domestic ones any more, she doesn't want them around any more than people. what she keeps exactly is five vehicles in perfect working order and a beebee gun and a regular .22. not counting the small adobe in which she cooks and eats and possibly reads and undoubtedly muses, an open tall shedlike garage where she was parking her new shiny blue vw sports model, an outhouse, a tiny cave log room guest dwelling and a compost affair and she still sleeps in the dodge pickup or the pickup detached from the truck in which she lived for a couple of years riding all round the u.s. and canada till she found the proper mesa. when we drove away i said it didn't seem as if we were driving off a mesa, she said that's because we drove off the back end. anyway she keeps all her machines in good shape. before we woke up she polished her green truck, a '48 chevie, she said. the jeep we didn't see because she keeps it in town in case the roads've been more washed out than usual. i didn't see how we made it in in her white dodge truck returning from taos there must've been some rain and the dodge had zilch traction so i kept ditching off to the side to a standstill and somehow retreating backtracking and then racing forward as though to hit your mark meaning staying on the road as in archery if there's a wind you shoot or aim way off target in order to hit it or even boomerang yourself. after the first night there she gave us a vacation and we went to taos. i was relieved in a way since the telepathy is pretty heavy and i had had a nightmare and the scrutiny is relentless and while she completely disarms you she then flatly contradicts you and as i've indicated i was fearful of exposing what could only be a profound political disagreement between us. i read a hilton kramer review she had there of her retrospective in philadelphia and couldn't help saying the reason she doesn't have the reputation hilton kramer says she should have is because she's a woman. but agnes knows exactly who or what she is or isn't she shot back i'm not a woman and i don't care about reputations. i said well i wouldn't come to see you if you weren't a woman. she concluded the argument saying i'm not a woman, i'm a doorknob, leading a quiet existence. in taos jane thought of buying her an enamel doorknob we saw there but we brought back some cheese and syrup instead. also jane bought some eggs milk and apples and agnes said that was exactly what she needed so as concerned the food we were in perfect agreement. another safe thing was finding out more about agnes, i never asked her much before, i never seriously wondered why she was so different and a natural woman of the universe, or even why i felt close to her while knowing she had her life a lot more together. i never knew she was scottish for instance, but i didn't know how scottish i am until recently either. i think the first thing i asked her over the apple pie and french soup bouillabaisse was where did she come from. then i asked her if she likes the bagpipes and she replied oh yes. a half a mile away. she doesn't come from scotland herself actually. she was born and grew up in saskatchewan, somehow i always thought it was vancouver. i thought vancouver was a wild uncharted territory, but i happen to be in vancouver right now and i can see how agnes couldn't possibly have come from vancouver, i never inquired what saskatchewan is but it sounds northern and wild and right for where agnes would have to come from. she's a mountaineering camping pioneering frontier type of woman whose unnatural habitats for reasons of turning out to be a painter were vertical claustrophobic cities like new york. she's climbed big mountains alone for years so i can only imagine how she felt going three hours upstate new york with me and thalia poons one summer for a little two day cook and sleep-out next to a crick river and 20 yards in from the macadam but she never mentioned what an elementary tourist trip it was. the crick was deep enough to submerge and swim a few strokes around where we camped and she seemed happy tearing off her clothes yelling at last at one with nature and doing so. it was there that she divined my future and said i would go insane again which i did. another fairly safe thing to talk about is insanity since i suppose we would both agree that nobody knows anything about it except the insane. i think it was at the very end of the summer that i did go out again and agnes and thalia were the ones who rescued me up in brewster where i abandoned my car and called them and waited for them to drive up in somebody's vw bug and didn't take the whole bottle of thorazine that agnes suggested i should but rather about 400 mcs or mgs or whatever they are. possibly agnes asked me what was wrong with me and i said i was afraid to die. yet in her wall and body of water game in which she asks people what sort of a wall you imagine or body of water and when you imagine it if you could cross it or go over it and if so how you would do it i was the one apparently who had the correct answer, at least to the wall question, and that was that the wall was transparent so naturally i could walk through it and whatever was on the other side was the same as on this, so it doesn't seem reasonable that i was afraid to die unless the game we played occurred later on and i was by that time dead or dead on the one hand and alive on the other so it didn't matter. on her mesa in the desert agnes told us the women in her family live a long time although her mother died young, at 75. she told us all about how she died, how it took two years and how happy she was when it happened, i mean how happy her mother was, and agnes's final pronouncement on death was that you go out either in terror or in ecstasy and clearly her mother was ecstatic. she said her mother was one of the little people. agnes isn't very tall herself but partly because of being full and solid of body she appears a medium height. she says at 60 your body begins to fall apart, whether she is or not it doesn't seem to cramp her style, when we emerged that first morning from the log cave guest dwelling she was standing on a ladder hurling handfuls of mud at the wall of her adobe. by little people i believe she was alluding to the fairies of old celtic scotland. the rest of what i found out about who she is or where she comes from was that an ancestor was the scottish poet who was the author of flanders fields and her father was an essayist and there weren't any painters in the family. she thinks everything happens according to destiny and i objected on grounds of social oppression which was one more instance of my political tactlessness. i was saying that my mother painted lobster pots and boats in the harbor at sunset and that her potential for being an artist or an artist's artist or an artist to herself and nothing else was undeveloped for social reasons but i was saying altogether too much. someone has to be absolutely quiet when the other holds forth agnes remarked. and she talks all the time when people come in order not to know more than she wants to know. but i was thinking some of the time how to get agnes's attention. jane had the idea that sometimes she must feel awfully heavy to herself and then i thought she hasn't had enough people respond to her humor and jane said yeah they're probably too busy at her feet. were we supposed to ask her the meaning of life questions. do people go in order to ask her the meaning of life questions. i guess they would. but she doesn't have any answers, for nobody can tell anybody something they don't already know. she says what she knows for what she knows is what she is and what that is is perfect for her and she is still on the path herself. she says one thing she has a good grip on is remorse. and that suffering is necessary for freedom from suffering. and that the wriggle of a worm is as important as the assassination of a president. and that our work is very important but that we are not important. and that what you want to do is your work and what you want to want to do is your work. and that people ask her whats going to happen in art, where is art going and she says gosh, i hope it's going to go in all directions. and that a sense of disappointment and defeat are an essential state of mind for creative work. a working through disappointment to further disappointment to defeat. what does it mean to be defeated. it means we cannot move . . . but still we go on, without hope, without desire, and without dreams, then it is not i, then it is not us, then it is not conditioned response . . . without hope there is hope, we go on because there is no way to stop, going on without hope and desire is discipline, going on without scheming or planning is discipline and without striving or caring is discipline . . . defeated you rise to your feet like dry bones, these bones will rise again . . . undefeated you will only say what has already been said . . . defeated having no place to go you will await and perhaps be overtaken . . . defeated, exhausted, and helpless you will perhaps go a little bit further. helplessness is very hard to bear, helplessness is blindness, in helplessness we feel as though some terrible mistake has been made, we feel cast into outer darkness as though some fatal error has been made . . . feelings of loss and catastrophe cover everything and we tremble with fear and dread but when fear and dread have passed as all passions do we realize that helplessness is the most important state of mind . . . lack of independence and helplessness is our most serious weakness as artists and that's the way agnes goes on in her 4000 word speech that i heard at the pasadena museum and a few of those things she said to me and i think her critical attitude her relentless scrutiny her voices of perfection her examination of your words and deeds is all in the spirit of improving your character for otherwise why would you go such a distance to see a woman who is herself on the path of perfection which is to say to becoming most totally who she is. she said sitting in the adobe or someplace if only i could get non resistance. she understands remorse but she needs non resistance, that's clear isn't it. yet while walking seems to cover time and space in reality we are always just where we started. i went for a little walk along the rocky edge of the canyon behind her adobe and was amazed to see a tremendously long procession of small black ants in an orderly line up and down this rock facing down into the canyon some going up and some going down with a few stray dissenters or were they the lost ones. i picked up a sandstone to take back to the world. i returned to eat supper. i didn't do much else there. i did take a shot out her door with her beebee gun at a can she placed for my aim after a quick lesson in how to hold the thing i hit the can and quit while i was ahead. also i thought there was a sudden rainbow just to commemorate our visit and i said i'll bet you rarely have a rainbow here and agnes replied yes we do, all the time, it's forever raining when the sun is shining. but the last perfect double rainbow i saw was a couple of years ago in mendocino so i was in and out of her adobe ooing and ahing catching it out in the open or through one window or another watching its aspects and fading disappearing act. about 6 p.m. the wind was blowing in the canyon. by nightfall we were in bed, there isn't any electricity, and i had another nightmare. there was of course just a little bedtime story, of multiple rapes in cuba, a most dangerous part of the country apparently. but agnes had a nightmare too, she was quite indignant about it, she said she knew those nightmares weren't hers, and that's why she can't be around people, because she takes on their . . . she picks up their . . . and jane told her i needed to live among people and agnes said then i must have more pain. i could of course consider exchanging the pain for the nightmares in the desert. yet i could say like her that pain is necessary for freedom from pain. anyway if we are always just where we started there isn't anyplace to go and we might's well be where we are. i was reading recently about merlin who retreated from the world into his forest hermitage. it was said that at the sight of a crowd of people his madness breaks out anew. it was said also that his laugh was especially well known, the result of his more profound knowledge of invisible connections. agnes has this laugh or this cosmic giggle, but i wish to say she isn't any magician. she disavows magic adamantly. she hates magic and fetishes and superstition and the i ching, she says superstition is a belief in power, that there've been whole ages where art was only fetishes and that superstition is the enemy of art. she is also as a classicist as a cool artist a woman who looks out with her back to the world a painter who paints not about ideas or personal emotion but who paints the desert in her head as a classicist she is also eloquently opposed to romance and romanticism. she said she never met anybody who wasn't searching for love. she thinks this is a great mistake. she described a time of her own enslavement in this respect and how she became definitively done with it. the voices of perfection. of being alone with your self. of everything being the same. of not having any verticals. of lots of time to herself. of not much time for other peoples problems. of solitude and loneliness and contentment with one self. the union of opposites without trying to do so. a zen sort of person who never studied zen. a woman perhaps who's endured many insults, and who forgives everybody — and nobody. a woman who doesn't believe in influence unless it's you yourself following your own track. a woman it seems to me absolutely fearless of saying what she thinks. after all she doesn't depend on people. the work is what counts and the work is so fine and the people like the work so much that they pay her to live without any people. once she took a freighter around the world and someplace in india they took her off the boat and confined her in a hatch because she'd gone into a trance. no doubt the people on the boat were altogether too much. the boat in the desert is a beebee gun a .22 and five vehicles in perfect working order and i'm not without a little remorse that i went to see her myself. do we have to give honor in person to our sages standing outside the affairs of the world. or bother them with ideas of themselves that they don't have themselves and be bothered ourselves by ideas of ourselves they may have that we don't or bother at all. i don't know. in albuquerque after she drove us out and we were having lunch in la placita i asked her if she didn't think she was leading an exemplary life and once again she knocked the whole thing, oh my no, i'm a murderer, i'm a this and a that, i'm working out the hairy ape in myself, i'm just beginning, and so on, and i remembered how she leaned forward intensely in the adobe and said somewhat incredulously and you realized how mean we all are and i nodded yes, so how could i exempt her from her own conclusions about life. the work is the thing. the grid is still because the whole can be grasped by the eye and mind at once. the value she places on the known rather than the seen suggests innate ideas which she sometimes calls a memory of perfection. agnes martin: a study in the memories of perfection. "the ocean is deathless/ the islands rise and die/ quietly come, quietly go/ a silent swaying breath/ i wish the idea of time would drain/ out of my cells and leave me/ quiet even on this shore."

—*September 20, 1973*

At the Crotch of Dawn

September 14 arrived surprise lake at 4 p.m. i thought it could've been called lake suddenly since you come upon it suddenly. and life is fool of surprises. the united flight boston to seattle september 7 contained a whole fastpitching softball team called the kawanis club and i've never flown in a plane full of goon boys who yell things like let me outa here when the plane is landing and taking off. and i've never flown with a couple celebrating their 58th wedding anniversary. and i've never flown with carol strawberry. and i've never been in point roberts which snowshoe tells me is probably the most inaccessible piece of land attached to the continent. to me the most inaccessible peace of anything i've been to was this surprise lake 4800 feet above sea level and nobody flew me there. it may be one of those points from which the desire to travel is more interesting than traveling. i didn't want to stay there long myself. about 5 p.m. i said i thought one night would do. i was cold and i felt strange and we'd forgotten to pack in mayonnaise. also i wanted a martini. and snowshoe was cooking up beef stroganoff with sour cream out of a package and the mushrooms she was frying to go with the package fell in the dirt so i had to wash each one off individually in the lake. and she wasn't happy herself that she'd forgotten a jello cheese cake mix she says she never goes without. she showed me the guide book with pictures and maps and told me if we kept on going today, that was the next day, these're some of the things we'd pass by. i'd already passed by the whole snoqualimie national forest on the pacific crest trail system and i thought i might have to have the cartilege in my right knee removed like my left from when i fell out of bed once. i kept referring to my knees. the day after when i couldn't walk, i kept referring to my calves. that particular trail was not recommended for cow travel. or rather horse. i wanted to know what mountain we were climbing and snowshoe said all these mountains have names but she'd have to look on a map to see what they are, none of em are famous mountains, tho that's a very human way of looking at it, tho what i meant to say was that what she told me mainly was we weren't climbing any mountains at all, we were hiking. i deduced therefore that for an outbacker like snowshoe who by the way was carrying 40 lbs. next to my three that climbing 4800 feet which she said is a lot more than our eastern mt washington which is our highest is a sort of a stroll over a slightly rising mole. she stopped to rest quite a bit on the way up though. i asked if every trail goes to a lake. she said no to peaks and meadows and shelters but lakes are the favorites. i could see why. they're not polluted by humans and they sit all still deep blues greens like a nest in a steep bank of branch. way up are these white vulva gulleys that're snow passages. way up were these meadows of stone heaps that avalanche down in the winters of snows. way up top of all that're the peaks that snowshoe doesn't know the names of. the mountain you can see around pt. roberts and vancouver is mt. baker. all i know about vancouver is you can walk to the beach from almost any part of it and you can't ever get lost cause you've always got the mountains to guide you. i saw the whole thing with embalmed freighters in a still life harbor out of jane rule's picture window and what she told me is that toronto is a city and vancouver is a womb with a view. i have no idea what toronto has to do with it. as i said i arrived at pt. roberts and that's where snowshoe came in her mother's toyota corolla squareback to take me down to gold bar and turn me into a rockicrucian mountaineer or rather a mere hiker whose knee cartileges would split and have to be excised and whose calves would assume a permarigid condition who anyhow would never be recommended for travel on any more horse trails. snowshoe arrived at the crotch of dawn while i was in the arms of carol strawberry with whom i flew united as i said. s. told me my horoscope for that day was i was not supposed to make any binding contracts, and the next day was auspicious for travel and romance, so she guessed i'm supposed to travel in romance on a free lance basis. every shroud has a silver lining. we accept whatever situation arises. i'm enjoying being sentimental. and i had to pack my fresca bottle out of the snoqualimie national forest. i wouldn't've packed it in if i'd known, three lbs. is a lot of lbs. climbing five miles, and s. had plenty of these packages with flavored powder for our drinking supply. she says it's a joke in the outback that anything to drink is good. we drank this grape mix all the way up. only city bunnies like me drag in their fresca bottles. there was a yuban can somebody'd thrown in a small pool this side of the lake that s. wanted to pack out too, but 40 lbs. is already a lot, and i wasn't adding to my three, which included the empty fresca bottle. on the way there were all sorts of mushrooms, even some papery thin orange ones, and white white white ones with fluted undersides like jane rule's white crepe pants. there was marmots pikas chipmunks no bears no snakes. i looked a pika straight in the eye beside the lake surprise. i said i'd like to study biology again, basically to find out how everybody reproduces. snowshoe said she just wants to know what to eat. at bottom we never know how it has all come about. i didn't actually see a marmot. i heard one whistle. i thought it was a boyscout leader, then the same whistle on the way out past the same place a cemetery of rocks and trees from avalanche and s. informed me the marmots'll lie out in the sun and roll over on their tummies n tickle themselves and play around then when they see somebody coming they'll whistle and dive for cover into the rocks. a good smart life. i can't even remember to take my mayonnaise along myself. nonetheless i have the cents to take a plane to the most inaccessible piece of land attached to the continent. when you cross the border around here there's a white peace arch that says Children of a Common Mother. that means canada is the legitimate child and we're the bastards. after being legitimate on king george highway for about 20 minutes however if you're going to pt roberts you cross another border into the u.s.a. again into our natural bastardy, pt roberts being a u.s. possession. four candles one bowl of salad one woman sleeping. analogies, affinities, correspond-ences, and repercussions. the feeling of strangeness which she conveyed, and yet of having known her always. i was immediately attracted to her because she was beautiful, eternite, infini, charite, solitude, angoisse, lumiere, aube, soleil, amour, beaute, inoui, pitie, demon, ange, ivresse, paradis, enfer, ennui, embrasse, etc . . . as sacred as 36,000,000 new born poodle dogs. switchback or sailboat tacking. in the woods snowshoe said oh by the way if you see any snakes don't worry 'cause none of them're poisonous. as for the bears, they're not grizzly. anyway i was pretty involved in these huge trees. i said there wasn't any lake, meaning we'd never get there. i said it's raining and s. said we call this sprinkling. i said my feet were falling off and s. said if i had the equipment very soon i'd get right into it too. i said lookit these enormous leaves, which were sun dappled, and s. said if i think they're big here i should go out to the olympic rain-forest, the leaves there're like the amazon basin. coming down i kept saying we should be recrossing the footbridge soon and s. said it's a foot log not a foot bridge. i said we were making it down in double time and s. agreed. although that was about three hours fast walking, or fast for trails not recommended for horse travel. the last 16th of a mile when we emerged from the trail onto a gravel road stretch crossing a crick and a railroad track back to where the toyota corolla was parked my mind told my body it was through so the remainder was a terrific sludge. i mean my mind had told my feet it was over but they had to go another 16th of a mile. this indicates to me that you could travel tremendous distances on foot and not mind it a bit until your mind registered the end, distance being absolutely relative an all. and space. the moving thin line of white far below was raging torrent. all you have to remember is your jello cheese cake mix. all i had to remember was the thing i never liked about camping was when you got to the campsite. then i never knew what to do. that's why i said to snowshoe i felt strange. i like just moving along, paddling down the rivers or trudging up the trails, oohing and ahing over the wilderness. but at the campsite i would feel dirty and sticky and useless and stand there poking at the fire and not looking forward to a night on the hard ground in a blue nylon tent flapping madly in the glacial wind and wishing i was looking out somebody's picture window at a bunch of embalmed freighters in a stilllife harbor. sdrawkcab spelt backwards spells backwards. the last thing on the way out were the great martian-like towers of the electrical transmission lines that stalk across the earth under which we passed on the way in and i heard for the first time the humming sizzling drone of the wires that had turned on la monte young as a boy in the west. if the winged victory of samothrace had kept her head she might've smoked a cigarette in a long jade holder. i got back to the cabin in gold bar and had a martini and a mayonnaise sandwich. — this is snowshoe's postscript that i asked her to write: time passes slowly up here in the mts. steel guitars and stars, mountain lakes and blackberry ramble. hey jill is this a letter to you? anything i can say is only about existing on a different time scale. four and a half miles up the trail is not the same as four and a half miles down the trail. leading a reasonable existence comes down to leading an invisible one. the singular technology of wilderness. surfboards, a co-op senior pack, bluet camp stove, poly bottle in the side pocket. we did spend a lot of time talking about trees. cedar trees and fir trees. the whispers tell of growing in a softly breathing world, a hundred years just to become young. richard and i lying on the snow, goofing on acid and getting drawn into the life trees swirled across the mist and dripping snow. the world we have is not the world we want but the forest seems satisfied. how remote. the nervous bustling trivial 20th century. where have you gone lita lepie? it was a long distance search. a long distance hike. an alpine lake with a happy personality. lake surprise. find it if you can. enough of salvation, back to civilization. go ahead and listen to helen reddy when you get back home. its so cute it'll just make your mind fall out. mind did. luckily as a rockicrucian that doesn't bother me at all. none of this is scary energy. like bears in the cascades. dark space outside the tent and no flashlight. i still believe you could relax and laugh with them and the bears would really dig ya. i talked with one when i was eight, it was cool. i'm in my own pocket. save our mother ocean. maybe my mission in life is to pass out surfer t-shirts to my friends. you're gonna laugh but we're gearing up for action. mind trips even. being in this time is being in no time at all. possession in a past space, and peace in another. hello lake carol lake diana lake robin lake vicki lake trina lake sandy hurricane heather mt debbie mt francis lake circumspect lake becky lake white cloud lake jane trapper past surprise creek hidden lake mt alison mt betty lost river & lake jill. goodbye from lake laziness.

—September 27, 1973

Valentein for Stine

I had the intention of commemorating gertrude which i have but not again today even though i didn't know it was her birth year. 1874 allegheny and my grandmother 1872 i have no idea where. why should i defend stein against her male detractors, the work is available for more and more of everyone to see for themselves even lifting belly should be out soon if it isn't now: insignificant work. interesting personality so was my grandmother. my long life. my long life. that was the bleak sum of mother's wisdom. she has purpose and passion but no perception or possibly no passion but almost certainly no purpose no purpose at all. she had a poor attitude. she didn't apply herself. or something exactly like that. suddenly i know tomorrow is going to be very great. old car junk buried besides what. these are words & words are fine. optimum reassurance. that's a sign in your flavor. a dome on the mountain. a palm to sea. a stein to mug. loud & monotonous or soft & complicated. did you ask an answer. did you answer ask. did a remark be introduced at this point. did this because there'd be no story events happen. did approach object this reverence with. did what who object care did is strange. if you have no problems buy a goat they say they say. they say so many things. influential but unread. i would say bought and unread and who is not influential and does it involve reading and don't you have to buy it and read it if they're dead. we know that the dead are powerful rulers. my grandmother was completely influential and unread. nobody read her because she didn't write and she was unread herself and she never heard of gertrude stein. who ever heard of gertrude stein. i heard of nelson eddy and jeannette macdonald through my grandmother and when at last long after my grandmother was dead i read the autobiography of alice b.t. i thought it was written by alice b.t. that's how much i knew of gertrude stein and now they're saying i was right i mean that this first success of hers when she was 57 or 60 or so can be explained away as an imitation outright of the spoken style of alice. every example encourages imitation. i suppose it matters. dear ann landers would i want my daughter to look like *that*? dear ann o. minity, you'll see it when you believe it. don't ask me nothing about it. the whole question of questions and not answer is not necessarily very interesting as gertrude stein herself would agree although she once remarked that it was and in fact addressed her very last remark to alice in the form of a question in that case she said what is the question after a pause when alice said nothing in reply to the question what is the answer. at least according to alice's version as richard bridgman put it i wonder what other version there could have been possibly since alice attended her into the hospital and outside the operating room before she never saw her again. in a world increasingly saturated with meaningless words. why cannot you speak in pieces and say no matter the matter in matter. the words & the words well anyway she's going in her bed which is a preparation for going to sleep. she followed her brother to europe and maintained her difficult style in the face of ridicule and charges of obscurantism. the charge of the heavy brigade. brigid teresa field saints aid ade er rather why should we understand. it's just words & words are fine. the yellow brick brook. the white rainbow airplane bird rail tracks. telephone football penny foolish. floor flower flaw. virtuous indignation real and assumed. room dreams my grandmother again old car junk buried anxiety what besides these fine words. also someone to make a pieta with two women nuns magdalen extremely sexual but don't mention it. mannish and defiant. hermetic and solipsistic. a colossal ego and a publicity seeker. etseculara. they were awfully sorry that it is too much trouble and excitement to be partly left alone without as much as it is made carefully in extenuation of their needing even which it is more than an affectation to be deprived of it amounting to that. she definitely feels that. the stirrings. stir soup jig pen box bin but can you come over she said can you come over and we know people by what they repeat. very profound and eventually published she wasn't intended. you weren't either and neither was i. but her parents bridgman informed us had set a limit of five children for their family and only after two of the stein children had died in infancy were leo and then gertrude conceived so her very existence struck her as having been threatened before it began. at last the whole world lies under an embargo of impossibility. soon there was nothing but sighs

& birdsong. the future isn't what it used to be or something not necessarily exactly like that. economy of xplanation/unity of solution. the references to the foetus are all slightly twisted. she refused to trim off contradictory feelings in order to achieve a smooth result. my mother's parent who was my grandmother had a limit of one for her family and that was my mother and subsequently as it would seem my own parent that is my mother also had a limit of one for her family which made us finally one and one and one. every example encourages imitation. women don't invent they receive. insignificant personality. uninteresting work. a discriminating eye for painting. indefatigably autistic. the most interesting person after all was the brother or even the wife being in this case the wife of a wife or a woman or a freak.

we understand. man has always been thinking equally well. any other solution they attempt is equally beset with difficulties. an inventive woman leaves us autochthonous again and that problem has been solved by levi-strauss. all the versions are correct and gertrude would agree. when mary maxworthy in *the making of americans* unexpectedly finds herself pregnant, gertrude stein resolutely ignores the male responsibility. mary simply "had something happen to her that surprised every one who knew her." one sign of her incipient reconciliation to her private vision came when she confessed that she preferred to write about women. asked what she thought of the atomic bomb she said she'd been unable to take any interest in it. she liked to read detective and mystery stories. what was the use she said if atomic bombs are really as destructive as all that there is nothing left and if there is nothing there nobody to be interested and nothing to be interested about. here, her meaning is reasonably clear. need we more. are you having fun, darling? are you beside yourself? are you peculiar? are you discreetly concealed but incapable of protrusion? do you cede the initiative and wait whatever is to come? are you righteously impenetrable? are you merely experimental? do you bless this cow? i bless this cow. it is formed, it is pressed, it is large, it is crowded. it is out. cow come out. cow come out and shout. entertaining conversationalist. saloon woman. no purpose at all. a poor attitude. didn't apply herself. sat by the window on the sunporch rubbing her arthritis. never wrote a thing. never heard of gertrude stein. who ever heard of gertrude stein. steins were from allegheny and california then paris and my grandmother wasn't from anyplace except a half of a house in little neck. funny i don't know from where except remotely germany possibly and i never thought of visiting her grave i don't know where that is exactly either yet it seemed correct and even urgent to visit gertrude and alice in the pere lachaise on the outskirts of paris. wonder wonderfully. by by the by. in sight. prevented preventing inordinately relieving which in best best of believing this mingled frantically remarkable extravagantly letting it alone. an account on account in in to be dismissed by that time. finally to say so. sap wordlings fine just fine but what else they say they say so many things. everything that's clear to them has no relevance. when there is no obstruction they invent one. it's out in the nature of continuing on thinking equally well. and if you have no problems buy a goat. herself gertrude stein had always liked little pigs and she always said that in her old age she expected to wander up and down the hills of assisi with a little black pig. bless this pig. she did prefer naturally to see through the subjective prism of her own consciousness. she never incests. she refused a smooth result. she refused whatever she wasn't. she never learned. she couldn't put two or two. or even finish medical school. or even write her final exam for william james. she could only read everything with studied inattention. she could follow her brother to europe. have a discriminating eye for painting and influence the importance of being earnest. no hems no haws. he goes or i goes alice said and leo went too. she was in earnest that's that that's it about it. i'm completing predictions and making others on many levels. suddenly i know tomorrow is going to be very great. she couldn't have the children she wasn't supposed to be only the one she is is is present presence prolonged. this is okay. also nelson eddy and jeannette macdonald. oh she liked edgar bergen too. and herbert hoover. when gertrude stein lectured the people said you speak so clearly why don't you write the way you speak and she said why don't you read the way you listen. invent and receive. insignificant personality. discriminating work. people who are ahead in their heads are very ordinary in their lives. i had the intention of commemorating gertrude which i have but not again today. let us now praise famous grandmothers.

—*February 24, 1974*

Muttering & Doddering

may 13 monday 11 am flight 159 united kennedy to portland
stopover chicago, i've been thinking a lot lately about connections
but not the ordinary ones, the official connection in this case was a
"gay conference" at evergreen state college in olympia which is
between seattle and portland, i more or less flipt a coin to determine
portland although my connection there was not any clearer than i
thought seattle would be and i'm not necessarily looking for a clear
connection but lately i'm more conscious of flying blind and seeing
how i pin the donkey when i get there. i was traveling book heavy
and clothes light so i figured my basic connection enplaning was my
literature and my seatmate was the perfect nonperson, young sallow
dour knitted pink properly connected and reading a michener novel,
i made a few inexplicable exclamations as usual, to which she
responded by continuing to read her michener so i felt free to pursue
my own abstractions and we were 10 or 15 minutes in the air when
i sensed this enormous presence nearby and looked up to meet the
eyes of a big friendly male freak with large features and lots of reddish
brown hair in a seat across the aisle the row was originally empty
except for an ossifer next to the window. we engaged for several
minutes in an autistic exchange, making faces and gestures and
flashing objects, he had a record book identical to mine, his brief of
books papers memroarbilious etc. was just as funky as mine and then
he produced a flask just like one i had in my minds eye that a lover
talked about giving me it was medium small leather bound with
gold initials and i think that was the first thing he said was that the
initials stood for his father who died when he was 12. he had a heavy
father story. what was your fathers name i asked im. jack. mine's jill
i said. i thought so he replied and we went on from there. he's daniel
himself and he's writing a novel called i am the great american novel
and he's living in eugene oregon with a beautiful "psychotic angel"
whose name is faith who's "very high and she doesn't use any drugs"
and who goes to a guru he doesn't like although he's looking for a
"teacher" himself and we talked a little about gestalt along with the
cosmos and everything until we landed in chicago. actually i was

somewhat bored and repulsed by his father & son story which included such items as . . . never mind. daniel was my connection from new york to chicago, i was blown out and trapped for the layover in the terminal near my gate too high to be tripping on the layers of archaelogical consciousnesses speeding by me in 20th century costumes the ticket agents wouldn't let me back on the plane right away so i was hovering around the dock there when my new connection came along — she was blond blue young athletic allamerican and "linda" she said as she shook my hand after asking me if i was me and telling me she'd have to "get past her star trip" to relate to me as a regular person to which i replied thanx i would too. i was grateful for the opportunity to be a regular person. i changed my seat and we obtained two together near the back next to a woman at the window in an immaculate white rayon pants suit reading *dibs* and wearing earphones. linda asked me what i like to do best. nobody's asked me anything like that in a long time. i thought about it and told her well i think i like to think the best. a few days later in seattle i mentioned this exchange to snowshoe who said it sounded like the sort of question a therapeutic kind of person would ask and i flashed that this was true that linda projected attributes of a therapist and otherwise what she does i learned is work in the post office play softball fall in love with people and read a lot. i've been reading dick alpert's (alias ram dass) *the only dance there is* concurrently with philip slater's *earthwalk* and if you can get past the sexism of the former he has many useful offerings, i.e., ". . . you get stuck in roles. & the life process, the spiritual contact, turns off the minute you think you're somebody doing something. as long as i think i am speaking to you and i'm doing something to you . . . i'm keeping you out there as them." much woman's talk and movement ideology has revolved around roles, cultural role stasis and role models and the termination of them. i've been thinking lately more about their flexibility or interchangeability since as long as we're living in a culture anything we do can be identified in some role sense and there's nothing wrong with roles except for their stasis in conditions of change. what we may need is attitudes of willingness to assume roles that are best or most effective for the moment. how can we play mutter & dodder to ourselves forinstance. this was one of the subjects raised by a woman at the workshop i conducted may 16 at evergreen in olympia. the familiar subject is placed in a strange setting. so that one can sit back and look and be amazed. or the familiar role. i didn't think of linda as a therapy type on the plane but i was a little amazed by her question and three days later after i was totalled from assuming role of mediator for three hours at evergreen she turned it around more obviously and became my "healer" and she's a woman 21 years old if that makes a difference or a sameness. anyway my connection from chicago to portland even ended up putting me on the plane the day after evergreen that was may 17 along with five other amazons seattle back to new york. throughout all these roles there's a connection. the role that most interests me now is that of mediator. life is an interstellar communication network and sometimes the connections are ruptured as wires in a storm and a repair crew is required to hook up the services again. i have more farreaching ideas about technological service connections along the lines of their replacement over a period of industrial time for correspondingly atrophied psychic functions but i'm dropping it here, it's a connection i'm exploring elsewhere. here's a passage from alpert alias ram dass's book on roles: "i've got to feed in one experience that i had that seems relevent. i was in england and i was with a psychiatrist by the name of ronnie laing. ronnie and i decided to take lsd together. and he said to me, 'how much shall we take?' i said, 'well, why don't we take about 300 micrograms?' and he said, 'well, that's a little much for me. but as long as you're along, i guess it's all right.' now by his saying that he put me into the role of sort of being his protector. that is, he cast me into the role of being the guide, which bugged me a little bit. but o.k. i don't know this guy. if that's the trip i'm supposed to play, i will be john responsible. and he can flip around the room. right? and my usual model of what's going to happen is i'm going to take it and i'm going to create a pleasant environment. i'm going to put on miles davis records (in those days) and we're going to lie around and you know, do it. so we take this and the first thing that happens after we've taken the chemicals is he takes off all his clothes but his shorts and he starts to stand on his head. this doesn't fit into my model of what you do when you have psychedelics. i don't know anything about yoga, and it all seems absurd to me. this is five, six, seven years ago. so i watch with a certain, you know, disbelief, then he walks over to me and he looks into my eyes and his face looks like the most defenseless child, just like my model had been that i'm going to have to take care of him . . . i'm going to be the guide. he looks like a totally defenseless child. he arouses in me every nurturant impulse i have, i feel tremendously protective of him. and i just feel like saying, 'oh ronnie . . . i'm not saying anything but i'm like, ronnie, it's all right i'm here.' you know, 'count on me.' he's just like a little child, wide open. and we were no sooner in that role than his face takes on the sublest change, just muscle patterns like, it's as if a thought in his head manifests in a change in his face — he now looks like the most protective fatherly, warm, nurturant being — and he arouses in me all those uncooked seeds of being a little, dependent child. see. and i become, 'oh, ronnie, oh, wow, you will take care . . . you are going to be my . . . oh ronnie, i can do it this time. oh, wow.' the minute i'm in that, his face changes again. and he is now the student and he's asking me questions. this is all silent. it's all mime and all just facial things. it's all thought forms." (lower case mine). — so we were descending into portland and by this time we were talking to the woman at the window in the immaculate rayon white pants suit who was reading *dibs* and she was confirming my suspicion that she was some sort of a therapist (about to become a "guidance counselor" she said) and daniel had passed by on his way to the lav looming big friendly large glowing redbrown eyes lots of hair and told me he'd been talking all the way from chicago to a "gestalt therapist" (a woman). *his* new connection i thought. and . . .

—June 6, 1974

Jill Johnston Meets The Argentine Firecracker

The Voice is Interested in This Woman and I Am Too but Probably Not for the Same Reason

I never heard of Fanne Fox until the day before I met her which was November 21 and *The Village Voice* never sent me on an errand before. They call it an assignment and in 15 years I was never assigned. Now it's November 23 and I'm personally acquainted with a stripper and I've suddenly become a journalist. And I was just thinking of giving up both. Just before you start something, it's wise to give it up. I have but I'm here to record the event, or the transition. In case anybody questions the sexual politics of the assignment, they're right. It should be commercially amusing to send a lesbian to interview a stripper. Moreover, I never heard of Wilbur Means of the Ways Committee I went to Washington once but only to see Bella. Later I wrote publicly about driving around in Bella's car in New York, but nobody took a scandalous interst in Bella being seen with a lesbian. Possibly because the police didn't stop us and neither of us fell in the lake. What I heard the day before I met Fanne or Anna, Anna Battistella, her real name, was that she was caught being seen in a congressman's car and the congressman was a very important person of that sort and she ran into the tidal basin. I had a lot to find out, including the nature of the tidal basin (I'd never heard of it), I assumed everybody assumed that Fanne or Anna was having an affair with this Senator Wilbur of the Means and Mills so I wouldn't bother asking her that. Why would a Wilbur from Arkansas hang out with a South American stripper. I have the regular Western imagination. An editor at *The Voice* suggested I might ask her why she jumped in the water and how Wilbur got that blood on his face if it wasn't from Fanne's fingernails. This was the first mention of blood. The editor thought Fanne must have leapt into the tidal basin to escape the clutches of this man and that this was good judgment on her part and I agree. The main thing was to get to the Pilgrim Theatre in Boston where she's currently doing a two week stint and catch her act. It was arranged I would talk to her at 12.30 p.m. for an hour before she went on. I should ask at the box office for Jimmy and Mr Barrack and look for David Ryan, a photographer from the *Boston Globe*, and give him $25 I didn't have to pay the $3.50 to see the show. Jimmy and Barrack were appropriately seedy and Barrack was most informative. He said Fanne has doubled their normal business and that she'll be here in five minutes then you can go backstage and do anything you want with her. I said "anything?" and he smiled crookedly. Fanne is being billed there as the tidal basin bombshell. I was dying to see the show and find out about the basin. I thought this might be the most professional act I'd seen since the Crazy Horse in Paris. In London the stripping is awful. In San Francisco I saw Carol Doda once but all I could think about was silicone. In New York I've done some strippng myself and otherwise I've only seen it done by friends or lovers. I never bend my knee and then snap my legs straight and then point my toe when I take off my pants. I don't really care about any of it actually. *The Voice* is interested in this woman and I am too but probably not for the same reason. Everything is an omen. My initiation into sex originated in and around Boston and that included one trip to the Old Howard which featured Sally Rand who had a virtuosic pair which she flung around her soldier like a continental shoulder (although I don't know if I saw Sally cause I never heard of her then and I don't know why I went there since I was an innocent schoolchild.) The Pilgrim Theatre is in its second year, and like the Old Howard, the only burlesque in Boston. It's a cavernous dilapidated movie house with operatic pretensions in its balcony boxes. There were a few jerkers down front in the orchestra watching a porn flick that alternates with a live act. Fanne entered the foyer in a big brown or red curly wig and checked herself out in a news clipping pinned up in Jimmy's office. We went downstairs in her dressing room which was full of feathers. She wasn't relating to me except as a potential nuisance. I guess she likes the publicity but she's bored with reporters. I didn't know how to relate to her myself much less to her feathers. Basically, I wanted to find out her origins and ancestry and why she would end up doing what she's doing and what else she does or wants to do and in order to do that I should insinuate myself into her confidence by asking the boring questions about the senator's car and her fling in the basin and the blood on the senator's face from possibly her fingernails. So I tried to mobilize my interest in an incident that Fanne herself or Anna as she says her friends and family call her (or "Bayba") later told me. "They make it sound so big and it was nothing at all." Or "Some people enjoy watching somebody come down from a pedestal." I was confused by her preparations for the act. It didn't seem right to be there. I'd adjusted to the feathers but suddenly she had no hair or what little there seemed of her own as she removed her big brown red curly wig and appeared in another bigger one and in just a lacy bra sitting there smiling theatrically at me beginning to relate to my function. Then the bra was coming off. Then a lackey called Tony entered bearing an item or a message. Then a comic who precedes her number was in the doorway smiling crookedly, and offering a complimentary opinion about one of her outfits hanging up among the feathers. "I'm not an interior decorator but I know a good looking woman." Then she was sitting in a short terrycloth robe facing the mirror applying makeup and I was sitting in a chair facing her mirror image and the photographer David Ryan was waiting until she had her gear together. I thought there couldn't be two more different people in the world than her and me if differences are defined by style. Yet I prostituted myself as a dancer at one time too although it was euphemistically defined as an artform not that Anna hasn't done this sort of dancing too. Anyway, in two or three installments she told me what happened the night she became the Argentine Firecracker or Bombshell. She'd known Mr Mills for a year, they (and his wife, Mrs Mills) were friends, they lived in the same apartment building, a party of seven (not Mrs Mills) went out October 9 for a dinner party for Anna's cousin who came from Argentina on vacation with her son and was leaving in the morning. "We had only two bottles of wine the whole meal and we were only seven people so that is not enough to make anybody drunk." They were driving possibly a little over the speed limit and had forgotten to put their lights on. Anna thinks the police recognized the licence plate then called two more cars plus the reporters before they were actually stopped. And that was on the bridge over the tidal basin. I asked her why she ran into it. She said she fell into it. I had to picture the scene. Besides the seven people, the scene involved Anna's bare feet and a broken Coke bottle and a stomach ache and antibiotics and a small argument over who would drive the car. It seems Anna always drives "Mr Mills' " car. She said. "Please let me drive" but he said she was in no condition to drive. She'd been on antibiotics every three hours for a bronchial infection and she had a stomach ache. "I'm not used to taking anything so a friend Mr Capaldi was driving. Also I don't like to wear my shoes so I took my shoes off in the restaurant. I didn't want my stockings dirty and ruin them and there was a broken bottle of Coca Cola in the car. I'd cut my foot and didn't know it so when I got out of the car I sort of fell down the police said I collapsed to the ground, it looked embarrassing for a congressman to have a ticket, two newspeople already were there so I got out of the car to explain so I started yelling please here is my driver's license. I was trying to get them to talk to me instead of go to the car, but they paid no attention to me — so I threw it on the seat of the car cause they didn't want to see it. I walked over to the railing, a little railing on the bridge and jumped up on it, and fell backwards into the water (which was 12 feet below the bridge) and as I fell I turned to go in in a dive the police officer jumped after me almost on top of me. I was mad 'cause he tried to help me. I was mad 'cause I can swim very well, instead of helping me he was drowning me — he sounded so desperate you know, he thought I was drowning when I tried to swim away from him, then he was drowning and hurting me in a lifesaving clutch . . . by this time they'd thrown in some tires and he said please hold onto the tires lady . . . I'd been swimming since I was four and for style since I was seven . . ." You're very athletic, I interposed. "Yes I can scuba dive. I can ski. I play the guitar. I speak three languages. Spanish, Italian. I like to sail. I'm learning Papiamenpo, (a dialect of Spanish, Portuguese, and Dutch). I accompany my husband on the piano. I *try* ice skating. I can't skate but at least I never go to the floor." Also Anna has four children: Aida. 19, Grace, 18, Alex, 16 and a half, Mary, 15. One of them adopted. On October 16, she was divorced from her husband. Her breasts are full, high, and firm looking so it crossed my mind I wondered if she had silicone. But not til after the first show. In the dressing room still trying to develop a relationship while i sat pen poised and looking serious I'm sure and demure in dykes denim asking about the basin and the blood ("I don't know how he got blood on his nose . . . cut under his eye from his eyeglasses possibly. . . he was trying to stop me from getting out of the car . . . he bleeds from the nose easily") I felt flustered and unnerved inside myself by her latest preparations — standing up applying leg makeup in the mirror to what she explained were her stretchmarks or the scar tissue from an operation from same. I said I think scars are very attractive possibly the essential expression of body art. Anyway she was very skinny as a child and her own children weighed nine, 10, and 11 pounds when they were born so that's how she has the stretchmarks. She told me during one of these shows in Boston a young man was very nasty and asking her things like how was Wilbur. "He was very young and I told him he had a very young mind. He said you have a very old body and I said you know why that's because I'm a 38-year-old mother, what's *your* excuse?" — "but everybody's treating me very nice." A manager appears in the door and her voice lowers several decibels: "hello sweetheart." By this time she was practically ready in a sparkling green business bra and color coordinated Frenchies with another Frenchy with an ass fringe on top, then a whole bunch of feathers including a headdress the size of an icebox. She said it was pheasant, ostrich and cock feathers. There was also a lot of Maribou around. That's a little bird so it takes zillions of maribous to make a burlesque skirt. I wasn't disappointed by her act and if it's commercially amusing to say so, I *was* turned on, but I didn't have my hands in my pocket. I have plenty to amuse me besides burlesque. Anyhow ladies are very turned on by themselves but of course they're not supposed to be. As for any feminist issues involving prostitution I wouldn't take a position against it without analyzing all the social components which still exist that make it essential. In any eve(nt) we're all prostitutes in the extant system and why one particular woman exhibits her body per se and another washes dishes or writes books or sells insurance is an academic question relating to our particular backgrounds. After the act, I went downstairs to the dressing room to ask Anna about hers. At that point my friend Sam arrived and then i felt emboldened to say I (we) were lesbians. Her face lit up under a Turkish towel and she said oh that crossed my mind before. "I know a lot of lesbians" she added. Some of her best friends are no doubt. I took it for granted she was herself, but I didn't ask. Whether she is or not she's "always proud to be seen with Mr and Mrs Mills," but we'd already settled the Mills ways and committee means affair. Her last remark was that Profumo was finished. I had some serious questions. Where did she come from. When did she start "dancing." She drew a map of Argentina for me and placed a dot on Buenos Aires and a dot for the small town not far away where she was born. Both her parents were nurses at the first aid station. Anna was a school teacher for a while but she didn't like it. She's always wanted to be a doctor. As a teenager she danced with her sister and entertained the local government at their functions. She danced the malambo "dressed like a man"— the malambo is a man's dance — there was no pay. I suppose the town gave them trinkets and dresses. Anna was married at 20. She left her country in 1961, going to Peru than Panama and Costa Rica. Eleven years ago, she came to America and was dancing in a supper club in Miami. She began stripping because the pay was better, last year she stopped "dancing." The idea was that her children were growing up and she would go back to school. She says she's been accepted as a pre-med student at Maryland University. I don't think she has any illusions about her present publicity. She's just stretching the moment for what mileage it's worth. I had to rush for a 6.50 plane to Iowa. On my way out Jimmy said. "Don't forget honey, push the theater, give it a good boost." Before I left I did ask Anna if she'd had silicone. She said yes but it was removed, and her left breast is still hard. She showed me how her right one is soft and normal. About her act, she told me. "I'm a very stubborn person. I do what I feel. I never could learn the regular routine of a stripper I made up my own according to what I feel comfortable. I don't like to be obscene or ridiculous. And I know when my show is good." I noticed a marked scar on her forehead. I think to myself she's had a rough time surviving. Possibly they've given her a year to live because of everything. But she has credit cards the length of a Continental. An american interlude. I have no doubt she'll go home eventually to help her people and be a doctor the way her parents were nurses.

—*December 2, 1974*

A Critique of Male Voices

yesterday i overcame myself and a fundamental resistance i've had to reading this newspaper for some time. long before it was recently bought from the people who bought it from somebody else actually and fearfully but courageously read quite a few items, even those items i never could understand or decipher and the ones i knew might arouse the sort of primal rage that made me stop reading the media altogether. i still can't understand or decipher the ones i never could, but apparently i have some new interpersonal perspective on the "male problem" including both their reaction to and/or ignorance of feminism and i feel more detached from the whole thing and even deluded by what appear to be token gains or advantages. what i never could understand were the exposure or muckraking articles concerning stolen goods or injured parties. i tried reading one yesterday about nursing homes and i couldn't keep the cast straight although it was clear to me who the villains were. i don't think there were any good guys. usually there's at least one prosecutor. the victims were the old people who live in the nursing homes but this was understood. what i'd really like to know is something about the psychology of the family in western culture which creates nursing homes in the first place and how this is integrated with the political-economic system i already know that any institution is ripping off somebody else who in turn is also etc. the cast of characters alters from year to year. this is as interesting as a new line of soup labels. or the name of a new president. i want to know why we *have* these institutions. an article exposing some guy and his wife and cronies who run lousy nursing homes and milk the taxpayers for them and make a lot of bread off of them as well may be a good thing if we want good nursing homes and we can define what that is. i question their existence. the conditions of every institution for exiled citizens are relatively bad. the conditions of every institution are relatively bad. the conditions of life are difficult. why do tremendous numbers of old people let themselves be herded into nursing homes. old people should be getting healthier and happier, shedding the body is a natural process that can happen anywhere. the animals of the universe don't die in nursing homes. articles about bad nursing homes and bad ambitious people who own them presuppose both the value of the homes in some way and the inherent corruption of ownership — neither of which are put directly in question. in order to see a fish you have to watch the water. actually when you see the water you see the true fish. anyway spearing a fish is still a lot more interesting to people than just watching the water. i wouldn't be criticizing nursing homes myself if i could just relax and watch. then besides watching all i have to do is stay out of them myself and the more of me who stay out of them the less we'll need them. even so, it's presumptuous to image that other people shouldn't need what you don't. it may be the most revolutionary thing to be exposing crooked nursing homes. what else did i read in the newspaper. i read that a man and his wife in israel were killed. i read that robert redford is very goodlooking. i read about abbie hoffman and couldn't figure it out, a man called dezse was involved and i got kind of stuck on that name or idea. there are many articles by and about boys. it does make sense that boys chiefly comment on themselves. the ones who spear the fish should be best acquainted with their own equipment and we might not need any newspapers if we were just watching the water. the boys watch each other carefully and report as many of their evil deeds as possible. they concede victories to themselves and gloat over their failures. they make and break heroes daily by the dozen. they keep their daddies in line and deplore their own system when they can't and they root for their sons. when it means a break in daddy's defenses then go after the sons when the sons have obviously established themselves as the new daddy. the identification of any new quarterback or lineback is very important. since culture is a zero-sum contest — someone wins only if someone else loses — and the media is the cultural medium for transmitting information about these wins and losses naturally the newspaper is all about this. it's rarely ever all about anything in itself. that would involve merely watching and being. then we'd be just as contented to see the newsprint floating down the river with the fish. until recently i had a vital interest in fish myself. i still do to a certain extent, but not for the same reasons i did. i was interested in saving the whales and finding the save the whale people. if you can't spear something you can try to save it. women are particularly vulnerable to this form of being outstanding and in fact project jonah is headed by a woman. i've been fascinated by whales for a long time and then when i heard that they needed to be saved i believe i mobilized my last fantasy of social responsibility. that is, what could i do for certain victims by lining myself up somehow with the prosecutors againt the villains. i would have to fight the japanese for one thing and i still feel badly about hiroshima. then it occurred to me that possibly the whales are being exterminated for ecological reasons that we know nothing about. i speculated that whales have victimized shrimp and plankton to an ungovernable degree and that the real object of concern may be the maintenance of shrimp and plankton. i speculated that whales got too big for things that move around. even mountains can be scary although they don't seem to move. even ocean liners are recycled or transformed or sunk if necessary. and i wondered how many whales had to pay for the sinking of the whaleship essex in the pacific around 1830 by a white whale who was angry by the attack on his brood or school and who started it all. i was about to become a major champion of yet another minor issue when the major issue is who started it all and what for. then we can find out how it works and whether we want it or not. anyway i am still very interested in whales but for my original reasons: because they're so enormous and i've never seen one. i hope to see one before they're exterminated. this new book assembled by the woman who heads project jonah, joan mcintyre, called *mind in the waters*, is a wonderful book. i love whales for the facts about them. the tongue of the blue whale weighs as much as an elephant — the largest land animal that ever lived could stroll through the blue whale's mouth. i could read a newspaper all about a whales mole. we already know about nursing homes and how bad they are and how goodlooking robert redford is and how abbie hoffman is in trouble again and how rocky owns more money than anybody else. nearby is a large mass of water called the sea. is there an explorer in our midst who can travel to a previously unknown region in order to learn something about natural features there. and i'm not thinking about cousteau and his gang. the newspaper would love to send me to interview cousteau five miles down to the bottom of the ocean. actually i'd be interested to find out why cousteau goes to such scientific and physical trouble investigating other creatures. i might even like to know who he's ripping off to do it and who the people he's ripping off are ripping in order to give it to him etc., i'd be sure to find a villain somewhere, and i'd cast about for some victims, and i'd watch the man carefully because he's famous and he might not have a right to be and the best we could do is to make him infamous. zero-sum winners are always eventually exiled anyhow in the inevitable cultural ritual of vengeance. that's why we have nursing homes to contain the people who were so mean to us by having us. if we don't make them (in)famous we can hole them up somewhere. then we can write about how mean we are to do it. the least we can do is blame it on somebody else. then it makes sense for a sorehead like me to come along and blame the people who're blaming people who enjoy reading so much blame & shame. i'm glad i read the newspaper i'm having a really good time. the people who claim they can't understand or decipher my own work here should find this completely comprehensible. kali herself walking the streets in the world she's destroying. the knife without a handle that lacks a blade. oppression at the hands of the man with the purple kneebands. the token gains or advantages of women in a male world are confusing to me or at best don't necessarily mean anything to me. the great argument of the movement turns around on whether we want this world or not. the major assumption of feminism thus far is that we do. it's a tacit consensus. thus when a male friend tells me "girls can't necessarily do it better" i agree with him. who could do anything better in a zero-sum contest system. we could give it a whirl with women presidents but i question the existence of presidents and i doubt that women would've invented them. women merely gave birth to them. all the time i'm reading paul cowan's impressive piece of journalism on a textbook controversy i'm thinking about the absurdity of the school system itself. the question of what sort of books or ideas the school should have, not whether the schools themselves are valuable or not. clearly everybody is

right about what they should have and the big interest is who
will win. when somebody wins, another beseiged county will be
located to document a new football game. while all this is going
on we ignore the possibility of high level communications with
whales. it wouldn't be interesting to people to just relate and
watch the waters. at some point in the history of survival (male)
people started talking about killing everything that moved. even
mountains had to be conquered. if it exists it has to be conquered
but the major issue of existence itself, the way to enter the mind
of the whale is to *enter* the water. i have something more organic
in mind than schools and nursing homes. organic networks are full
of inconsistency. they arrive at some balance through spontaneous
blundering toward multiple accommodation. the real feminism
that nobody knows about yet is not known because it's been
invented, then when it's invented we still won't know what it is
because it will continue in a state of invention. as soon as you
call it something so far as i'm concerned it's a male institution. all
we'll know is that we're living & dying in harmony with the
butternut leaves. we'll probably be butternut leaves ourselves.
bemeantimes we're busy developing many fantasies & strategies.
i have an intense media fantasy and i want to take over the whole
media to execute it. it's a typical male fantasy of seizure and control.
so long as i have a token advantage in the male system i'm only
exercising my rights. as a feminist who presupposes that the
world we have is valuable i want more & more rights. the wrongs
are that i don't have enough rights. i want the nursing homes
& schools & everything to be nicer. but since i'm a media person
i want to take that over. my villains would be whoever stands in
my way. that would probably be everybody. the victims would
be thousands of media people put out of a job as soon as i
take over. i'd ship them out to some renovated nursing homes
and hire a prosecutor to make sure the profit off them is lower
then rocky's off anaconda rubber. i'd make sure they had some
good whale movies to watch. movies of (in)famous people would
continue to be included. we don't want the whole operation
to lurch out of control during the planning stages. i don't

question their existence. everything we have is already just enough
& as much.

—*December 23, 1974*

Media Knots and Future Shots

i was saying about my rights and how i needed more of them. that as a feminist who presupposes that the world we have is valuable i want more & more rights. the presupposition of a media women's conference is that the media we have is desirable and as such women should compromise 51 per cent of the force in power. for myself i just want to take it over. the males who work with it are never satisfied till they run the whole thing and i don't know why i'd be participating in such a powerful medium myself unless i wanted to seize it and run it the way it should be run. certainly i wouldn't run any more stories about nursing homes by the time i seized the media there wouldn't be any homes to talk about. everybody would've forgotten about them as we lurched into the post-technological era of pure communications. i wouldn't run any stories about media women's conferences either and what a poor showing women are making in the business. we don't want to complain about anything or imagine that things shouldn't be better than they are right now. what we want is to just begin communicating and stop relating stories about what everybody appears to be doing. newsprint would probably become obsolete immediately. the medium for communication will become ourselves for a change. i think everybody must feel exactly the same way. the stories are very confused by now and the differences of opinion concerning the details of the identities of stolen goods and injured parties have created a tremendous babble of dissatisfaction. we should let ourselves be guided by what is common to all. however we can't be guided by what is common to all without first acknowledging our critical differences. the purpose of my media seizure would be to do just this. before we can become our own medium of communications we have to find out who we are. as we do our cultural technological instruments by which we convey our ideas about ourselves will gradually self destruct. we need an alternate media institution that will self destruct in sequential interrelated stages according to the pace of its participants in discovering its absurdity through its transitional usefulness. the ones who won't participate will be the ones who don't use it or don't know what it is. people who still gather coconuts in the middle of australia or wherever they are. these're the people who've known who they are presumably for millennia. eastern peoples know a lot better than europeans and europeans much better than americans & canadians and i don't know what's happening south of florida or the panama canalzone. the principle is that the further a civilization is into its technology the further away it is from its sources of knowledge about itself. (much learning does not teach understanding.) the second principle is that we *use* this form of selfalienation called technology to find our way back & out. over & out. as for newsprint hopefully each person would acquire their own xerox equipment to broadcast their personal stories. i have to make a distinction between types of stories at this point. i alluded above to those stories about what everybody else is doing and how confused they are because they involve many differences of opinion concerning the details of the identities of stolen goods and injured parties. the media as it now exists is a kind of giant finger pointing exercise. if i am as right as i am, you are wrong. entire lives are lived with this sort of thinking and the media is the official machinery of our judgments. if i-then you. either-or. black-white. etc. means we can't live without taking sides. you say you are right and our neighbor is wrong but there may also be a place where you are wrong and s(he) is right, and both of you may be wrong and both right. and at still another place, all this may be forgotten. that's when we become ourselves the pure medium in the wind and rain both coconut & newspaper civilizations are blown away like flies. newsprint in its present form is still about everybodyelse. if women comprised 51 per cent of the force in power we could write more about other women. we could point the finger at more of the right (or wrong) people. certainly the coverage of a media women's conference would occupy as much space as the report of a murder in england. recently in this paper there was practically a novelette about a murder in england and by contrast a few notes about what a poor showing women continue to make in the media. the inference clearly is that nobility in england is still of much greater consequence to the people in america than the condition of more than half the population in america itself. certainly i enjoyed the murder too. it was a lot more entertaining than the dreary news about how badly women are doing. and besides i'm currently seeking an audience with the queen over there. i want my rights in england as well as in america naturally. i was conceived in the middle of the ocean between the two and i bear my english father's name in america and my mother's american father's name in england. i'm very mixed up and all i know is that i want my rights. if the fathers are of any value and we still bear their names we should reclaim them. the great work of reclamation is just beginning. the one constant in the american environment has been the wilderness in its varying forms of forest, plain, mountain & desert. at the source of the american experience lies the fatal opposition between two worlds, two races, two realms of thought and feeling. the women will join the indians as we go back to the land the tension between blood knowledge & brain knowledge will converge in the wilderness of the imagination. i don't know what will happen to all the presidents. after my great seizure i'll be able to admit that i don't know anything. our present task is to run through all the male commodities as fast as possible. i really do have this intense media fantasy. it's particulars are undeveloped, the general idea is a massive psychoanalytically based assault in every language through a sort of united nations exchange system employing relays of people in deep hypnotic rap groups exposed constantly on every available tube & satellite station thruout the world beamed into each little (nursing) home. a prime objective would be to retrace our steps in order to find out why a father had to become a president and thus how fathers and presidents are synonymous entities and how queens were merely the wives of very early presidents. women would immediately become feminists by realizing that the part of their name considered culturally the most important is not really their own and whatever it was that was their own has been lost in the antiquity of a patriarchal revolution. who says that "girls can't necessarily do it better." the reason girls are in a position to do it better is that we've lost our names and we have to invent them. we speak across centuries of namelessness. the great argument of the movement turns around whether we want this world or not. the major assumption of feminism thus far is that we do.

feminism in its present state is a kind of male institution because we continue to use all our brothers' and fathers' names with the idea that we can make their "things" better or turn their institutions into nicer places. a woman with her father's name would make a better president since she's a woman. this is a misunderstanding of the temporary necessity of using or reclaiming the father's name and things. the idea as i said is to *run through* their things. as the boys retraced their steps they would walk right back into the womb of mother and that's where we want them. that is, we want them to know where they really are. their motion will enter its centripetal stage. the overall objective is the encouragement of *all* peoples to re-group in compatible and manageable units of relative selfsufficiency and united by the best aspects of a vestigial technology: communications & transportation services in their purest sense short of the ultimate forms of telepathy and astraltravel — a global village driven into its (dis)organization by methods suggested in orwell's *1984* which is close upon us anyway. the agent will just be big sister instead of big brother who's watching you. the governments will automatically fall. the goal is the establishment of many selfgoverning units connected by primitive trade agreements as well as by the services above mentioned. organic networks which arrive at some balance through spontaneous and continuous blundering toward multiple accommodation. the way to do this is to rediscover our uncommon denominators. first we have to acknowledge our critical differences. in america particularly this is critical. "to an unrecognized extent we are a collection of religious ethnic & generational tribes who maintain an uneasy truce. we had to conquer this continent in order to exploit its vast resources. but we were never able to conquer our own atavistic hatreds and loyalties to live comfortably as a single people." (cowan). the crash groups appearing on the boobtube would be rapping intensively & incessantly among themselves about their names & origins & "family" transactions. human beings are constantly thinking about others and what others are thinking about them and what others think they are thinking about the others and so on. and this is what we want to hear about not how we're sending arms to israel or legs to turkey or vutnot. the global project is decentralization and internationalization by therapeutic overkill. the great unconscious middle crasses would be violently absorbed into the two ethics at either end of the social spectrum who would also converge in some new grey total indeterminate center. the tribal christian local suspicious prejudiced backcountry conservatives would meet the liberal meltingpot media mcluhan baby situational ethnic people coming & going as they both absorb the huge mucky indecisive and authority laden masses. one has to go this way because one has never been this way before then one has to come back to the middle. human society was once so much something or other (probably women) that it had to go all the way the other (obviously male) in order to sort itself out again. things make reparation and then do justice to one another according to the order of time. the uproar of feminism is proportionate to the time of our demise. the agony of feminism is the apparent necessity of a clamor which contradicts its aims. a group of women in st louis call themselves a cuntspiracy of amazon artists doing this anarchy which they refer to as tomatoe whenever it seems advisable. another group a lot further north is originating a "feminist" institution with a name and a bunch of teachers and courses, even a course on anarchism! an old woman in france (de Beauvoir) says she's no longer interested in comunisme and socialeesme so much as she is in human relationships — she's giving up the institutions of her male mentors. nonetheless i think we can *use* their institutions. we have their names so we might as well. for myself i want to know who my family is. and i don't mean (necessarily) my regular biological immediate family at all. i know many completely uprooted and disoriented anglican protestants like myself. the peoples who came here recently or who came here long ago may know more about themselves. i came here very recently but my mother was an uprooted american anglican heathen and i too was assimilated into the vast privileged unconscious displaced anglican majority. some of the minority groups refuse to talk about their families because they're so familiar with them and because they wish to be assimilated too. in our "agnostic post-linear multicultural multi-ethnic space age world" we're very knowledgeable and adrift. but the closed modern family is a tangle of knots of stories concerning thoughts about what everybody is thinking about everybody else's stolen parties & injured goods. these family tangles are projected thru the media in the guise of public spectacular scandals. by exposing our "internal" dissensions resolutions feelings transactions etc. by this rather fascist method that i have in mind of opening up all box stations to the incessant rattling of heads & bodies however difficult & embarrassing i think the people would soon see thru the projections of their media representatives who are talking about everything but where we're coming from. possibly many people would return to europe and asia or south of florida: certainly the great american pretense is clomping to a close. if the boys can't figure it out the women will do it for them. the women will lead the way thru brain knowledge back to the blood of the indians and the land. the tribal reorganization of society will bring us back to the boundless world of the mother. the paradox is that in such a world we are better contained. there'll be literally thousands of different sorts of containments, depending on which kind you want to join or originate. and there'll be many transients or dropouts as well and hoot knows anyway. the boys who still have karmic warrior problems to work off will be encouraged thru this fascist media seizure operation to group themselves in tournament organizations on secluded property where they can happily kill each other and even have the opportunity to register their victories & defeats back at the media home office for all the other people who still have karmic spectator needs. women who have to be warriors will do their thing too. the impact that i'm trying to make here is that we don't want to reform, we want to regroup. the problem is centralization. the solution is diffusion. the goal is telepathy. the end is obsolescence. the sum is wind fire & rain. the fairest universe is but a heap of rubbish piled up at random.

—*January 6, 1975*

Trick or Trek

dear p and b: so far i've come this far now i only have so far to go. by the time you read this i'll be. by the time of the high sierras i'm halfway to noplace again. on flight something out of hartford to oklahoma via chicago the pilot mentioned the place where four states meet: arizona utah colorado & newmexico. someday i'll do a one armed handstand where the states of seaweed and dry grass intersect at the meridian of the terminal central. i'm reading here that mind changes the universe. mind is as strong an evolutionary force as teeth or claws or glaciers. i'm fixing my teeth but only for cosmetic reasons. i still like pretty people but the blue of the sky is likely to become a somewhat duller blue after prolonged gazing. i want to write a mushy letter to lc but all these explanations are secondary. i'm flying american flt 126 sandiego to kennedy. pauline isn't speaking to me so i saw alan kaprow instead. i have a healthy attitude this trip. i want whatever i can get. i want to write about the work of the wives of artists but i didn't see alan's wife vaughn who published a beautiful book of photos of an icebox. i think anita has my copy. i like anita's work too if she would do it but she isn't the wife of an artist. if people were as amused by life as i am we wouldn't have any electricity in our houses, right? if parrots were the same as balloons we could watch hotdogs fly around the cathedrals right? new thought: if i pride myself on not falling down i fall down. otherwise i could have the kind of luck you only get when you don't care. in oklahoma i cared about the pa system so we all had to wait an hour while i sat obdurate and immovable arms folded across my lower breasts in an archaeology department office until they located the system. the audience was patient since i agreed to go there for much less than they were paying angela davis. for their woman's week they appropriated all their funds to bring angela. i can understand that since she's black and was honorably acquitted from jail. if amelia earhart is alive we'd certainly want her too. i want whatever i can get and i told the audience which was a wonderful throng that i accepted their chickenfeed cause it was taking me the rest of the way across the country to sanfrancisco where my daughter was meeting me at the airport. you can't hire destiny. can you hire destiny? anyway they kept telling me how deadly oklahoma is or didn't i think oklahoma was backwards. so i guess if there was any excitement around there i brought it with me. i told them all i knew about oklahoma was a musical my mother took me to see once. yesterday in losangeles i was awakened at 4 a.m. to be driven out to a ranch to see the swami muktananda who wears red hats and drives a mercedes. the meditations begin in the dark in the rain. i sat next to a fire warming my back staring into the gloaming morning while shadowy figures slipped furtively into the improvised temple with their pillows and beads and blankets. the throne was empty until the swami occupied it a lot later on. i saw sally kempton who looks fresh and happy and saved. she asked me what i was doing there. i wanted to say it was a prize arrangement of the irresistible force meeting the immovable object but i told her i went with ellie and that was true. it's always the main things that're true. the secondary thing was a man in a red hat who drives a mercedes. hello i'm your teacher and i go to the bathroom. the bathroom for ladies was out in the rain so i went to the braves. it said braves on the door. old thought: why does a man kill? he kills for food. and not only for food: frequently there must be a beverage. for you pam i looked for some special chocolates but i found another cut-out coin to protect myself from the swami and that wasn't necessary since he seems like a nice guy and i kept imagining gloria or amelia or angela on the throne. i'm very western and woman. c'est la vis a vis. the coin is our lady of liberty 1942 50-cent piece. she's walking into the sunrise or set. didn't set have a brother? i'm pretty high. about 37,000 feet and three silver women around my neck. in frisco there were four of us for dinner at fanny's. we liked ourselves together so much that we had dinner the next night at the tivoli savoy and then joe from city lights bookstore came in with ferlinghetti who was supposed to meet me at breakfast the following morning. joe is a cheerful funny extrovert with a hairy chest. ferlinghetti has glazed blue eyes and a stubbly whitish beard. i told him i'd tell everybody back east that i met him. he looks like conrad carrying coleridge's albatross. if i washed up on a southsea island i'd find him there living alone in a thatched bamboo hut. joe thinks my work is like this man around there who writes visceral illhumored things by name bukowski with whom joe identifies. laurel was deeply offended, she said bukowski is a pig and i have nothing to do with him. page loved the way laurel was huffy. her style is dignified terrorism. page's style is eloquent comic relief and i wanted to package her right away, she might even fly to places like oklahoma for nothing where i know she'd have some new fast answers to the regular species propagation questions. how can we concern ourselves with propergation of the specious when the urgent interest is banana and chocolates. anyhow there'll always be some old sow & stud left to lumber back into the primordial waters. of much more immediate concern is an "endangered species called the gay photographer" according to a tall thin blonde ectomorphic intensive strangely gorgeous woman who is the sort of species she described and whose neighbors are cows and apple orchards. nancy sunflower said she saw her on main street in a whiskey ad holding hands with another woman. extra thought: who was it said that beyond a certain point all dangers are equal. trick or trek. trench or trail. tape or worm. wheel & whoa. waste & repetition. reefs stretching far out where the waves're breaking white and at sunset people just look and look. a pair a dux. it's so dangerous looking. i looked at the swami or the mook as he may fondly be called and he looked at me too. i like his style. the shades and red hat and orange dress and nervous quick gestures. i liked watching all the 70 people or so worshipping him in the new morning light. i stayed warming my back by the fire. i felt high on the chanting and didn't pay attention to the words. i fondled my liberty woman coin in my pants pocket. i drank their tea and ate their porridge. i put my arm around ellie. i kissed sally kempton goodbye. i laid down the length of me on my back on a big long counter. i observed the ritual of the man holding court after the chanting and wondered whether i would've received more gifts in oklahoma if i'd sat on a throne with a candle and flowers and worn a red hat. hello this is your teacher and sometimes i masturbate. i'm also suffering from terminal honesty. the reason i'm addressing you both is that i'm uncertain who's receiving this any more. i'll try to be honest and slick. hopefully this may be slick enough not to mean anything at all. i want to be slick as a glacier or a cosmetic tooth. i want whatever i got. i want to write the lives of the wives of the artists. i talked with alan driving to sandiego about the artists and why they're so awful. he says artists were bred to believe that all artists were "queers" and therefore in order to be artists against in most cases the wishes of their fathers they had to prove what very tough guys they were. this makes them tougher & scarier than businessmen or even politicians or truck-drivers or hairstylists. however all tough guys are monotonous — like playing cards with a deck that's all aces. and that's why i lost interest in them and i always liked their wives anyway and now their wives are doing this vital interesting work. braced thought: maybe pauline would speak to me if she wasn't a tough successful artist who needs a nurturant supportive wife. side thought: maybe alan is becoming his wife's wife. weak return: the women at the mook ranch meditation rain porridge & fireplace were mysterious to me. the main thing is i enjoyed being there being high on their high on highness. i was only minimally irreverent. a busy woman aide said i should get off the counter cause that's where they serve the food. i said if it was good enough for the food it was good enough for me. if porridge were the same as balloons we could watch bananas fly around the temples, right? if people were as amused by life as i am we wouldn't have these airplanes, right? are airplanes good? are we going climbing in the cascades when you have a vacation? are we slowly unfolding this everything else? are we in a period of craving need and struggle or a period of satiety and rest or are we finding repose in change or vise virtue or just interesting repetition with waste and tartar sauce on the side. i had shrimp in la & sf and scallops in s diego at the reuben e lee which is a boat restaurant overlooking the airport and just when a scallop was approaching my mouth i felt really woozy and thought i was drugged by the kind people who took me there when they reminded me i was eating on a boat. since we were discussing the past it was appropriate to be abroad. the path that leads to noplace eventually. the dream of a half of a dress or a robe that was indian. waking up to praise the morning moon. the theatre of the indian gods in the hills of the andreas fault. the encouraging possibility of blaming everything on oil and the arabs. the difference between knowing nelly from frank or frank from alan and alan from vaughn and the reassurance of felice waiting in the car to drive us back to la. the ritual of holding court i thought you'd like. the gifts were coffee dried fruit and oranges and written things and a black dog and a box with something in it and a pillow and a new red hat and all. actually the black dog was borrowed by the master who beckoned her over and draped his white socked feet over her back. the pillow he threw back at the donor and i thought he didn't want it but ellie told me he was probably blessing it. he blesses things or people by sort of swatting them. a friendly hit with an open palm. a blonde huge tall nordic guy prostrated himself at the swami's feet and he received this blessing on his head. he stayed there much too long apparently because the interpreter told him at length that he should get up. i thought if the dog was there why couldn't the man stay too. i enjoyed everything until the swami held hands a long time with an older man who was presented to him and was probably the owner of the ranch and that made me think about money and oklahoma and amelia earhart and the second chakra and a one armed handstand where the states of seaweed and drygrass intersected the meridian of the terminal central. the whole trip, nothing but the trip. a totally peripheral thought. a dog who sings a mushy letter about our bodies. a glacial evolutionary tooth. a liberty woman in a ranch rain moonrise. a daughter in an airport. a teacher who lectures in a quicksand. see ya soon. so far i've come this far now i only have so far to go. love, jill.

—*February 17, 1975*

do it yourself, mr steele

I

this may be a piece with caps and paragraphs but i wouldn't know where since i'm not putting them there. a capital letter is a major consideration. this is the way we were brought up. i was brought up on castor oil and little lulu. if you had castor oil and little lulu you wouldn't want to change to exercises and hannah arendt. here's a new paragraph. you can do it yourself by putting your finger on the period and turning to talk to a friend. if you're tired of your friend you can fry an egg or fly a kite. this is then moving on and finding a new way to end an old idea or begin again the way it went before before before before six sentences in search of a paragraph. the way to do it is easy if you were brought up right you indent. an indentation is a notch or a recess in a border. the border never bothered any of us his name was mr shoemaker. now you wouldn't capitalize a shoemaker. a mr steele is different but i don't know any. my grandmother only had a border called shoemaker. his recess was a room on the second floor overlooking the backyard and in back of that was a lot with a few trees that i climbed with walter or florence or mildred. mildred's mother was mrs lindbergh and she was a sad woman and she sat sadly on her back porch in her print cotton dress when she finished doing things inside and that's all i remember about mrs lindbergh who wasn't important except to me for existing. the important people came on sundays in the newspapers it was understood. we were trained properly. some other important people came on the covers of dixie cups. i loved the good humor man the bellsound of his white truck. that's an old paragraph, i mean to get on with the business or borders proper and names, which are proper to capitalize on. i was capital myself. i was more important than my teddy bear or my desk or my marbles or mr shoemaker but it was only assuming what was proper was not my place to question what was proper. some things are proper and others aren't. although a mr steele was different and i didn't know any later i would learn there was a difference between mr shoemaker mr steele mrs lindbergh and cheese chairs or chicago.

II

the important thing about geography was the capital of each state. next came the occupation of the state but agriculture wasn't capital unless it was owned by somebody so we then began to learn about ownership and how capital that was. in this way the convention itself assumed capital importance and what was there to question if we had our marbles and teddy bears and trees to climb. everybody could own something. even so the death of a grasshopper was considerably less important than a man in a wheelchair called roosevelt although we didn't know this man and his doings and me and mildred and walter and florence etc. conducted an elaborate funeral for a grass-hopper even so. this paragraph has hope as origin. think of all these sentences and not to be annoyed. after all what is the difference between it and you. everybody has said they are happy. if two sentences make a paragraph a little piece is alright because they are better apart. now feebly commence a sentence and remember that gertrude's life remains much more important than her sentences by which we know gertrude and all and that isn't all or major. a sentence should be arbitrary it should not please be better. this is then moving on and finding its own way of beginning or ending itself the way it went before in selfconsuming variations six or many sentences in search of a paragraph the way it started was arbitrarily inventive and derived from my attachment to kinds of historical and contemporary painting and a certain experience of myself as a multitude of selves solvent and spatio temporally contingent.

III

the kinds of art that excited me were schwitters cornell pollack rauschenberg and mark tobey and so of course they and many more were important to me to be exciting. i liked things all over as they said about tobey and pollack about their dripping and white writing and so on or the way the dripping and writing was dense and reached all the borders and without punctuation except as mutually important parts or events. now think of a sentence. all these are parts. this sentence comes to the same place as all they said and it's moving on.

if you want to reach the border prepare your passport. if you pass the port you may miss the border. the borders are beautiful and i like to reach all the ends of them and pass them if possible if they're all over and sense i wouldn't know the difference if i'd passed or not. if it's all filled up it's as good as nothing and everything is getting someplace. i still like little lulu and i've added hannah arendt but i've changed from castor oil and capitals to water and exercises and the sense of the tremendous importance of a grasshopper although this week i'm concentrating on dogs. that is alright. so there we are just as all the same. it should not be disturbed. that is one of the best i've done. do it yourself by putting your finger in the period and turning to talk to a friend if you're tired of your friend what can anybody do. we exist importantly. we still love the good humor and the funny papers. this is not easy because it isn't trained. i made it up. a sentence is from this time i will make up my mind. the problem of time in reading is a problem of our time. in time we read and stop read and stop as though the book is really going someplace. in painting we see the thing all at once and then we may notice its details but these details are not separated in time. in space they act in concert as integrally necessary to each other.

IV

a tapestry made easy by being seen. how are ours received. a capital letter is a major consideration. the renaissance is still alive in writing in the renaissance in painting you have foreground and background. in the foreground is the prince or patron. in the background his wife and landscape and glimpses of his castle. the peasants of breughels romping in a field were all over. possibly painted for his own satisfaction. otherwise it was essential to please a patron and that's capital mr steele do it yourself. see mr steele in his playroom assembling the bits of his life in cartoons toytrucks pistolcaps soldiers marbles wood rope metal feces deadbirds nests all over the floor filling up the whole place he might even include a few remaining tinker toys or bits from a construction set from christmas but as he grows up trained properly capitalizes and paragraphed he'll stay in his corner with the tinker or construction set only assuming what was proper was not his place to question what was proper was given. what made schwitters and rauschenberg shoe or shitmakers which mr steele would later convert into money or filthy lucre i don't know and i do think mr steele if he doesn't do it himself could enquire into the original workings of his subjects. his sentences are capital. how has he hurried. that is a paragraph because it means gone. a verb ever after. a noun should always be replaced by now. by now this is truly related.

V

i did it in the beginning making up my own mind with sentences as though a sentence was an old bed or a bottle in the gutter or a knife in the garbage or a torn spattered shirt or a new shiny urinal or a wheel or a shovel and i collected and hoarded these sentences like pieces of an unknown jigsaw which would be an arrangement of (un)collected sentences. at first i put these sentences together end to end without connecting tissue. i was more involved in the sentences than the sense of a piece. the sense came later and then i selected sentences more to fit the sense or a subject or several subjects connected by sentences. at first i was merely enthralled by sentences. i thought they were capital and i left them as i found them with some letters higher or lower than others but i needed to fit them end to end to see the pattern of sentences. this was 1967 or '68. i typed out these sentences i had heard uttered or that i read in papers or books then took scissors and cut them out so they were separate appearances on narrow rectangular strips of paper which i laid out along the floor the length of them a few yards or so of these stripped sentences. then i walked or crawled along side of them looking for one sentence i wanted to begin since you have to begin somewhere if you begin you need to select something and that isn't easy because in an important way i felt that one was really as good as another and that made selection difficult at the same time i had no inclination to toss them all up in the air and by some chance operation let one select itself so somehow i would select myself one to begin. it was quite a selfconscious operation. the confrontation of apparently unrelated fragments as a literary method is not new but it was new for me and it was new for an american newspaper. anyway this is an example. that's a good enough sentence. it's very difficult to think twice. history is twice. being once we wouldn't bother and i like these ordinary sentences.

VI

if it's embarrassing and inappropriate it's still interesting and essentially happening. so here we are. a capital well brought up sentence selfconscious trees desks marbles borders chairs cheese chicago mrs lindbergh mr shoemaker the running togetherness of things of things separate leaving please. every page should be considered in its entirety as though it were a picture. the title is a sentence cut into fragments that are distributed throughout. i never mentioned the title the title is what is journalism and if you know what journalism is what is literature? what is you know is mentioned. hurry with a sentence. what are you doing tomorrow. this is characteristic of the sort of industry in that particular state of the union. they're all coming to the same end. these three are examples of what i mean. snatches of conversation, routine phrases and clichés following without transition or apparent thematic connection. in june 1968 i wrote something for the newspaper called the grandest tiger which was a piece of sentences from everyplace jammed up against each other with no air between them except the space between the letters. i was more involved in the sentences than the sense of the piece although any perceptive person could see that the grandest tiger was r f kennedy who'd recently been assassinated and i felt the event intensely but i hated public sentimentality since that's the way we were brought up to regard the least excessive display of emotion unless possibly you were a girl swooning over a prince or a girl hysterically in trouble in case it provided any local prince to come and save you otherwise the display of emotion generally even in private to a friend or lover or mother or yourself was as unthinkable as accepting little lulu and the good humor man and so even though i felt the event of the r f kennedy assassination intensely i don't know now i couldn't tell you whether i really felt it or not that is if i did it was a mystery even to me which is not an uncommon state of mental affairs in american puritan culture to feel something and not to know it. anyway whether i knew it or not i wrote a short piece of sentences jammed up against each other mostly about death as i now perceive it. the sentences i found at that time were primarily exotic. the banal came later. the clichés were always difficult. i wanted to be clever. i had to be clever to be printed by an american newspaper. the woman who accepted my copy would say sometimes this is not a literary journal jill and frankly i wasn't thinking of literature or a journal or anything. i was preoccupied with survival. nonetheless i commenced my career of self important writing about the importance of not being important. (this is the beginning of an extended essay with the working title what is journalism and if you know what journalism is what is literature? — dealing with the history of my origins and attachment and formation as a writer in relation to the *village voice* — with roundabout thanx to mr and mrs shoemaker and the steeles.)

—*March 24, 1975*